A T O M I C   S T E P P E

ATOMIC STEPPE

How Kazakhstan Gave Up the Bomb

TOGZHAN KASSENOVA

STANFORD UNIVERSITY PRESS
Stanford, California

STANFORD UNIVERSITY PRESS
Stanford, California

© 2022 by Togzhan Kassenova. All rights reserved.

Printed in the United States of America on acid-free, archival-quality paper

Library of Congress Cataloging-in-Publication Data
Names: Kassenova, Togzhan, author.
Title: Atomic steppe : how Kazakhstan gave up the bomb / Togzhan
    Kassenova.
Description: Stanford, California : Stanford University Press, 2022. |
    Includes bibliographical references and index.
Identifiers: LCCN 2021050058 (print) | LCCN 2021050059 (ebook) |
    ISBN 9781503628465 (cloth) | ISBN 9781503632431 (paperback) |
    ISBN 9781503629936 (epub)
Subjects: LCSH: Nuclear disarmament—Kazakhstan—History. |
    Nuclear weapons—Government policy—Kazakhstan—History. |
    Nuclear weapons—Kazakhstan—History. | Nuclear weapons—
    Kazakhstan—Testing—History.
Classification: LCC JZ5665 .K365 2022 (print) | LCC JZ5665 (ebook) |
    DDC 327.1/747095845—dc23/eng/20211018
LC record available at https://lccn.loc.gov/2021050058
LC ebook record available at https://lccn.loc.gov/2021050059

Cover design: Rob Ehle

Cover photograph: Kazakhstan Steppe, photo by the author

Text design: Kevin Barrett Kane

Typeset at Stanford University Press in 10/14 Minion Pro

To Ragna Kassenova and Oumirserik Kassenov

CONTENTS

MAPS, TABLES, AND PHOTOGRAPHS

ACKNOWLEDGMENTS

In November of 2020, after months of being stuck in a city (Washington, DC) in pandemic quarantines and lockdowns, I found myself in the middle of the Kazakh steppe. The vastness of the open space was overwhelming. This was my last trip to eastern Kazakhstan before completing this manuscript, and I felt immense gratitude for the privilege of telling the story of my land and its people.

This book was more than a decade in the making. I am fairly certain I won't do any other writing that will have the same level of professional and personal importance to me. This book has been a labor of love, and I will be forever grateful to so many who helped me in this journey.

Over the years, several institutions provided me an intellectual home. Most of my writing took place at the James Martin Center for Nonproliferation Studies, the Carnegie Endowment for International Peace, and the Center for Policy Research at the University at Albany, State University of New York (SUNY). I gratefully acknowledge the fellowships and grants that made my research possible: a predoctoral fellowship at the International Institute for Asian Studies (Leiden University); a postdoctoral fellowship at the James Martin Center for Nonproliferation Studies; a Stanton nuclear security fellowship and grant support from the Carnegie Corporation of New York at the Carnegie Endowment for International Peace; and a Gerda Henkel Foundation grant that helped with my field work and production of this book.

The best part of this research was meeting people who lived through or shaped the events I describe. I am grateful to all the Kazakh, US, and Russian former and current officials, experts, scientists, and survivors of nuclear tests who agreed to talk with me and share their stories. Those who can be are named in the book.

I am incredibly grateful to all the librarians and archivists whose enthusiasm for what they do makes me think that their profession is one of the
best in the world. My gratitude goes to the staff of the Archive of the President of the Republic of Kazakhstan, the Library of the Academy of Sciences
of Kazakhstan, the Central State Archive of Film and Photo Documents and
Sound Recordings (Kazakhstan), the Center for Modern History Documentation (Kazakhstan), the US Library of Congress, the George H. W. Bush Presidential Museum and Library, the National Security Archive, the William J.
Clinton Library and Museum, and the Hoover Institution Archives. Special
thanks to the former librarians at the Carnegie Endowment for International
Peace—Kathleen Higgs, Christopher Lao-Scott, and Alex Taylor—who found
impossible-to-find titles. I will wear the badge "the scholar who orders most
obscure titles" with honor.

My thanks go to several generations of brilliant junior fellows and staff
at the Carnegie Endowment for International Peace who helped me with my
research—Zoe Benezet-Parsons, Wyatt Hoffman, Thu An Pham, Lauryn Williams, William Ossoff, Chelsea Green, Alexandra Francis, and Jacyln Tandler.

There are so many people who helped with my education and career,
shared their expertise, read parts of my manuscript, offered feedback, asked
questions, or reminded me when needed the most that this was a worthwhile
project. My first word of gratitude goes to two individuals—one Kazakh and
one American—who not only played historic roles in the events I describe but
generously spent hours and hours over the years answering my questions about
the intricacies of US-Kazakh nuclear negotiations. These are Tulegen Zhukeev
and William Courtney.

I am indebted to David Holloway, William Potter, George Perkovich, Susan
Koch, Andy Weber, Kairat Kadyrzhanov, James Goodby, Eric Howden, Byron
Ristvet, Ed Chow, Toby Dalton, Matias Spektor, Martin Sherwin, Bryan Early,
Rita Guenther, Stephen Shapiro, Svetlana Savranskaya, Thomas Blanton, Lyn-
don Burford, Frederic Wehrey, Sarah Chayes, Alimzhan Akhmetov, Oleg Bu-
tenko, Larissa Pak, Timur Nusimbekov, Rico Isaacs, Nargis Kassenova, Zhar
Zardykhan, Julia Khersonsky, Gulshat Kozybaeva, Kleoniki Vlachou, Haytham
Yaghi, Ahmad El Tannir, Juan Carlos Davila, Fatos Kopliku, Natalia Saraeva,
Sheryl Winarick, Saida Taulanova, Bayan Kozhagapanova, Margarita Kalinina-
Pohl, and so many others. A writing group of incredible female scholars—
Anne Harrington, Kathleen Vogel, Jennifer Giroux, and Lorraine Bayard de

Volo—offered support, camaraderie, and inspiration. Lisa Sanders Luscombe read and edited my first drafts and guided me toward better writing with poise and kindness.

I am very grateful to Isabel Adeyemi. She cared about my book as much as I did and was the first to read all my drafts. She always found time to provide feedback despite being in the middle of writing her PhD dissertation and raising a newborn baby.

Special thanks go to Yelena Kalyuzhnova and Christoph Bluth, who played a pivotal role in opening the doors of postgraduate education in Great Britain, where I first developed an interest in nuclear politics.

So many authors and books inspire me, but for this particular project, I especially drew inspiration from David Holloway's *Stalin and the Bomb: The Soviet Union and Atomic Energy, 1939–1956*, Sarah Cameron's *Hungry Steppe: Famine, Violence, and the Making of Soviet Kazakhstan*, Kate Brown's *Plutopia: Nuclear Families, Atomic Cities, and the Great Soviet and American Plutonium Disasters*, and David Hoffman's *Dead Hand: The Untold Story of the Cold War Arms Race and Its Dangerous Legacy*. Toshihiro Higuchi's *Political Fallout: Nuclear Weapons Testing and the Making of a Global Environmental Crisis* inspired me with its prose and related subject matter. Kazakhstan's writers—Medeu Sarseke with *Semipalatinskaia tragedia* [Semipalatinsk tragedy] and *Kanat Kabdrakhmanov with 470 bomb v serdtsce Kazakhstana* [470 bombs in the heart of Kazakhstan]—offered invaluable contemporaneous records of events that unfolded in the region during the period of Soviet nuclear tests.

Preliminary research from chapters 1–5 and 11 appeared in "Banning Nuclear Testing: Lessons from the Semipalatinsk Nuclear Testing Site," *Nonproliferation Review* (copyright © 2017 Middlebury Institute of International Studies at Monterey, James Martin Center for Nonproliferation Studies, reprinted by permission of Taylor & Francis Ltd, http://www.tandfonline.com on behalf of Middlebury Institute of International Studies at Monterey, James Martin Center for Nonproliferation Studies).

One of the best things I did for this book's fate was to sign up for a writing class in New York City, where I met Francis Flaherty, editor extraordinaire. Any author would be lucky to work with Frank, who always asked the right questions, pushed me to add "treats for readers," elevated my prose, picked up on any inconsistencies, and—most importantly—understood and cared about the story I was trying to tell.

Above all, I am grateful to Stanford University Press for believing that Kazakhstan's nuclear story is worth telling. I am indebted to Alan Harvey, Caroline McKusick, and Gigi Mark for making this book a reality, to Stephanie Adams for help with marketing, and to everyone on the Stanford University Press team for continuing to bring new books to life despite the global pandemic. I was lucky to have Susan Olin as the copyeditor of my manuscript. She improved my manuscript with thoughtful care; it remains a mystery how she was able to pick up on my typos even in foreign-to-her Russian words. Rob Ehle designed the beautiful cover and Erin Greb produced the maps.

This was as much a scholarly journey as it was a personal one. The family I was born into predetermined my desire to start writing this book and helped me find the will to finish it.

Almaty and Washington, DC

August 29, 2021

Thirty years since the shutdown of the Semipalatinsk Nuclear Polygon

EXPLANATORY NOTES

I have used the Library of Congress transliteration of Russian words and names throughout the manuscript with the following exception: for well-known individuals or places, the most commonly accepted transliteration has been used. Some notes and bibliographic entries reflect the transliterations used in published sources. All translations are my own unless otherwise noted.

The term "Semipalatinsk region" refers to the general vicinity of the Semipalatinsk Polygon without reference to the formal administrative units of the territory. The city of Semipalatinsk was renamed Semey in 2007. Alma-Ata was the capital of the Kazakh Soviet Socialist Republic and independent Kazakhstan from 1929 until 1997. Alma-Ata was renamed Almaty in 1993.

The Communist Party system was at the core of the Soviet political system. For example, the First Secretary of Kazakhstan's Communist Party was the head of Kazakhstan, and the First Secretary of Semipalatinsk Oblast (an administrative unit of a territory) was the top local governor.

The Soviet legislative system consisted of Supreme Soviets at the level of republics (for example, the Supreme Soviet of the Republic of Kazakhstan) and at the level of the union (USSR Supreme Soviet). In 1989, as part of his reform agenda, Mikhail Gorbachev introduced a new legislative organ, the Congress of People's Deputies of the Soviet Union. The Congress increased the role of the competitive election process as it expanded the number of elected lawmakers. The Congress had the power to elect the USSR Supreme Soviet.

Kazakhstan is a multiethnic society. Unless specifically noted, terms such as "Kazakh government" and "Kazakh officials" signify connection to the state of Kazakhstan, not ethnicity.

ABBREVIATIONS

CIS   Commonwealth of Independent States

CSCE   Commission on Security and Cooperation in Europe

CTBT   Comprehensive Test Ban Treaty

CTBTO   Comprehensive Test Ban Treaty Organization

CTR   cooperative threat reduction

DOD   Department of Defense

DOE   Department of Energy

DTRA   Defense Threat Reduction Agency

FBIS   Foreign Broadcast Information Service

HEU   highly enriched uranium

IAEA   International Atomic Energy Agency

ICBM   intercontinental ballistic missile

IPPNW   International Physicians for the Prevention of Nuclear War

ISTC   International Science and Technology Center

JVE   Joint Verification Experiment

KGB   Komitet gosudarstvennoi bezopasnosti
           [Committee on State Security]

LEU   low enriched uranium

MAEK   Mangyshlak Atomic Energy Combine

MFA	Ministry of Foreign Affairs
NATO	North Atlantic Treaty Organization
NGO	nongovernmental organization
NNSA	National Nuclear Security Administration
NPT	Treaty on the Non-Proliferation of Nuclear Weapons
NSC	National Security Council
NTI	Nuclear Threat Initiative
NWFZ	nuclear-weapon-free zone
START	Strategic Arms Reduction Treaty
TPNW	Treaty on the Prohibition of Nuclear Weapons
USSR	Union of Soviet Socialist Republics
WMD	weapon of mass destruction

ATOMIC STEPPE

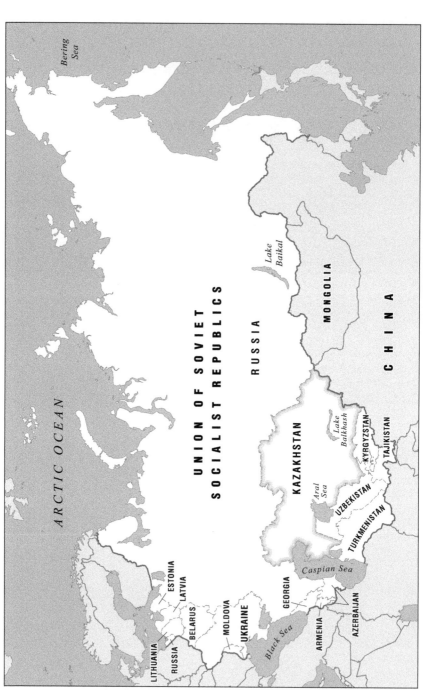

MAP 1   The Union of Soviet Socialist Republics.

PART 1

RULED BY RUSSIA, SCARRED BY NUCLEAR TESTS

Kazakhstan Under the Russian Shadow

PROLOGUE

I AM KAZAKH, and the two main topics of this book—the Soviet nuclear tests in the Semipalatinsk region of Kazakhstan, and the nation's early days of independence—are very personal to me. Despite living abroad since the age of nineteen, my ties to my homeland are deep. I treasure the memories of my youth, even those of such turbulent times as the collapse of the Soviet Union and the struggle of my newly independent country to find its place in the world. Kazakhs have a particular attachment to their place of birth, and I still call my hometown—Almaty—my first love. My heart skips a beat when my plane lands in Almaty, and I see the majestic Zailiiskii Alatau mountains that surround the city.

The family of my father lived in the city of Semipalatinsk, just 120 kilometers (seventy-five miles) from the nuclear test site. I was named Togzhan after a young girl loved by Abai, Kazakhstan's most famous writer and himself a native of the Semipalatinsk region. My bond to the region also stems from my father's life work. In the 1990s, as the head of the country's first analytical institution (the Center for Strategic Studies, which later grew into the Kazakhstan Institute for Strategic Studies), he helped the Kazakh government make nuclear policy decisions. I chose the nuclear field as my profession because I understood how central the nuclear story was to Kazakhstan's nation-building. I also wanted to follow in the footsteps of my father, who passed away too young.

NUCLEAR TESTING

The first part of this book is devoted to Kazakhstan's experience with Soviet nuclear tests. For more than forty years, the Soviet military tested its nuclear bombs in the Kazakh steppe, with devastating consequences for the people and the environment. Archival documents and memoirs paint a picture of disregard by the Soviet government for local residents during the decades of testing. All the early documents that discuss the suitability of the site for nuclear tests focus on the geographic advantages of the site, describing the area as "uninhabited," and giving little, if any, consideration for the local population.

Through the years, I met many people from the Semipalatinsk region. Some of them were small children when the nuclear tests took place. They told me how nobody warned them not to gaze at the nuclear mushrooms as they helped with herding cattle or collecting hay close to the Polygon, the Soviet term for a military testing site. These Kazakhs were innocent, kids who did not know why they encountered lambs with two heads or no limbs. What struck me in my conversations with them was how they longed for the pain of their families to be acknowledged, but, at the same time, they did not want to be portrayed just as victims. People from the Semipalatinsk region wish their land to be known for its history and culture, for the richness of its flora and fauna, and not only for the hardships they faced.

The Soviet government's disregard for Kazakhs during the nuclear testing period fits a general pattern of careless long-term and short-term policies toward them during the era of Soviet rule. There were the political repressions of 1937–38, for example, when the Soviet government imprisoned and executed the Kazakh intelligentsia, and the bloody suppression of youth protests in Alma-Ata, then Kazakhstan's capital, in 1986. But perhaps the most infamous episode of Soviet brutality was the collectivization of the 1930s. In this effort to "industrialize and modernize" Kazakhstan, Stalin's government forced farmers and livestock breeders to live together in one place and to join "collectives" to supply meat and grain to a common state-controlled pot for national distribution. For Kazakhs, whose herds and livelihood depended on a nomadic lifestyle, being forced to become sedentary was a death sentence. Livestock numbers plummeted, and 1.5 million people died (1.3 million of them were ethnic Kazakhs).

Ethnic Kazakhs in rural areas near the testing site suffered the most from nuclear tests because of their use of land for livestock herding, but they were not the only victims of the Soviet nuclear program. The city of Semipalatinsk was home to a multiethnic community, including many ethnic Russians who settled there as the Russian Empire expanded. In Soviet times, Stalin chose Kazakhstan (and the rest of Central Asia) as the remote place to forcefully move political exiles and ethnic minorities—Koreans, Crimean Tatars, Chechens, and others—from the European part of the Soviet Union. In the 1950s, Nikita Khrushchev's "Virgin Lands" campaign, an attempt to increase grain production in Kazakhstan, drew in youth from all Soviet republics. These voluntary and involuntary migrations contributed to Kazakhstan's multiethnic fabric. All locals, no matter their ethnic background, suffered from the nuclear tests.

Although, for reasons I explain below, hard numbers are difficult to find, the nuclear tests imposed a high human cost, with more than a million people in Kazakhstan harmed in some way by them. Some had to move, ejected from the lands appropriated by the Soviet military. Many others lived in areas exposed to radioactive contamination, causing thousands of them to get sick from radiation and thousands more to die from it.

But the human toll of the nuclear tests was not all; the tests exacted a huge price on the environment, too. I will never forget the first time I saw the former nuclear test site, during a helicopter flyover in June of 2015. To observe that enormous piece of land, entirely and artificially flat, with the tracks of heavy trucks forever tattooed into the ground and the carcasses of cement structures littering the site, was a stark reminder of the abuse this land took. The steppe's animals, such as the saiga antelope and the wild sheep known in English as argali and in Kazakh as *arkhar*, with their wondrous curved horns, suffered greatly. Their habitat was overtaken during the forty years of nuclear tests, and it was only years after the last nuclear test that they returned to the area.

However, while the cruelty of some Soviet policies and choices shocked me, I did not want to paint the Soviet leaders as a bunch of villains hurting people and the environment for no reason. The Soviets were rushing to equalize their power with the Americans, who already possessed nuclear bombs. Both countries found themselves locked in an arms race, each believing its nuclear program necessary for its survival.

In addition, although I started my research mostly concerned about the people of Kazakhstan, I quickly realized there were other victims of the Soviet nuclear program. The builders of the Polygon, many of them Soviet prisoners or rank-and-file soldiers, worked in horrible conditions. Many of them perished. The Soviet nuclear scientists and other military personnel at the site faced many hardships as well, especially in the early years of the program when housing conditions were poor and families not allowed. Eventually, their living conditions improved, and their lives could even be described as privileged, with special foods and consumer goods that were unavailable to other citizens, but they always lived under the watchful eye of the KGB and were never entirely free. I also did not want to skirt over the fact that most scientists and military who participated in the nuclear testing program made sacrifices for the cause they believed in—helping their country protect itself. Many rightfully felt pride in the scientific and military breakthroughs.

In my quest to tell the story truthfully, I relied on documentary sources as much as possible. I wanted to see the data for myself, read the memoirs of scientists and military officials who created and tested the bombs, find contemporaneous records of the experiences of people who lived near the testing grounds, and search through all the available archival material for clues. How much and how soon did the Soviet government understand the human harm of nuclear tests? What did the local government in Kazakhstan know? Most importantly, what did the people who lived through the tests experience?

The hardest question to answer was this: What was the full impact of the nuclear tests on the people and the environment during the nuclear tests and many years after? Three decades after the last nuclear explosion at the Semipalatinsk nuclear testing site, I cannot provide the reader with a complete answer. The secrecy surrounding the entire Soviet nuclear program meant that whatever data the Soviet military collected was classified. Nuclear weapons remain today at the core of Russia's national security, and for that reason sensitive information related to the Soviet/Russian nuclear program is still mostly out of reach. In the archives in Kazakhstan, I came across requests from Kazakhstan to Russia to provide the data that could help understand the health impact of nuclear tests on its people. I did not find responses.

Adding to these research difficulties are the contradictions among the different narratives over the human consequences of the nuclear tests. What the military medics said differed from what the clinical data suggested. But because the clinical data remain incomplete, it is hard to give exact answers; I can only provide the reader with the different, conflicting versions of what was happening in the Kazakh steppe. The concluding chapter of the book summarizes some of the more recent studies, which, while limited in scope, afford at least a glimpse of the long-lasting effect of nuclear tests on the people of Kazakhstan.

My research into the testing period wasn't all dark. It was wonderful to learn about people of integrity and courage both in Russia and in Kazakhstan. Some of Russia's most prominent scientists—Andrei Sakharov and Evgenii Velikhov, to name two—became opponents of Soviet nuclear tests. In Kazakhstan, I was moved by writers, scientists, and political leaders—such as Mukhtar Auezov, a famous writer and a native of the Semipalatinsk region, who first talked about the Semipalatinsk Polygon at an international conference in Japan in 1957; Dr. Bahiia Atchabarov, who led clinical studies of test victims in the 1950s; and local governors of Semipalatinsk, such as Mukhametkali Suzhikov in the 1950s, Mikhail Karpenko in the 1960s, and Keshrim Boztaev in the 1980s—who were among those who publicly questioned the tests. And, of course, above all, I was in awe of the millions of regular people of Kazakhstan who, in the 1980s, led by the writer Olzhas Suleimenov, launched the antinuclear movement called Nevada-Semipalatinsk. These people brought to an end nuclear testing in Kazakhstan.

I used the archival documents to the best of my ability. Even if my topic is still sensitive, for which reason not all records are available, I still got a sense of how no consequential action (or inaction) remains hidden forever. Contemporaneous documents, even if sometimes written in an obfuscated way to muddy the real facts, provide good hints at decision-makers' motivations, courage, or lack thereof if studied closely and cross-checked against other sources. Interviews with a wide range of participants provided rich material and added a human touch to my writing, but I was always aware that how we remember things tricks us all, and individual memories might not fully reflect reality. To the extent possible, I tried to use multiple sources to minimize inaccuracies.

NUCLEAR NEGOTIATIONS

The second part of my book is devoted to the first years of Kazakhstan's independence. When the Soviet Union collapsed, Kazakhstan found itself with a daunting inheritance it had not sought—more than a thousand Soviet nuclear weapons. That legacy would have made Kazakhstan the world's fourth largest nuclear power, but, after complex and high-stakes negotiations with the United States, Russia, and others, it decided to spurn that option and instead become nuclear-free.

I tell the story of this journey by again relying on primary documents found in the archives—memos, cables, and policy papers as well as interviews with the diplomats, officials, and experts who were active participants in the relevant events. As a scholar, not bound by political correctness or government narrative, I have written a story which might appear messy but is, I hope, more nuanced and more accurate than would be a glossy celebration of US-Kazakhstan achievements in diplomatic denuclearization.

As with the first part of the book, the second part presented research issues. Sifting through archival documents felt like a treasure hunt. It was interesting to see how Kazakhs and Americans interpreted the same events, how each side prepared for negotiations, and what they thought about each other.

Time presented a different challenge in the research. If you talk today to Kazakh and American participants in those 1990s events, they describe them with warm nostalgia and mutual respect. The passage of time has allowed them to zoom in on the good, important moments and perceive history as a neat progression of wise decisions and laudable cooperation, all leading to a culmi-nation of which they are rightfully proud: a nuclear-free Kazakhstan. This rosy narrative would suggest that the Kazakh leadership immediately knew what to do with its nuclear arsenal (give it up) and that the United States never worried about Kazakhstan's inclinations.

But the primary documents—the diplomatic cables, internal memos, and media interviews from the early 1990s—tell a more complicated story. Ac-cording to those contemporaneous records, for the decision-makers from the United States and Kazakhstan, the nuclear negotiations were shot through with uncertainty, anxiety, and apprehension.

These worries make sense. Kazakhstan was then a brand-new country. Its leaders were understandably anxious about its future. Whether to give up nu-clear weapons and the nuclear infrastructure and how to do it in a way that would help, not detract, from the country's security, were not easily answerable questions, especially as two of Kazakhstan's neighbors, Russia and China, were nuclear powers. Similarly, on the US side, understanding Kazakhstan's inten-tions was not a given in the beginning. There was no certainty about what Ka-zakhstan would do.

As a scholar, I wanted this book to reflect as accurately as possible the com-plexities of that period. But I also believe that, in the end, those complexities render the eventual achievements even more impressive. A young country whose leaders were not allowed to make any significant decisions of their own under Soviet rule made life-changing decisions that benefited a new nation diplomatically, economically, and in terms of security. Kazakhstan, poor and in crisis, negotiated with the world's superpower on an almost equal footing. As for the United States, it achieved its main objective of assuring the removal of Soviet nuclear weapons from Kazakhstan, and it did so through thoughtful and skillful diplomacy. Specifically, the United States offered Kazakhstan what it needed most—support for its sovereignty and security, the financial and technical means to help dismantle weapons infrastructure and secure vulnerable nuclear material, and direct foreign investment and political and economic assistance.

A KAZAKH, A SCHOLAR

Like the story of the nuclear tests and of Kazakhstan's early years of independence, my own Kazakh heritage is nuanced, both in its effect on me and on my preparation of this book.

"Aren't you happy Kazakhstan got rid of those nasty Russian colonizers?" was the most frequent question I got when I started living and studying abroad. Fellow graduate students from Western countries, informed by textbooks written by Western scholars who never lived in the region, assumed the only emotion people in Central Asia could feel about the Soviet collapse was joy. The truth was way more complicated.

My childhood, lived under Soviet rule, could not have been happier. My parents loved each other, and they loved us, their two daughters. Our parents' circle included people in politics, history, arts, and literature. They would regularly host interesting people for dinners. We never sat at the "kids' table." Our parents often struggled financially, just like most of the Soviet intelligentsia, but we never felt deprived. I felt safe, loved, and happy.

I also distinctly remember feeling pride for the Soviet Union. Usually, it was during international sports events that I felt it most strongly. Soviet teams winning dozens of gold medals in the Olympics. Soviet gymnasts dazzling world audiences. And my favorite of all—Soviet figure skaters—performing incredible pirouettes on ice. My heart skipped a bit when I heard that triumphant Soviet hymn:

> The unbreakable union of free republics
> Great Russia united forever.
> Long may it live, created by the will of the people
> United, mighty Soviet Union!

But there were also things that did not make sense, things that were part of living in a Soviet state. In elementary school, the teachers told us that we were expected to love Grandpa Lenin more than anyone else. "Mum, is it okay that I love Dad more than I love Lenin?" a six-year-old me asked, seeking reassurance. "Absolutely," my mother responded. She, forever a nonconformist, never joined the Communist Party even though it was expected of all university professors.

The fact that Kazakhs were second-class citizens in their own republic or that non-Slavic ethnicities were considered inferior to Russians was also something I could not fully grasp until much later. As a little girl, I internalized Soviet standards of beauty. Female beauty was someone blonde with blue eyes, not Asian with almond-shaped eyes, like me. I even disliked my name—Togzhan. An unusual Kazakh name did not sound feminine enough in Russian because it did not end with a vowel. It was only as a young adult that I embraced my name, which can be translated from Kazakh as "full, satisfied soul."

The Soviet system officially prided itself on interethnic harmony, but the reality was very different. In the Soviet republics, most top positions—in governing bodies or big industrial facilities—were awarded to ethnic Russians. The deputies would often be the representatives of local ethnicity.

Local culture and language were also relegated to second place, after Russian. In my home city of Almaty, there were only a handful of schools that allowed teaching in Kazakh. There was no Kazakh language heard on the streets of Almaty or other big cities. One had to travel deep into the rural countryside to hear Kazakh. As a child, I was oblivious to how the Soviet state suppressed Kazakh identity.

In terms of this book, my Kazakh heritage afforded clear advantages in my familiarity with my nation's history, geography, culture, and language, and my access to my father's papers. But that heritage also posed dangers, particularly in the area of potential bias and undue exaggeration. The scholar in me wanted to tell my country's story as fully and objectively as I could. But because I am a Kazakh and because my father was a major figure in Kazakh nuclear policymaking, this journey wasn't without a struggle.

On an emotional level, the hardest part of research and writing concerned the Soviet nuclear tests. As someone who grew up in Kazakhstan, I knew about the history of the tests and the endless victims. But visiting the former nuclear test site and reading contemporaneous documents about the period elevated my understanding of the tragedy to a new level. On more than one occasion, my blood boiled when I came across particularly cruel or tragic material.

Meeting Kazakh victims of the Soviet tests or reading about their experiences proved especially hard. Those were my people—the people who looked like me, who shared my culture and affinity for the land, people who did nothing wrong but ended up paying the price for the Soviet "nuclear shield." The stories of these people are heartbreaking and continue to haunt me. But I have tried my best to research and report this story with scholarly discipline and impartiality.

Please read this book with an understanding of both my heritage and the emotions it engenders, and of my desire as a scholar to write a book that is as objective and comprehensive as possible. It took me more than a decade to research and write this work; I hope you find it to be a full and fair treatment of the issues discussed. My hope is that it is a worthy tribute to my father and those who, like him, navigated the complexities of building a new state, and to the people of Semipalatinsk, who paid the price for Soviet nuclear might.

CHAPTER 1

THE STEPPE

Summertime is here. The full heat of July
Stands over lush meadows
Where sedge and wildflowers grow tall.
An auyl comes to this roaring river
To settle while the summer lasts,
Among pastures so high that the horses
Can hardly be seen. They're well-fed beasts—
The colts and mares and stallions.

—Abai, Kazakh poet and writer, native of Semipalatinsk region (1845–1904)

THE DISMEMBERED BODIES of animals covered the ground. Farther out from the blast site were animals that had survived. Some, including birds hit midflight by light radiation, lay on the ground, while others roamed in shock, their skin and fur burnt. Medics and soldiers carried dead and wounded animals to their vehicles.[1]

Before the blast, scientists and military personnel had scattered thousands of animals—sheep, goats, pigs, dogs, rabbits, mice, rats, and guinea pigs—across the testing grounds to gauge the power of splitting an atom. It was August 29, 1949: the date of the Soviet Union's first detonation of an atomic bomb at the newly built testing site in the steppes of Kazakhstan.

The vast territory of the Soviet Union offered seemingly endless choices for such a site. A special government commission considered different options. Ultimately, the commission chose a spot in the middle of Kazakhstan, one of its republics on the border with China, where the remote geography offered the most favorable conditions. The Kazakh steppe—a flat grassy plain similar to a prairie—stretched for thousands of miles. The chosen site was ideal for future atmospheric nuclear tests since the military could build all the necessary infrastructure on and underneath its flat surface. With time, underground nuclear tests would be conducted in mountain ranges nearby. The Irtysh River, one of the largest rivers of the continent, stretched from China via Kazakhstan to Russia, providing access to water. Plenty of construction material—wood, sand, and stone—was available as well. Away from major cities and far from major transportation hubs, the future testing site would also be hidden from public view.[2] This testing site, which at more than 18,500 square kilometers (more than 7,100 square miles) was the size of Belgium, would become known as the Polygon, the Soviet term for an area used to test weapons or conduct military exercises.

Soviet officials referred to the area as almost uninhabited. In fact, only 120 kilometers (75 miles) away lay the city of Semipalatinsk, home to 120,000 residents at the time (the city's population would grow to 350,000 over the years). Thousands of people lived within an 80-kilometer (50-mile) radius of the site in rural settlements that dotted the land.

Semipalatinsk was a multiethnic, culturally diverse city. It was home not only to Kazakhs and Russians but also to many other ethnic groups. This diversity was the result of Stalin's policy of exiling ethnic minorities he deemed untrustworthy to remote parts of the Soviet land.

The population in several villages consisted mostly of ethnic Kazakhs who bred sheep and horses. Some other villages near the chosen site were home to many Russians, Ukrainians, and other ethnicities. Before the Soviet military arrived, Kazakh shepherds roamed the generous land that provided food for their cattle. These villages supplied high-quality meat and dairy products. In the city of Semipalatinsk, the meat-processing factory was one of the largest in the Soviet Union; its canned meat and sausages had fed the Soviet army during World War II.

During the more powerful tests, these people would experience firsthand the immediate and long-term consequences of explosions. Radiation would poison their air, water, and food, irrevocably changing their lives.

THE SEMIPALATINSK REGION: A TROVE OF NATURAL BEAUTY AND A CRADLE OF KAZAKH CULTURE

What appeared as harsh and barren terrain to the Soviet military was, to Kazakhs, a treasured ancestral land. Kazakhs feel a deep affinity for their land and place of birth, and the Semipalatinsk region, in the country's east, has always held an especially sacred place in the Kazakh consciousness. This esteem stems from the region's beauty, its hallmark nomadic culture, and its role as the birthplace of Kazakh literature and center of intellectual life.

Since ancient times, the endless steppe and limitless blue skies of the region have signified freedom to the nomads who long occupied it. At the horizon, the steppe meets the skies, dividing what you see into two blocks of color, with nothing to obstruct the view—no trees, no bushes, nothing. Just like a Rothko painting. The vast steppe changes color from season to season. Vibrant green in spring, by summer the land has been scorched golden by the sun. In autumn, the air smells of rain and fresh grass. In winter, falling snow cloaks the curves of the landscape in silent white.

Despite its massiveness, the steppe morphs at points into hills, low-range mountains, pine forests and, along the Irtysh River, areas of lush foliage. Silver-leaf poplar and willows line the river, where bass, pike, and other fish live. In the pine forests, dotted with maple and elm and suffused with the almond-like fragrance of the meadowsweet bush, roe deer, elk, wolves, and lynx take shelter. In the skies above soar steppe eagles, skylarks, kites, and rooks. On the steppe itself, the many gophers, hamsters, mice, and other rodents form an indispensable part of the ecosystem, for they are the primary source of food for larger animals, including the ones humans rely on.

The steppe is also famous for its saiga antelope. Cave paintings from the seventh to the fifth century BC often feature saiga antelopes, hinting at the important role they played,[3] but, by the second half of the nineteenth century, their population had plummeted due to aggressive hunting for their valuable horns. By the 1950s their numbers had rebounded to about two million, but, tragically, that is also when the Soviet nuclear testing program began to significantly harm Kazakh flora and fauna.

Living in close harmony for centuries with Kazakhstan's natural beauty were the region's most iconic figures, the nomads. Although not all Kazakhs were nomadic—some lived in oasis cities that served as centers of trade—most of them were, and their lives were governed by rhythms now long gone. To survive, each small community of nomads, connected by family ties, migrated along predetermined routes and searched for new pastures each season to feed its sheep, horses, and camels. They carried all their possessions with them, including the traditional round, domed tents known as yurts. Simple but brilliantly engineered, yurts consisted of only three main parts and could be easily assembled. The nomads covered the yurts with felt on the outside and

PHOTO 1   Kazakh steppe, Semipalatinsk region, 2020. Photograph by Togzhan Kassenova.

decorated them with carpets on the inside, rendering them warm in winter and cool in summer.

Summer was the highlight of the nomads' year. Their cattle quickly gained weight from abundant grass, they could comfortably sleep under the open sky, and the summer season was filled with weddings and competitions in singing, music, and physical strength. The memories of summer helped the nomads to endure the harsh winters when the cattle had to eat frozen or dry grass and the freezing wind blew unobstructed across the flat steppe.

In addition to its natural beauty and its hallmark nomadic culture, the Semipalatinsk region was also the cradle of Kazakh literature and the home of many of the most educated and enlightened Kazakh leaders. Kazakhstan's most revered poet, philosopher, and composer, Abai, born to a well-known local landowner, lived in Semipalatinsk in the late nineteenth century. In Kazakhstan, which long had an oral literary tradition, Abai is considered the father of the nation's written literature. His writings focus on his countrymen and display a deep love for his region and for nature. Abai's magnum opus, *The Book of Words*, is a philosophical treatise inspired by the Western Enlightenment. In it, Abai muses about humanity and his people's culture and history, and he appeals to Kazakhs to value literature, education, and hard work. Fluent in several languages, Abai also translated into Kazakh works by Pushkin, Lermontov, Goethe, and Lord Byron.[4] Several other notable figures—Shakarim (a student of Abai), for example, and Mukhtar Auezov—solidified Semipalatinsk's reputation as the birthplace of Kazakh literature.

Song was another art in which the region excelled. The first singer to represent Kazakhstan abroad in a singing competition was born in the Semipalatinsk village of Kainar, whose residents would later become the first victims of Soviet nuclear experiments. The singer, Amre Kashaubaev, enchanted the audience at the Paris Expo of 1925 and came in second in the competition. The French newspapers marveled at his unique voice, and George Gershwin befriended him.[5]

Semipalatinsk was also home to prominent Russian intellectuals, many exiled there from tsarist Russia during the years between the second half of the nineteenth century and the early twentieth century. Evgenii Mikhaelis, a member of the Russian revolutionary movement in the 1860s as well as a close friend of Abai, studied the geology of eastern Kazakhstan during his exile. Mikhaelis developed navigation maps of river basins and collected economic and geographic data.[6] Fyodor Dostoyevsky, the legendary writer, spent several years in compulsory military service in Semipalatinsk. (He had already spent years imprisoned in Siberia after being accused of reading books banned for their criticism of tsarist Russia).[7] These and other talented Russian individuals studied the Semipalatinsk region, developed strong bonds with the Kazakh intellectual elite, and helped to make the area a center of literature, science, and education.

SEMIPALATINSK: AT THE HEART OF KAZAKH-RUSSIAN HISTORY

It is no surprise that the Soviets ended up conducting their nuclear testing in the Semipalatinsk region. Kazakhstan's relationship with Russia dates to the sixteenth century, and the Semipalatinsk region has been the principal theater of that relationship. Russia had long exercised domination over the area, disrupting and controlling nomadic Kazakh life. At the same time, Russian hegemony also prompted the development of Semipalatinsk itself into a bustling modern city, a site of international trade with a special multicultural environment.

The Semipalatinsk region was the site of Russia's earliest military settlements in Central Asia, a part of the Russian Empire's expansion. Paramilitary groups of Russian Cossacks began building forts at the northwest edge of Kazakhstan in the early sixteenth century, over time expanding their reach into the north. By the early eighteenth century, they had expanded into northeastern Kazakhstan, gradually consolidating control over the territory inhabited by Kazakhs.[8] In 1718, Russia built a fort on the bank of the Irtysh River, next to the remnants of a Buddhist monastery. The name "Semipalatinsk" ("seven chambers") stemmed from the seven buildings that made up that fort. The settlement gradually became a link between Central Asia and the Russian Empire and blossomed into a thriving merchant city.

At the time, the Kazakh tribes were divided into three hordes (tribes)— the Small Horde, Middle Horde, and Great Horde. Each horde was ruled by a khan, a title reserved for sovereign or military rulers in Turkic tribes. The hordes struggled to defend themselves from Mongol tribes that sought to get control of land and oasis cities in the south of Kazakhstan. In the early eighteenth century, Abulkhair Khan, the leader of the Small Horde, led 30,000 warriors against Mongol invaders. But he knew that the Kazakhs would not be able to defend their land alone. So he sought help from Russia. By 1730, the Russian Empress Anna Ioanovna had decided to help the Kazakhs as she feared that the Kalmyks would overtake the Kazakh steppe, a move which would threaten Russia's own plans for expansion as well as Russia's position in southern Siberia. Abulkhair Khan thought that his alliance with the Russian Empire would be temporary. However, it in fact laid the foundation for Kazakhstan's eventual colonization by Russia. Gradually, the other two hordes also fell under Russian rule.

Large bazaars started appearing in Semipalatinsk in the late eighteenth century. Merchants, customers, and goods from Russia, Europe, and all of Central Asia would mix in a lively cacophony of sounds, languages, colors, and aromas. One could find anything—from food to clothes to livestock. Central Asian merchants sold embroidered caftans, colorful blankets, and exquisite leather goods. From the Silk Road cities of Bukhara and Turkestan merchants brought saddles and silver ornaments for horses. At the European part of the bazaar, Russian merchants sold flour, European clothes, and other goods unusual for

PHOTO 2   Palace of Labor, Semipalatinsk, 1929. Photograph by I. Golovanov.
SOURCE: Central State Archive of Film and Photo Documents and Sound Recordings,
Kazakhstan. Image #5–2555.

Central Asia, such as guitars and felt hats. Caravans from the heart of the Kazakh steppe would arrive at the bazaars as well, with camels and horses laden
with wool, furs, and camel's milk.[9] As the city grew, new industries such as
leather-making emerged, as well as new mining ventures that sought silver,
gold, lead, and copper.

Meanwhile, more and more Slavic people, mostly Russians and Ukrainians,
were drawn to Central Asia by offers of land. By the late nineteenth and early
twentieth century, 1.5 million of them had settled in Kazakhstan. The tsarist government forcibly seized Kazakh land and governed through violence and cruelty.
Kazakh nomads had less and less territory in which to find pastures for their
cattle—their only source of livelihood. The process of turning the Kazakhs into
a sedentary people had begun. The consequences would be painful and tragic.

In the nineteenth century, the ever-expanding Russian control over this
part of Asia triggered several uprisings by Kazakhs to claim independence. All

of them failed. Then, in the early twentieth century, the Kazakh elites established a Kazakh independence party to promote and defend the interests of
the oppressed majority Kazakh population. Among the founders was Alikhan
Bukeikhanov, the highly educated son of a khan, who had been arrested on
multiple occasions by the tsarist government and would spend years in exile for
his political activism.[10] The new party was called Alash—in Kazakh mythology,
Alash was the khan and the warrior who in the first half of the fifteenth century
united different Turkic tribes and founded the Kazakh nation.[11]

During the brief period that followed the abdication of Tsar Nicholas II,
Alash leaders were hopeful that the new regime, led by liberals, would lessen
Russia's colonial pressure on Central Asia. Taking advantage of this opportunity, Alash promoted the idea that Russia should become a democratic federal
republic in which each state would have autonomy. In just a few months, however, that February Revolution was over. The Russian Provisional government
fell and, following the October Revolution, the Bolsheviks took control. The
new political situation changed the calculations of Alash, as one of its leaders,
Akhmet Baitursynov, explained:

> Kazakhs understood and joyfully welcomed the first [February] revolution be-
> cause it freed them from the tyranny and the violence of the tsarist government

PHOTO 3   Purchase of sheepskin, Semipalatinsk, 1916. Photograph by F. Belosluidov.
SOURCE: Central State Archive of Film and Photo Documents and Sound Recordings,
Kazakhstan. Image #B-2481.

and strengthened their hope for a cherished dream of self-governance. It is easy
to explain why Kazakhs did not understand the second [October] revolution:
Kazakhs [did] not have capitalism and class differentiation; property [was] not
as divided as in other nations. The October revolution terrified Kazakhs with
its external manifestations. In remote areas, the Bolshevik movement used violence, robbery, abuses [of power] and dictatorial power. [In] other words, it often represented not a revolution but complete anarchy.[12]

In December 1917, Alash established a Kazakh autonomous government,
called Alash Orda. This government, centered in Semipalatinsk, created an
education commission, militia regiments, and adopted legislation under the
leadership of Alikhan Bukeikhanov, the highly educated founding member and
longtime Kazakh activist. Alash Orda, with Bukeikhanov as its prime minister,
lasted for three years, until it was forced to surrender to the Russian Bolsheviks
in 1920. Kazakhstan was incorporated into Russia as an autonomous republic,
and the Alash Orda leaders were imprisoned and labeled "bourgeois nationalists" and "enemies of the state." Stalin, who consolidated his power in 1929,
executed those bright Kazakhs in his Great Purge of the 1930s.

In 1936, Kazakhstan received the status of a Soviet republic, ushering in
the Soviet period of Kazakhstan's history. The Central Committee of the Soviet Communist Party in Moscow made all major decisions on behalf of the
republic, from how much meat, wheat, cotton, or minerals Kazakhstan should
produce to how many schools and kindergartens should be opened. In Kazakhstan, the Central Committee of Kazakhstan's Communist Party received orders
from Moscow and instructed the executive organ—the Council of Ministers of
Kazakhstan—on their implementation.

Becoming a part of the Soviet Union was both a blessing and a curse for
Kazakhstan. It prompted the republic's modernization, bringing asphalt roads,
electricity, and other infrastructure. Kazakhstan's people benefited from the
universal health care and education promoted by the Soviet government. They
received access to Russian science and literature through Russian language
training, which almost all urban and many rural dwellers had to learn.

Yet Russian and Soviet rule also brought extreme national tragedies. During
the Soviet collectivization between 1929 and 1934, Stalin's government forcibly
consolidated individual peasant households into collective farms. This policy
devastated the many Kazakhs who had led a nomadic pastoral life and had
roamed in small groups with their cattle. The imposition of a sedentary lifestyle
and the requisitioning of livestock from Kazakh herders to feed other parts of

the Soviet Union deprived millions of Kazakhs of their only source of food. Of the 40 million head of cattle that Kazakhs possessed at the start of collectivization, only 4.5 million survived three years later. More than 1.5 million people (1.3 million of them ethnic Kazakhs), a quarter of the population and a third of all ethnic Kazakhs, perished from famine because of collectivization. The Soviet government shut the borders so that the many starving Kazakhs could not leave. Some managed to escape to Mongolia, Turkey, or Uzbekistan, losing family members en route to cold, hunger, and violence from the Soviet soldiers.[13]

With these actions, the Soviet government completely changed the ethnic and social landscape of the Kazakh steppe. Kazakhs were now a minority in their own land. And they were forced to abandon their nomadism. Their way of life was forever altered.

But the rush for the Soviet nuclear bomb would bring a whole new trial for the Kazakh nation.

THE SOVIET NUCLEAR PROGRAM

Stalin and his military advisors did not see the natural beauty and cultural heritage of the Semipalatinsk region. They saw only its potential as an advantageous site for their nuclear experiments. Thanks to Soviet intelligence services, Stalin had known since the early 1940s that the Americans were working on a nuclear bomb. But at that time the Soviets were busy fighting World War II, defending their home against Nazi Germany's incursions. The Soviet government threw all scientific efforts into the immediate war effort—developing and building conventional weapons, such as tanks and artillery. The turning point for Stalin came in 1945. At the July Potsdam Conference, US President Harry Truman privately boasted to Stalin about the Americans' possession of a novel weapon of unusual destructive force. The very next month, on August 6 and August 9, the United States dropped two atomic bombs, on Hiroshima and Nagasaki, instantly killing roughly 100,000 to 120,000 people. Many thousands would die soon after from the injuries they sustained.

Stalin immediately tasked his government and scientists with developing a Soviet nuclear weapon. The Soviet Union, which had already started working on nuclear matters during World War II but had not made them a priority, now rushed to equalize its power with the United States.[14] At that time, the Soviet Union was reeling from the devastating losses of the war, in which more than 26 million of its people had perished. Despite this, the government spared nothing to build the ultimate weapon. Stalin apparently told the scientists to ask for anything they needed to build a bomb: "If a child doesn't cry, the mother doesn't know what he needs. Ask for whatever you like. You won't be refused."[15]

Stalin's right-hand man, Lavrentii Beria, personally oversaw the Soviet bomb project and ensured that it operated in complete secrecy. He would come to the Semipalatinsk test site regularly to observe the most important tests and keep tabs on sensitive work. Beria was infamous for the persecution and deaths of thousands of Soviet citizens during Stalin's reign. A man of pathological cruelty, he enjoyed torturing people personally and was believed to have kept truncheons in his office desk. Given that Beria was in charge, the scientists who worked on the first Soviet bomb knew that the stakes were high, that any failure on their part could lead to their execution.

Yet Soviet nuclear scientists also saw a patron in Beria. He possessed exceptional organizational skills, secured unlimited resources for the nuclear program, and made sure its participants enjoyed benefits to which no other Soviet citizens had access. Yuli Khariton and Yuri Smirnov, leading Soviet nuclear scientists at the time, described him as "the very personification of evil in modern Russian history" but at the same time "courteous, tactful, and simple when circumstances demanded it."[16]

The leader of the scientific effort was Igor Kurchatov, a nuclear scientist in his early thirties. He spent substantial amounts of time at the Polygon, personally overseeing the tests. Uniformly respected by the scientists, optimistic by nature, and jovial in personality, he had a reputation for being attentive and patient. Kurchatov also managed to have a good working relationship with Beria, even though Beria was a person of a completely different character and notably less sophisticated in science than Kurchatov and his colleagues.

Yuli Khariton, a chief designer of the first Soviet atomic bomb, was another key figure at the Polygon. The urgency of the Soviet nuclear project saved the Cambridge-educated Khariton, an ethnic Jew, from Stalin's purges. He was the only child of Mira Burovskaia, a successful theater actress whose stage name was Mira Birrens, and Boris Khariton, a famous journalist who perished in the Soviet Gulag.

In 1947, the Soviet government began to assemble manpower for the testing program. Soldiers, officers, and engineers were selected en masse and sent to the Semipalatinsk testing site. Refusing to go was not an option.

The initiative was conducted in complete secrecy. Before arriving, the first military personnel, who were to build the Polygon, received little information aside from their titles and salaries. Their superiors did not disclose the location of the new assignment. Only a five-digit number—52605—denoted the new military division. Everyone was sworn to secrecy, and the words "atom," "Polygon," and "Semipalatinsk" were forbidden from use. Some of the arrivals sought to be sent back home, exhausted from years away from their families during World War II. But the majority followed orders, driven by the knowledge that they were part of a major state project.[17]

The government used a lengthy questionnaire to carefully vet every single conscript, ensuring that those who would work on this crucial project did not have a criminal background or connections with foreigners. The questionnaire even asked where dead relatives were buried.[18] Such information could give the government a good idea of the person's background, religion, and roots. Did the person have several generations of ancestors in the Soviet Union and was not some foreigner who had infiltrated the Soviet system? Some conscripts dreamed of trips abroad, mistaking this process for the background check on Soviet citizens before foreign travel. Instead, those chosen for the secret mission were summoned to Zvenigorod, a twelfth-century town on the banks of the Moscow River. They stayed at a military sanatorium in an idyllic setting near the beautiful Savvino-Storozhevskii monastery, a preferred place of worship of the Russian tsars.

At Zvenigorod, Mikhail Sadovskii, the deputy director of the Institute of Chemical Physics, who would become scientific director of the Polygon in 1954, interviewed the conscripts.[19] Soon after, they were assigned to various institutes in Moscow and Leningrad, depending on their specific skills, expertise, and the anticipated needs of the testing program. Once trained and ready to be deployed, the early rank-and-file soldiers received train tickets. First, they traveled to Novosibirsk in Siberia, where they then boarded a southbound train to Kazakhstan. Even the tickets were part of a state-level disguise, listing their destination as Charskaia, the final stop. In fact, they stepped off the train one station early, at Zhana-Semey.[20]

They disembarked only to face harsh weather in a barren place with no infrastructure. In winter, temperatures plummeted to -50° C (-60° F).[21] Snowstorms made it difficult to see or walk.[22] Construction workers suffered from chilblains due to relentless northern winds.[23] The rough winters gave way to beautiful but short springs followed almost immediately by scorching summers. Dry conditions on the steppe led to frequent fires.[24]

The first few years of building and operating the Polygon were the hardest. For two years, 1947 and 1948, work continued from dusk to dawn. Construction personnel slept in dugouts. The Polygon was built by 15,000 soldiers, officers, and construction workers, who were joined in the effort by thousands of prisoners shipped in from camps overseen by Beria. The prisoners were forced to carry out the most arduous work, and many of them perished. Disturbed by the human activity, many animals left the area. Even mice escaped, running away from the soil as it was dug over.[25]

Conditions were similar to those of wartime, with dugouts, camp meals, and the full control of life by the state. The letters that construction workers received from family and friends were stamped "Checked by military censorship." Newspapers arrived at the Polygon site with a four- to six-day delay. Starting in 1948, when the site got its first radio, tired men gathered every evening around the post on which the radio was mounted to hear the national and global news. Broadcasts of soccer games attracted particularly huge, and rowdy, crowds.

On Saturdays—movie night—films were projected onto a white bedsheet hung between two poles. Because the Soviet Union produced hardly any films of its own in the early postwar years, the scene was striking: in the middle of the Kazakh steppe, amid the construction of the first Soviet nuclear testing site, soldiers watched movies that were made in the West. Most were war trophies stolen from Germany, such as *The Woman of My Dreams*—a musical about a theater actress—and *Ohm Krüger*—an anti-British propaganda movie telling the story of South African politician Paul Kruger and his defeat by the British during the Boer War. On one occasion, when new movies could not be delivered due to some logistical issue, everyone watched a movie based on Puccini's *Tosca* three Saturdays in a row. The bored men joked that the repeated showing was a real *toska* (Russian for melancholy or anguish).[26] The extreme weather, poor living conditions, and constant surveillance by Beria and his men created an extraordinarily harsh environment, physically and psychologically.

Despite all these hardships, the Polygon pioneers built a sprawling nuclear testing site. The Kazakh steppe, which had been entirely free of man-made structures just two years earlier, was soon populated by giant buildings and complex equipment. At the testing field, a circular area that had been completely flattened, thousands of miles of wires and cables ran under the ground. At its center, engineers built a 30-meter (100-foot or twelve-story) metal tower from which the first bomb would be detonated in August 1949.[27] In all directions from the heart of the testing site, the workers erected 10-meter (32-foot) iron-and-concrete structures that looked like huge geese (and were so dubbed by the military). These were special buildings to store the measuring equipment. Scientific labs, and even a vivarium for studying animals during nuclear tests, were also now part of the landscape.

THE FIRST ATOMIC TEST

By the summer of 1949, the atomic bomb team began transporting equipment by rail from the Institute of Chemical Physics in Moscow to the Polygon. The train, with its special freight, made brief stops at platforms emptied in advance of its arrival.[28] Four planes carried the bomb components from a secret town in Russia called Arzamas-16, the home for Design Bureau 11, which had built the bomb.[29]

Still, despite the preparations and evident infrastructure, no one dared to whisper the word *bomb*. "Until the last moment, I did not even know what I guarded. Of course, I had my guesses, but I did not even try to mention it to anyone, and no one mentioned anything to me," recalled a military officer tasked with Polygon's security.[30] The night before the test, those not directly involved were instructed not to wake up early or go to the canteen until 8 a.m.[31]

The weapons team, eager to understand the potency of their bomb, had built an entire miniature city in the testing area, including buildings, parts of a railroad, a highway with a concrete-reinforced bridge, an electric power station complete with diesel generators, a subway tunnel, and military equipment. More than a thousand animals were placed in cages or tethered to the ground across the testing field.

On August 29, 1949, as preparations for the test continued into the early hours, the weather deteriorated. Gusts of wind and cloudy skies threatened to cancel the test. Rushing against the worsening weather conditions, the state commission in charge of the first nuclear test ordered the explosion to take place an hour earlier than planned.

With everything at stake for their country, top military and scientific personnel, overseen by Beria and Kurchatov, anxiously awaited the test from an observation point. At 7 a.m., in the rain and wind, the Soviet Union conducted its first nuclear explosion.[32] At the first ray of explosive light, the observers jumped up, hugged, and screamed, then dropped to the ground just before the blast wave roared. Meanwhile, the flame was pulling up clouds of dust and sand with it, forming the foot of an atomic mushroom. The temperature inside the fireball was 300,000° C (540,032° F). While many shouted in happiness again, Kurchatov remained calm and said simply: "It worked!"[33]

Nuclear physicists Veniamin Tsukerman and Zinaida Azarkh, a married couple, recalled:

> What remarkable words these are: "It had worked! It had worked!" Physicists and engineers, mechanics and workmen, thousands of Soviet people who had worked on the atomic problem, had not let the country down. The Soviet Union had become the second atomic power. The nuclear balance had been achieved.[34]

Beria asked Kurchatov to give the bomb a name, and Kurchatov told him that one of the bomb designers had already given it one—RDS-1. RDS stood for "Rossiia Delaet Sama," or "Russia Does It on Its Own." From then on, all Soviet nuclear bombs would be designated RDS-2, RDS-3, and so on.[35]

Beria called Stalin in Moscow, where the local time was a little after 4 a.m. When Beria woke Stalin with news of the successful test, the premier—keen to keep his closest aide in his place—curtly responded "I know" and promptly hung up.[36]

While Beria posed for photos in front of still-smoking buildings destroyed by the explosion and next to mangled pieces of military equipment, the scientists and military officers were impatient to check the damage their creation had caused at the epicenter.[37] A mere twenty minutes after the explosion, the first tanks rolled toward ground zero.

"The view was striking: destruction all around, heavy dead silence, burnt soil, dead burnt birds," wrote one test witness. "An eerie feeling."[38] In place of the metal tower on which the bomb had been detonated was a crater, a meter and a half deep, of molten soil. Buildings and other structures within a 50-meter (160-foot) radius of the epicenter were gone. The railway bridge had been torn out of the ground and thrown across the field by the force of the explosion.[39]

Animals placed at different distances across the testing field provided Soviet scientists and military a first glimpse of the bomb's power. Close to the epicenter, some animals had been incinerated. The dead and injured animals were transported back to the vivarium where the scientists studied them there and attempted to cure those that survived to gain insight into treating human victims of a nuclear war.[40]

The dosimetry teams, tasked with checking radiation levels across the testing field, donned their protective gear and received instructions on how to proceed. However, scientific curiosity pushed some to disobey the rules, driving within 2 kilometers (1.3 miles) of the epicenter when they had been warned not to approach within 2.5–3 kilometers (1.6–1.9 miles). The radiation safety crew roaming the field in a special tank screamed at those dosimetrists to get away. Though tensions were high, the dosimetrists "badly wanted to collect more data," as one admitted. On return, his gas mask was filled with "enough sweat to fill half a glass."[41] That day, radiation at the epicenter of the explosion reached extremely high levels—more than 5,000 micro-roentgen per second (5,000 micro-roentgen per *year* is the maximum allowed dose for occupational exposure for a US worker today).[42] On return, everyone had to shower, sometimes more than once, to remove radioactive dust.

Other teams checked on the recording and measuring equipment secreted in bunkers and other structures across the testing field. Eight-millimeter movie cameras were checked for the few seconds of explosion footage they recorded before the blast destroyed them.[43]

In one of the nearby villages, Mutan Aimakov, a newly appointed head teacher recalled the day of the first test: "At 6 a.m. on August 29, the soldiers ordered all villagers outside. The explanation was simple but unclear: 'An event will take place shortly. You should all lie face down to the ground. Close your eyes, don't open them, don't raise your head! If you disobey, your life will be in danger.'"[44] Aimakov, who spoke some Russian, helped the soldiers communicate with the villagers, and soon, at 7 a.m., everyone heard the roar followed by the earth shaking, the walls of clay houses breaking, and windows shattering, as a dark nuclear mushroom filled the skies:

> Village dogs suddenly started to howl, as if at someone's command, all facing east. The cows began to moo. The camels howled. They howled not like female camels looking for their colts, but melancholically, as though complaining about something. Some cows ran up a heap of cinder and started kicking it. The horses came back from pastures at full gallop and grouped in fright in the center of the village. The noble animals clearly sensed some kind of trouble—or were they seeking help from people?[45]

The first test would turn out to be the most harmful in the entire history of Soviet nuclear tests. Within hours, a radioactive cloud blanketed the area, spreading as far as Russia's Altai region a thousand kilometers (more than 600 miles) away. Some people who worked outside when the radioactive cloud passed suffered radiation burns.[46]

Back in Moscow, the leadership celebrated a new chapter of Soviet might. State honors were bestowed on scientists and military personnel. But the awards ceremony was held behind closed doors, and no newspaper made any announcements because the government decree listing the awards was classified. Igor Kurchatov and a few others became Heroes of Socialist Labor, the highest title in the Soviet award system.

The program's scientists, who along with the rest of the Soviet society had led modest lives, were elevated to a previously unimaginable level of prestige. They were given dachas, and, in the case of a few key personnel, legendary, sleek *Pobeda* (Victory) cars. Igor Kurchatov and Yuli Khariton received rare seven-seat luxury ZIS-110 automobiles. These cars required heated garages and special oil, among other things, which proved to be too high-maintenance and expensive for the modest and busy nuclear scientists. In the late 1950s, both cars were sold via secondhand shops to Orthodox Church officials.[47]

The children of the honorees could study at any school of their choice.[48] The most unusual reward, conferred on key scientists and their spouses, was dubbed the "magic carpet": the right to unlimited, lifelong, free travel on any mode of public transportation across the Soviet Union. Their children could use this right until turning sixteen.[49]

Had the first test failed, the principal scientists and military personnel would have been sent to Siberian labor camps or shot. Despite the rewards and accolades, they continued to straddle the fine edge between celebration and punishment in the culture of surveillance and fear that permeated life at the Polygon.

The first nuclear test opened the forty-year history of the Semipalatinsk Polygon. The total yield of nuclear explosions at Semipalatinsk would reach 17.7 megatons, the equivalent of a thousand Hiroshima bombs.[50]

CHAPTER 2

FORTY YEARS OF NUCLEAR TESTS

FOR THE NEXT FORTY YEARS, under pressure to maintain parity with the United States, the Soviet government poured money, brainpower, and manpower into growing its nuclear program. The brightest minds toiled on the bomb project, and Soviet nuclear science made impressive breakthroughs. To turn theory into practice, Soviet scientists and the military conducted more than seven hundred nuclear tests, with more than 450 of them at Semipalatinsk between 1949, when the Polygon was established, and 1989, when Kazakhstan's antinuclear protests stopped them.[1]

More than a hundred additional tests were conducted in the Russian Republic between 1955 and 1990, at Novaya Zemlya—two islands in the Arctic Ocean. Unlike the Semipalatinsk Polygon, Novaya Zemlya was far from a major population center and uninhabited after about four hundred locals, mostly Nenets, a Samoyedic ethnic group native to northern arctic Russia, were relocated to the Russian mainland. Another hundred-plus nuclear tests were carried out at other sites across the Soviet Union.

The United States conducted more than a thousand nuclear tests of its own—most of them at the Nevada Test Site and in the Pacific Ocean. The United Kingdom, a close ally of the United States, carried out more than twenty nuclear tests on the Australian territories and in the Pacific Ocean, and another twenty-plus tests with the United States at the Nevada Test Site. France followed with tests in Algeria and French Polynesia, and China with tests in Xinjiang province, home to a Muslim minority of Uighurs. In a striking similarity, all five governments chose territories primarily inhabited by indigenous peoples, ethnic or religious minorities, or otherwise vulnerable groups. India, Pakistan, and North Korea also tested nuclear weapons, and Israel is suspected of being involved in a joint nuclear test with South Africa.

In Kazakhstan, as the Cold War raged on for four decades, more than a million people living near the Polygon were at the mercy of Soviet and American politicians. Nuclear explosions ripped through the Kazakh land, harming people in the Semipalatinsk area and their homes. The explosions and shock waves damaged buildings, and people were injured from shattered glass. But the more sinister and long-term danger was an invisible one—radiation.

Following a nuclear explosion, radioactive particles mix with dust in the air and spread into the atmosphere. In unfavorable weather, this radioactive dust sweeps up into the clouds and rain, traveling far beyond the test site. The radioactive fallout from the Polygon contaminated not only grazing lands but also water wells, soil, and vegetation. Animals fed on contaminated pastures, and people who lived in the vicinity of the Polygon drank polluted water and milk and ate meat laced with radioisotopes. This meant that people and animals not only were exposed to external radiation but also internalized it. Ingested radioisotopes lodged in their bones, thyroids, and blood.

LIFE AT THE SECRET TOWN

To house scientists and military officers working at the Polygon in the late 1940s, the Soviet government built a new settlement about sixty kilometers (thirty-seven miles) from the testing field. Tucked away on the banks of the Irtysh River and not marked on any maps, it was known initially as the "Bereg" (Riverbank) or Site M (after its secret designation as Moscow-400). Later it became Semipalatinsk-21, a code name derived from the nearest civilian city, Semipalatinsk, and the last two digits of the postal code. In 1974 the settlement was officially designated a town and named after Kurchatov to honor the father of the Soviet atomic weapon. The residents of the town mostly came from Russia. Only a handful of Kazakh officers lived there, unlike at the Polygon, where approximately 5,000 soldiers from Kazakhstan joined soldiers from throughout the Soviet Union to do menial work.

The early years of the testing program—the late 1940s and early 1950s—were hard on everyone. Residents at the military settlement lived in tight quarters in shared rooms with no gas or hot water and few electric stoves. The social dynamic reflected its artificial composition. Few women lived there, and as one woman described it, "men fell in love with just anybody."[2]

During those first years, no families of military officers or scientists were allowed at the site, and no vacations were authorized. Beria and his underlings kept a close eye on everyone, scrutinized the mood, and even monitored scientists' discussions. The KGB censored personal letters and prevented any information from leaking to the outside. During the periods leading up to and following the tests, Polygon staff were not allowed to write letters or send telegrams to their families or friends. Other times, postcards and letters were regularly "lost."

Life on the steppe was lonely and void of entertainment, except for the occasional party and movies projected on a big screen on Saturdays. Site workers watched the same films over and over, learning some of them by heart. Despite the bleak conditions, an officer reminiscing about the 1949 New Year's party (held in the vivarium for lack of a more appropriate accommodation) noted, "we were young [and] optimistic."[3]

By the early 1950s, the soldiers' families could finally join them, and the place began to look more and more like a regular town. A kindergarten and a school opened. Families started tending to gardens and small plots of land near their homes, growing tomatoes, watermelons, and other fruits and vegetables.[4] As the town expanded, social life improved. With more women present, the residents could enjoy dance parties on weekends.[5] Locally organized plays and concerts became a favorite pastime, in part because residents had to rely on themselves for entertainment. They did not have access to television, and no visiting shows were allowed.[6]

By 1952, the town had good grocery stores. With time, the supply of food and other goods in this secret settlement exceeded those in the average Soviet city. Stores stocked good wine and chocolate, even tins of crabmeat and canned fruits—goods considered luxuries by regular Soviet citizens. By the late 1950s, every officer's family had an apartment, and by 1956–57 the military town offered some of the best living conditions in the Soviet Union.[7]

New apartment buildings sprang up, wide streets were built, more trees were planted. The population soared. Residents could now enjoy cultural events in the newly built Culture House and Officers' Club. With time, the town built more schools, kindergartens, its own stadium, a polyclinic, and a hospital. Meanwhile, residents in nearby rural settlements struggled. They lacked fresh food; living conditions were dire; and medical services were basic.

ATMOSPHERIC TESTS AT THE SEMIPALATINSK
POLYGON (1949–62)

Throughout the 1950s and early 1960s, the United States and the Soviet Union developed and tested increasingly advanced weapons. In 1952, Americans triggered the world's first thermonuclear explosion on the Marshall Islands in the Pacific Ocean, proving that multimegaton blasts were possible. A thermonuclear explosion uses two stages to create an impact hundreds of times more powerful than a simple atomic explosion. The nuclear fission of the heavy elements uranium-235 or plutonium generates the enormous heat that makes it possible for light elements to fuse, with an enormous release of energy.[8] America's first thermonuclear weapon had a power equal to seven hundred Hiroshima-sized bombs.[9] Later, Soviet scientists dismissed this achievement, saying the 82-ton installation could not be called a bomb since it looked like a building—"a two-story laboratory structure with thermonuclear fuel stored in a liquid state close to absolute zero."[10]

By 1953, the Soviets were ready to test their own thermonuclear weapon. But before the test could take place, an announcement came in early March that Stalin had died. The news shocked all Soviet people, including the nuclear scientists who did not know what Stalin's death meant for the nuclear program. Hundreds of thousands of mourners filled the streets of Moscow.

After a brief power struggle for the top spot in the Soviet hierarchy, Nikita Khrushchev officially became the First Secretary of the Soviet Communist Party. Khrushchev, the son of a coal miner in Ukraine, worked as a mechanic in his teens and later as a machine repairman at a coal mine. He joined the Communist Party in his early twenties and, by the time of Stalin's death, had risen to the highest ranks of the Soviet ruling elite. Khrushchev and his allies were keen to get rid of Beria, who continued to be the most important figure in the Soviet nuclear program. In June 1953, two months before the scheduled test of the first Soviet thermonuclear weapon, Khrushchev had Beria arrested.

The pretext for the arrest was a specially arranged meeting of the Communist Party leadership, to which Beria had been summoned. There, he was accused by Khrushchev and others of treason—specifically, of selling state secrets to British intelligence. Marshal Zhukov and a group of armed military officers stormed into the meeting room and arrested a shocked Beria on the spot. The operation had to be carefully planned; Beria was formally in charge of both the secret and regular police. In order to avoid a confrontation with his men, who were waiting for their boss, Beria was taken out of the Kremlin under dark of night in the back of a car. He was eventually imprisoned in an underground bunker.

Within two weeks of the arrest, the government newspaper *Pravda* announced Beria's fall.[11] He was convicted at a special tribunal of treason and allowed no appeal. He was shot in December 1953. His wife and son were sent to one of the Siberian labor camps that Beria had established. The fate of this mass murderer and torturer had come full circle.

When Beria was arrested, nuclear weapons scientists were worried about their future; after all, the main man behind their weapons effort had fallen in disgrace. A nuclear scientist who was at the Polygon during that time recalls:

> One evening, when we got together in our temporary dorm at the testing site, listening to homemade radio, the radio host suddenly announced that a government statement would follow. Indeed, what followed was an announcement that Beria had been arrested for being a state enemy and foreign agent. We were shocked! What will happen next? To sit here at the Polygon until things become clear—Beria oversaw the entire nuclear weapons program![12]

However, when Khrushchev appointed Vyacheslav Malyshev as the new head of the program, the preparations for testing the first thermonuclear weapon proceeded as planned. Malyshev was a well-known manager of large-scale military projects. During World War II, he had led production of military tanks, which were indispensable for the Soviet army.

THE SOVIET THERMONUCLEAR BREAKTHROUGH

The scientist behind the Soviet thermonuclear achievement was Andrei Sakharov. The son of a physics teacher, Sakharov followed in his father's footsteps, studying physics under the legendary theoretical physicist Igor Tamm. Sakharov was only thirty-two years old when he designed the first Soviet thermonuclear bomb.

Sakharov worked on his bomb at the secret town code-named Arzamas-16–the same place where the first Soviet atomic bomb was developed. Originally named Sarov, Arzamas-16 was historically a pilgrimage site for worshippers in the Orthodox Church. The famous Sarov monastery housed the remains of Saint Serafim, known for his powers of healing and prophecy. The water of the local Sarovka River was believed to possess healing powers, too. In 1923, following the establishment of the Soviet Union, the ruling

Communists closed the monastery, killing many of the priests and destroying several religious buildings.

In 1946, the Soviet government erased Sarov from all unclassified maps of the Soviet Union and established there the All-Russian Scientific Research Institute of Experimental Physics—a secret nuclear weapons design facility. Renamed Arzamas-16, the site became one of the Soviet Union's secret cities, hermetically sealed to outsiders. For eighteen years, from 1950 until 1968, the secret city would be home to Sakharov and his family.

By late summer of 1953, Sakharov and his colleagues had succeeded in developing the first Soviet thermonuclear bomb. Yuli Khariton, the chief weapons designer, oversaw the process of building the new weapon, to which Sakharov gave a benign name—Sloika, translated from Russian as "layer cake." The bomb was built with layers of fission and fusion material, which allowed for a more powerful yield. The fissile core was enveloped with alternating layers of unenriched natural uranium and deuterium (a hydrogen isotope) and surrounded by a chemical explosive. The teardrop-shaped device weighed more than four tons.[13] In the United States, Sloika was historically downgraded to a description of a "boosted" fission bomb rather than a true two-stage super bomb (which the Russians would develop later).

Once Sloika was ready, it was moved by rail to the Semipalatinsk Polygon. One train carried military personnel, engineers, scientists, and the supporting equipment; the other transported the new device. Sakharov traveled with Yuli Khariton and a few others in Khariton's private railway car, gifted to him back in the 1940s by Beria. Sakharov and other key scientists were deemed so valuable that they were not allowed to fly for fear of a plane crash, but an advance team had flown earlier to Semipalatinsk and was waiting anxiously at the Zhana-Semey station for the trains' arrival.[14]

TESTING SLOIKA

The plan was for Sloika to be dropped from a tower in the middle of the testing site. Until the last moment, nobody gave thought to the fact that the radioactive fallout from such a powerful explosion would spread beyond the site. But then the point was raised by the lone voice of Victor Gavrilov of the Ministry of Medium Machine-Building, an agency with a misleading name that was charged with overseeing the nuclear weapons program. Sakharov admitted: "We had all been so busy preparing the device, organizing the test, and performing calculations that we simply lost sight of the fallout problem." The new chief of the

TABLE 1. EFFECTS OF RADIATION

DOSE RECEIVED	EFFECT ON HUMANS
50 rem*	Dose that causes damage to blood cells
	Lowest dose that could cause acute radiation syndrome
100 rem	Dose for which risk of getting cancer increases from about 22% (average risk of cancer in the United States) to about 27%
400 rem	Dose that results in death for 50% of those who receive it
1000 rem	Dose that results in death for 100% of those who receive it

* A unit measuring the biological effect of radiation.

SOURCE: Adapted from "Radiation Thermometer," Centers for Disease Control and Prevention, https://www.cdc.gov/nceh/radiation/emergencies/radiationthermometertext.htm.

nuclear weapons program, Khrushchev-appointee Malyshev, was furious: "We were ready for the tests, everything was going beautifully, and then all of a sudden Gavrilov pops up like an evil genius, and now everything's a mess."[15]

In a rush, Sakharov and others made calculations about the fallout. Sakharov and his team concluded that everyone within the zone where radiation could exceed 200 roentgen would have to be evacuated if the test proceeded. They also estimated that a dose of 100 roentgen would injure children and people of vulnerable health.

There were two choices: to delay the test for months and prepare for a different method of explosion—from a plane instead of a tower—or to evacuate the locals.[16]

The military bosses chose the second option, marshaling more than a thousand military personnel, the Kazakh government, and local officials to launch a large-scale evacuation. A convoy of more than six hundred army trucks relocated 2,000 people and 40,000 livestock from homes within 120 kilometers (75 miles) of the epicenter.[17] More than 12,000 people who lived in settlements beyond the 120-kilometer radius were ordered to leave their homes and gather in several other villages for easier evacuation in case of emergency, and some 300,000 livestock were moved to safe areas.[18] A Kazakh soldier named Musa Sharipov, who served at the Polygon and helped with the evacuation, described a scene of confusion: "Why? Where? Neither the soldiers nor the shocked locals knew. Panic reigned in the steppe; bewildered people waited for something terrible [to happen]."[19]

Sakharov was worried about the confusion and panic, and about the danger of the fallout to the population. But the military director of the tests, Marshal Vasilevskii, told him and a few others, "There's no need to torture yourselves. Army maneuvers always result in casualties—twenty or thirty deaths can be considered normal. And your tests are even more vital for the country and its defense." A fellow scientist also tried to reassure Sakharov: "Don't worry, everything will be fine. The Kazakh kids will survive. It will turn out okay."[20]

On August 12, 1953, on a beautiful summer morning in the steppe, the Soviet Union carried out its first thermonuclear test. The engineers had mounted Sloika onto the tower in the center of the testing field and placed hundreds of measuring and recording devices in an underground bunker a few meters away. The bunker's steel and cement walls were two meters (six-and-a-half feet) thick, designed to withstand the enormous power of a hydrogen explosion.[21] To learn the effects of the weapon on infrastructure, the engineers had installed electrical lines and built several multistory brick houses, an industrial building, a railway, and a railroad bridge, and they brought a steam locomotive and two train cars onto the tracks.[22] Planes, tanks, mortars, and other pieces of military equipment as well as animals were placed in the testing field. The scientists expected a yield of 400 kilotons, the equivalent of 400,000 tons of TNT, but, as designers admitted, its full impact remained "largely unpredictable."[23] For comparison, the atomic bomb that the US military dropped on Hiroshima in 1945, which killed 70,000–80,000 people by blast and firestorm, had a yield of less than 15 kilotons.

A test participant described the blast: "A black cloud with red licks of flame covered the entire Polygon. A pillar of a black-red mass of crushed, sizzling dead matter of several kilometers in diameter—went up to the skies. And there slowly rose a bright-orange fire sphere."[24]

A member of the safety team described the impact on the ground: "As the blast wave reached the first five-story building, it disappeared in the dust, and when the dust settled, there was no building. Just ruins."[25] The steel tower supporting the bomb had evaporated into an enormous crater of black-green cinder and a thick layer of dust. Soil across hundreds of meters had melded into a glassy yellow crust.[26]

PHOTO 4   Infrastructure at the Semipalatinsk Polygon, 2016. Photograph by Timur Nusimbekov.

PHOTO 5   A replica of the Moscow subway at the Semipalatinsk Polygon, 2016. Photograph by Timur Nusimbekov.

Close to the epicenter of the explosion, everything disintegrated. Further out one could see maimed pieces of equipment and ruined buildings. Animals near the testing site, tied so they could not escape, perished. Those further out stayed alive, but the sides of their bodies facing the explosion were burnt. Many died later from burns or radiation.[27]

"The gigantic testing field looked like a fantasy illustration in a book on extra-terrestrial civilizations," recorded a test participant. "Steppe eagles, disturbed by humans, were observing this sight from above. A pity that all these beautiful birds [were] burnt or blinded on the day of the test."[28]

About 95 kilometers (60 miles) from the Polygon lay the village of Karaul, home to Kazakh meat and dairy farms. Before the test, Karaul residents had been told to leave the village and take their livestock with them. The government promised each resident 500 rubles for the trouble, roughly a month's salary. The last car carrying Karaul residents had departed August 4, and soon after the military abandoned the village as well.

Talgat Sliambekov was a twenty-eight-year-old accountant at a local government office. He was one of a small group ordered by the military to stay in Karaul, along with some other low-level government workers, teachers, and other professionals. Just one among their number was a woman—a sales clerk from a grocery store. Sliambekov and the others were guinea pigs, although they didn't know it. When the blast came on August 12, they watched with their mouths open, unable to comprehend what was happening.[29] According to Sliambekov, "They chose the most conscientious, as though for an important task. We, not knowing a lot and due to inexperience, stayed. . . . Without suspecting much, we even admired the explosion, went outside to [better] see an unusual mushroom-shaped cloud. . . ."[30]

Soon after the test, soldiers showed up in Karaul, wearing white protective suits. They drove Sliambekov and the others 50 kilometers (30 miles) away to the mountains. As Sliambekov continued, "There they measured the dose of radiation each of us received . . . and made us drink 200 grams of vodka, which they themselves poured for us. . . . They made us drink, whether we wanted or not."[31] The soldiers believed that vodka helped protect the body against radiation. Sliambekov had no idea he had been exposed to extreme amounts of radiation or what a horribly inadequate remedy vodka would be.

The military kept the group under observation in another village for two more weeks before returning them to Karaul. They were only in the village for a few days before the military showed up again and ordered the group to the hospital, where medical personnel drew their blood for analysis. Then the military were absent for nearly a year until, in the summer of 1954, they arrived in the village to order several of the group to go with them to Semipalatinsk. Sliambekov was one of them:

> They examined us for a month and a half. They drew blood, gastric juice, urine. When they let us go, they gave us some certificates and told us that everything was done for the sake of the people and science. We stayed in the regional hospital. All doctors were military, from Moscow. . . . Among the people who stayed behind during the test almost everyone died. Most died before reaching the age of fifty.[32]

Later three of Sliambekov's children died, one at the age of two from a brain tumor. His family's third generation continued to be unhealthy, with a grandson born with congenital paralysis.[33] In the late 1980s, Sliambekov described his experiences as a test subject in a letter to a local official:

> Back then we were not told [the bomb] would be dangerous for life and health, and we knew nothing, suspected nothing. It was only thirty-six years later that we found out that we were left in the danger zone as though we were rabbits in a lab experiment. Because of this dangerous experiment, many died or became disabled.[34]

Kabden Essengarin, a local health official, lived in Sarzhal, a village in the vicinity of the Polygon known for livestock breeding. He had spent several days in evacuation after the test but was soon asked to return to Sarzhal to sort out the cattle of different households that had gotten mixed up after the residents evacuated. There he saw dogs and cats that had lost all their fur, and later on observed that returning villagers drank water from the open wells. "Nobody warned them that the water could be radioactive," Essengarin said.[35]

Families in the area would suffer the effects of radiation both immediately and for generations. Not atypically for these families, Essengarin's granddaughter Samantha, named after an American girl famous for her letter to the Soviet leader Yuri Andropov about a nuclear war, would be born with Down syndrome.[36]

The thermonuclear test resulted in radioactive contamination of more than 1 roentgen up to 400 kilometers (250 miles) away from the testing site,[37] more than triple the recommended per-week exposure level established by the International Commission on Radiation Protection in 1950.[38] Residents of nearby settlements who could not evacuate before the test received 10–40 roentgen,[39]

133 times more than the weekly limit. Whether the massive evacuation protected locals from radiation remains an open question; some experts say that the fallout also occurred in the zone where people were relocated.[40]

For Andrei Sakharov, Sloika's creator, the test planted the first seeds of doubt about the ethics and morality of nuclear weapons. He himself suffered from an undiagnosed bout of fever and nosebleeds and produced abnormal blood tests a couple of months after the test. These same symptoms resurfaced again in a milder form a few months later. Sakharov never learned the reason for his condition but wondered if he had received an overdose of radiation when examining the aftermath of the nuclear test with the chief of the nuclear program, Malyshev. Malyshev died in early 1957 of acute leukemia.[41]

Despite Sakharov's early doubts about the morality of developing nuclear weapons, two years after the first thermonuclear test, he and his team were ready to test a more advanced thermonuclear device that was even more powerful. The Soviets were half-a-year ahead of the Americans with a portable thermonuclear weapon.[42] Whereas Sloika had a yield of 400 kilotons, the new thermonuclear bomb had a potential yield of 3 megatons. It was scaled down to 1.6 megatons for the test, but that was still four times Sloika's yield.

Sakharov again traveled to Semipalatinsk in Khariton's private railway car, and this time he was accompanied by two "secretaries"—armed bodyguards who now protected him and followed him everywhere he went.[43]

Unlike in the first thermonuclear test, the new thermonuclear bomb was to be dropped not from a tower but from a plane. The test was scheduled for November 20, 1955. That day, the plane with its nuclear cargo was already in the air when the weather changed. The pilot had doubts about the ability of the optical systems—which were supposed to aim the bomb and monitor the explosion—to perform in such weather, so the test was aborted. The plane and its undetonated bomb would have to land at the city of Semipalatinsk, and those in charge of the test were anxious because the runway was iced over. But an army unit cleared the airfield and the plane landed safely with its lethal cargo.[44] The test was rescheduled for three days later.

Although the bomb was more powerful this time, the military's disregard for locals was the same. A nurse from Chagan, a village about 110 kilometers (70 miles) from the epicenter, described the scene:

> On the eve of the test, the military came to our village and gave instructions. In the morning, after breakfast, around 10 a.m., we walked all the patients outside, put them face down to the ground and covered them with bed sheets. We

covered the windows with mattresses, and carried all the dishes outside. We opened all the doors wide, secured them. . . . We were warned not to raise our heads and not to look at what was happening around us.[45]

That day, a bomb outfitted with a parachute fell from a plane, exploding at a height of 1.5 kilometers (5,000 feet) and with a yield of 1.6 megatons.[46] A fireball grew upwards and sideways, chased by the dust plume which rose and mixed with the clouds, creating an enormous pitch-black vapor that crept toward the labs and residential area of the military town. The power of the explosion sent heavy tanks flying and tore structures of iron and concrete from the testing ground. An enormous heat wave reached the observers who lay on the field, roughly 30 kilometers (20 miles) away. Even at such distance, they had to wear special glasses.[47] Three minutes after the explosion a powerful shock wave reverberated through the ground.

This time, with a 1.6 megaton explosion, it was felt even farther from the test site. A declassified CIA report describes the account of an unidentified man who worked at one of the factories in the area:

[He] experienced a significant change in pressure in his eardrums. This pressure was not sharp and painful but was of sufficient intensity and duration to cause him to turn from his work to determine the cause of the pressure. For a few seconds he was unable to hear. As [he] turned from his work, the ground began to tremble and pulsate.[48]

In the military town, about 60 kilometers (37 miles) from the test site, doors, window frames, and light walls crumbled. Windows shattered.[49] The force of the explosion damaged houses in dozens of villages and towns. In the city of Semipalatinsk, the industrial lights in its large meat-processing factory shattered into the ground beef below.[50]

In the village of Malye Akzhary, a three-year-old girl was killed in a bomb shelter. On the authorities' instructions, the villagers had hidden there, but after the initial flash of the explosion, the adults went outside while the little girl remained inside the shelter playing with toy blocks. The shock wave that followed the explosion destroyed the shelter, burying the girl beneath the collapsed ceiling.[51] This was not the first tragedy in the life of the girl's mother, an ethnic German who was deported to Kazakhstan in the 1940s under Stalin's policy of exiling ethnic minorities to remote parts of the country.[52]

Dozens of locals suffered multiple injuries, including concussions and broken bones.[53] In the women's ward in one hospital, half a dozen patients were injured when the ceiling crashed down on them.[54] Thirty-five kilometers (22 miles) from ground zero, Soviet soldiers waiting in trenches found the soil collapsing on them. Five soldiers were injured, and one, a young boy who had just joined the army, died.[55]

After the test, Andrei Sakharov joined the crew that retrieved the films and recorded the data from the measuring equipment. He described the scene of devastation in his memoir:

> We walked past the buildings that had been specifically constructed to determine the effects of the shock wave and heat radiation. Many were damaged or obliterated. Fires blazed in several places, water jets shot up through the ground from broken mains, and glass from shattered windows crunched underfoot, bringing back memories of the war. An oil tank had ruptured, and the oil, ignited by the heat radiation, burned for several days, sending thick black smoke drifting along the horizon. Special crews retrieved the experimental animals (dogs, goats, and rabbits). I found it painful to watch their suffering, even on film.[56]

The tragedies that accompanied the 1955 test and the enormity of the bomb's power deeply disturbed Sakharov. He would later describe the experience as transformative. He struggled with contradictory emotions, fearing that thermonuclear power could "slip out of control and lead to unimaginable disasters." The deaths of the little girl and the young soldier haunted him.[57]

Sakharov wrote about that moment in history:

> We, the inventors, scientists, engineers, and craftsmen, had created a terrible weapon, the most terrible weapon in human history; but its use would lie entirely outside our control. The people at the top of the Party and military hierarchy would make the decisions. Of course, I knew this already—I wasn't that naive. But understanding something abstractly is different from feeling it with your whole being, as the reality of life and death. The ideas and emotions kindled at that moment have not diminished to this day, and they completely altered my thinking.[58]

Sakharov grew particularly concerned about the biological effects of nuclear tests. In 1957, two years after his second thermonuclear accomplishment, Sakharov wrote "Radioactive Carbon from Nuclear Explosions and Nonthreshold Biological Effects," an article in which he voiced his concerns about the increase in risks of cancers and damage to the immune system from nuclear explosions. What worried him most was the impact of radiation on heredity and DNA. He recognized that "a single ionization event is sufficient to cause irreversible change—a mutation—in a gene."[59]

The sheer scale of destruction brought by the second thermonuclear test and the inescapable evidence that atmospheric tests harmed people's health prompted the Soviet government to declare that from then on, the most powerful tests could take place only at Russia's Novaya Zemlya, the uninhabited, isolated testing site in the Arctic Circle, established in 1954 to host large-scale atmospheric and underwater tests.[60] The site, consisting of two islands in the Arctic Sea, could be used for underwater tests, similar to the ones the United States carried out on Bikini Atoll in the Pacific Ocean.

At the same time, the Soviet defense ministry decided it needed more space at Semipalatinsk to continue its tests there, and it ruled that several settlements cede their lands to the Polygon. The local official tasked with informing residents they would have to abandon their homes tried to reassure them: "I praised [the new location], told them there was railway there, that it would be easier for them to live there, but people did not accept our proposals. In the end, they would agree, but they were apprehensive." The scene was deeply distressing for the local official: "They were killing their livestock, saying farewell to the land and graves [of their loved ones], crying, and it was hard to look at them."[61]

THE BAN ON ATMOSPHERIC NUCLEAR TESTS

Into the late 1950s, politicians from the nuclear powers—the United States, the United Kingdom, and the Soviet Union—could no longer ignore the damage of atmospheric nuclear tests on people and the environment.

The international public pressure to stop nuclear tests was growing. The US thermonuclear test Castle Bravo at Bikini Atoll was among the particularly egregious cases that made the international headlines because of its immediate victims. The 1954 test, with a yield equal to 1,000 Hiroshima bombs, resulted in heavy radioactive fallout. At the time of the explosion, the twenty-three-man crew of a Japanese boat, the *Lucky Dragon*, was fishing for tuna outside the danger zone declared by the United States in advance of the test. But the test was so powerful that the fallout went far beyond the indicated zone. All the men fell victim to acute radiation sickness and suffered for weeks, with one man dying.[62]

And the United States and the Soviet Union were also increasingly worried about the arms race and the potential for new nuclear powers. Banning nuclear tests was a way to prevent other countries from developing, testing, and per-fecting nuclear weapons.

And so, in late October 1958, representatives of the three nuclear powers de-cided to start negotiations on a comprehensive test ban treaty. They assembled in picturesque Geneva—far from the ongoing destruction in Kazakhstan—to negotiate a ban on nuclear tests following preliminary talks involving experts earlier that summer. Khrushchev, Eisenhower, and UK Prime Minister Harold McMillan informally agreed not to conduct any nuclear tests during the nego-tiations. The three-country test moratorium meant that, for a brief period from November 1958 to August 1961, the Semipalatinsk Polygon went quiet.

The negotiations in Geneva focused on disagreements over verification between the United States and Britain on one side and the Soviet Union on the other. The main point of contention was on-site inspections. The US gov-ernment insisted on twenty on-site inspections a year.[63] The Americans and the British favored on-site inspections to determine, say, whether a suspicious event was an earthquake or an underground nuclear test. The Soviets opposed on-site inspections, which they considered too intrusive as well as possible openings to US spying on the Soviet program.

On May 1, 1960, progress further stalled when the Soviets shot down a US U-2 spy plane, piloted by Francis Gary Powers, in Soviet air space. Several months later, the moratorium on testing collapsed to a large extent because of pressure from the military in those two countries, and the Soviet Union and the United States tested more than two hundred devices in 1961 and 1962.

In anticipation of a ban agreement, Moscow rushed to conduct as many tests as possible during this period. It performed seventy-nine atmospheric tests in 1962 alone, more than half of them at Semipalatinsk. The yields ranged from 0.001 to several kilotons.[64] The total release of energy through nuclear tests in 1961 and 1962 (at both Semipalatinsk and Novaya Zemlya) amounted to 220 megatons—more than 70 percent of the megaton total in the four-decade history of Soviet nuclear testing.[65] The United States also quickened its pace. In 1962, it conducted a total of ninety-two nuclear tests, the most in any year in the entire history of US nuclear testing. It also conducted two additional tests in cooperation with the United Kingdom.[66]

Nevertheless, the desire of Washington and Moscow to negotiate a test ban treaty not only persisted but grew, given their fear of other nations acquir-ing nuclear capability. However, in October of 1962, the Cuban missile crisis interfered with resuming such negotiations, as the Soviet Union and the United States found themselves one step away from a nuclear confrontation.

THE CUBAN MISSILE CRISIS

The events that led to the Cuban missile crisis had begun a year earlier. In 1961, the United States started installing intermediate-range ballistic missiles in Turkey and Italy. Those missiles could reach the western part of the Soviet Union, including Moscow. The Soviet Union felt vulnerable and, in response, secretly transported some of its nuclear weapons and missiles to Cuba. By stationing them there, Soviet leader Nikita Khrushchev also signaled military support to communist Cuba following the CIA's attempted overthrow of Fidel Castro during the failed Bay of Pigs invasion.

Once US spy planes revealed a military buildup in Cuba, an island just 140 kilometers (90 miles) from the US mainland, some of President Kennedy's top advisers urged him to authorize a strike against the Soviet military installations. Kennedy, fearing that a military confrontation with the Soviet Union could escalate into nuclear war, preferred to exhaust other options first. He authorized a naval quarantine around Cuba to prevent any further buildup and to signal Washington's resolve to counter the Soviet incursion while giving Khrushchev time and space to deescalate.[67]

For thirteen days, the world was on the brink of nuclear war. After tense negotiations, involving letters sent directly to each other, Kennedy and Khrushchev managed to resolve the crisis and walk back from the standoff. The Soviet Union agreed to dismantle and remove its weapons from Cuba, and the United States pledged not to invade Cuba and to remove its missiles from Turkey (it subsequently removed missiles from both Turkey and Italy).

The experience affected both Kennedy and Khrushchev profoundly. Having narrowly avoided nuclear war, both the Americans and the Soviets were keen to make progress on banning nuclear tests. However, fundamental differences persisted over on-site inspections. The Soviet Union wanted to avoid inspections while US and British experts continued to argue they were necessary, especially in cases of suspected underground tests. Failure to agree on verification measures meant a comprehensive test ban treaty, one that would ban all nuclear tests, was out of reach.[68]

In June 1963, a few months after the Cuban missile crisis, Kennedy delivered a passionate appeal for peace in his commencement address at American

University in Washington, DC. The speech followed private letters between Kennedy and Khrushchev in which they discussed restarting talks on the ban treaty, and it generated goodwill in the Soviet Union. The Soviet government even translated and broadcast Kennedy's speech on television and printed it in state-controlled media.[69] Secret direct interactions between Kennedy, Khrushchev, and Britain's McMillan sparked the renewal of high-level trilateral negotiations in Moscow on a limited test-ban treaty.[70]

Thanks to a decision not to include underground nuclear tests in the agreement, thus avoiding the issue of on-site inspections, the parties moved quickly to agreement. On August 5, 1963, the foreign ministers of the three countries signed the Partial Test Ban Treaty. The treaty forbade nuclear tests in outer space, the atmosphere, and under water. With a new ban in place, the Soviet Union continued only with the underground testing it had begun in 1961. The era of atmospheric tests, the most damaging for the environment and health of the people of Kazakhstan, had now ended. But it left a trail of tragedies and health problems that would persist for generations.

UNDERGROUND NUCLEAR TESTS AND PEACEFUL NUCLEAR EXPLOSIONS (1961–89)

Nuclear testing moved fully underground, less visible to the naked eye. Until 1989, underground nuclear tests rocked the mountains near the Semipalatinsk Polygon. In total, the Soviet military conducted at least 213 underground tests (295 explosions) in tunnels and shafts dug at the Polygon.[71]

The first area for underground tests—181 tunnels in Degelen Mountain—spanned 33,100 hectares. It was the world's largest underground nuclear test site. With no equipment available to perform the task, construction workers dug horizontal tunnels by hand, each tunnel hundreds of meters long.[72]

The maximum yield for tests in the Degelen tunnels was limited to 30–50 kilotons. Many of these tests measured the effects of nuclear explosions on various kinds of military equipment. For more powerful tests, a new site was developed at the Polygon: Balapan—Kazakh for "child"—covered 100,000 hectares. In contrast to the Degelen tunnels, deep vertical shafts at Balapan could be drilled without manual labor, making them easier to build. Shaft tests were also carried out at the Sary-Uzen, Murzhik, Telkem, and Aktan Berli sites, also part of the Semipalatinsk Polygon.[73]

Secrecy continued to envelop the testing program and the conscription of soldiers to serve at the Polygon. Anatolii Yegai, a young man from the southern Kazakh town of Kyzyl Orda, was drafted by the Soviet army in 1971 to serve at Semipalatinsk. Unaware that they were headed for the Polygon, Yegai and his fellow soldiers eagerly anticipated serving near one of the major cities. The new recruits imagined a rosy picture: "On Saturdays and Sundays in our new military uniform we will explore Semipalatinsk, an ancient city of merchants, and go dancing with the girls." These daydreams were abruptly dispelled. At the military recruitment office, Yegai and his companions encountered a man who had served at the Polygon. He warned the new recruits that it was a "bad place" they were going to. "As the future showed, there was truth in his words," admitted Yegai. He described persistent safety problems during the era of underground nuclear tests: "Soldiers, officers, and civilians did not receive any individual dosimetry devices in order not to provoke panic. Otherwise, nobody would agree to work or serve. . . . Many soldiers died because they did not follow safety rules and were not careful."[74]

Although underground tests were less dangerous than atmospheric tests in terms of above-ground radioactive fallout, they still caused serious harm. The land shook with the force of the underground explosions, changing the geography of the region.[75] The underground craters created by explosions would fill with water or gas, sometimes collapsing on themselves. The most potent underground tests registered above 6 on the Richter seismographic scale, rocking buildings more than a hundred kilometers from the epicenter. The aftershocks lasted for days.[76] Locals gave up on fixing walls and ceilings that cracked so regularly. Underground tests damaged sewage and water supply systems and contaminated the groundwater. Tremors destroyed the deep wells that supplied water to large areas and livestock barns. Entire pastures were rendered useless. Local authorities spent significant amounts of money in a futile, Sisyphean endeavor to rectify the damage.[77]

Almost one in three underground tests led to radioactive gases escaping the depths of the earth, adding to the general contamination of the environment. Local people continued to use nearby land to graze their livestock and collect hay, work in which schoolchildren often joined adults. The son of a shepherd remembers cutting hay near Degelen Mountain.[78] Another local remembers: "We witnessed nuclear tests and observed the military's day-to-day work. They came in six buses at six in the morning and left at five in the evening."[79] As Soviet military experiments continued, everyday life in Kazakhstan went on.

ATOMIC LAKE

Both the United States and the Soviet Union explored the use of nuclear explosions not only to develop nuclear bombs but also to move earth for potential industrial and agricultural applications. In the United States, one such experiment was carried out in 1962. The purpose of the Storax Sedan project at the Nevada Test Site was to see how nuclear detonations could be used in mining. The explosion ejected more than 12 million tons of soil and created the largest man-made crater in the United States. As a result of the explosion, massive amounts of iodine-131—a radioactive substance that can cause thyroid cancer—traveled across several states. Millions of people in Iowa, Nebraska, South Dakota, and Illinois were exposed to the fallout.[80]

Soviet scientists followed up with a similarly grandiose and harmful experiment of their own. Soviet innovators explored how large craters, created as a result of nuclear detonations, could be turned into bodies of water—canals and reservoirs. In this effort, the Soviets carried out thirty-nine "peaceful" nuclear explosions at different sites in Kazakhstan during the years 1965–88.[81] These explosions were usually lower in yield than weapons tests, but they still contaminated the environment.

The first and largest such experiment created an artificial lake on the grounds of the Polygon. The project team from Russia had chosen a spot in the bed of the Chagan River. In a rush to meet the deadline, the construction workers labored in harsh winter conditions, battling snow and frost. The work did not end with sunset; powerful lights illuminated the dark sky as the crews worked through the long nights.[82]

Nevertheless, extreme cold and chilly winds delayed the nuclear excavation experiment by a few days. Finally, on January 15, 1965, a 140-kiloton underground nuclear explosion expelled 4 million cubic meters of soil from the ground. The resulting crater measured 400 meters (1,300 feet) wide and 100 meters (330 feet) deep. Nearby rivers filled this newly created reservoir with more than a million cubic yards of water.

The lake, however, posed an extraordinary danger to human health. The fallout from the explosion contaminated ten villages and towns, and the wind carried radioactive substances as far as the city of Semipalatinsk 120 kilometers (75 miles) away. The residents of Znamenka, many of them grain farmers, were exposed to a radiation dose exceeding 1 roentgen, far beyond the then-international standard of 0.3 roentgen per week.[83] A government commission from Kazakhstan concluded that the internal radiation dose in the thyroid among children had reached 53 roentgen equivalent man (rem).[84] Rem is a unit measuring the biological effect of radiation. A dose of 50 rem causes damage to blood cells.[85]

The fallout from the explosion also contaminated water in uncovered wells. The milk from cows that grazed on contaminated pastures contained radioactive iodine-131. When consumed, iodine-131 is directly absorbed by the thyroid gland. As the iodine-131 decays, it damages the gland, sometimes leading to thyroid cancer. The amounts of radionuclides in milk and meat were hundreds of times higher than the maximum level allowed by Soviet standards.[86]

The locals dubbed the lake Atom Kol (Atomic Lake, translated from Kazakh). After the lake experiment, Semipalatinsk health authorities again raised with Soviet officials the issue of radiation poisoning and contamination.[87] But Soviet military officials denied that the nuclear experiments posed a health danger. In a letter to Kazakh leader Dinmukhamed Kunaev, Avetik Burnazyan, the Soviet official in charge of medical issues in the nuclear military complex, and Efim Slavskii, the head of the Soviet Ministry of Medium Machine-Building, which oversaw the nuclear weapons complex, insisted that underground nuclear tests were safe because they were conducted deep underground. At the same time Burnazyan and Slavskii admitted that a shift in the wind had led to some contamination of nearby settlements with short-lived fission products. They blamed the leadership of one of the military divisions stationed near the Polygon for incorrectly assessing the situation, which, in their words, had led to rumors.[88]

PHOTO 6   Atomic Lake at the Semipalatinsk Polygon, 2019. Photograph by Oleg Butenko.

Slavskii was an enthusiastic supporter of nuclear energy for both military and civilian purposes and, according to Sakharov, not terribly concerned about the victims of nuclear tests.[89] In an act of defiance aimed at his critics, Slavskii even swam in the lake to prove that it was not dangerous.[90] Local Kazakhs called it "dead lake" but continued to graze their cattle nearby.

More than fifty years later, the lake remains contaminated and locals worry that it poisons underground waters. Even in the 2000s, residents of nearby Sarzhal complain that "when the wind blows from the direction of the lake, the air thickens with unbearable stench."[91]

MOSCOW AND WASHINGTON: SCALING DOWN NUCLEAR TESTS

Throughout the 1960s and 1970s, both the United States and the Soviet Union regularly conducted underground tests, many of them incredibly powerful. But in 1974, the two countries agreed to sign the Threshold Test Ban Treaty, prohibiting underground tests with a yield exceeding 150 kilotons. Two years later, in 1976, they signed a similar treaty, with the same 150-kiloton ceiling, for nuclear explosions for peaceful purposes (Peaceful Nuclear Explosions Treaty). For decades, neither country ratified the treaties but promised to comply with the treaties' provisions before ratification.

The arrival of Mikhail Gorbachev, a younger and more liberal leader, in 1985, led to profound changes within the Soviet Union and in its relations with the outside world, including the United States. Gorbachev represented a new generation. Unlike the old Politburo leaders, who viewed the outside world with suspicion, Gorbachev was keen to engage with the international community. He enjoyed traveling abroad with his wife even before he took the helm of the Soviet Union.

US President Ronald Reagan and Gorbachev agreed that the complete cessation of nuclear testing was the ultimate goal for both countries. In July 1985, Gorbachev announced a unilateral moratorium on nuclear testing, to which Moscow adhered until February 1987, when it resumed testing at Semipalatinsk because Washington had failed to join the moratorium and had continued its nuclear tests. The Soviet leadership, conscious of its international image and consistent with Gorbachev's policy of glasnost, decided not to keep its tests secret but rather announce them via Soviet official media outlets "to avoid negative rumors." Occasionally, the Soviets would admit that tests were for weapons purposes.[92]

The Soviet and US governments began negotiations in Geneva on the ratification of the Threshold Test Ban and the Peaceful Nuclear Explosion Treaties. In an echo of an issue that had arisen in the test-ban negotiations of the early 1960s, the ratification process had stalled due to disagreements over methods for verifying that the yields of nuclear tests did not exceed 150 kilotons.

Washington insisted that the seismic method—measuring elastic ground motion after the test to evaluate the yield—was not sufficient. One problem was that underground cavities could lead to decoupling of seismic waves, thus impeding distant seismic measurement. Notably, some in the US scientific community contended that their government used this argument to delay discussing the next step—a complete ban on nuclear testing.[93] Whatever the case, in its negotiations with the Soviets, the United States insisted on using the hydrodynamic method for verification. This approach measured the yield of an explosion by taking an on-site measurement of the shock front. A shock front is an area through which a shock wave travels—akin to a real wave that rolls through air and earth as energy is suddenly released in one place and disturbs everything around it. The Soviets, in turn, claimed that allowing Americans to be physically present at their test sites, as required by the hydrodynamic method, would make the Soviet nuclear program vulnerable to espionage.[94]

Then, however, thanks to an overall thaw in the bilateral relationship that accompanied Gorbachev's ascendance to Soviet power, in an unprecedented move, Moscow and Washington agreed to conduct a Joint Verification Experiment (JVE) that would allow the two countries to use all verification methods. The plan called for Soviets to come to the Nevada Test Site, followed by a visit of Americans to the Semipalatinsk Polygon. Never had American and Soviet nuclear scientists stepped foot onto each other's nuclear sites.

The arrival of Soviet scientists at the Nevada Test Site in August 1988 opened a new chapter in the nuclear relationship between the two countries. The *Los Angeles Times* reported on the day of the test, "Exactly on schedule and under ideal conditions, Soviet and US technicians made history."[95] The 6.5-metric ton (15,000-pound) device, sealed in a steel container and painted in red, white, and blue, exploded more than 600 meters (2,000 feet) underground. The Soviet and American scientists used hydrodynamic and seismic methods to measure the yield, and both sides called the first part of the Joint Verification Experiment a success.

The following month it was the turn of the Semipalatinsk Polygon to host Americans. The Americans flew five military cargo planes full of drilling and verification equipment to the site. The planes, known as C-5s, flew from Dover Air Force Base via Frankfurt to Semipalatinsk, more than 9,600 kilometers (6,000 miles) away.[96]

Victor Alessi, an American nuclear physicist who was one of the JVE participants, recounts his impressions on arrival: "We stopped to watch the sunset over the Irtysh River. It was spectacular. The sky was a fading red. The river, which was quite wide and fast-flowing, seemed almost out of place in this barren landscape."[97] Most of the forty-five-strong American team stayed in a dormitory-style camp not far from the testing grounds. The VIPs remained in the town of Kurchatov, a town which once had not even appeared on Soviet maps due to its secrecy.

Hopes and worries ran high. Alessi sympathized with the Soviets, who seemed to him anxious. He wrote in his travel diary: "Only a month ago the United States was in the same position at the Nevada test site. In the back of everyone's mind was the fear that, when the time came, nothing would happen, and all the preparations would have been for naught."

One thing that surprised Alessi was how physically close the Soviets were to their tests:

> In Nevada, we used a fixed building as a command center from which the test was observed on TV. It was located many miles away from the actual test. In contrast, the Soviet command post was portable and placed only four kilometers away from the explosion, and we had a clear line of sight to ground zero.[98]

Finally, the moment came to carry out the test. Alessi recalled:

> The ground shock beneath me occurred almost simultaneously [with the blast]. . . . It felt as though I had been standing on a table and someone had hit the underside of the table with a sledgehammer. My notions about the power of nuclear explosions—a mental image until now—suddenly became a reality. Had the weapon exploded at ground zero's surface or above ground, instead of a half a kilometer below the surface, I would have been killed instantly. . . . Nuclear weapons suddenly were no longer abstractions and scientific calculations.[99]

The dust from the explosion rose and blew away. Americans and Soviets broke into applause, celebrating a second successful joint endeavor that provided both sides more confidence in verification methods. At a press conference that followed the test, Alessi absorbed the moment: "It was hard to believe that I, with 44 other Americans, was standing only a little more than two miles from a Soviet nuclear explosion within sight of ground zero at a place that had to be one of the most secret in the Soviet Union."[100]

The Joint Verification Experiment certainly symbolized a new era, but it was not only symbolic. Thanks to the JVE, the two countries now had enough technical data to negotiate verification methods for the two treaties that awaited ratification—the Threshold Test Ban Treaty and the Peaceful Nuclear Explosion Treaty.[101] Moscow and Washington moved quickly, and in 1990 both treaties banning nuclear explosions of more than 150 kilotons were officially in force. The two countries had taken one more step toward a complete ban on nuclear tests.

Nevertheless, the forty years of nuclear testing in the Kazakh steppe had claimed thousands upon thousands of victims. People drank contaminated water and milk and ate meat from animals who had fed on pastures laced with radioactive isotopes. Thousands of families continued to go through the heartbreak of losing loved ones to cancers and other diseases. Women suffered from miscarriages or had babies with birth defects. The everyday life of people living in the Semipalatinsk region was mired in the stress of constant bombardment from nuclear explosions and the long-term suffering that was their aftermath.

CHAPTER 3

THE HUMAN TOLL

IN THEIR RUSH TO DEVELOP A NUCLEAR ARSENAL, Soviet leaders gave little thought to protecting the locals and the Polygon's workers. Nor did they know enough about the immediate and delayed dangers of nuclear explosions. During the early years of the testing program, scientists left animals on the test sites to study radiation's impact on living organisms, but not much was known about how radiation affected humans specifically.

Within a few years after the first test of 1949, however, the Soviet government began to monitor the health of the local population, gaining insights into the effects of radiation on people. But throughout the decades of nuclear testing, contradictory narratives were presented on these effects, sowing confusion and uncertainty. Officials and medics from the Semipalatinsk region reported to authorities in Alma-Ata and Moscow that people were suffering from deteriorating health. However, Moscow stood firm in defense of its testing program and claimed that the nuclear tests did not harm people. The military insisted locals' health problems stemmed from poor diet and living conditions.

The Soviet ways of hiding and dismissing evidence that nuclear tests made their people sick were similar to those in the United States. The American Energy Commission dismissed concerns about radioactive contamination. People who lived in states close to the Nevada Test Site, where the US military carried out more than nine hundred nuclear tests, ingested radioisotopes with their food and milk that resulted in a spike in cancers years later. As with the Semipalatinsk Polygon, most of the contamination occurred during the atmospheric nuclear tests of the 1950s. The rural town of St. John, Utah, home to a Mormon community, is one example of a hard-hit area. Like rural settlements near the Semipalatinsk Polygon, almost no family in St. John was spared from tragedy. Native tribes in the affected states, who, like ethnic Kazakhs, very much relied on land in their everyday lives, suffered from similar ailments as the Kazakhs halfway across the world. Cancers became commonplace.

In a notorious case that still haunts Hollywood, almost half of the two-hundred-member crew that worked on the movie *The Conqueror* in St. John and in nearby desert locations in 1956 developed cancer by 1980. Forty-six of them died, including the movie's stars, John Wayne and Susan Hayward. While nobody could tell with certainty—and some thought the alcohol and chain-smoking of the Hollywood crowd could also be blamed—radiation contamination of the area likely played a hidden role.[1]

Away from the continental United States, people in the Pacific islands had even less influence over their well-being and future. As a result of more than sixty nuclear tests from 1946 to 1958, their land became contaminated, even rendering one of the Marshall Islands—Bikini—uninhabitable. The US National Cancer Institute estimated that, because of the tests, the Marshallese over their lifetimes would suffer from five hundred additional cancer cases—"about a 9% increase over the number of cancers expected in the absence of exposure to regional fallout," in the institute's words.[2] In the 1980s, the United States agreed to set up a $150 million Nuclear Claims Trust Fund for medical and property damages caused to the Marshall Islands people by its nuclear testing program.[3]

The people of the Semipalatinsk Polygon shared with movie stars, American downwinders, and Pacific Islanders the host of ills caused by nuclear testing.

TAKING RISKS

At the Semipalatinsk Polygon, the military bosses themselves took health risks and pressured their subordinates to do the same, especially in the early years of the program. The top officials did so partly because of the rush to catch up with the Americans and partly because they did not fully appreciate the dangers. Episodes described by test participants attest to that. Shortly after the first test in 1949, secret police General Avraami Zaveniagin—one of the chiefs of the nuclear program—ordered an engineer to open the mock subway tunnel built in the epicenter to check the explosion's effect on the infrastructure. When the engineer explained that doing so would be too dangerous, since radiation levels were still high, the annoyed general screamed at him.[4]

In an incident following another test, Zaveniagin drove to the testing grounds and his car got stuck. He got covered in highly radioactive dust when he got out of the vehicle. The general's contaminated uniform and shoes set off the radiation measuring devices when he reached the sanitary facility at the Polygon. Witnesses recalled that the head of the sanitary division asked him to take a shower and change into clean clothes. The general initially resisted and only obeyed after prodding by sanitation services.[5]

With the military brass acting so heedlessly, it is no surprise that Polygon workers, sometimes unknowingly, sacrificed their own health. Acute radiation sickness was never officially reported, making it hard to know how common it was. But individual anecdotes reveal a culture of ignorance and secrecy. In 1956, for example, while retrieving films after a nuclear test, several cameramen were exposed to extremely high levels of radiation, to which their bodies reacted violently. One minute they burned from fever, the next they shivered under fur coats. Their faces turned red from the damage to their skin cells, and the lymph glands in their necks swelled—all effects of radiation. "Stupidity and enthusiasm" were at play, one of them admitted, but also a dearth of knowledge: "What did we know about radiation? Nothing pretty much! A lack of information is to blame for what happened to us."[6]

In another case in 1962, eight young dosimetrists disregarded safety rules while working in the epicenter after a test explosion and likely received a radiation dosage of 250–300 roentgen per hour. Spending more than an hour in 100 roentgen per hour conditions can be fatal. Like the cameramen, the dosimetrists did not know much about the acute radiation sickness from which they would suffer—fever, skin and gum bleeding, blood in the urine and excrement. It would take them four weeks to recover.[7]

Melgis Metov was one of thousands of Kazakh soldiers who served at the Polygon. An engineer by training, he toiled at the testing field with his teammates, setting up and fixing equipment to measure electromagnetic waves before and after nuclear tests. "We did not have real protective gear," Metov, now in his seventies, said with tears in his eyes.[8] Protected by nothing more than the standard issue cotton overalls, army boots, and a simple filtering half-face mask, Metov went to the testing grounds after each explosion to retrieve the recorded measurements during his two years of service at the Polygon, from 1961 to 1962. This added up to many trips. The Soviets conducted more nuclear tests in Semipalatinsk in 1962 than in any other year, as the anticipated ban on atmospheric testing loomed.

Metov would spend the rest of his life suffering from poor health. But because he was a citizen of Kazakhstan, he did not receive any compensation for his sacrifice. Russian legislation authorizing benefits to "atomic soldiers" like him did not cover citizens of other republics, and Kazakhstan's similar legislation awarded benefits only to civilians.[9] His first name—Melgis—consists of the initials of Communist ideologues and leaders (Marx, Engels, Lenin, Stalin). In a sad irony, he grew to hate the Communists for what the ideology and its adherents had done to him.[10]

IMPACTS ON PEOPLE

The weather was monitored more attentively at the Polygon than anywhere else in the Soviet Union. Before each test, scientists and military personnel studied the forecasts to predict the movement of radioactive plumes and avoid contaminating nearby settlements. In some instances, they waited for better weather, but sometimes, under pressure to deliver results, they proceeded with tests despite weather that could shower contaminants on innocent populations.

When more powerful tests were scheduled, the military, aided by local authorities, would on rare occasions evacuate people from nearby settlements to safer areas. Soldiers remained on standby near the evacuated towns to deal with damage and radioactive fallout, equipped with glass to fix broken windows as well as foaming devices to put down fires, cement machines, and other technical equipment to repair structural damage.

During the first few years, locals were not warned about the tests and carried on with their everyday lives. Only in 1953 did radio announcements start to warn residents in the military town and nearby settlements to leave their houses before a high-yield test. Tests of nuclear weapons with the explosive power of more than 100 kilotons were scheduled for days when people were off work or during early morning hours when fewer people were outside. Sometimes authorities advised residents to leave buildings during a seismic wave.[11] In settlements lacking radios, authorities dropped message bags that contained information about the time of the explosion and safety measures to be taken.[12]

"Yes, I remember the tests," recalled a woman whose family lived in the military town. "I remember my grandma waking me up on Sundays, asking us to go outside. The radio announcements were usually broadcast during lunch break when people would go home to eat."[13]

Such were the measures taken. They were nowhere enough to protect people living and working in the vicinity of the testing.

The nuclear tests disrupted the lives of both local civilians and military families. Since the government was not compelled to explain anything, people were left without reliable information and could only guess at the causes of their health problems. Those problems did not stop at injuries and exposure to radioactivity in the immediate aftermath of the tests. Contamination of water, food, and soil meant that, long after each test, people continued to absorb radioisotopes.

One Russian officer who worked at the Polygon described the disruption of daily life:

> My daughter was born on February 1, 1953. During the tests, in the middle of winter with temperatures below -20 or -30 Celsius [-4 or -22 F], my wife had to leave the house with the baby in her arms after opening and propping up the windows and doors and propping them up with special wedges [to prevent them from breaking]. Sometimes the tests got canceled, and she had to go back inside the cold house. The next day everything repeated itself [as the tests continued]. . . . After a nighttime explosion, when all the residents had to stay outside and saw the illuminated skies, she developed a fear of the tests. All military personnel were required to be at their work stations during the testing, and their families had to make decisions on their own.[14]

Though military personnel like this officer had to endure nuclear tests during their stints at the Polygon, their postings were temporary; the locals experienced these conditions for decades. One of them was a Kazakh woman named Gulsum Kakimzhanova, who was born in 1952, three years after the testing program started. Kakimzhanova, who grew up in a small settlement near a rail station not far from the Polygon, described her childhood in the testing zone:

> I remember I was a little girl, maybe eight or nine years old. . . . My dad woke up to find all his hair had fallen out on the pillow! . . . It was only later that I understood the reason why. . . . He had worked for the railway. They probably never even covered their heads, and there were atmospheric nuclear tests up until 1962. He was exposed to radiation and became sick for a very long time.[15]

She also recalled an early morning spent out on the steppe: "When I came home, I felt very sick; my nose was bleeding. I felt weak and slept the whole day."[16] In her adulthood, Kakimzhanova would establish an NGO to help victims of nuclear tests.

It didn't take long for people in the Semipalatinsk region to suspect that the Polygon was making them sick. However, daunting government bureaucracies stymied their search for help. In the mid-1950s, a Semipalatinsk resident's appeal had to be routed first to Semipalatinsk officials, then to the government of Kazakhstan in Alma-Ata, and only then to the Soviet government in Moscow. The veil of secrecy and the helplessness of local Kazakh officials and regular citizens in the face of the central government and the military-industrial complex prevented locals' concerns from being recognized.

The chief radiologist from Kazakhstan's Ministry of Health, Saim Balmukhanov, recalls that in the early 1950s on one of his visits to Semipalatinsk, a chief doctor from a regional hospital described the unusual illnesses of the locals. Balmukhanov noticed that the pathology looked similar to what victims of Hiroshima and Nagasaki attacks had experienced. Balmukhanov and his colleagues conducted some small-scale surveys in the areas near the Polygon. But these were not enough to prove the damage to locals' health was from nuclear tests.[17]

CLASHING NARRATIVES

In the 1950s, the Soviet and American governments already knew well their nuclear tests were harmful to people, but they did not know precisely how a nuclear war would impair its own and its enemies' troops and population. The exact impact of the ionizing radiation was hard to grasp. The animals left on the testing field during explosions provided some idea; the skin of baby piglets, for example, was somewhat close to human skin. But no animal could provide all the answers to how radiation would affect people.

With only limited data from the Hiroshima and Nagasaki bombings available to them, the Soviet military sought to understand the impact of radiation on humans.[18] What information the Polygon staff did collect and analyze on radioactive contamination, however, was not shared with civilian health authorities for reasons of secrecy surrounding the nuclear program. That meant health authorities had to rely on guesswork, with no support from others for safeguarding the health of the local population.

The Soviet government did not engage in any meaningful monitoring of public health until 1956, seven years into nuclear testing.[19] Following the first test in 1949, medical authorities examined only ten inhabitants of a nearby village. After the first thermonuclear test, in 1953, the authorities examined two hundred people in one area near the test site. But there is no public record of how the government used these early data.

The first systematic Soviet radiation survey and comprehensive medical examinations were conducted after a nuclear test carried out on August 24, 1956. A nuclear device dropped from a 100-meter (more than 300-foot) tower produced a yield of 27 kilotons. Because of rain, the radioactive contamination spread beyond the Polygon. The radioactive cloud traveled directly over the rural settlements and the industrial city of Ust-Kamenogorsk.[20] In the wake of that test, the Soviet Ministry of Health received reports of significant ground contamination outside the testing site.[21] Reportedly, 638 people ended up in hospitals with "radiation poisoning," four times more than after the Chernobyl nuclear power plant later exploded in 1986.[22] People's skin turned red, and the tests revealed changes in the composition of their blood. Spurred by the large-scale contamination and numerous hospital admissions, the government authorized expeditions of experts from the Institute of Biophysics to the Polygon area to understand the extent of contamination.[23]

Following the public outcry, the Soviet government also established two special clinics in Kazakhstan to monitor locals' health—Dispensary No. 3 in Ust-Kamenogorsk, where most of the fallout had occurred after that test, and Dispensary No. 4 in Semipalatinsk. The Ust-Kamenogorsk clinic was closed within a few years.[24] Dispensary No. 4 remained and became the primary facility for monitoring the effects of radiation on people.

One persuasive explanation for why the government began collecting data was the desire to understand how radiation impacted humans, since that information would be valuable for military planning.

From 1956 to 1960, several expeditions conducted radiological and health surveys across the region. The teams were made up of specialists from the Institute of Biophysics in Moscow, an institution affiliated with the Soviet military program, as well as from Dispensary No. 4 in Semipalatinsk, which was created under the umbrella of the nuclear program but staffed with civilian doctors. Starting in 1957, the Kazakh Academy of Sciences also sent its own expedition, staffed by the scientists from the Institute of Regional Pathology, which examined thousands of people living near the test site over the course of three years.[25]

The Military Narrative: The Institute of Biophysics

The Institute of Biophysics and Dispensary No. 4 conducted joint medical expeditions in 1956 and 1957 to the Semipalatinsk region. The two organizations wrote separate reports; they had similar findings but divergent recommendations.

In its top-secret report, the Institute of Biophysics concluded that the radio-active fallout from nuclear testing negatively affected the population's health and the environment. In the worst cases, the report noted, the level of radio-activity of butter in Sarzhal—a settlement close to the Polygon—was 58 times higher than the norm, while one Semipalatinsk storehouse contained grain with radioactivity 20 times higher than usual.[26]

Of the nearly five hundred people examined by the specialists on one of their trips, more than three hundred suffered from common illnesses such as brucellosis, tuberculosis, and heart disease, while more than a hundred demon-strated "symptoms occurring in cases of chronic radiation illness."[27] The mili-tary medical experts concluded that only 10 percent of those examined were in good health. The Institute of Biophysics staff cautiously concluded: "The role of ionizing radiation could not be excluded."[28]

Military doctors recommended discontinuing ground tests (atmospheric tests where nuclear devices explode at ground level rather than in the air), the most hazardous type of atmospheric testing, during the harvest season. But in what became a familiar narrative, the military medical specialists emphasized poor conditions in the area as the principal culprit behind the local popula-tion's health troubles. Accordingly, the doctors recommended that the govern-ment rectify "the unsanitary conditions," provide a better supply of fruits and vegetables, and improve health care services.[29] Their prescriptions did not in-clude a call to end nuclear testing.

The Civilian Narrative: Dispensary No. 4

Despite the main purpose of Dispensary No. 4, it was disguised as an antibru-cellosis clinic. Cattle are the primary victims of brucellosis, a chronic infectious disease. Humans who drink unpasteurized milk or eat dairy products from in-fected animals succumb to bacterial infection, leading to muscle pain, fevers, and night sweats. Brucellosis, widespread in the region due to cattle breeding, provided a convenient cover story for the Soviet military keen to study the im-pact of radiation.

It was not long after Dispensary No. 4's founding in 1957 that its doctors began raising the alarm about locals' health. In February 1958, in response to a request from Mukhametkali Suzhikov, then the highest-ranking Communist Party official in the Semipalatinsk region, a group of Dispensary No. 4 doctors sent a classified letter.[30] Suzhikov had come to the job only a month earlier, but he was known for tackling difficult issues head on. In his prior position as the head of Kyzyl Orda region, in the southern part of Kazakhstan and famous for its rice production, he persuaded the Soviet leadership to invest in the rice industry and raise the prices for rice to help this region. He also took it upon himself to resolve the devastating problem of leprosy there, pushing the Soviet government to adopt a regional program to fight the disease.[31]

The letter from Dispensary No. 4 to Suzhikov described the widespread radioactive contamination in Semipalatinsk. In some places, soil radioactivity was eleven to forty times greater than normal, and staple foodstuffs also registered higher than normal radioactive levels. The radioactivity of meat bought at Semipalatinsk markets was double or triple the norm, and the levels in wheat flour, buckwheat, and rice were four to five times the norm. Local hospitals, kindergartens, and nurseries bought grains from city stores, which meant that even the most vulnerable—the sick and the young—ate contaminated food.[32]

As for health impact, specialists from Dispensary No. 4 reported the same data points as the Moscow-controlled Institute of Biophysics. But their conclusions were different. Unlike the institute, with its timid recommendation to halt ground tests during harvest season, the Dispensary No. 4 staff called for a full cessation of all nuclear tests. The report from Dispensary No. 4 stated that the nuclear tests "[led] to contamination of soil, food supplies, grass and create[d] a significant danger to public health." Also, it advised the government to improve the supply of fruits, vegetables, meat, butter, vitamins, and essential medications to the Semipalatinsk region.[33]

Suzhikov, upon reading the Dispensary staff's alarming reports, sent a secret letter to the Soviet leader, Nikita Khrushchev, and to Kazakhstan's leader, Nikolai Beliaev (a native of Russia, appointed by Moscow), sharing the data with them. In response, the Soviet government authorized only insignificant financial and medical assistance to the region.[34] Many believe that Suzhikov's direct appeal to the Soviet leadership was behind the loss of his job as the head of the Semipalatinsk region. He was dismissed under the pretense that his region failed its meat production quota.[35]

Suzhikov was not the only one courageously raising his voice. In 1957, one of Kazakhstan's most prominent writers and a native of the Semipalatinsk region, Mukhtar Auezov, carried the story of his fellow citizens to the world at the international antinuclear conference in Tokyo. This was a bold move during the time of complete secrecy surrounding the Soviet nuclear testing program.[36]

A deep worry about his native region motivated Auezov. In 1958, he shared with his friend, President of the Kazakh Academy of Sciences Kuanysh Satpaev:

> Rumor has it that in the villages neighboring the Polygon—Sarzhal, Karasu, Kainar, and many other places—the youth succumb to suicide. Would you believe it? Teenagers of fifteen or sixteen years are giving up on life. This is a horror that our Kazakh children have never before known in their lives! The youth of yesterday, who looked after cattle and chased balls, suddenly go into the corner of the barn in the middle of the night and hang themselves. Why? Because an accursed atomic bomb rumbles above them . . .[37]

In 1962 a top Semipalatinsk official named Mikhail Karpenko, a native of Siberia, wrote to Dinmukhamed Kunaev, who by then was the republic's leader as the highest party official in Kazakhstan, requesting help with his region's overcrowded and unhealthy housing. Karpenko also mentioned radioactivity and that the local people understood what took place at the Polygon, despite being told nothing by the authorities. He implied that popular discontent was growing.[38]

A few days later, Karpenko wrote another letter to Kunaev after a failed nuclear test. On August 7, 1962, a missile carrying a nuclear charge had failed to explode in the air, instead detonating on the ground. Then the winds changed in the direction of populated areas. Massive amounts of dust rose into the atmosphere as a cloud that then carried radioactive fallout to Semipalatinsk and other nearby settlements. Karpenko again asked Kunaev for help with funds to build housing for the local population and for better supplies of meat, milk, butter, fruits, and vegetables. He stressed again that the populations of Semipalatinsk and the rural settlements not only know but "many *see* and *feel* external manifestations of the tests."[39]

In the wake of the botched test, Soviet military-industrial officials continued to insist to the Kazakh local leaders that radiation levels were normal—despite possessing hard data showing that the radioactivity levels in grain were 10–60 times higher than usual, and speaking plainly of radioactive contamination in their own internal secret documents. Several Soviet officials representing the nuclear weapons complex—the Polygon's military division, the defense ministry, and the health ministry—responded to Karpenko. Radioactive pollution, they said, was "insignificant;" radioactivity levels satisfied the standard for "special sanitary zones," defined as areas hosting facilities with higher impact on the environment and health, such as industrial plants that produce highly toxic materials.[40] Soviet officials advised regional authorities to send contaminated grain to other parts of the country to even out the radioactivity levels. Still, they did not want radioactive grain to be exported outside of the Soviet Union, presumably to avoid negative publicity.[41]

While government officials in Moscow buried the complaints that came through official channels, the KGB was closely monitoring the correspondence of Semipalatinsk residents who had nothing to do with the military program. Intercepted letters from Semipalatinsk locals to their family and friends described frequent explosions and the rumbling of the shaking earth that locals had grown to detest. The letter-writers also complained about polluted air, contaminated water, and mysterious health problems.

A local whose letter was intercepted by the KGB in 1966 reveals the residents' growing wariness of the nuclear tests:

> Everybody is fleeing, especially the last fifteen days. Now [the authorities] inform us in advance of the tests. At 12 p.m. [on test days], we go outside—it is dangerous to be inside. At the factory, everything stops, and everyone gets out onto the street. It feels like everything might collapse—[it's] so scary. All sorts of rumors are going around, and that's why everybody . . . is leaving this place.[42]

Despair filled the letters. Non-Kazakhs with relatives in Russia, Ukraine, or other republics were eager to leave. One resident wrote, "As soon as I retire, I will leave Semipalatinsk, for I do not want to be a guinea pig and hear the rumble of explosions." Several cited the bleakness of the area as their impetus for leaving: "We want to leave for Ukraine. It is becoming difficult to live here. I feel sorry for the people; there is nothing except for sand, not even fruit. The air is very polluted, especially in winter. Children are sluggish, with dark circles under their eyes. Our houses are always swaying from tremors. In other words, we'd better leave this place soon."[43]

For those who remained, health problems dogged whole families for generations. "My husband died of cancer at the age of fifty-four. My son was born in 1961 with encephalopathy and eye nystagmus [brain damage and uncontrollable eye movement]. . . . My grandson was born with six fingers on his hand. I have an allergy, joint pain, and heart and liver problems." Another local resident recounted her family's grim medical history: "My grandmother, uncle, and sister died from stomach cancer, my brother from lung cancer. I am losing my eyesight rapidly, and my arms, legs, stomach, and liver hurt."[44]

Unlike non-Kazakhs who had relatives in other republics and could move there, ethnic Kazakhs had nowhere to go. Decades after the tests ended, their stories paint a picture of the individual and collective tragedy that enveloped the region.

The mayor of Mukur, a village of a thousand people near the testing site, has her own family story:

> At the age of fifty-two, my father passed away from lung cancer. Our world turned upside down because we always perceived him to be a healthy and strong man. When my mother became a widow, her youngest child was only six years old. We had been brought up to work hard—this had been our father's motto—and we did. We were left on our own, without much help from the outside. When my mother turned sixty-four, she had a stroke and was bedridden for four years before she died. My older brother's life ended at fifty-seven. A blood disease took him away from us. My younger brother suffered from neuroderma-titis. My sister and I have problems with blood pressure.[45]

A man named Nesipbai Diusekeev, an educator from Abraly, recalled the cost of the tests on local children:

> I have lived in Abraly since 1950. Before I retired, I worked as a school director for many years. During the atmospheric and underground nuclear tests, we were told that they were harmless, that all safety measures were being taken. But from then on, locals started developing illnesses that we had not seen before—leukemia, for example. I am not a doctor, but I've seen sick people whose bones broke with the slightest movement. Among the children, there are many who are already thirteen or fourteen, but they look like they are only two, three, or four. Many children, born disfigured, always sit at home. Some died at thirteen or fourteen.[46]

Children often observed the horrible consequences of nuclear tests on their surroundings without realizing the cause. Aliia, a native of Chagan, a village near the Polygon, recalls:

> Every summer, I visited relatives in the Kumurza grasslands, where my uncle looked after the cattle. The road to the pastures was right on the way to the test site. I saw a newborn lamb with two conjoined heads with my own eyes. A lot of newborn cattle were born without body parts (like noses or ears) or with differ-ent pathologies and deformities of the skull. At that time, I found it interesting

and strange, and I didn't even think about how it had happened. Only when I grew up did I understand the reason.[47]

The darkest side of the human tragedy unfolding in the Kazakh steppe was the rise in suicides and mental illness.[48] Suicide was previously such an alien

PHOTO 7   Victims of Soviet nuclear tests, Semipalatinsk region, circa late 1980s. Photograph by Yuri Kuidin.

concept to Kazakhs that they had no word for it. But now it loomed large for many, such as this woman from Sarzhal, a small settlement directly affected by nuclear contamination: "Two of our sons hanged themselves when they were 14 and 20 years old. The third son suffers from mental illness. My husband died from heart disease. There is no doubt the nuclear test site is to blame for everything."[49] Her family was only one of many who suffered this experience. Dozens of people from villages close to the Polygon committed suicide each year, primarily by hanging.[50]

The Kazakh Narrative: The Institute of Regional Pathology

It was hard to ignore the Polygon's curse. In 1956, Bahiia Atchabarov, director of the Institute of Regional Pathology in Alma-Ata, visited his native town of Karkaraly. His friend, Syzdyk Takumbekuly, described the tragedies that beset the locals in their hometown:

> Under the guise of night, young men commit suicide. We are haunted by leukemia and other diseases, when blood suddenly gushes from the nose, the heart pounds, there is shortness of breath, and the body becomes covered with spots. The saddest of all is the rise in births of babies who are mentally or physically disabled. Some were born without arms and legs, or with disfigured faces.[51]

Takumbekuly appealed to his friend, now the head of an entire institute in the capital: "Why don't your doctors check [what is happening]?" Atchabarov explained to his friend that anything connected with the Polygon was for the military doctors to examine. His institute's mandate, he said, was to study and prevent professional injuries at the large industrial enterprises.

But Takumbekuly's plea stayed with Atchabarov, and in 1957, like writer Auezov, he shared his worries about the region with the president of the Kazakh Academy of Sciences, Kuanysh Satpaev. Atchabarov asked Satpaev to allow his institute, which was part of the academy, to conduct a clinical expedition in the region. Satpaev, a leading geologist who founded metallogenic science in Kazakhstan and was a highly respected scientist, gave his authorization. The initiative also had the support of Soviet Health Minister Mariia Kovrigina, despite the serious problems it could potentially cause her with the Soviet military establishment. Kovrigina was known for her courage and professionalism.[52]

For three years, from 1957 to 1960, the doctors conducted clinical observations of 3,500 people in the area around the Polygon, and of 2,000 people from other areas around Kazakhstan, who served as the control group.[53] This was the

PHOTO 8   Victims of Soviet nuclear tests, Semipalatinsk region, circa late 1980s.
Photograph by Yuri Kuidin.

first and last medical survey led by doctors from Kazakhstan during the Soviet
period.[54]

Dr. Atchabarov led a Kazakh research team that reflected the multiethnic
composition of Kazakhstan, including Kazakhs, Russians, Jews, Germans, and
others. These scientists faithfully recorded everything they observed, including
information that would be damaging to the Soviet nuclear program, and did so

despite enormous personal risks. They could have been accused of state treason for describing how the country's most important national security project was ruining the health of their countrymen.

Their account was a clinical record written in medical jargon, but it painted a heartbreaking picture of innocent people suffering from the effects of nuclear tests through no fault of their own. The scientists noticed that people living in the settlements closer to the Polygon suffered from a range of ailments. The neurological pathologies made people tired and caused headaches and dizziness. Many locals were losing their swallowing reflex—the body's important defense mechanism against choking on food. In the villages of Kainar, Sarzhal, and Dolon-1, only about a third of residents could be considered neurologically healthy.[55]

Atchabarov and his team also observed that blood circulation problems in the brain were more common and more severe among people living in the contaminated settlements than in the control group. For the people with long-term exposure to high amounts of radioactivity, there were also changes in the threshold for pain sensitivity, and in the senses of taste and smell.[56] Women in the contaminated settlements suffered from disrupted menstrual cycles, pathologies in genitalia, and other gynecological problems.[57]

The Institute of Regional Pathology team found that low doses of ionizing radiation caused nose, ear, and throat changes among locals who lived close to the testing area.[58] Inhabitants of villages close to the Polygon aged prematurely as a result of infectious and somatic diseases (a condition where extreme focus on pain and fatigue leads to emotional distress) and generally unfavorable living conditions. In Kainar, for example, the villagers appeared to be ten years older than their actual age.[59]

The specialists also studied animals, plants, and the overall environment. Animals were exposed to radiation even more than humans, since they spent all their time outside, eating contaminated grass, in constant contact with soil that absorbed radioactive particles. They suffered from deteriorating health, with blood and liver diseases, damage to their lungs and bleeding in their respiratory systems, mouths, and genitals. Even their brain tissue was altered.[60] Postmortem tests found strontium-90 in the bones of sheep and dogs.[61] Strontium-90, a product of nuclear fission, has earned the terrifying nickname of "bone-seeker" because it lodges in bones and bone marrow and causes cancer of bone, nearby tissues, and leukemia.

Soil and vegetation in the rural settlements near the Polygon were seriously contaminated, irradiating people and animals not only externally but internally. In the village of Kainar, for example, the experts said that the soil was full of tiny radioactive particles (up to five microns). Such particles were "most aggressive," they explained, because they easily traveled into humans' bloodstream when breathed in, delivering a large dose of internal radiation.[62] It did not help that villagers lived in adobe houses they had built with raw bricks made of contaminated soil. As a result, even when indoors, they continued to be exposed to radioactive contamination.[63]

Around 1958, Atchabarov and Saim Balmukhanov, the chief radiologist at Kazakhstan's Ministry of Health and part of the expedition, also talked to Mukhametkali Suzhikov, the head of the Semipalatinsk region, who, as mentioned earlier, had bravely brought up the issue of the Polygon to the Soviet government and lost his job because of it.[64]

The Atchabarov team concluded that the environment's radioactivity levels were 20 to 300 times greater than maximum permissible levels. In some settlements, the radiation was 650 times higher than normal.[65]

The findings of the Institute of Regional Pathology, which filled twelve volumes of classified documents, were sent to Moscow. The Institute of Biophysics, the military-affiliated organ whose earlier expedition had recommended nothing more than a pause in nuclear explosions during harvest time, called the team's conclusions "tendentious." Members of the Soviet military-industrial complex complained that local doctors blamed all health problems on radiation and "said nothing of sanitary and socioeconomic factors." They argued that "the examination results do not present data on the sanitary state of inhabited settlements, living conditions of the inhabitants, nor the quality of food—dominating factors in the development of some diseases."[66] This was in fact a false criticism, since these reports from Kazakhstan's doctors did acknowledge difficult living conditions and infectious diseases as contributing factors to the poor health of the Semipalatinsk locals.[67]

These officials, addressing the Communist Party Central Committee and the government of Kazakhstan, requested that Atchabarov be recalled and given an administrative punishment. Evidently, the Kazakh government resisted, as Atchabarov was not punished. "At the same time," Atchabarov noted, "we never heard open disapproval of nuclear weapons testing at the Semipalatinsk Polygon from the Kazakh government."[68] The Kazakh team was eventually forced to stop their clinical studies.

In his memoirs, Atchabarov writes that the president of the Kazakh Academy of Sciences, Kuanysh Satpaev, told him, "I protected you as long as I could.

This time, however, General [Avetik] Burnazyan [Deputy Health Minister, who was in charge of health issues in the military] followed me around demanding an end to the expedition. Your work has already made a difference."[69]

Those words marked the end of the expedition.

After the brief moratorium on nuclear testing between 1958 and 1961 (during the test-ban negotiations between the United States, United Kingdom, and the Soviet Union), Soviet nuclear tests resumed. But the statistics on cancer and mortality rates in the Semipalatinsk area remained classified.

Dispensary No. 4 continued to observe the effects on locals. From 1961 onward, the medical personnel from Dispensary No. 4 examined 20,000 people: 10,000 local inhabitants from areas exposed to radiation—the Abai, Beskaragay, and Zhana-Semey districts—and 10,000 from elsewhere in Kazakhstan, as a control group. The 10,000 locals from affected areas had been exposed to radiation at doses ranging from 10 to 150 rems.[70] To put this in perspective, in 2021, the annual limit of exposure for US emergency responders was set at 5 rem.[71] Because Dispensary No. 4 began its first large-scale surveys of the radiological situation and people's health only in 1961 and 1962, three years after being established and twelve years into the atmospheric testing, data on the immediate impact of radiation on people was lost.[72]

The clinic at Dispensary No. 4 housed only fifteen to twenty hospital beds—it was designed to collect data, not treat locals, despite its disguise as an antibrucellosis facility. Meanwhile, doctors in regular hospitals were instructed to falsify the records of illnesses caused by radiation—to classify them as other illnesses or leave patients without a diagnosis.[73] Kabden Essengarin, the health official from the local village of Sarzhal, explained that "if somebody died of stomach cancer, we couldn't report that. . . . We had to write down 'stomach problems' or something like that. People from the KGB came to make sure we said nothing more."[74] In 1965, the Soviet Health Ministry forbade any studies to be conducted in the city of Semipalatinsk, thus restricting scientists and medics to studying rural settlements.[75] This restriction was likely motivated by fear that researching health issues in a big city like Semipalatinsk would lead to breaches of secrecy.

From the reports of the Institute of Regional Pathology, made available to scholars in Kazakhstan after the collapse of the Soviet Union, and from appeals by local government officials in Semipalatinsk, we get a rare glimpse into what Semipalatinsk, Kazakh, and Soviet authorities knew about the impact of nuclear testing on the local population starting in the 1950s. Some local officials in the Semipalatinsk region rang alarms early on, but, as Atchabarov suggests above, the Kazakh government was unable to stand up to Moscow. The Soviet government, backed by the military-industrial complex, continued to deny that nuclear tests harmed people and the environment while at the same time it monitored the health of 10,000 people for scientific purposes, without treating them.

As the Soviet Union entered a stage of profound transformation with the advent of liberalizing perestroika and glasnost, the people in Kazakhstan rose up to demand the closing of the Semipalatinsk Polygon forever. Forty years of nuclear tests had wrought so much devastation that popular anger had swollen.

CHAPTER 4

THE NATION RISES

ON DECEMBER 16, 1986, for the first time in the republic's history, Kazakh youth openly protested Moscow's rule. On that gray winter day, an estimated 30,000 young men and women gathered in Alma-Ata's main square. They were revolting against Moscow's removal of Kazakhstan's popular leader, Dinmukhamed Kunaev, an ethnic Kazakh, and the appointment of Gennadii Kolbin, a Soviet official with no prior ties to Kazakhstan, to replace him.

The KGB acted swiftly. It sent troops to brutally suppress the protest, killing 168 protesters, beating 1,700, and detaining some 8,500. Many protesters received criminal sentences (revoked when Kazakhstan gained independence in 1991). Students who participated in the protest lost their places in universities. In sum, Moscow waged a campaign of intimidation and silencing against those who dared to voice disagreement.[1]

The crackdown was "a slap in the face" to Kazakhstan, according to Murat Auezov, the son of legendary Semipalatinsk writer Mukhtar Auezov. A culturologist by training, Auezov believed this suppression resonated among the populace because it coincided with a period of Kazakh self-awakening. Seminal works of literature, film, and other forms of artistic expression promoting Kazakh identity now nourished growing self-respect.

In literature, for example, folklore works that depicted authentic Kazakh traditions and culture were making a comeback. One was the poetic folk legend "Kyz Zhibek" (Silk girl). The poem is partly a love story of a beautiful proud girl and a warrior, and partly an examination of Kazakh history in the sixteenth century, a period of feudal fights. During the Soviet times, works like "Kyz Zhi-bek" were condemned for their "antipopular" sentiment. One of the reasons: Kyz Zhibek and her warrior lover were both from rich Kazakh families, and Soviet communism treated any material capital with suspicion. In the 1980s, stories like "Kyz Zhibek" received renewed attention in Kazakhstan, adapted for the theater and translated into Russian for greater distribution.

The December events hung heavily over the republic. Those who protested against Moscow were ethnic Kazakhs, and those who were sent to suppress them were mostly Russian. For Kazakhstan, which was home to more than a hundred ethnicities and prided itself on its interethnic harmony, the tension between Kazakhs and Russians in the December unrest undermined confi-dence in Soviet rule from Moscow and was itself a tragedy even beyond the death and the violence.

In this polarized environment, popular resentment against the decades of nuclear testing in Kazakhstan reached its peak. The protests were ampli-fied because this was the era of Mikhail Gorbachev, and the Soviet Union was in the midst of dramatic social and political transformation. Gorbachev, who had risen to power in 1985, opened the floodgates to changes, which even he proved unable to control. Glasnost—greater freedom to express one's views—made dissent possible, and Gorbachev's perestroika—an attempt to modernize a stagnating political system—unveiled the depth of the Soviet Union's social, political, and economic decay. Most non-Russian republics, tired of being gov-erned by Moscow, sought greater independence. A collapsing Soviet economy, along with the republics' perceptions of long-term exploitation by Moscow, deepened their frustration.

By 1988, as part of Gorbachev's reforms, the Soviet Union had relaxed the rules for establishing political and social organizations. What Gorbachev did not expect was that the groups he did allow—those with environmental, history, and language agendas—would become vehicles for nationalist and pro-independence movements.[2] Kazakhstan's antinuclear movement was one of them.

The major shifts in domestic and foreign policy during the Gorbachev era sharply affected the Semipalatinsk Polygon. Gorbachev was keen to demilita-rize Soviet policy and to slow the nuclear arms race with the United States. With the latter goal in mind, he instituted a unilateral nuclear testing moratorium in 1985, soon after becoming the Soviet Secretary-General. The moratorium lasted a year-and-a-half, but continued US testing pushed Gorbachev to resume So-viet tests. Although Gorbachev remained convinced that a nuclear test ban was necessary, the powerful Military-Industrial Commission of the USSR Council of Ministers, led by Igor Beloussov, demanded that tests continue. Beloussov, a naval engineer by training whose background included building nuclear submarines, led the Soviet Ministry of Shipbuilding before becoming the second in command of the Soviet government and the head of the Military-Industrial Commission. Because of his position, Beloussov would become the face of the Soviet military establishment in the eyes of Kazakh local leaders.

The standoff between a more liberal Gorbachev and Soviet hard-liners also extended to Moscow's dealings with the republics. Gorbachev was eager to preserve the Soviet Union, but he believed that, without greater autonomy, the republics would eventually revolt against Moscow. The hard-liners insisted that reining in the republics—through brutal crackdowns if necessary—was necessary to preserve the Soviet Union.

Meanwhile, against this tense backdrop in Moscow, the people of Kazakhstan demanded an end to nuclear testing. The nuclear power plant accident at Chernobyl in 1986, which had killed dozens and injured untold numbers of people, afflicted 134 others with acute radiation sickness. It also contaminated vast parts of Ukraine and Belarus, and in Kazakhstan it intensified the growing public fear of the atom.[3]

The immediate catalyst for Kazakhstan's antinuclear outcry was an underground nuclear test that rocked Degelen Mountain on February 12, 1989. Nothing out of the ordinary, the blast followed two decades of underground tests at the Semipalatinsk Polygon. No one expected that the test would become a symbolic flashpoint for the Polygon's ultimate demise.

During that test, the radioactive gases xenon-133 and xenon-135, which are products of uranium-235 fission, escaped through cracks in soil that had been damaged by years of testing. In the past, venting of colorless, odorless gases during underground tests occurred regularly and went mostly unnoticed, as the plumes quickly dissipated in the atmosphere. Xenon is used, in controlled amounts, in radiological medicine. Inhaled in large quantities, it can cause nausea, dizziness, and even loss of consciousness and death.

As a matter of routine, testers would wait for the winds to blow away from the military settlements in the vicinity of the Polygon before conducting nuclear tests. On February 12, however, the wind suddenly changed direction. A huge radioactive cloud, up to 200 meters (650 feet) high and more than a mile wide, traveled across the military settlements and then on to populated civilian areas.

In the military town of Chagan, the base of a Soviet strategic air force division, safety devices registered radioactivity hundreds of times above natural levels. The division's military commander, General Pavel Berdikhin, fearing the worst and not fully sure what the spike in radioactivity meant, canceled classes at school and breakfast for military staff at a canteen.[4]

In the atmosphere of glasnost under Gorbachev's rule, the general was reluctant to hide the results of radiation probes in Chagan and confirmed the release of radioactive gases to the top local official in Semipalatinsk, Keshrim Boztaev. It was the first time that a nuclear test and radioactive contamination were acknowledged by a representative of the military. Meanwhile, the Polygon's director, General Arkadii Il'yenko, reported to Moscow that the test was successful and did not raise radiation levels. These conflicting reports frightened and angered local people and the Semipalatinsk authorities. But just five days later, on February 17, another underground explosion shook the testing grounds.

Three powerful factors—the unprecedented publicizing of test information, the opportunity to act that Gorbachev's reforms allowed, and the rising Kazakh self-awakening—converged and brought the Kazakh nation to its tipping point. The February 12, 1989, test unleashed an antinuclear movement whose supporters and sympathizers eventually numbered in the millions and came from all corners of Kazakhstan. Fear, despair, and resentment at the Soviet nuclear program finally crested in an enormous wave of protest.

Olzhas Suleimenov, one of the most prominent Kazakh literary figures of his generation, rallied the nation to the fight. In Semipalatinsk, Keshrim Boztaev, who became the head of the region in 1987, committed himself to the Polygon's closure. And in Alma-Ata, an ambitious Nursultan Nazarbayev—the new young leader of Kazakhstan—sought avenues to persuade Moscow to stop the tests. Gorbachev was now caught between the powerful Soviet military-industrial complex and the increasingly vexed people of Kazakhstan. The shifting political and social environment in the Soviet Union provided fertile soil for Kazakhstan's antinuclear movement to grow into a formidable political force.

THE BIRTH OF THE NEVADA-SEMIPALATINSK MOVEMENT

From the moment in 1984 when Olzhas Suleimenov became a deputy of the USSR Supreme Soviet (the Soviet top legislative body), he received desperate letters from people living near the Semipalatinsk Polygon, and other testing grounds in Kazakhstan, complaining about deteriorating health and hard living conditions. It was the February 12 test, however, that spurred Suleimenov.

He received a call from Chagan to alert him that the test had caused the leakage of radioactive gas. Suleimenov later explained: "Gorbachev, democracy, and glasnost made that call possible."[5] With the military's confirmation of the radioactive contamination, Suleimenov stepped into action.

Suleimenov, who was running a reelection campaign for his USSR Supreme Soviet seat as a representative of one of Alma-Ata's election districts, was scheduled to speak about his political platform on national television on February 25—less than two weeks after the test. But Suleimenov went off script and shared what he had learned about leaked gases after the underground tests, and, more broadly, he decried the decades of nuclear testing that had wreaked devastation on Kazakhstan's people and land. On live television, he read a statement demanding that Moscow curtail the testing program. Suleimenov and three other senior Kazakh elected representatives had signed the statement, which was addressed to the USSR Supreme Soviet and the Kazakhstan's Supreme Soviet. It read:

> We, the people of Kazakhstan, more than anyone in the world, have the right to express our concern and demand that production and testing of nuclear weapons stop. For the health of today's and future generations, for life on Earth, expressing the will of multiethnic Kazakhstan, we demand the shutdown of nuclear testing sites in our republic.[6]

In concluding his speech, Suleimenov urged opponents of the nuclear tests to join him for a rally three days later in Alma-Ata.

Thousands of people answered Suleimenov's call and assembled at the Writers' House, a gathering place for Alma-Ata's literary professionals. The building's main hall had capacity for only four hundred people, so thousands of others stood outside on the cold streets. Tall and handsome with jet-black, wavy hair, Suleimenov was naturally charismatic. Murat Auezov, who was present at the rally, recalled, "The atmosphere was electric, Suleimenov's energy was spellbinding. . . . I had goosebumps when he spoke."[7]

Suleimenov, a skillful orator, galvanized the crowd:

> The life expectancy in developed countries is increasing while in our republic it has shortened by four years compared with a decade ago. One of the main reasons is the increasing radioactivity levels in soil, water, and food. . . . Forty years of peace? No, those were forty years of silent war! The government is waging secret nuclear war against its people. . . . To be or not to be. We face Hamlet's dilemma . . ."[8]

Several speakers from the Semipalatinsk region took to the podium to tell their painful stories. A female obstetrician from one of the villages who had delivered babies for thirty years shared her damning evidence: "In the last six months, out of forty-eight births, twelve were tragic. Six newborns died, and six were born either without limbs or with Down syndrome." She implored: "I demand as a doctor and as a mother, stop nuclear tests!"[9]

On the spur of the moment, Suleimenov called for the creation of an antinuclear movement, to which the audience responded with thunderous applause. Suleimenov stepped outside to speak to the gathered crowds. They, too, wholeheartedly expressed their support for an antinuclear movement.[10] Sergei Shafir, a cameraman who filmed the historic rally and later became a movement activist himself, recalled: "Suleimenov gave us a feeling of self-esteem and faith in our human power."[11]

"When I woke up that morning, I wasn't thinking about it," Suleimenov recounted, reflecting on his spontaneous call to begin a movement. The raw emotions of the people at the rally inspired him. That day—February 28, 1989—marked the birth of the most powerful public movement in the history of Kazakhstan and the world's largest movement against nuclear tests. Initially, the movement members called it Nevada to feel united with the downwinders in the United States fighting to stop nuclear tests at the Nevada Test Site. Later, it became Nevada-Semipalatinsk. The movement's logo, designed by the art critic Umyt Sakharieva and her husband, the immunologist Zhamil' Issin, depicted a Native tribe elder from Nevada offering a peace pipe to a Kazakh elder from the Semipalatinsk region.[12]

Among the hundreds of people at the rally was Tolegen Mukhamedzhanov, a famous composer. He had grown up in a village not far from the Polygon, and in his boyhood he had admired the nuclear mushroom clouds without care. At the Writers' House that day, he cried as he suddenly grasped several tragic truths about his family. "Finally, I understood why I lost my father at such a young age, why my older brother died at the age of twenty, why my sister died at the age of twenty-seven, why my best friend committed suicide at the age of twenty-four."[13] Moved by the emotion of his fellow countrymen, Mukhamedzhanov wrote a melody that would become the hymn of the Nevada-Semipalatinsk movement. The poet Ulykbek Esdauletov wrote the lyrics. The song "Zaman-Ai" (Oh, such times) became a tribute to the suffering endured by Kazakhstan's people and land. The pain of the Kazakh experience was so steeped in the melody and lyrics that even those who did not understand the Kazakh language were deeply moved upon hearing it.

Immediately after the rally, a number of Kazakhstan's prominent writers, journalists, filmmakers, and scientists joined the Nevada-Semipalatinsk organizing committee and sprang into action. Suleimenov's office in the Writers' House became a site of nonstop activity; advocates were busy planning, coordinating, and campaigning to capture the attention of Moscow and the international community as well as to galvanize the people of Kazakhstan. Some composed and typed speeches; others worked all available telephones.[14] Galina Kuzembaeva, a talented journalist, disseminated the movement's message across media networks. Described by her fellow Nevada-Semipalatinsk activists as "the heart and soul, the backbone of the movement who knew the media outlets across the country," Kuzembaeva enabled Suleimenov's appeal to spread rapidly even without the benefit of the internet or social media.[15]

This massive public outcry unified Kazakhstan and helped heal the wounds and ethnic tensions that had arisen from Moscow's bloody suppression of the 1986 youth protest. More than a million people of different nationalities and ethnicities, professions and occupations signed the Nevada-Semipalatinsk petition to end nuclear tests at the Polygon.

Murat Auezov described the great impact of the movement on Kazakhstan's long-standing quest for independence from Moscow:

> The antinuclear movement helped to cleanse the psychic stain of the events of 1986. It restored the fabric of Kazakh national identity by uniting all the ethnicities of Kazakhstan around the same cause to stand up to Moscow. This time, however, the movement for greater national autonomy proceeded in an organized manner, motivated by a single, noble goal—the cessation of nuclear testing.[16]

Auezov saw the birth of the Nevada-Semipalatinsk movement as redress not only for Moscow's brutal crackdown at the December 1986 protests but also for Russian oppression of the Kazakh independence movement Alash Orda and for the execution of Kazakhstan's educated elite by Stalin in the 1930s.[17] In other words, the Nevada-Semipalatinsk movement tapped into the broader resentment in Kazakhstan with rule from Moscow.

Meanwhile, Olzhas Suleimenov dropped out of his reelection campaign in Alma-Ata, partly because one of his competitors—a representative of the working class—was expected to win, and partly because Mikhail Gorbachev invited Suleimenov to join him on a trip to London to meet with Margaret

PHOTO 9   Olzhas Suleimenov, poet, leader of Nevada-Semipalatinsk movement at the rally in the rural area near the Semipalatinsk Polygon, 1989. Photograph by V. Pavlunin.
SOURCE: Central State Archive of Film and Photo Documents and Sound Recordings, Kazakhstan. Image #2–104147.

Thatcher. Suleimenov later asked, "Why did Gorbachev support me, take me to London, even though we never spoke until that moment? He needed an antinuclear movement. We helped him, and he helped us."[18] Gorbachev faced the strong opposition of the military, keen on maintaining a robust testing program, which he was not powerful enough to overcome. To stop the testing, he needed active, vocal popular support.

On his return from London, Suleimenov resumed his political career. The Kazakh political leaders encouraged him to run for a seat in the USSR Supreme Soviet—this time to represent not Alma-Ata but the Semipalatinsk region. His victory allowed him to push the Nevada-Semipalatinsk agenda in the highest legislative organ in Moscow.

ON THE GROUND IN SEMIPALATINSK

The antinuclear agitation was not just a popular local movement but also a national political one, and in 1989 Kazakhstan's leadership had to walk a tightrope between the two. On the one hand, Kazakh leaders used the February 12 test and the growing popular anger as an opportunity to push back against a central government in Moscow that was losing its grip on the republics. On the other hand, Kazakhstan was still highly dependent on Moscow and had to move carefully and gradually against the Polygon. Too slow, however, and the leadership would face mounting impatience at home.

A courageous, native-born leader of the Semipalatinsk region, Keshrim Boztaev was a metallurgical engineer by training. He rose through the party ranks and by 1987 had become the regional head. Boztaev learned about the released radioactive gases from General Berdikhin shortly after the February 12 test. When Gorbachev requested a status report from the Kazakh government on the local state of affairs after the test, Boztaev had a chance to appeal directly to the Soviet leader with the blessing of Nursultan Nazarbayev, the head of the Kazakh Council of Ministers. Nazarbayev was second in command after Gennadii Kolbin, the Moscow-assigned head of Kazakhstan whose appointment had ignited the anti-Moscow youth protests in Alma-Ata in December 1986. In a telegram marked "Secret" and sent directly to Gorbachev on February 20, Boztaev pleaded for the suspension of nuclear tests at the Polygon, or at least a reduction in their frequency and yield.[19] "This was the voice of the victimized steppe. . . . They [Politburo members and the military-industrial complex] could not have expected that a telegram like this could come from the most senior party official in Semipalatinsk."[20]

Kazakhstan's Communist Party also took action, dispatching its representatives to visit the Polygon area. Those officials returned to Alma-Ata with broader concerns about the Polygon's operation. They criticized the lack of studies on how underground nuclear tests changed rock formations, the failure of Polygon officials to inform the local authorities about emergencies, and the reluctance of Soviet military doctors to share with local authorities the health data they had been collecting for decades. Kazakh party officials also complained that the extreme secrecy surrounding the Polygon and the testing program had bred rumors that stoked popular paranoia.

Further, they said, if they did not receive any guidance or data to back them up, they could not convincingly explain to the local population the merits of the testing program—as their party bosses had ordered them to do. They demanded that the tests be better planned to avoid the accidental release of radioactive gases and that the Polygon's security apparatus be strengthened to prevent people and animals from entering contaminated areas. They highlighted the need for the Soviet authorities to share medical data with the local health authorities to improve treatment for the afflicted population, and to make available seismic assessments of buildings following tests. Finally, without asking for an outright ban on nuclear testing, the officials broached the idea of a "potential relocation of the Polygon" due to increased social tension in the region.[21]

The government of Kazakhstan established a commission to monitor the environmental situation in the area, led by Erik Assanbaev, deputy chairman of Kazakhstan's Council of Ministers.[22] The Soviet government also created a commission, which arrived in Semipalatinsk on February 28. In a meeting there between the Moscow delegation and the local authorities, the head of the Moscow commission, Vladimir Bukatov, who was an official from the Soviet Council of Ministers and a prominent specialist on naval engineering, claimed that no breach of radiation safety had occurred on February 12. Nevertheless, Keshrim Boztaev pressed the Soviet officials to offer his region compensation and to disclose the data collected by Dispensary No. 4, the institution set up to monitor radiation effects on the local population.[23]

Bukatov could not just wish away the growing tensions between locals and the Polygon program. To help dispel hostilities, Bukatov's commission proposed to lower the number and yield of tests and to place nuclear devices deeper underground to avoid the release of radioactive gases. The commission also recommended public outreach with the hope that providing more information on the tests and on the ecological situation would calm the populace. Unsurprisingly, the Moscow commission did not call for the end of nuclear tests.[24]

In late March of 1989, Boztaev wrote a detailed memo to Gennadii Kolbin. "For decades, mortality rates in the Semipalatinsk region have been 5 to 10 percent higher than average in the republic,"[25] Boztaev noted. He pointed particularly to higher cancer rates and higher child mortality rates—33 out of 1,000 newborns died. He also shared local veterinary labs' findings of high concentrations of radioactive cesium, strontium, and polonium in the hay that was used to feed local livestock. This last finding was particularly alarming in a region that prided itself as a major meat producer for the entire Soviet Union. Like Semipalatinsk officials before him, Boztaev demanded increased measures to deal with the region's health, environmental, and seismic problems. He, again, pushed for less frequent and lower-yield nuclear tests and for relocation of the Polygon to another site.[26]

The same month, Kolbin (then the highest official in Kazakhstan appointed by Moscow), Nursultan Nazarbayev (a native of Kazakhstan, the chairman of the Council of Ministers of Kazakhstan and the second in command), and several Soviet defense officials wrote a letter to the Central Committee of the Soviet Communist Party. The letter cited appeals from lower-level, regional officials such as Boztaev as well as the growing popularity of the Nevada-Semipalatinsk movement to make a case for lower-yield and fewer nuclear tests at Semipalatinsk. But the letter did not question the necessity of continuing nuclear tests per se and did not demand their cessation, acknowledging, "The United States continues to test. We are forced to test too."[27] The letter did point out, however, that the local population demanded an end to all testing.

In response, the Central Committee of the Soviet Communist Party ordered the military-industrial complex to improve the safety of nuclear tests at Semipalatinsk and to consider revising plans for tests scheduled for the remainder of 1989. The Soviet party bosses also called for a report on the February 12 test to be published in the Kazakhstan press.[28]

Controversy about the February 12 test continued through the spring of 1989. The Soviet military newspaper *Krasnaia Zvezda* published an interview with a Soviet defense official who argued that naturally occurring radioactive gases released during underground tests presented no danger to the population. The official claimed that the lack of information could breed rumors. He also dismissed complaints about the seismic impact of underground tests, suggesting that "the power of jolts during tests was insignificant. . . . You can compare it to a train station building trembling when a train passes."[29]

Nazarbayev traveled to Semipalatinsk and reassured local officials that the republic's leadership was doing its best to change the region's circumstances. Seeking to assuage local anger, he told them, "Today I have all the numbers; I did not know them before." Nazarbayev agreed with the Semipalatinsk authorities that the frequency and yield of nuclear tests had to be reduced. He promised them, "This is the first step, and then we will see. We are working, so that you will know. We are working, not sparing anything."[30]

Meanwhile, Erik Assanbaev, the leader of the Kazakhstan government commission on the impact of nuclear tests, shared his report on the situation at Semipalatinsk with the Central Committee of Kazakhstan's Communist Party. Assanbaev told his colleagues about petitions sent directly to the Council of Ministers that demanded the full cessation of nuclear tests in Kazakhstan. Bolstered by the voice of the populace, the ministers cited higher-than-average mortality rates in the Semipalatinsk region and demanded from Moscow a reduction in the frequency and yield of tests, with the ultimate goal of ending all tests.

Nazarbayev used the growing antinuclear movement to entrench his political power in an increasingly independent Kazakhstan.[31] He argued that the Soviet military must first scale down testing and later halt it altogether. A back and forth between Alma-Ata and Moscow on the fate of the Polygon followed. On the one hand, the Soviet government, especially the military and the military-industrial complex, continued to downplay the negative impact of nuclear tests. On the other, even they could not deny the facts on the ground. On occasion, Moscow appeared sympathetic and ready to offer social, economic, and medical help to the Semipalatinsk region. But at the end of the day, the Soviet central government did not stop its nuclear tests there. Gorbachev, who on a personal level was in favor of demilitarizing the Soviet Union, could not overrule the system.

MOSCOW STANDOFF AND THE FIRST PUBLIC CONFERENCE ON HEALTH PROBLEMS

The broad popular appeal of the Nevada-Semipalatinsk movement and its ability to mobilize large numbers of people took nuclear mandarins in Moscow by surprise. As a direct result of the pressure generated by the Nevada-Semipalatinsk movement, the Soviet Military-Industrial Commission cut the number of nuclear tests planned for 1989 from eighteen to nine and reduced their yield as well. Meanwhile, Olzhas Suleimenov continued to use his platform as a deputy at the USSR Supreme Soviet in Moscow to draw attention to the antinuclear cause.

In July 1989, Soviet authorities allowed representatives of the Nevada-Semipalatinsk movement and the press to observe an imitation underground test carried out with conventional explosives instead of a nuclear device at the Polygon's Balapan range. The government hoped the experience would help quell the criticism surrounding the tests. Observers stood out on the steppe, about 3 kilometers (2 miles) away from the explosion. Despite the distance, they felt a tremor equal to a 4.0 magnitude earthquake. According to Murat Auezov, who witnessed the test, "the water splashed from the glasses when the test happened . . . large cracks appeared in the ground."[32] Putting on a full show for the visitors, immediately after the test a cement truck appeared on the range, and a team garbed in protective suits emerged and quickly poured cement into cracks in the ground. "These would be required safety measures," a military officer in the observation area explained. "In three to four hours [after a test], inert gases might attempt to escape."[33]

After the simulated test, all visitors gathered at the Officers' Club in Kurchatov, where General Il'yenko, the head of the Polygon, tried to convince them that underground nuclear tests were safe. In response, Murat Auezov asked the military officers present: "How many of you know the poetry of Abai, Shakarim, [Mukhtar] Auezov?" These were the names of Kazakhstan's most consequential literary figures—the last of them Murat's own father. All these writers had roots in the Semipalatinsk region and their works reflected the beauty and the special place of the region in Kazakh history and culture. Met with silence, Auezov tried to call out the military on the disruption the tests brought to the animals of the region: "Do you know how many groundhogs have died since testing began?" The little animals are an indispensable part of the steppe's fauna. Il'yenko was taken aback: "What groundhogs?!"[34]

Also in July, another "first" followed the unprecedented visit of antinuclear activists to the Polygon. A public conference on the health and environmental issues of the testing program was held in Semipalatinsk thanks to the efforts of local authorities. The meetings focused on the findings of a Moscow-authorized government commission led by Anatolii Tsyb, the leading Soviet specialist in radiology, oncology, and radiation therapy.[35] Both Soviet and Kazakh medical professionals and scientists participated in its work.

Professor Tsyb's commission calculated that the radiation doses absorbed by the local population during atmospheric nuclear tests could lead to significant increases in mortality and cancer rates. They also confirmed that underground nuclear tests contributed to accumulated radiation doses thanks to the leaking of radioactive gases into the atmosphere.

The scientists noted that at some points during the years of nuclear tests, people in the Semipalatinsk region died in greater numbers from cancers than anywhere else in the Soviet Union, with stomach cancers being most common. Pathologies present in almost 70 percent of women in Semipalatinsk and rural settlements near the Polygon complicated their pregnancies, leading to miscarriages and abnormal fetus development. In rural areas, where people spent more time outside, such skin diseases as pigmentation, keloid scars, and precancerous illnesses were common. High child mortality, childhood diseases, genetic abnormalities from chromosomal changes—these were among the somber facts that the commission recorded. Suicide rates were 1.5 to 2 times higher than those in the rest of the Soviet Union. More than 40 percent of locals suffered from neurosis.[36]

The conference was just the beginning of a painful and difficult search for truth that continues to this day. The conference ran over several days and local newspapers reported in detail on heated discussions. Most speakers, including from the Soviet civilian health institutions, presented evidence that nuclear tests harmed local people. For example, the head of the cytogenetics lab at the Soviet Academy of Medical Sciences, Alexander Sevan'kayev, shared that samples from dozens of people revealed the following trends: in Semipalatinsk, the level of spontaneous chromosomal aberrations in blood lymphocytes was 1.5–2.5 times higher than average, and in rural areas up to 2.5 to 4.5 times higher. His colleague from the academy, Professor Matvienko, described the growing rates of endocrine diseases. In the village of Dolon, for example, a staggering 75 percent of residents suffered from endocrine disorders.[37] Doctors from Kazakhstan provided damning statistics showing that mortality and cancer rates near the Polygon were far higher than the average across the republic. Yet some visiting speakers resisted the notion that the Polygon represented any radiation hazard. The head of a scientific lab in Obninsk, for example, said that the radioisotope levels in more than a hundred samples of soil and water collected near the Polygon did not exceed maximum allowed levels.[38]

Some conference participants from Kazakhstan thought that the commission's findings were muted and did not reflect the true scale of the tragedy. A few months after the conference, Professor Tsyb authored an article entitled "Semipalatinsk Polygon: Legends, Lies, Truth" in *Pravda*, the largest Soviet newspaper, that toned down some of the commission's data. In response, Professor Atchabarov, who in the late 1950s had led the medical expedition to examine the health of locals in the Polygon's vicinity, responded to Professor Tsyb in *Izbiratel'* ("voter" in Russian), a newspaper published by the Nevada-Semipalatinsk movement. Professor Atchabarov protested the attempt to downplay the negative impact of radiation on people in the Semipalatinsk region.[39] In articles marked by polemic, the Kazakh press picked up the controversy surrounding the article and the findings of the Tsyb commission.

But the fact that the Tsyb commission's official report acknowledged the harmful effect of nuclear tests, however reluctantly, was a sign of the times. Social tensions had reached a boiling point. Any further attempts to deny the deteriorating health of Kazakhs exposed to nuclear testing were simply not sustainable. The conference had opened the eyes of the population to the price they had paid and continued to pay for the nuclear tests.

Soon after the conference, on the August 6 anniversary of the US bombing of Hiroshima, the Nevada-Semipalatinsk movement organized a rally attended by thousands. The gathering took place near a mountain range about two and a half miles away from Karaul.[40] As noted earlier, in the early days of testing, Karaul had been the site of a cruel experiment in which the military forced a small group of locals to stay behind during a thermonuclear test. Now those present joined in ceremonies infused with Kazakh symbolism. They walked between two fires, signifying the act of cleansing or catharsis.[41] They hurled rocks into a large pile to create a burial site for the evil nuclear threat. They tied pieces of white cloth to a tree, hoping their wishes would be granted.[42]

Instead, their hopes were crushed. The tests continued.

But during this summer of 1989, popular unrest spread across Kazakhstan. Miners there and elsewhere in the Soviet Union protested poor working conditions and meager salaries, and sought greater economic autonomy from the central government. Kazakh miners made an additional demand: More than 130,000 of them from Karaganda, one of the world's largest coal-producing regions in the center of Kazakhstan, threatened to strike should nuclear tests continue at Semipalatinsk. Workers from Semipalatinsk, Pavlodar, Ust-Kamenogorsk, and Dzhezkazgan supported them.[43]

On September 1, 1989, Nevada-Semipalatinsk activists organized a series of peace lessons in schools across Kazakhstan on the first day of the new term. Midway through the lesson in Kainar village, a military helicopter appeared above to announce an upcoming test.

> The children knew that a helicopter was a sign of an impending test, and seeing
> that the helicopter [was] preparing to land, they left their desks and ran outside,
> screaming. The children ran to where helicopters usually landed. There they
> threw stones into the sky, screaming, the younger ones crying. Those children
> wanted to prevent another test. They did not allow the helicopter to land.[44]

Though the peace lesson made students act, and they had successfully disrupted the landing, the next day, an underground test thundered across the steppe. Nevada-Semipalatinsk representatives sarcastically called the test "a gift" to the schoolchildren. Keshrim Boztaev, the head of the Semipalatinsk region, again wrote to Gorbachev. Boztaev lamented the illnesses, stress, and

damaged infrastructure caused by the tests: "The region received no compensation, and not a single facility was built to help the people." He described the
thousands of letters he had received from locals. In response, Gorbachev requested that the Soviet officials in charge of the military-industrial complex
"return to the problem again."[45]

The Soviet Council of Ministers did authorize economic and social assistance for the Semipalatinsk region, but on October 4 the military conducted
yet another nuclear test, this time at Degelen Mountain.[46] At a protest rally
outside of the Soviet Defense Ministry in Moscow, Olzhas Suleimenov appealed to Gorbachev and Bush to announce a moratorium on nuclear tests.
Suleimenov and Andrei Sakharov, who by then had become one of the most
important antinuclear voices in the Soviet Union, established an independent parliamentarian group, "For a Nuclear-Free World," at the USSR Supreme Soviet.

Simultaneously, the Soviet Health Ministry issued an order to examine residents in the areas close to the Polygon and to fund the improvement of health
facilities in the region. Two weeks later, on October 19, another test rumbled
from the Balapan mountains.[47] After that test, Kazakh shepherds threatened
a strike if the military carried out any more tests; they would lock all sheep
in paddocks and refuse to herd them,[48] disrupting the local wool and meat
economy. Protest rallies erupted across Kazakhstan.

The Kazakh government, facing continued stonewalling from the central
government, replaced its timid proposals to reduce the yield and frequency of
tests with outright demands to stop all tests immediately. The Council of Ministers, in coordination with the Central Committee of Kazakhstan's Communist Party, submitted a proposal to the Soviet Council of Ministers to cease all
nuclear tests at Semipalatinsk. Weeks later, in November, the Supreme Soviet of
Kazakhstan appealed to the Soviet government and the USSR Supreme Soviet
to immediately cease all nuclear tests.[49]

That same month, a delegation led by Igor Beloussov, the person in charge
of the Soviet Military-Industrial Commission, visited Semipalatinsk, the town
of Kurchatov, and several other settlements near the Polygon. In Znamenka, at
Boztaev's insistence, all the local mentally disabled children were brought to a
local hospital for Beloussov and his people "to see with their own eyes." Boztaev
recalled "a terrible scene: twenty-nine mothers with their disabled children."[50]

"Do you love your child?" Boztaev said, addressing one of the mothers,
though he was conscious of the insensitivity of the question.

PHOTO 10   Antinuclear rally organized by the Nevada-Semipalatinsk movement at a
rural area near the Semipalatinsk Polygon, 1989. Photograph by Yuri Kuidin.

"When a long-awaited child is born with defects, his mother feels special
love toward him because it wasn't his fault that he was born this way. . . . It's we
who are to blame," she replied.

"It'd be better if they drank less," remarked one of the visitors flippantly.
Taken aback, Boztaev asked: "Did you come here to say things like that?" The
visitor did not respond.[51]

Despite the growing social unrest, the most that the Soviet Council of Ministers offered, in a decree in late November, was to stop nuclear tests by January 1, 1993, and to cap nuclear tests at nine per year until then. But as the military and the military-industrial complex pressured the Kremlin to continue the tests, Kazakhstan intensified its call on the Kremlin to halt them.

In December 1989, the heart of Andrei Sakharov, the creator of the Soviet thermonuclear weapon who turned into one of the harshest critics of the nuclear race, stopped beating. As fate would have it, his last interview, recorded just three hours before his death, was devoted to the Semipalatinsk Polygon. Sakharov gave the interview to a film crew from Kazakhstan in the Moscow hotel room of Olzhas Suleimenov.[52] The next day, Sakharov and Suleimenov, both deputies of the USSR Supreme Soviet, were scheduled to vote on the fate of the Soviet Communist Party—on whether it would remain the guiding force in Soviet politics.[53]

Into 1990, the Soviet government continued its tactic of appearing responsive to Kazakhstan's demands while not taking meaningful action. In February 1990, the Soviet Council of Ministers issued a resolution that proposed to *consider* the cessation of nuclear tests at Semipalatinsk and reiterated plans to help with economic recovery. The Soviet Health Ministry ordered an examination of all areas at both the Semipalatinsk and Novaya Zemlya sites.

But by April, with the Soviet system shaken by reforms that allowed more freedom for the republics, the conversation between Alma-Ata and Moscow had shifted to not *if* but *when* nuclear tests should stop. Several officials from Kazakhstan, including Assanbaev, Boztaev, and others, traveled to Moscow to discuss the timing of the cessation with Beloussov. Three days later, Beloussov sent a letter to Nazarbayev seeking his support for a decree allowing the tests to continue until 1993. The Soviet leadership understood that tests would have to end at some point, but they pushed to squeeze a few more tests out of the Semipalatinsk Polygon.

Kazakhstan, however, stood firm. Boztaev wrote to Nazarbayev, "Our noble fight against nuclear tests at the Semipalatinsk Polygon is coming to the final stretch. I am convinced we will reach our goal with some effort." Boztaev also conveyed his mistrust of Beloussov: "Beloussov-led intrigues and speculative maneuvers around the Polygon are not calming down.[54] . . . I learned recently that Beloussov's commission is trying to secure the continuation of tests with a decree of the Soviet President."[55]

All of Kazakh officialdom rallied to prevent any new nuclear tests in Kazakhstan. Preempting the Soviet decree to continue tests until 1993, the

PHOTO 11   Protest rally near Karaul. Photograph by Yuri Kuidin.

Supreme Soviet of Kazakhstan, under the leadership of its chair Erik Assanbaev, issued a decree of its own in May, demanding from the Soviet government "an immediate and full cessation of nuclear testing at Semipalatinsk" and
compensation for the incurred damage as well as additional benefits for the region's population, which had suffered from so many decades of nuclear tests.[56]

Moscow then sent the Minister of Atomic Energy and Industry, Vitalii Ko-
novalov, to meet with Nazarbayev to discuss two compromises. The first proposed three smaller explosions with yields of up to 20 kilotons in 1991. The
second promised the cessation of testing starting on January 1, 1992—a year
earlier than the previous deadline set by Moscow—in exchange for the ability
to carry out explosions with yields of up to 0.5 kilotons indefinitely. These com-
promise proposals failed to gain traction. At its 27th Congress in June 1990,
Kazakhstan's Communist Party voted to support the republic's Supreme Soviet
decree and submitted a proposal to the USSR Supreme Soviet for the full cessation of nuclear testing in Kazakhstan.[57]

SEMIPALATINSK: BATTLEGROUND OF
THE INTERNATIONAL FIGHT

While Kazakhstan's officials negotiated with Moscow, the Nevada-
Semipalatinsk movement pressed its campaign, holding rallies across Kazakhstan and engaging both domestic and foreign groups.

Kazakhstan's antinuclear activists longed to be heard and supported by the Americans who were waging a similar campaign in their own country. Prominent members of the movement, including its charismatic leader Ol- zhas Suleimenov, traveled to the United States to tell the Americans about their struggles. In 1990, Murat Auezov, the Nevada-Semipalatinsk activist and son of the writer Mukhtar Auezov, visited several American states and cities. His fondest memory is of a night in San Francisco when he met some US activists who were eager to meet him. "What wonderful people those were!" Auezov reminisced. "They were the ones who blocked roads, got arrested. . . . They shared their experience, and brought lots of valuable literature with them."[58]

Back in Alma-Ata, movement leaders arranged for a live televised conver- sation with victims of the nuclear bombings in Japan. They also published ap- peals to the Soviet government in the press and organized rallies across the country.[59] The largest event was the International Congress of International Voters for the Prevention of Nuclear War, held in Alma-Ata in May 1990 in cooperation with International Physicians for the Prevention of Nuclear War (IPPNW). The American and Soviet leaders of IPPNW, two cardiologists—Dr. Bernard Lown from Harvard's Institute of Public Health and Dr. Evgenii Chazov from the Soviet Institute of Cardiology—were among the first to sup- port the idea of hosting the congress in Alma-Ata. The friendship and collegial- ity of Lown and Chazov symbolized the fight of Soviet-American civil society against nuclear war. The congress brought together four hundred participants from twenty countries—teachers, lawyers, environmentalists, physicians, nu- clear physicists, students, survivors of the Hiroshima and Nagasaki bombings (Hibakusha), and "downwinders"—people who lived downwind from nuclear test sites in the United States.[60] Twenty thousand Kazakhs gathered to greet the foreign guests.[61]

Jacqueline Cabasso, an American activist who had participated in antinu- clear protests in Nevada, described the scene at the congress:

> When our plane landed . . . , the airfield was filled with hundreds of welcoming Kazakhs in traditional clothing, carrying trays of bread and holding signs that read: "Let the Generals Build Their Summer Homes at the Nuclear Test Sites." A huge billboard was mounted on the wall of the airport with the logo of the Nevada-Semipalatinsk movement, a Western Shoshone elder passing a peace pipe to a Kazakh elder. At that moment, I realized that I was part of the global majority—and not a marginalized minority.[62]

The participants in the congress traveled to Semipalatinsk and Karaul, and their visits left a lasting impression. Dan Young, the president of the American group Physicians for Social Responsibility, recounted his experience:

> In Karaul, two or three thousand [people] met us and mingled with us in a large field, as dozens of their fellow villagers told the sad stories of Soviet downwinders. American downwinders and *Hibakusha* from Japan told their stories as well. While the stories were tragic, the atmosphere was that of a great celebration. Kazakh musicians and dancers entertained us; our hosts in Karaul gave us a glorious feast in yurt[s], some forty of which had been erected for the occasion. The children—who had never seen foreigners before—circulated everywhere asking us to sign their papers.[63]

A medical doctor from Canada representing International Physicians for the Prevention of Nuclear War, Mary-Wynne Ashford, described how after a full day of events on the hillside in Karaul, at almost 11 p.m., the rally participants celebrated with feasts held in Kazakh yurts:

> Dinner was in traditional Mongolian tents called yurts, with 20 people in each. Inside, the vertical walls were covered with thick, bright rugs. A circle of low tables separated guests from the host who sat in the centre. A feast of vegetables and nuts, dried fruits and conserves, steaming dishes of spicy lamb in sauce, pungent horsemeat and chicken were piled overlapping in a kaleidoscope of colour. Horse milk and fragrant tea were passed along with vodka and cognac.[64]

Ashford described the beautiful dark sky and bright stars that night as the antinuclear activists from around the world celebrated their coming together in the middle of the steppe. After the dinner, a Kazakh elder suggested that everyone sing a song, and the group broke out into "We Shall Overcome." "It was so moving," Ashford remembers, "I cried."[65]

American peace activists drew inspiration from the Kazakh movement, which in turn had been inspired by the Nevada antinuclear protests. For Cabasso, the 1990 Congress laid the groundwork for global antinuclear movements.[66] Young described his emotions after a trip to Kazakhstan:

> We found ourselves inspired—maybe a little proud to have stood by the side of these extraordinary people. But we were also a little ashamed as we saw how much they are risking to awaken their government, while we sacrifice so little and seem to achieve so little.[67]

The Soviet government continued its promises to improve medical services in Semipalatinsk and to construct clinics and hospitals throughout the region, including a specialized Institute of Radiation Medicine and Ecology in Alma-Ata that would have a satellite facility in Semipalatinsk. A Soviet decree in July 1990 mandated a survey of the population's health and also contained a timid admission that the tests could have been detrimental to locals' health: "In case it is revealed that some diseases are the result of nuclear testing . . . [relevant agencies] are to make suggestions on [providing] benefits to those affected."[68]

But the decree was met with criticism. The chairman of the Council of Ministers of Kazakhstan, Uzakbai Karamanov, condemned it for failing to mention a date for the cessation of nuclear tests. The decree also said nothing about compensation to victims, about the declassification of documents that would shed light on the radiological impact of the tests, or about financial assistance for medical equipment and medication, hospital and clinic construction, or food products.[69]

On the ground in the Semipalatinsk region, tensions rose between antinuclear groups and the military supporters of the nuclear program. Heated polemic spilled onto newspaper pages and often turned personal. Major Nikolai Petrushenko, for example, was vilified in the region for his support of continued testing and his dismissive attitude toward Kazakhs. The Soviet army had sent Petrushenko, born in Belarus, to Kazakhstan to serve as a political commissar. He had successfully run in an election to become a Soviet Congress of People's deputy (a new supreme legislative body established by Gorbachev in 1989). A true believer in the Soviet military and its programs, Petrushenko argued adamantly that nuclear tests were harmless. To prove his point, he even swam in the Atomic Lake, just as Efim Slavskii, the man in charge of the Soviet nuclear industry, had done before him. Not only did Petrushenko swim himself, but he made his teenage son swim with him.

At the height of tensions, Petrushenko brought more than a hundred Soviet Congress of People's deputies to Semipalatinsk to seek to quell negative perceptions of the Polygon. But Petrushenko and his colleagues were not interested in meeting local people and were dismissive of local authorities, which further inflamed hostilities. They went straight to the military town of Kurchatov and met behind closed doors with the Polygon's chief, General Il'yenko. Boztaev complained to Moscow about the circumstances surrounding the visit,[70] and almost nine hundred medical professionals bemoaned its secrecy in a letter to Nazarbayev and Gorbachev.[71] The people wanted to be heard.

According to one witness privy to the meeting:

> Petrushenko arranged for a visit to the Polygon, but all meetings promoted the idea that testing was harmless. . . . Petrushenko talks about the rural doctors and their methods of treatment in an insulting manner, without providing any facts. . . . [He] calls witnesses of tests—alcoholics and criminals.[72]

Petrushenko allegedly accused Semipalatinsk doctors of advising locals to "breed lice because they suck radioactive blood, and to give vodka to their kids for disease prevention." In a statement published in a local newspaper, the antinuclear activists wrote: "This is an insult . . . to the people in Semipalatinsk region."[73]

National and local newspapers published both letters of support for the tests and statements in protest, often in the same issue. In a letter to *Rudnyi Altai*, a daily newspaper, testing-program personnel countered complaints that the nuclear tests disrupted economic activity and rejected reports about the deteriorating health of locals as baseless. Another letter, signed by more than three hundred residents of the military town of Kurchatov, further attacked the testing program's critics:

> An absolute majority of these claims are incompetent and often absurd, which end up with requests for aid with a supply of food and staples. . . . Local and national officials use the Polygon as a convenient object to channel energy of social dissatisfaction. Some beginner politicians use it to build their political capital. [. . .] We are especially disturbed by the leaders of Nevada-Semipalatinsk who use the parliament, rallies, and miners' protest movement to manipulate awakening public conscience, monopolize glasnost, and drive a wedge between the army and the people.[74]

The signatories, most of whom were not from Kazakhstan but rather temporary workers in Kurchatov, concluded: "We support banning nuclear tests but [other countries] continue testing. It is necessary to think about the entire Soviet nation, not just the region."[75]

On the anniversary of the Hiroshima nuclear attack, August 6, the Nevada-Semipalatinsk protesters again held a memorial rally. At the event, a Kazakh veteran of World War II wondered:

> Will our descendants curse us? It is a tragedy that women give birth to deformed children. We are so passive; we have stopped thinking about our children. . . .

Because of the Polygon, there are cracks in the earth that stretch for thousands and thousands of kilometers.[76]

At the end of the rally, children and adults placed paper boats with lit candles onto the waters of the Irtysh River as a reminder of the victims of Hiroshima, Nagasaki, and Semipalatinsk.

The next month eighty Americans (including members of the Shoshone tribe in Nevada and downwinders from Utah), several Japanese, and a few Russians who lived near the nuclear testing sites joined the people of Kazakhstan for an International Peace March to protest nuclear tests.[77] Almost two hundred participants gathered at a stadium in Alma-Ata and from there, by plane, bus, and on foot, they traveled across Kazakhstan, stopping in small cities and small villages. Their final destination was the town of Kurchatov.

PHOTO 12   Antinuclear International Peace March, Kazakhstan, 1990. Photograph by Yuri Kuidin.

"We marched for the entire month," recalls Mariiash Makisheva, who helped the Nevada-Semipalatinsk movement as a translator. Her memories of the Peace March are vivid: "They were participants of all different ages—from a five-year old girl, Melissa, to a seventy-five-year-old man."[78]

In keeping with traditional Kazakh hospitality, in every village, town, and city that the marchers visited, local authorities did their best to welcome them. Long tables with delicious national food—dishes with lamb and baursaks (small pieces of freshly fried round bread)—awaited them. In places where there were not enough buildings to house everyone, the international crowd put up tents or slept under the open sky. Makisheva remembers with a smile: "Americans had those wonderful colorful heated tents. We were given the military green ones."[79] One tent brought to the Peace March had itself become an attraction. Its owner, an American veteran in his seventies, lived in it for four years near the Nevada nuclear testing site. He planned to keep his tent up until the Nevada tests ended.[80]

The joy of camaraderie in the pursuit of a noble goal was tempered by the trauma of witnessing conditions in the Polygon's vicinity. Makisheva recounted that "we saw with our own eyes how local people struggled while military in the town of Kurchatov enjoyed a good life." One of her haunting memories was "a man who looked like a mallet—no arms, no legs, an eye in the middle of his face."[81]

One Kazakh participant in the Peace March, twenty-two-year-old Karipbek Kuyukov, was born without arms. Friends that he met through Nevada-Semipalatinsk gave Kuyukov new meaning in his life.[82] Later, he learned to paint by holding a brush in his mouth and became an artist; his art would reflect the pain inflicted by nuclear tests. Kuyukov would also become an internationally known antinuclear activist.

The antinuclear movement prompted the Kazakh government to keep pushing for the cessation of testing. On October 25, 1990, Kazakhstan's Supreme Soviet adopted a Declaration of State Sovereignty, a precursor to declaring independence. A month later, it passed a resolution prohibiting nuclear testing at the Semipalatinsk site. Despite overwhelming opposition within Kazakhstan, however, Moscow stood firm. The Soviet mass media reported that tests would continue until January 1993. Nineteen more tests were still planned.[83]

MOSCOW OFFERS A DEAL

In March 1991, Nazarbayev again wrote to Gorbachev. The letter reflected the continuing frustration of Kazakhstan's leadership with Moscow, and its tone

PHOTO 13   Karipbek Kuyukov, artist, victim of Soviet nuclear tests at the memorial rally, 1996. Photograph by V. Pavlunin.
SOURCE: Central State Archive of Film and Photo Documents and Sound Recordings, Kazakhstan. Image #2–104136.

showed increasing assertiveness in establishing the republic's sovereignty: "Kazakhstan fulfilled its patriotic obligation to the country—the Soviet Union achieved nuclear parity with the United States." However, he stated, that act of patriotism had come at a severe cost to the health of Kazakhstan's people and environment. Nazarbayev lamented the lack of "a single program for the medical and biological protection of the population." Neither numerous requests for help and compensation or appeals to declassify written materials about radioactivity had produced any tangible results. The Kazakh leader warned Gorbachev that if the tests were resumed in spite of the Kazakh Supreme Soviet's ban on them, "unpredictable consequences, clashes between the population and the Polygon staff," would ensue. Nazarbayev no longer minced his words: "In this situation, the pressure from the military-industrial complex on you to continue testing until January 1, 1993, is an attempt to undermine the trust of Kazakhstan's people in the USSR's president."[84]

Moscow continued to push tests while offering small concessions. In July 1991, the Soviet Council of Ministers issued a new resolution, "On the Cessation of Nuclear Weapon Tests at the Semipalatinsk Test Site," calling for two final nuclear tests in 1991 with yields under 20 kilotons. It also proclaimed that all nuclear tests at the site would cease on January 1, 1992.

The local authorities in Semipalatinsk were ready to accept Moscow's deal. At the Polygon, one nuclear device had even already been placed underground —there was no way to extract it safely. Semipalatinsk authorities worried that some within the military-industrial complex would renege on promises of compensation and measures to improve the well-being of local people if the two tests did not take place.[85] Boztaev explained:

> There are moments in life when one needs to retreat to achieve a greater victory. In this case, we deeply believed that [by] agreeing to two more tests of limited yield we would show a degree of flexibility, prioritizing people's social well-being above politics. We knew we would encounter great difficulties—first and foremost from the public.[86]

Boztaev was correct in his prediction of public objection to the two tests. The Nevada-Semipalatinsk movement, for one, disagreed with the Semipalatinsk local government. Along with public organizations across Kazakhstan, the movement sought popular support to resist the resumption of nuclear tests and prepared for massive protests on August 29, 1991—the forty-second anniversary of the first Soviet nuclear test at Semipalatinsk.

But, meanwhile, hard-liners in Moscow attempted to overthrow Gorbachev between August 19 and 21. Confusion in Moscow created an opportunity for the Kazakhs to act.

CHAPTER 5

THE SWAN SONG OF THE SOVIET UNION

ON AUGUST 19, 1991, in the midst of summer vacations and a slowed political life, Soviet citizens woke up to the score of *Swan Lake* airing nonstop on all state-controlled radio and television channels.[1] Families in Kazakhstan and elsewhere in the Soviet Union felt uneasy. Had Mikhail Gorbachev died?

The broadcast of Tchaikovsky's ballet had long been an ominous sign of political upheaval. During the 1980s, repeated programming of the work had accompanied a quick succession of deaths of frail and aging Soviet leaders. Leonid Brezhnev died in late 1982, and his successor, Yuri Andropov, succumbed in 1984 after a mere fifteen months at the helm. Then Konstantin Chernenko died in 1985 just thirteen months after taking the highest office.

In fact, Gorbachev *was* alive, despite the Tchaikovsky. He was trapped in his summerhouse in Crimea, *Zarya*, cut off from his government and the world by a group of military and KGB leaders who had staged a coup against him. All telephones to Gorbachev, including secure government lines, had gone silent. Gorbachev described the moment he knew he was sealed off from the outside world:

> Since the whole communication system was with me—the government line, the normal line, the strategic and the satellite communications—I picked up a receiver of one of the telephones—it was dead. I picked up a second receiver, then a third, a fourth and a fifth—they were all dead. Then I picked up the internal telephone—it had been cut off.[2]

Not only was Gorbachev held incommunicado but, more critically, he had lost control over the entire Soviet nuclear arsenal. His "nuclear suitcase," the system that allowed him to control the launch of Soviet nuclear weapons, was in someone else's hands.[3] The coup potentially threatened the security of nuclear weapons in Russia, Ukraine, Kazakhstan, and Belarus. In Kazakhstan alone, there were forty heavy bombers capable of reaching America and more than a thousand nuclear warheads that could be deployed on giant SS-18 intercontinental ballistic missiles. Who was in charge of the nuclear codes? What were the risks?

That fateful August set off a countdown to the final days of the Soviet Union. Although the coup itself failed, it exposed the illegitimacy and fragility of the Soviet system. Within months, the Soviet Union would dissolve, bestowing on Kazakhstan a nuclear inheritance that it did not seek, enough to make it the fourth largest nuclear power in the world.

THE RUN-UP TO THE COUP—THE NEW UNION TREATY

In the mid-1980s, economic and political inefficiencies were coming to a head in the Soviet Union. When Gorbachev assumed power in 1985, he introduced a more open, albeit far from completely free, political environment. However, this greater freedom of speech allowed expressions of dissent and disillusionment, and tension became more public. The planned economy was deteriorating, and the fifteen Soviet republics were becoming increasingly disenchanted with rule from Moscow. Some dissenters took to the streets, and in 1989 the Soviet army forcefully suppressed a peaceful protest in Georgia. But that crackdown only made Georgia more determined to seek its independence.

By early 1991, the Soviet economy was collapsing. Store shelves were bare, and people could not buy even basic foodstuffs such as meat, flour, eggs, or milk.

In January, Gorbachev signed a decree for what would become the last Soviet monetary reform. It was nicknamed the "Pavlov Reform" for the Soviet Minister of Finance, Valentin Pavlov, who had hatched the idea. Under this decree, the Soviet government announced the withdrawal from circulation of fifty- and hundred-ruble banknotes that had been printed in 1961. The official reason for the move was to counter the smuggling of counterfeit rubles into the Soviet Union from abroad.[4] But the real purpose was to remove a substantial amount of paper cash from circulation. The Soviet government printed bills in large quantities in the 1980s. There was money but nothing to buy. By removing some bills from circulation, the government hoped to ease the consumer goods shortage.

The decree came out of the blue. The government unveiled its plan on television at 9 p.m. in Moscow (midnight in Kazakhstan). Stores had already closed for the day, but people immediately rushed to exchange their soon-to-be useless banknotes anywhere they could. They bought air and rail tickets for future trips because those offices were still open, and they traded their bills with taxi drivers who hadn't heard the news yet. Citizens in all Soviet republics were given three days to exchange a mandated maximum number of old banknotes for new ones. Further, there were limits on the amount of cash that could be withdrawn from bank accounts. This and subsequent hyperinflation resulted in many people losing their life savings. Across the Soviet Union, people were angry and disillusioned with the central government.[5]

The economic crisis went hand-in-hand with the turbulent politics of Gorbachev's era. The Kremlin was losing its grip on Soviet territory. In January 1991, in an echo of its crackdown in Georgia two years earlier, the Soviet army took over several government buildings in Lithuania—one of the three Baltic republics—to prevent its impending separation from the Soviet Union. Fifteen people died in the clash. The Soviet military killed thirteen civilians, another suffered a fatal heart attack, and one Soviet soldier was killed by friendly fire.

Meanwhile, the Soviet establishment was a battleground of different factions. Gorbachev recognized that the republics needed greater autonomy from Moscow to keep them in the union and, in that way, guarantee its survival. But Soviet hard-liners, fearful that Gorbachev would dismantle the old system and lose control over the republics, were determined to prevent any changes.

In these conditions, Gorbachev, along with Boris Yeltsin, the leader of the Russian Federation, and Nursultan Nazarbayev of Kazakhstan, spearheaded development of a New Union Treaty, which would grant more autonomy to the republics. The treaty would create the Union of Soviet Sovereign Republics. The republics would own land, mineral resources, water, other natural resources, the plant and animal world. They would be allowed to establish diplomatic relationships with other countries. At the same time, there would be single currency and one army under the union structure, and the union would act as a successor to the Soviet Union and conduct foreign policy on behalf of the whole. The New Union Treaty promoted "free choice of ownership and methods of economic management," which was a big step toward modernization of the Soviet economy based on state ownership.[6]

Yeltsin favored the treaty because he sought greater autonomy from the Soviet government and wanted to disassociate Russia from the crumbling Soviet empire. Nazarbayev signed on because he wanted more economic independence for his republic, but he also feared it might not survive completely on its own since its economy depended entirely on ties with the other Soviet republics. And Gorbachev planned to appoint Nazarbayev as the prime minister of the new union.

As Gorbachev rushed to secure the New Union Treaty,[7] he also chipped away at the Communist Party's predominant role in Soviet political life. This was a major source of irritation to the Soviet establishment.

The battles for the future of the Soviet Union played out both openly in the halls of Communist Party congresses and behind the scenes. Vladimir Kryuchkov—the head of the KGB as well as one of the coup's masterminds—placed Gorbachev under surveillance. The KGB bugged the government compound at Novo-Ogarevo in the Moscow region, where Gorbachev, Yeltsin, and Nazarbayev worked on the draft treaty. Unaware of the surveillance, the three men discussed two sensitive plans—to sign the New Union Treaty on August 20, and to remove from government any hard-liners who opposed it.[8] Six republics, including Kazakhstan, were to sign it without delay, on August 20, in St. George's Hall in the Kremlin.[9] These plans prompted the hard-liners to act.

Rumors about a potential coup against Gorbachev had been circulating in Moscow. As early as December 1990 Gorbachev ally and Soviet Foreign Minister Eduard Shevardnadze had resigned, warning, "dictatorship is coming." In June 1991, Moscow's mayor Gavriil Popov had warned US Ambassador Jack Matlock about the risk of a coup, and Matlock had relayed the message to Gorbachev. US President George H. W. Bush also warned both Yeltsin and Gorbachev. Although Gorbachev agreed the situation was volatile, he brushed aside Bush's warning of a coup as "1,000 percent impossible."[10]

On August 4, Gorbachev left for vacation a few kilometers from the Crimean beach town of Foros. With him were his wife Raisa, daughter Irina, son-in-law Anatolii, and a small granddaughter. The next day, several KGB and military leaders joined high-level Soviet officials from the anti-Gorbachev camp to gather at a secret KGB house outside Moscow and plan the coup.

Meanwhile, Yeltsin was spending a weekend in Kazakhstan visiting Nazarbayev. On Friday, August 16, Yeltsin and Nazarbayev signed a treaty of bilateral friendship between Kazakhstan and Russia that included agreements on economic cooperation under the anticipated New Union Treaty.

Yeltsin and Nazarbayev were in good spirits and enjoyed the many pleasant things that Alma-Ata and its surroundings had to offer. They even visited a horse-breeding farm where Nazarbayev gave a black stallion to Yeltsin. The Russian president, uninhibited due to generous alcohol consumption, immediately decided to ride it, to the great anxiety of his bodyguards and Nazarbayev. The two presidents also went to the nearby mountains, where Yeltsin insisted on swimming in an ice-cold mountain river.[11]

Yeltsin left Alma-Ata in the evening on August 18, a few hours later than initially scheduled. He blamed the tardy departure on Kazakh hospitality:

> Nazarbayev wouldn't let us go, and persuaded us to stay another hour. After a large ceremonial dinner, there was a concert of Kazakh folk music, then another performance, and another . . . Choirs, dance collectives, the clanging of national instruments, colorfully dressed girls whirling around. Frankly, my eyes were already starting to glaze over from it all. Our flight was postponed for an hour. Then another hour. Nazarbayev was playing the Oriental host—not imposingly, but gently, delicately. Still the grip was just as strong.[12]

But Kazakh eyewitnesses pointed to Yeltsin's alcohol intake as the culprit behind his late departure. "He couldn't walk," one of them said.

Yeltsin would later speculate that the delay saved his life. According to his questionable account, the coup plotters had ordered the Soviet Air Defense Force stationed in Kazakhstan to shoot down a plane that would take off from Alma-Ata for Moscow at 4 p.m. on August 18.[13] Departing four hours later, Yeltsin's flight encountered no resistance. (Yeltsin's theory is somewhat dubious: if coup organizers had planned and had the ability to shoot down the plane, a few hours' delay would have been unlikely to change their plans.) What was indisputable was that while Yeltsin was *en route* to Moscow and Nazarbayev sound asleep in Alma-Ata, several individuals appeared unannounced at *Zarya* and put Gorbachev under house arrest. Military, border patrol, and intelligence forces blocked the roads and shut down the local airstrip. Armed men guarded the garage that held Gorbachev's cars, which were equipped with radiotelephones.[14]

Gorbachev found himself a prisoner in his summerhouse. The unexpected guests represented the self-proclaimed "State Committee on the State of Emergency." Later nicknamed the "Gang of Eight," the committee included Gennadii Yanayev, the Soviet vice president; Valentin Pavlov, the Soviet prime minister; and Vladimir Kryuchkov, the head of the KGB.

The State Committee gave Gorbachev an ultimatum: transfer his powers to Soviet Vice President Yanayev and agree to a state of emergency or renounce the presidency altogether. Gorbachev lashed out at them, calling them "scumbags," and refused to accede to their demands. He also warned that declaring a state of emergency would lead to civil war since people would never want to return to the old dictatorial ways of governance.[15]

Yeltsin and Nazarbayev, as well as everyone else in the Soviet Union, would wake up the next morning to *Swan Lake* playing continuously on television and radio. Every thirty minutes a news announcement about the state of emergency punctuated the ballet.

THREE DAYS OF THE ATTEMPTED COUP

On the first day of the coup, the plotters seized control of all Soviet state communications and shuttered independent media outlets. Soviet state radio announced that Gorbachev was sick and had stepped down and that power had been transferred to Yanayev. The coup organizers' public declaration that Gorbachev was gravely ill prompted fears back at *Zarya*.[16] Unsure whether he would make it out alive after hearing this announcement, Gorbachev wrote a statement to the people of the Soviet Union and recorded a video of himself reading it.

More than five hundred tanks rolled into Moscow, and armored vehicles and military units controlled by the coup leaders surrounded the Russian parliament building (dubbed the White House) and awaited orders to capture it. Over the next three days, the battle for power played out there. Thousands of Muscovites poured into the streets, constructed barricades, and formed human chains to protect the parliament from the coup's military forces.

Yeltsin woke up at his *dacha* after just a few hours of sleep. He had returned to Russia from Kazakhstan at daybreak, but his daughter had soon awakened, screaming: "Papa, get up! There's a coup!" Yeltsin described his initial reaction: "Still half asleep, the first thing I said was, 'That's illegal!' . . . It was so stupid. I said to [her], 'Are you kidding me?'"[17]

Yeltsin donned a bulletproof vest under a brown business suit and headed to the Russian parliament in the city to meet the other leaders of the Russian (not the Soviet) government. In those early hours of the attempted coup, Yeltsin showed tremendous courage. Despite the personal danger, he felt the urge to address the crowd gathering outside. He waded into the center of the turmoil, climbed onto a tank and addressed the people. He dismissed all the actions of the coup leaders as illegal.

For Yeltsin, that moment on the tank was a turning point:

> I had a sense of utter clarity, complete unity with the people standing around me. The crowd was large and some people were whistling and shouting. Reporters, television crews, and photographers were everywhere. I took out the piece of paper with the text of my appeal and held it in my hands. The shouts died down and I read the text loudly, my voice almost breaking. Next I greeted the commander of the tank upon which I was standing and talked with the soldiers. From their faces, from the expression in their eyes, I could see they would not shoot us.[18]

As a result, Yeltsin emerged as the symbol of the new Russia fighting against the Soviet edifice. By the end of the day, the crowd in front of the Russian parliament had swelled to 70,000 people.[19]

In Alma-Ata, Nazarbayev feared the worst. His direct phone line to the Kremlin was not operating. His official car did not arrive at his residence to take him to work. Nazarbayev would later claim he expected the KGB to arrest him. His car did turn up. According to one version of events, the delay was caused by a technical malfunction. Another version offers a more plausible explanation—his driver had parked the car out of sight in the shade of some trees to avoid the August sunshine.[20]

After rushing to his office, Nazarbayev received a phone call from Yeltsin. The Russian leader did not have much information, only that a coup was underway, and tanks now occupied Moscow's main streets. "Anything could happen," Yeltsin told Nazarbayev. Minutes later, Yanayev, a member of the Gang of Eight, called Nazarbayev to inform him that Gorbachev was too sick to govern the Soviet Union. KGB head Kryuchkov and Soviet Prime Minister Pavlov also telephoned Nazarbayev that day seeking his support.[21]

Nazarbayev did not know whether the coup organizers would declare a state of emergency in Kazakhstan and seize control. He worried that the so-called State Committee on the State of Emergency would send troops into Kazakhstan if interethnic clashes or nationalist protests erupted.[22] With all this uncertainty, Nazarbayev trod carefully. On the first day of the coup attempt, he neither supported nor denounced the State Committee on the State of Emergency. Yeltsin was disappointed that the reaction of Nazarbayev, as well as the leaders of Belarus and Ukraine, was "too calm." They told Yeltsin

they had too little information to come up with a clear position on the unfolding events—to which Yeltsin responded that he had the information and
that it was a coup.[23]

Instead, that evening, Nazarbayev made a televised address to the people of
Kazakhstan as well as the Soviet military and KGB-controlled military forces
stationed in the republic. He asked his fellow citizens to remain calm, stress-
ing interethnic harmony. He called for Soviet soldiers stationed in Kazakhstan
not to use force and to avoid bloodshed. Nazarbayev was afraid of a repeat of
the tragic events of December 1986 when the Kremlin suppressed protests by
Kazakh youth against Moscow.[24]

Some in Kazakhstan observed with irony that four of the five leaders of the
Central Asian republics reacted to the coup by following the Eastern wisdom:
"Sit tranquilly at the riverbank, and your enemy's corpse will float by."[25] Only
the leader of Kyrgyzstan, Askar Akayev, quickly and forcefully denounced the
coup. In a way, he could afford to be bold because, unlike Nazarbayev, he had
less to lose. Nazarbayev was a contender for the position of prime minister if a
union could be preserved.

While most people in Kazakhstan anxiously but passively observed the
events unfolding in Moscow, political activists huddled together to plan. Evgenii Zhovtis, a member of the anti-Soviet democratic movement in Kazakhstan,
remembers his emotions during the first day of the coup: "I met the day, to put
it mildly, with fear, anxiety, and annoyance. By then I already had a clear view
of the world and of where I wanted to live. And without a doubt, I did not want
to live in the Soviet Union, even less in a country that the State Committee was
trying to bring back."[26] Zhovtis, who would later become a prominent human
rights defender in Kazakhstan, described what he and his colleagues did on the
first day of the coup:

> We phoned each other. . . . We met up without delay in the morning to dis-
> cuss our actions. We went to the [city administration office]. They looked at us
> like we were complete idiots. We came out of there bewildered, not knowing
> what to do next. Then we went to the editorial office of *Zhalyn* magazine led
> by Mukhtar Shakhanov [a famous Kazakh writer]. This is where the anticoup
> group formed. . . . We even managed to get in touch with the representatives of
> democratic movements in other Central Asian republics.[27]

Among other things, they prepared and distributed anticoup posters inside
Alma-Ata's city buses.[28]

But frayed nerves were evident everywhere in Kazakhstan. In stores, while waiting in line to buy groceries, strangers shared their anxiety in hushed conversations. Lack of information bred fear of the unknown, except for the lucky ones with access to foreign-produced FM transistors that could catch broadcasts from Radio Free Europe/Radio Liberty.

While dramatic events unfolded in the Soviet Union, Washington was enjoying its usual August lull: Congress was in recess and the bureaucrats were out of town on vacation. President George H. W. Bush, on vacation just like Gorbachev, had fled Washington's stifling heat and humidity for his family's residence in Kennebunkport, Maine.

On the morning of August 19, Bush started calling foreign leaders. Frustrated and unsure of what to make of the developments in the Soviet Union, he told Canadian Prime Minister Brian Mulroney: "Our embassy did not know a damn thing. We were surprised like everyone else."[29] The US Ambassador in Moscow, Jack Matlock, would later dispute this characterization and criticize Bush's initial "muffled response" to the coup. In his autobiography Matlock describes his warning to Washington about a coup being possible but unlikely to succeed.[30] Bush himself had warned Gorbachev and Yeltsin about the danger of a coup back in June.[31]

Bush and several other world leaders tried but failed to contact Gorbachev. Gorbachev's telephone lines remained silent. Meanwhile, the US news media pressed Bush with uncomfortable questions, such as whether he had used a hotline to get in touch with Gorbachev and whether he knew who was in control of Soviet nuclear weapons.

At 5 p.m. Moscow time (8 p.m. in Alma-Ata), six of the Gang of Eight appeared together in a televised press conference intended to win public support. But their grim and ashen faces did not exude confidence, and the hands of the self-proclaimed Soviet president, Yanayev, were visibly shaking.

In Kazakhstan, Vitalii Voronov, a deputy of the Supreme Soviet of Kazakhstan, describes that day:

> I was restless at home the entire day. After watching the *Vremia* program in which they showed the Emergency Committee members and its leader—the Soviet Vice-President Gennadi Yanayev, mumbling something and his hands shaking, it became clear—the situation in the country was serious and unpredictable.[32]

Yanayev's shaky hands would become the symbol of a poorly planned coup attempt. Rumor had it he was drunk.

The next day, August 20, Gorbachev and his people remained trapped under the continuous surveillance of the KGB officers and soldiers sent by the coup leaders. Initially, small transistor radios were the only source of outside information for Gorbachev, his family, and his aides. They caught bits of the BBC, Radio Liberty, and Voice of America on a small Sony device that Gorbachev's son-in-law had with him. In one of the rooms of the sanatorium where they were staying, Gorbachev's aides also found a transistor radio that broadcast the Soviet main radio station Mayak.[33] Eventually, with the help of wire fashioned into a homemade antenna, Gorbachev and his associates restored the functionality of their television.[34]

US President Bush phoned Yeltsin, who confirmed that nobody could contact Gorbachev. Yeltsin sounded resolute about resisting the coup leaders, and Bush offered him his full support.[35] In Moscow, Russia's Supreme Soviet ruled that the coup was illegal and gave Yeltsin additional powers to remove local Russian authorities if they supported the coup organizers.

Meanwhile, in Kazakhstan, Nazarbayev informed the deputies of Kazakhstan's Supreme Soviet that he planned to fly to Moscow. Allegedly, Nazarbayev said he wanted to prevent bloodshed but all members of the Kazakh legislature firmly opposed Nazarbayev leaving, since the situation was too fluid, and they worried about his safety.[36]

Some public organizations did not wait to see how the attempted coup would play out. They forcefully denounced its organizers for their unconstitutional attempt to usurp power. The antinuclear movement Nevada-Semipalatinsk—as well as around twenty other public groups and parties, including the human rights organizations Memorial and Adilet, the environmental movement Aral-Balkhash-Aziia, the Social-Democratic Party of Kazakhstan, the trade union Birlesu, and the Unity movement—spoke out against the coup.[37]

In the evening, the coup plotters decided to take the Russian parliament by force, despite the thousands of people now gathered outside to protect it. They ordered an elite military unit to storm the building, but the soldiers refused. More and more military units began openly declaring that they would not obey orders from the self-proclaimed new leadership.[38]

That evening, Nazarbayev denounced the coup. In his second television address to the nation, he declared that the actions and decrees of the State Committee on the State of Emergency, including its declaration of a state of emergency, were unconstitutional and contravened the republics' declarations on state sovereignty.[39] He also announced he would leave the Soviet Communist Party.

By the end of the day, the coup organizers were quickly losing ground. But tragically, the night in Moscow ended in blood. Three young Russian men died while trying to prevent armored vehicles from advancing toward the Russian parliament building.[40]

On the final morning of the attempted coup, August 21, the Soviet defense minister Dmitrii Yazov, one of the coup plotters, ordered the troops to leave Moscow for fear that more civilians would be killed. Although the troops departed as ordered, the situation continued to be tense and unpredictable.

Amid all this drama, five coup organizers and some of Yeltsin's emissaries and parliamentary representatives flew separately to Foros to see Gorbachev. The coup organizers arrived in Foros first. "They looked defeated, their faces gloomy . . . they came to plead guilty," according to Gorbachev's aide Anatoly Chernyaev. Gorbachev refused to speak to them.[41] "Just by their appearance you could tell that they were finished," concluded Chernyaev.[42]

The envoys of the Russian government and the parliament finally also arrived and rushed to greet Gorbachev. After emotional embraces, Gorbachev, Russian Prime Minister Ivan Silaev, Russian Vice President Alexander Rutskoy, and others from the group talked for hours, filling each other in on what had transpired over the last few days. In the past, some from this group had fought bitterly with Gorbachev. They had resented and criticized him for not being enough of a reformer and for not turning entirely against the old Soviet guard. But on that day, as Chernyaev put it, "Politics evaporated for that moment, not to mention past disagreements, offenses, and quarrels."[43]

Once his telephone lines were restored, Gorbachev issued orders to the commandant of the Kremlin to seal the offices and cut the phone lines of those who participated in the attempted coup.[44] The same day the general prosecutor of the Russian Federation ordered arrests of all the coup participants. Minister of Internal Affairs Boris Pugo committed suicide by shooting himself the following day. General Akhromeyev hung himself on August 24.

Finally, Gorbachev spoke to President Bush. Bush could not hide his relief: "Oh my God, that's wonderful, Mikhail!" he exclaimed. It had been only an hour since Gorbachev had restored his presidential powers. Grateful to Bush for his support, Gorbachev reassured him: "We want to go ahead with you. We will not falter because of what happened," confirming his commitment to democratic reforms. Bush responded: "Sounds like the same old Mikhail Gorbachev, one full of life and confidence."[45]

Gorbachev also spoke with Yeltsin in Moscow, Leonid Kravchuk in Kyiv, and Nazarbayev in Alma-Ata.[46] The Soviet leader would later say that Yeltsin, Kravchuk, and Nazarbayev were the "greatest opponents of these illegal acts."[47]

Even though the coup had all but failed, there was still uncertainty in the air. Only once Gorbachev and his entourage—family and aides—were safely aboard their flight back to Moscow did the atmosphere grow relaxed and optimistic. Gorbachev said: "We are flying to a new country."[48]

A new country it was. Within four months, the Soviet Union would cease to exist.

ON THE ROAD TO COLLAPSE

Although the coup had failed, it had irrevocably damaged Gorbachev's legitimacy. He was too much a reformer for Soviet hard-liners but too sympathetic to the old guard for Russian liberals and the republics that wanted to leave the union. Further, the attempted coup had thrown into too-sharp relief the fatal deficiencies of the Soviet model. The country Gorbachev was trying to save was crumbling fast. Yeltsin had emerged as the face of a newly democratic Russia. The image of Yeltsin standing atop a tank rallying Muscovites in front of the Russian parliament became the symbol of a new country. Gorbachev never recovered his authority, and he was devastated that the people he had trusted had betrayed him: "The hardest thing that I suffered on a personal level was the treachery. That will haunt me for the rest of my life."[49]

The coup attempt shifted the balance of Soviet power. The hard-liners who had hoped to preserve the Soviet state in its current form, lost. But so too did Gorbachev, who now understood that he could not keep the republics from spinning away from the center: "Perhaps the most tragic result of the attempted coup is that those three days stimulated—gave a real boost to—the centrifugal tendencies in the country. There emerged a real threat that the state would fall apart and no longer be a union."[50]

Gorbachev still wished to rally the Soviet republics to sign the New Union Treaty, but its prospects grew bleaker by the day. The republics were turning away from Moscow, which was wholly preoccupied with the power struggle between the old Soviet system and the Russian reformers. Russian nationalists called for redrawing the borders in the union, taking land from the republics. This alienated the republics further.

The leaders of the republics worried about their own political fortunes and devised ways to remain in power while also leading their republics to independence. They were wary that under the proposed treaty Russia would continue to dominate their affairs. Yeltsin and his advisors were moving Russia away from the Soviet state while simultaneously making Russia the principal inheritor of the Soviet Union. Additionally, Yeltsin and the rest of the Russian government were sidelining Gorbachev more and more, making him irrelevant to the political process.

As the political power struggles continued, the Soviet economy went into free fall. Gorbachev appealed to the leaders of the major countries for immediate and substantial aid. In early November of 1991, he pleaded with the UK prime minister John Major, the coordinator of G-7, admitting that "the currency situation is close to collapse." In early December, the G-7 offered the Soviet Union US$10 billion; by then the country was near economic disaster.[51]

After the failed coup, the US ambassador in Moscow cabled a dire warning to the State Department: "How long central authority will remain in the USSR in any recognizable form is a question."[52] What Americans feared most was a nuclear superpower in disarray.

NUCLEAR FEARS BEGIN AND THE POLYGON CLOSES

During the coup, when Gorbachev lost access to the "nuclear suitcase" (called "Cheget" after a mountain in the Caucasus), who had controlled Soviet nuclear weapons? The nuclear launch authorization process, or "Kazbek," involved three devices assigned to three authorizing parties—the president, the defense minister, and the chief of the general staff. The president and the defense minister would send separate codes to the third device, which would then receive input from the chief of the general staff. The composed code would then be transmitted to the commander-in-chief of strategic forces to authorize the launch of nuclear weapons.[53]

In August 1991, the three individuals whose input was necessary to authorize a nuclear launch were Gorbachev (trapped in Foros), Defense Minister Yazov (a coup leader), and Chief of the General Staff Mikhail Moiseev, who returned to Moscow from a vacation on the first day of the coup. According to Gorbachev's aide Chernyaev, Moiseev was on the side of the coup plotters.[54]

When the coup leaders placed Gorbachev under house arrest, they ordered his nuclear suitcase to be brought to the Ministry of Defense in Moscow. There the officers in charge of the device disabled it.[55]

Under normal circumstances, the communication device of the president, as commander-in-chief, had priority power over the other two devices. The president's device allowed him to raise the alert level of the nuclear arsenal and to order a launch if an early warning system registered an incoming attack. The other two devices allowed their custodians to communicate with the commander-in-chief but not to generate an order to launch a nuclear attack. There were two important exceptions to this rule, however: if the device of the commander-in-chief had sent an order for a high alert status, or if it had remained silent for an extended period.[56]

The coup leaders used this second exception. Because Gorbachev's device had remained silent and the plotters had access to the other two devices—Yazov's and Moiseev's—they could raise the alert level of the Soviet strategic nuclear forces. If the Soviet early warning system registered a nuclear attack (whether real or perceived), the coup leaders could have ordered a retaliatory nuclear launch, too.

The details of what transpired during those few days remain murky, but at least two anecdotes suggest that the coup leaders controlled the nuclear arsenal and raised the level of alert of at least some nuclear forces. On August 19, all strategic submarines of the Northern Fleet located in the Murmansk region in northwest Russia were on high alert and could launch nuclear weapons from their base without leaving for the ocean. And at the air force base near Khabarovsk in southeast Russia, nuclear custodians loaded nuclear weapons onto a bomber. Its crew received two envelopes—one with the codes to arm the weapons and another one with the coordinates of a target. For an hour, the crew was on standby, ready to take off within sixty minutes of an order.[57]

The fact that Gorbachev did not control the Soviet Union's nuclear weapons during the attempted coup posed an immediate security risk. But the risks did not vanish with the coup's failure. The unsuccessful coup laid bare the risks that a disintegrating nuclear power posed.

At its zenith, in 1986, the Soviet nuclear complex boasted a stockpile of 45,000 warheads.[58] Thanks to the US-Soviet arms control measures, the two countries reduced their stockpiles over the years, but they still had several times more than needed to destroy the entire planet. By 1991, the disintegrating Soviet Union retained more than 27,000 nuclear warheads.[59] Uncertainty over the fate of these nuclear weapons made the United States extremely nervous. What would happen to these thousands of nuclear weapons, tons of nuclear material, and thousands of nuclear scientists who possessed weapons knowledge?

Meanwhile in Kazakhstan, as the forty-second anniversary of the first Soviet nuclear test at Semipalatinsk approached on August 29, thousands of people were on standby for the planned massive antinuclear protests. The Kazakh government rushed to prevent unrest. Atamurat Shamen, who worked on environmental issues for President Nazarbayev's administration, remembers the rapid-fire events of that day. In the morning, the president's staff prepared a draft decree to close the Semipalatinsk testing site for Nazarbayev's signature. "To somehow calm down the population, the plan was to, at least, show the draft decree on closing the Polygon, in case the president wouldn't sign it," Shamen recalls.[60]

For many hours, it appeared that the Nazarbayev would not sign it, because he spent the entire day in the building at the Supreme Soviet and it was impossible to reach him. Finally, however, at the end of that historically significant day of August 29, 1991, Nazarbayev "signed the decree at the last moment, not even in the president's office."[61]

With that signature, Nazarbayev closed the Polygon and, for the first time in its seventy years of Soviet history, Kazakhstan took its fate into its own hands.

FOUR NUCLEAR REPUBLICS

In September 1991, the American government dispatched its chief diplomat, Secretary of State James Baker III, on a tour of key Soviet republics. Three weeks after the August coup attempt, he visited Russia, all three Baltic states, and Kazakhstan. Baker wanted to understand the republics' plans for economic reform and future political arrangements between the Kremlin and the four states.[62]

Washington viewed Kazakhstan as key because, during the turbulent post-coup period, when the future of the Soviet Union was still up in the air, Nazarbayev had emerged as a pivotal player.[63] The Kazakh leader maintained a good relationship with both Gorbachev and Yeltsin and acted as an envoy between Moscow and the republics in the negotiations on the New Union Treaty—which Gorbachev still believed could succeed. Further, Nazarbayev enjoyed high levels of popular support throughout the Soviet Union. In a poll that asked Soviet citizens whom they would want to see in a coalition government, Nazarbayev came in second, behind Yeltsin and ahead of Gorbachev.[64]

The plane with Baker and his wife approached Alma-Ata on a mild midSeptember day. Baker recalled: "As I looked over the rugged peaks and stark land below, I felt for a moment that I had returned to Wyoming. I would soon learn that President Nursultan Nazarbayev definitely wanted me to feel at home."[65] That evening, Nazarbayev and his wife hosted the Bakers at their residence. The small private dinner was a family affair, with Nazarbayev's daughter playing the piano for the American guests.

According to Baker, Nazarbayev shared his anxiety about Kazakhstan's overbearing neighbor—Russia—and its "dangerous nationalism": "The Kazakhs, surrounded virtually on every side by a great power, wanted to reach out to the United States, the one power in the world that could ensure their peace and stability."[66]

The evening ended with Nazarbayey, Baker, State Department interpreter Peter Afanasenko, and US ambassador to the Soviet Union Bob Strauss enjoying a sauna. Baker humorously described the experience:

> So soon enough, [we] had stripped down and were sitting with Nazarbayev and our vodka in the presidential *banya*—a Russian sauna. . . . After about twenty minutes, Nazarbayev picked up a large bundle of eucalyptus branches and beat me on the back and legs in order to open pores and increase the therapeutic value of the heat. Upon seeing this, Strauss said he'd had enough and stepped out.[67]

Apparently, Strauss joked with Baker's security service: "Damn! Get me the president of the United States on the phone. His Secretary of State is buck naked, and he's being beaten by the President of Kazakhstan!"[68]

The official meetings started the following morning. Nazarbayev said he was still hopeful some kind of union could be preserved as a conglomeration of sovereign states—with a single currency, one military force, a single command of nuclear weapons, and a coordinated foreign policy, along the lines of the New Union Treaty that the attempted coup had derailed. At the same time, Nazarbayev did his best to sell Kazakhstan's economic potential to Baker and urged Washington to invest in his republic and help with energy development and integration into the world economy. With the Soviet Union crumbling and Moscow in disarray, Kazakhstan was ready for direct cooperation with the United States and welcomed the establishment of a US embassy in Alma-Ata.[69]

As for nuclear matters, Nazarbayev told Baker the opposite of what the secretary had hoped to hear. Nazarbayev said that Kazakhstan did not plan to renounce nuclear weapons and that, in his view, states with nuclear weapons on their territory should be the ones to control them. Nazarbayev added that Russia and Kazakhstan should make the decisions on the use of nuclear weapons together.[70]

All in all, Nazarbayev impressed Baker.[71] A senior US official from Baker's travel team told the *Los Angeles Times* that "Nazarbayev is clearly someone committed to maintaining some kind of coherence . . . to prevent the disintegration of the country. The guy is important, and [Baker's visit] is a way of giving him additional status. It is in the interests of Nazarbayev to be seen working with us."[72]

In the last months of the Soviet Union, Nazarbayev remained committed to common economic and military spheres. Although in October 1991 he created a seventy-five-man State Committee on Defense to oversee the military infrastructure and defense issues in the republic, to be led by General-Lieutenant Sagadat Nurmagambetov, Nazarbayev did not rush to create an independent Kazakhstan military force. There was no desire to call the newly created committee a defense ministry, since the Soviet defense ministry already existed. Nazarbayev envisioned the former Soviet republics as working in cooperation with joint military forces.[73]

Around the same time, in Washington, Larry Napper assumed the directorship of Soviet Affairs at the State Department. Napper feared that one or more countries with nuclear weapons on their territory would enter into an antagonistic relationship, if not conflict. He later recalled that "as we all looked at the impending breakup of the Soviet Union, this became for most of us, for me anyway, question number one: How are we going to manage this so that we did not wind up with four nuclear states on the territory of the Soviet Union instead of one?"[74]

As US government analyzed potential developments in the Soviet Union behind the closed doors, policy analysis conducted in academia was public. Academics at Harvard University, including Ashton Carter—who would later become Assistant Secretary of Defense in the Clinton administration and Secretary of Defense in the Obama administration—began assessing potential scenarios for those "four nuclear states," namely Russia, Belarus, Ukraine, and Kazakhstan. They published their findings in a report entitled *Soviet Nuclear Fission* in November 1991.

In the scenario most favorable for the United States, but also highly unlikely, the collapse of the Soviet Union would lead to complete Soviet nuclear disarmament and the dismantlement of all the weapons. The challenges in such a case would be twofold: ensuring the safe dismantling of the weapons and managing any geopolitical shift that might occur if neighboring states adopted more assertive policies toward the new, nonnuclear Moscow.[75]

A second scenario posited that only one of the four nuclear republics would inherit Soviet nuclear weapons. If Russia were the sole inheritor, the Harvard scholars argued, the United States would be in the best position. Moscow understood how to manage nuclear weapons, and, thanks to decades of arms control cooperation, it also knew how to deal with Washington on nuclear matters. But there were drawbacks to that scenario. For one, Russia would retain its nuclear superpower status. Also, to encourage the other three republics to relinquish their nuclear weapons, the United States would have to "pay the price" in the form of security guarantees—promises not to threaten the republics and to protect them in case of need. Finally, if the three non-Russian republics insisted on keeping their nuclear weapons in spite of Washington's preferences, the trajectory of the United States' relationship with them would be uncertain.[76]

Finally, in the scenario most frightening for the United States, all four—Russia, Belarus, Kazakhstan, and Ukraine—would emerge as nuclear states from the disintegrating Soviet empire. The latter three lacked the knowledge and capability to exercise command and control over nuclear weapons. What's more, nobody knew what kind of leaders would come to power in these republics and whether political stability could be maintained.[77] The National Security Council made this grim assessment of how wrong things could go: "The range of possible crises is large, from an accident involving a single weapon, to the loss of control of a weapon, the takeover of a storage site by terrorists, dissident military units or the like, to civil war, to war between two republics."[78]

Less than a month later the Soviet Union would collapse.

COLLAPSE

In Kazakhstan, Nazarbayev, who took over the top position from Gennadii Kolbin in 1989, remained the leader. He had held the title of president since 1990, when the position was first introduced in the republic, but he was appointed by Kazakhstan's Supreme Soviet, not elected by the people. That changed on December 1, 1991, when Kazakhstan held its first presidential elections and Nazarbayev, with a whopping 98.7 percent of votes, became the nation's first popularly elected leader.

On December 8, 1991, the leaders of three Slavic republics—Boris Yeltsin of Russia, Leonid Kravchuk of Ukraine, and Stanislav Shushkevich of Belarus—met at the state dacha in the Belovezh Forest in Belarus. There they adopted the historic Belovezh Accords, which proclaimed the dissolution of the Soviet Union and the creation of the Commonwealth of Independent States (CIS), a very loose confederation of former Soviet republics. The more tightly knit relationship of the republics that was envisioned by the stillborn New Union Treaty was now just a dream. The republics would instead be sovereign independent states and use the CIS to coordinate their "divorce" and, hopefully, to guide their future collaboration.

Yeltsin, Kravchuk, and Shushkevich called Nazarbayev and invited him to join them in Belarus. Nazarbayev, who was in Moscow that day, initially agreed but didn't show up in the end. Yeltsin was disappointed but could understand Nazarbayev's motivation:

> It was important to have Nazarbayev present, at least in an observer capacity, but he decided otherwise. I don't think he cancelled his flight to Belarus only because it was awkward to refuse Gorbachev [who had urged him to abandon it]. In those hours, Nazarbayev must have been thinking of the Eurasian context in which Kazakhstan was situated. To be sure, Kazakhstan shared extensive borders with Russia and common ties and interests. Still, situated as Kazakhstan was in the Central Asian region, Nazarbayev's neighbors were most important, too. They had ethnic and spiritual ties.[79]

Meanwhile, Yeltsin called Bush immediately to update him on the developments even before informing Gorbachev that the country he led was ceasing to exist. Yeltsin described to Bush "the economic and political crisis" that Gorbachev's policies had created and the other motivations for the accord:

> The system in place and the [New] Union Treaty everyone is pushing us to sign does not satisfy us. And that is why we got together and literally a few minutes ago signed a joint agreement. Mr. President, we, the leaders of three states, . . . noting negotiations to the new treaty are at a standstill, have seen objective reasons that the formation of independent states has become reality.[80]

Now that it had become abundantly clear to Nazarbayev that the New Union Treaty wasn't an option, he wanted to manage Kazakhstan's transition on his own terms. Two days after the Belovezh Forest events, on December 10, in the Palace of the Republic in Alma-Ata, a site of Communist congresses and cultural events, Nazarbayev was inaugurated as the president of Kazakhstan.

Two days later, Russia formally seceded from the Soviet Union. Other republics followed. From December 12 to 13, the leaders of the five Central Asian republics—Kazakhstan among them—met in Ashgabat, the capital of Turkmenistan. There, they agreed that their states would also join the CIS.

The US ambassador to the Soviet Union, Jack Matlock, described how Nazarbayev explained to him his decision about joining the CIS:

> In 1992, I asked Kazakhstan President Nursultan Nazarbayev what had caused him, despite his strong support for Gorbachev's union treaty, to lead the Central Asians into the Commonwealth of Independent States. He replied that, as soon as it had become apparent that the three Slavic republics were determined to leave the Soviet Union, he had realized that if the Soviet Union should break up with the Slavs in one group and the Turkic peoples in another, it would be a disaster for all. Though he had hoped for a stronger union, he had urged the Central Asian republics to join the CIS to prevent the formation of exclusive Slavic-Christian and Turkic-Islamic groupings.[81]

On December 16, 1991, the fifth anniversary of the first revolt against the Soviet government in Alma-Ata, Kazakhstan's parliament declared the country's independence. The people of Kazakhstan found out about it only the next day, from the newspapers. "Euphoria" was the word Kazakhstan's prominent public figures used to describe their emotions. For most of the country's population, especially the ethnic Kazakhs, this was the dawn of a new era. But there was also apprehension about the future. Would the new country retain its independence? Would it make it on its own? How would the relationship with Russia, its former patron, unfold? Nazarbayev, who felt acutely both the promise and the challenge of independence, commented: "I look at [the future] with optimism and hope that common sense will prevail."[82]

The same week as Kazakhstan declared independence, Secretary Baker was in Moscow meeting with Yeltsin. The US government, nervous about command and control of Soviet nuclear weapons in Kazakhstan, Ukraine, and Belarus, was seeking reassurance from the Kremlin. Yeltsin assured Baker that command and control would remain centralized.[83] The next day, Baker made his second visit to Kazakhstan. He was on a mission to convince Kazakhstan's leadership to give up the nuclear weapons on its territory.

When Nazarbayev talked to Baker in private, he echoed his comments back in September, informing the American diplomat that Kazakhstan was in no rush to give up its nuclear weapons. As long as Russia had nuclear weapons, Kazakhstan would remain a nuclear power. Nazarbayev further said that he had spoken with Yeltsin about a proposal to keep nuclear weapons in both Russia and Kazakhstan.[84] Nazarbayev added: "If the international community recognizes and accepts Kazakhstan, we will declare ourselves a non-nuclear state.

This is the best way that our territorial integrity will be assured. That's what we require."[85] After spending three productive hours with Nazarbayev, Baker returned to his room at 3 a.m.:

> He was a very impressive leader, one that could not be underestimated. His near future would undoubtedly be rough—he had a full plate of enormously complex issues to iron out in the days ahead and the Commonwealth meeting in three days would be pivotal. But Nazarbayev had both a vision of what was needed, as well as an acute sense of how to get things accomplished on the ground.[86]

Secretary Baker continued his travels. From the road he managed to get hold of Nazarbayev on December 20, just as Nazarbayev welcomed leaders of the soon-to-be-former republics of the USSR. Baker encouraged Nazarbayev: "I wanted to let you know as you go into these meetings that I wish you luck." Nazarbayev sounded optimistic and determined: "I have assurances from everyone here that we will be successful in creating this Commonwealth [of Independent States]. . . . I will not let anyone leave here without a deal."[87] Nazarbayev understood that the former Soviet republics would be better off having some kind of structure to support the transition from a union to independence. After all, Kazakhstan's entire economy still depended on ties to the disintegrating Soviet Union, and, having no army of its own, Kazakhstan was also unable to provide for its own security.

The next day—six days into Kazakhstan's independence—the leaders of eleven Soviet republics met at Alma-Ata. The heads of state for Georgia and the three Baltic republics—Latvia, Lithuania, and Estonia—declined to participate. In Alma-Ata, the eleven presidents confirmed the dissolution of the Soviet Union and reaffirmed the establishment of the Commonwealth of Independent States (CIS) by signing the Alma-Ata Declaration.

The summit produced the Agreement on Strategic Forces which gave a glimpse into how the disintegrating Soviet state planned to deal with its nuclear weapons. It proclaimed that Russia would control the nuclear arsenal in consultation with the three republics that possessed nuclear weapons on their territory. It was agreed that the president of the Soviet Union would resign on December 25 and transfer authority over Soviet nuclear weapons to the president of Russia.

After returning to Moscow from Alma-Ata on December 23, 1991, Yeltsin called Bush to fill him in on the details of the newly signed declaration. Yeltsin reported that Belarus and Ukraine had committed to becoming non-nuclear-weapon states and would eliminate all tactical and strategic weapons on their

territory. The declaration mentioned the destruction of nuclear weapons located in Belarus and Ukraine but was mum about Kazakhstan. In fact, Yeltsin
told Bush that "there will be some strategic nuclear weapons maintained in
Kazakhstan."[88] It was not clear whether at that point Yeltsin was open to the
idea that nuclear weapons would remain in Kazakhstan. As a minimum, Kazakhstan leadership managed to keep itself free of any written commitment
on the nuclear issue in the Alma-Ata Declaration. "We left ourselves space for
maneuvering. We persuaded Yeltsin."[89]

The Russian media reported that the negotiations on nuclear weapons were
"not that successful." Russian journalists wrote with alarm: "Kazakhstan, as
Nazarbayev stated in the beginning of the week, plans, it seems, to join the
nuclear club, and colleagues have given up hope of persuading Kazakhstan's
president otherwise."[90]

Washington viewed the meeting less pessimistically than did the Russian
media. Baker, who received a call from Nazarbayev as soon as the meeting was
over, thought the Alma-Ata Declaration was "definitely a positive step forward."
Nazarbayev recapped to Baker: "We are determined that there will only be four
nuclear republics, but that control of nuclear weapons will be handed over to
Russia. Ukraine and Belarus will transfer their nuclear weapons by 1998 to Russia, where destruction of all nuclear weapons will take place. Strategic nuclear
weapons will remain in Russia and Kazakhstan; however, Kazakhstan will declare itself a non-nuclear zone when it is admitted to the United Nations."[91]

On Christmas Day, Gorbachev called Bush to inform him that the Soviet
state would cease to exist the next day: "I have a decree of the president of the
USSR on my desk. As I cease to be the Commander in Chief, I transfer the
power to use nuclear weapons to the president of the Russian Federation."[92] The
next day the Soviet Union no longer existed, and Kazakhstan found itself with
the fourth largest nuclear arsenal in the world.[93]

On December 30, five days after the Soviet Union was formally terminated,
CIS leaders met in Minsk and reconfirmed their plans for the Soviet nuclear
weapons, more or less repeating what they had agreed on in Alma-Ata a couple of weeks earlier in a new Agreement on Strategic Forces that became part
of their Minsk Declaration. The brief two-page text proclaimed that Marshal
Boris Shaposhnikov would act as commander-in-chief of the Joint Armed
Forces of the Commonwealth and that, until the elimination of nuclear weapons from non-Russian republics, the Russian president would decide on their
use "in agreement" with the presidents of Belarus, Kazakhstan, and Ukraine.[94]

Russia's promise to consult with Minsk, Alma-Ata, and Kyiv was purely for political appearances. None of the three republics had any technical means to stop the launch of nuclear weapons from their territory if Russia decided to launch them. Further, this arrangement did not stipulate any practical means for the three non-Russian presidents to prevent a nuclear launch. As a consequence, Kazakhstan would run the risk of being drawn into a nuclear war without the consent of its head of state.

And again, as with the earlier agreement from the summit in Alma-Ata, the Minsk Declaration mentioned a process for weapon destruction in Belarus and Ukraine, while omitting any mention of Kazakhstan's nuclear arsenal.[95] The likely reason for the omission was Kazakhstan's decision to avoid any public commitments on nuclear weapons and to keep all its options open. Again, that was a win for Kazakhstan's leadership which had managed to maintain room for maneuver. The fate of Soviet nuclear weapons in the new nation of Kazakhstan was yet to be decided.

PART 2

FREEDOM DAWNS, BUT THE ARSENAL REMAINS

CHAPTER 6

FEARS IN WASHINGTON AND ALMA-ATA

Even if one-hundredth of one percent of the nuclear weapons in the Soviet stockpile falls into the wrong hands, destruction greater than the world has seen since Hiroshima and Nagasaki could result.

—Ashton B. Carter, statement before the Defense Policy Panel H
ouse Armed Services Committee, December 13, 1991

We did not want to become a Central Asian North Korea.

—Tulegen Zhukeev, State Counselor and Deputy
Chair of the Security Council (1992–94), Kazakhstan

AS THE SOVIET UNION WAS DISSOLVING, 104 Soviet nuclear missiles (code-named SS-18 by NATO) capable of striking the American mainland sat launch-ready at two secret locations in the Kazakh steppe.[1] Each missile could be armed with up to ten warheads. Americans called them "silo-busters, the hard target killing machines."[2] SS-18s were built to survive a first enemy strike and then launch. In addition, forty heavy bombers capable of carrying 12 tons of nuclear bombs could fly from Kazakhstan to the United States. All in all, more than 1,400 strategic nuclear warheads sat in Kazakhstan ready to be used. The fate of these weapons was suddenly uncertain.

Kazakhstan's nuclear inheritance was not limited to warheads and the missiles and planes that could carry them. Kazakhstan was also endowed with the world's second-largest uranium reserves.[3] The Soviet nuclear industry had developed uranium mines and built milling and reprocessing facilities to convert the uranium into nuclear material. Military testing sites added to Kazakhstan's weapons infrastructure. And the scientists and engineers from Kazakhstan

125

who worked at these facilities possessed sensitive expertise that could be sold to others or used by the Kazakh government to build its own nuclear program.

Amid the uncertainty surrounding developments in the Soviet Union, these questions loomed particularly large: What would the Central Asian republic do with its nuclear cache? Would Kazakhstan try to gain control over Soviet nuclear weapons stationed on its territory? Would new leaders try to use them as a bargaining chip to get economic and political concessions from the West? Would the Kazakh government sell nuclear goods to neighboring Iran? Would it be able to protect nuclear material in the turmoil of the post-Soviet transition and prevent would-be terrorists from stealing it and making a bomb? Would Kazakhstan decide to push its way into the exclusive club of nuclear nations? No one could answer these questions in 1991.

URANIUM: BLESSING AND CURSE

Kazakhstan's rich natural resources included the world's second largest reserves of uranium. Natural uranium is required to produce highly enriched uranium and plutonium, two nuclear fissionable materials that fuel the bombs. Due to its massive reserves, Kazakhstan became home to a range of uranium production and processing facilities.

Exploration for Kazakhstan's uranium began in 1948 at the Kurdai deposit, in the southern part of the country. The next year, the Ulba Metallurgical Plant was established in Ust-Kamenogorsk for the eventual processing of uranium and other metals such as beryllium, tantalum, and niobium. Uranium mining began in the mid-1950s, and soon Kazakhstan became indispensable for the Soviet nuclear program and for nearly every step of the nuclear fuel cycle—the process of producing nuclear fuel for both nuclear power plants and nuclear bombs.[4]

By 1964, in the town of Shevchenko (renamed Aktau in 1991) on the shores of the Caspian Sea, the Soviets had built a fast breeder nuclear reactor that produced plutonium. The reactor, identified by its Russian acronym BN-350 ("Bystrye Neitrony"—Fast Neutrons), desalinized water and supplied electricity while at the same time breeding plutonium.

Thanks to uranium deposits, nuclear-fuel producing facilities, and the fast breeder reactor, when the Soviet Union disintegrated the Republic of Kazakhstan was left with more than 14 metric tons of highly enriched uranium (HEU) and roughly 3 metric tons of plutonium. While most of it was in spent fuel form and would require processing to make it usable in a bomb, the total amount was enough to build hundreds of new weapons.

The most challenging step in building a bomb is producing nuclear material. Once it is obtained, building a simple bomb is relatively straightforward. This is why, with the turmoil in the Soviet Union, Washington was anxious about the fate of this material. Should a well-funded group or a state obtain just 15–25 kilograms (33–55 pounds) of HEU, only as big as a 5-pound bag of sugar, or 6–8 kilograms (13–17 pounds) of weapons-grade plutonium, only the size of a grapefruit, it could build (and detonate) a simple nuclear device.

From the Americans' perspective, even in stable times the security of Soviet nuclear material was questionable. The Soviet government planned only for contingencies in which the Americans or their allies tried to breach Soviet nuclear facilities or collect intelligence. For this reason, the Soviets built their nuclear facilities in remote areas and prevented the names of the secret cities from being printed on maps. The government did not worry about people working at the facilities—the insiders.

To some extent, that policy was understandable. In a police state such as the Soviet Union, the government controlled its entire population, and its grip on its nuclear force was even tighter. The KGB constantly monitored nuclear scientists, engineers, and custodians, their families included. Those who worked in the nuclear sector could not travel abroad or communicate with any foreigners without special state authorization. No nuclear worker could steal nuclear material in such circumstances, the government persuaded itself.

But peculiar Soviet methods of accounting for nuclear material meant that nobody knew the exact amount of such material in inventory at any given time—and therefore could not possibly know if any went missing. Specifically, the Soviet central planning economy relied on five-year production plans, and these plans inadvertently encouraged Soviet facilities, including nuclear ones, to manipulate their production numbers.

A nuclear facility might produce extra HEU or plutonium and then fail to properly register it; this practice furnished insurance against a possible shortfall from spills, overflows, or production inefficiencies the following year.[5] In other words, extra material produced one year could be counted for the next year. Computers in the former Soviet Union were a rarity during the early 1990s, and all the accounting was done on paper, with no real-time tracking of material quantities. If someone had quietly siphoned off nuclear material from a facility, the loss would not have been noticed quickly, if ever.

To make matters worse, the Soviet political crisis had dramatically diminished living standards and worsened working conditions for workers in the nuclear field. Before the collapse, they enjoyed stable salaries and the privileges that came with working for the state's most important industry. Now their financial circumstances were precarious. Some lost their jobs while others went unpaid for months, and morale was at an all-time low. Sloppy accounting habits and growing economic despair created a dangerous mix, with desperate nuclear workers tempted to sell off nuclear material to eager third parties. Very soon it became clear that this risk was not hypothetical.[6]

In a notorious case, Leonid Smirnov, a forty-six-year-old engineer at a nuclear plant in Russia, stole 1.5 kilograms (3.3 pounds) of HEU.[7] In an interview many years after his arrest and a three-year probation sentence, Smirnov admitted that stealing the HEU was not difficult: "I knew when I could take some and how much I could take that no one would notice. . . . It was possible to siphon off around one percent [of HEU] a month for yourself." Over the course of a few months, until he was discovered by complete chance, Smirnov quietly removed small quantities of HEU from the facility where he worked:

> I'd take a fifty gram vial. . . . So when no one was looking during a smoke break or just when no one was there, I would measure off a little from the box into a vial, shake it off (still in the box), wrap it up, then take it out of the box and place it on a clean rag in gloves and wipe the vial with a special chemical solution.[8]

Smirnov would then roll it in paper and hide it in his pocket before putting it in his bag to carry home. "That was it, and I'd take it out of the plant." Smirnov planned to ask $500 for his HEU, worth two years of his salary. He hoped to buy a new fridge, a new stove, and renovate his modest apartment.[9]

Like Smirnov in Russia, employees of nuclear facilities in Kazakhstan also faced unpaid wages. The facilities were civilian, not military, which meant no armed guards protected them against criminals or criminal organizations.[10] Stolen nuclear material could conceivably have left Kazakhstan's porous borders and ended up anywhere in the world.

Criminals and disgruntled nuclear workers were not the only security threats that worried American policymakers. Envoys of countries eager to build their own nuclear bombs could come knocking on Kazakhstan's door. Quite soon after the Soviet collapse, Tehran had tried to establish an Iranian consulate in Aktau, the town that hosted the fast breeder reactor BN-350, a source of plutonium. The Kazakh government had denied Iran's request,[11] but Iran's attempts continued. The CIA knew that Iranians had reached out to officials at Kazakh nuclear facilities on several occasions in search of nuclear material. In 1992,

Iran attempted to buy HEU from the Ulba Metallurgical Plant.[12] What Americans didn't know at the time was that roughly 600 kilograms (more than 1,300 pounds) of HEU, enough to build more than twenty nuclear bombs, was sitting in a building at the plant protected only with a padlock. Even without any official deals to sell HEU, the dangerous material could have easily gone missing.

NUCLEAR KNOWLEDGE AND FACILITIES

The possibility of desperate employees' selling not only nuclear material but also their nuclear knowledge was real. Days before the Soviet breakup, Secretary Baker delivered this warning in a speech at Princeton University:

> While the nightmare of Orwell's 1984 is past, the terror of 1994 is that a Saddam Hussein or Moammar Qaddafi will use the black market to buy weapons from rogue military units or blueprints from unemployed engineers. *We want to ensure that the creative talents of Soviet scientists and engineers are not diverted to dangerous military programs elsewhere in the world.*[13]

Soviet nuclear experts could have left to work in North Korea or Iran, for example. As William Potter, a US nonproliferation expert, warned, "a typical Soviet nuclear engineer[,] who makes less than a bus driver[,] would appear to be an attractive candidate for recruitment by a well-heeled, would-be nuclear weapons state."[14]

Kazakhstan's nuclear specialists were not experts in building and maintaining nuclear weapons, but they possessed a certain expertise from hosting their republic's nuclear facilities. This knowledge translated into high levels of proficiency in the production of nuclear material, thanks especially to skills obtained at the Ulba Metallurgical Plant in Ust-Kamenogorsk and the plutonium breeder reactor in Aktau. In other words, while technical experts in Kazakhstan did not know much about nuclear weapons, they knew a lot about nuclear material, an indispensable part of any nuclear weapons program.

In addition to the facilities in Ust-Kamenogorsk and Aktau, Kazakhstan's sprawling nuclear infrastructure included the nuclear testing sites at Semipalatinsk and part of Kapustin Yar (the site stretched across parts of Russia and Kazakhstan), and sites for peaceful nuclear explosion experiments at Azgir, Lira, and Say Utes. Kazakhstan also had a wide variety of other military and weapons-related sites. At Sary-Shagan, a testing site near picturesque Lake Balkhash in southeastern Kazakhstan, the military tested antiaircraft, antiballistic missile, and antisatellite defense systems. Year-round sunny weather and more than 480 kilometers (almost 300 miles) of unin-habited territory created near-perfect conditions for such tests. When the Soviet Union successfully tested its first antimissile system at Sary-Shagan, Soviet leader Nikita Khrushchev boasted to the world, "We now have au-tomated antiaircraft and antimissile systems that can shoot down a fly in space!"[15] In the Aral Sea, on Vozrozhdenie Island (Russian for "rebirth"), Soviet scientists tested biological weapons in the open air. A bioweapons fa-cility in Stepnogorsk, a secret town in northern Kazakhstan, could produce 300 tons of anthrax each year.

The first man in outer space, Yuri Gagarin, lifted off on his historic journey from Baikonur, a space launching site in Kazakhstan on the banks of the Syr Darya. Baikonur, Kazakh for "wealthy brown" due to the area's fertile soil and plenty of herbs, was actually the name of a mining town several hundred kilo-meters away. The Soviet military gave the site that name to keep the location secret and confuse outsiders.

All this WMD-related material, expertise, and infrastructure in Kazakh-stan concerned American leaders. But it was the nuclear weapons stockpile that caused their gravest fears.

NUCLEAR BOMBS IN THE KAZAKH STEPPE

As the weeks passed after the August coup and the republics sought to distance themselves from Moscow, the Americans' nuclear anxieties took on new ur-gency. They wondered, who controls the tactical nuclear weapons, relatively easy to transport? And who controls the strategic nuclear weapons that could be sent on a missile across the ocean to attack the United States?

A grim mood and separatist sentiments in the Soviet Union worsened this worry. In the words of Robert Strauss, the US ambassador in Moscow:

> The optimism that gripped the USSR immediately after the failed August coup has been replaced by a sense of drift and anxiety. The past two months have seen an accelerating decline in central authority and a corresponding rise in separatist feelings within republics. As more and more republics assert their determination to take on all the attributes of independence, including join-ing the UN and creating their own armed forces, how long central authority will remain in the USSR in any recognizable form is a question. Real power is devolving to the republics but the republics themselves are beset by internal divisions.[16]

High-level military and civilian officials in Russia assured American envoys that centralized control over Soviet nuclear weapons would continue. But the Americans could not be sure.[17]

For one thing, they wondered also if Kazakhstan's leader, Nazarbayev, would try to gain control of the nuclear weapons in his territory. Graham Allison, part of the Harvard group that assessed nuclear risks in the Soviet Union, offered his opinion of Nazarbayev:

> He now thinks of Kazakhstan as a nuclear state—but I suspect that he doesn't know what part of that thought is real and what is fanciful. When Russia stated last week that it would assert territorial claims against any republic that left the Union, Nazarbayev stated quite deliberately: any assertion of territorial claims against Kazakhstan could lead to war. He has closed the nuclear testing facility in Kazakhstan because of long-standing local environmental opposition. But he is acutely conscious that Western Kazakhstan, which contains the SS-18 fields [missiles able to strike the United States], is mainly populated by Russians and is certain to be the subject of intense dispute between an independent Russia and an independent Kazakhstan.[18]

Allison's assumption about what post-Soviet leaders would choose to do was pessimistic:

> Any independent small power adjacent to a large power with which it has substantial territorial and ethnic disputes has a security problem. No geopolitician would voluntarily choose to be a non-nuclear state facing a major power that was a nuclear state. Nor would any strategist advise them to. . . . Thus, as quickly as they recognize their real interest, they will be really interested in maintaining whatever nuclear arsenals they can.[19]

Meanwhile, halfway across the world, Kazakhstan's leaders grappled with the same questions that Allison was mulling.

KAZAKHSTAN'S NUCLEAR DILEMMA

As American leaders tried to guess what Kazakhs would decide about their nuclear legacy, the Kazakh leadership faced a whole gamut of social and economic crises in the wake of the Soviet breakup.[20] The newly independent country suffered from food shortages; supermarket shelves were bare. People waited in long lines to buy essentials as simple as bread. The country's coffers were empty; citizens waited for months to receive their salaries. Politically, the young

Kazakh government had to rebuild all its institutions. The painful divorce from
the Soviet Union and the yet-to-be-determined relationship with Moscow preoccupied Kazakh leaders. The nuclear dilemma was only one of many problems, but they understood that it was the most consequential.

To make the pivotal nuclear problem more difficult, Kazakhstan's policymakers did not know exactly what nuclear material remained on Kazakh territory. Nor could they predict how Russia would behave in the nuclear sphere,
nor how much leverage they would have with Moscow. After all, Russia still
was in sole control of the launch apparatus, even though the weapons were in
the territory of a now-sovereign Kazakhstan.

Only a handful of government officials and experts in Kazakhstan understood the enormity of the nuclear dilemma and had any say in resolving it.
President Nazarbayev was the ultimate decision-maker in all matters, and he
relied on his closest advisor, Tulegen Zhukeev. Trained in the technical field of
oil engineering, Zhukeev started his rise in the Communist Party ranks during
the mid-1970s. An intellectual with exceptional memory, he would later represent Kazakhstan in nuclear negotiations with the United States. His American
counterparts would nickname him "the Kazakh Kissinger" for his negotiation
skills.[21]

The nascent foreign ministry, which had only a few diplomats on hand at
the start of Kazakhstan's independence, provided reference material and wrote
memos for Nazarbayev but could not compete with Zhukeev, who had daily
access to the president. William Courtney, the US ambassador to Kazakhstan
in the early 1990s, recalled that "On key denuclearization decisions, it was only
Nazarbayev and Zhukeev. The Foreign Ministry had no role of which I am
aware. Nazarbayev authorized me to talk with Zhukeev. I never talked with
the foreign minister about this."[22] The defense ministry would be set up only
months later, in May 1992, so it was not a factor in Kazakh nuclear policy. Nor
was the nascent parliament, which was weak and conducted no substantive
discussions on the nuclear issue.

Independent policy advice on nuclear questions came from only one
source—the newly formed Center for Strategic Studies, which in 1993 would
be vastly expanded and renamed the Kazakhstan Institute of Strategic Studies
under the President of the Republic of Kazakhstan. Led by Oumirserik Kassenov, my father, the center was the single analytical outlet with enough sophis-
tication to weigh in authoritatively on nuclear matters. Kassenov received his
education in the Soviet Union's elite diplomatic institution, the Moscow State

Institute of International Relations. Fluent in English and well-versed in international affairs, he wrote policy memos for the government which placed Kazakhstan's nuclear dilemma in an international context.

In contrast to the United States, which relied on an interagency group with a wide number of experts and policymakers to deal with the Soviet nuclear questions, Kazakhstan had just a small circle of individuals during this critical moment when consequential nuclear decisions were made. Moreover, that handful were doing it while also trying to build a new nation.

FEELING INSECURE

History teaches that countries seek nuclear weapons when they feel vulnerable and keep them because they believe nuclear weapons make them safer. At its birth, Kazakhstan felt extremely vulnerable. Before declaring independence from the USSR, Nazarbayev had hoped some form of union could be preserved for a simple reason: To keep itself afloat, Kazakhstan depended on the common Soviet market and on economic ties with the republics. A fully integrated Soviet economy meant that all Kazakh industrial enterprises relied on the other republics for spare parts, technology, and other materials, and for markets to which to sell their products as well. But as hope for a meaningful union dwindled, Kazakhstan declared its independence and its leadership focused on strengthening its statehood and protecting its sovereignty.

Catapulted into independence with no military of its own, its state institutions weak and its national borders porous, Kazakhstan worried about looming threats from Russia on one side and China on the other. The new Russian leader, Boris Yeltsin, had hastened the Soviet demise by seeking independence for the Russian Federation, but many in Russia felt humiliated by the fall of the Soviet state and were not ready to accept the loss of the republics. China was growing rapidly and could potentially set its sights on Kazakhstan's vast land and resources to fuel growth. The risk from Kazakhstan's other neighbors—fellow Central Asian states—stemmed from their political and economic instability. Their demise or any severe problems could unsettle the region.

As Kazakhstan's former patron, Russia was now its most worrisome neighbor. Kazakh leaders feared that Moscow would not respect Kazakhstan's sovereignty and might even attempt to seize territory. Kazakhstan's troubled past—a colonial relationship extending back to the seventeenth century, with the last seventy years under Moscow's control which included the bloody crackdown on the *Alash* independence movement in the 1920s and 1930s, Stalin's devastating famine in the early 1930s, and the brutal suppression of anti-Moscow protests in 1986—fueled anxiety. The Soviet government had treated Kazakhstan as a remote land that could be used and abused—be it for siphoning out precious natural resources or conducting nuclear tests that devastated its environment and the health of its people. What could the Kazakhs use in defense against a well-armed neighbor? Certainly, one answer—retaining the nuclear arsenal already on its territory—crossed some minds.

However, Kazakhstan was also a deeply Russified society. Ethnic Kazakhs were a minority of the population, and most ethnic Kazakhs living in urban areas spoke Russian as their first language. Two million ethnic Russians, Ukrainians, and Belarussians had arrived in Kazakhstan in the 1950s, thanks to Nikita Khrushchev's costly "Virgin Lands" campaign to develop traditional pasturelands in northern Kazakhstan into new areas for grain production. By the early 1990s, ethnic Slavs represented more than 60 percent of the population in northern Kazakhstan.

In Russia, nationalists and hard-liners distraught over the Soviet collapse questioned Kazakhstan's right to statehood. They claimed that Kazakhstan was "devoid of self-history" and that it existed only because it had been part of the Russian—and later, Soviet—empire.[23] Aleksandr Solzhenitsyn, a Nobel Prize winner for literature and one of the most well-known dissidents of the Soviet era, had spent time in a hard labor camp in Ekibastuz in Kazakhstan for anti-Stalin comments. Now he added his powerful voice to the idea that Kazakhstan did not merit statehood:

> [Kazakhstan's] present huge territory was stitched together by the communists in a completely haphazard fashion. . . . It had been assembled from southern Siberia and the southern Ural region, plus the sparsely populated central areas which had since that time been transformed and built up by Russians, by inmates of forced-labor camps, and by exiled peoples.[24]

Solzhenitsyn also emphasized how few ethnic Kazakhs there were:

> Today the Kazakhs constitute noticeably less than half the population of the entire inflated territory of Kazakhstan. They are concentrated in their long-standing ancestral domains along a large arc of lands in the south, sweeping from the extreme east westward almost to the Caspian Sea; the population here is indeed predominantly Kazakh. And if it should prove to be their wish to separate within such boundaries, I say Godspeed.[25]

Russian nationalists openly demanded that parts of Kazakhstan with predominantly Russian population should become Russian territory. Within Kazakhstan, a separatist group called *Rus* advocated for Russian annexation of the large city of Ust-Kamenogorsk in northern Kazakhstan.[26]

Vladimir Zhirinovskii, the flamboyant and scandalous leader of the Liberal Democratic Party of Russia, was one of the loudest neo-imperialist voices. Born to an ethnically Jewish father and an ethnically Russian mother in Kazakhstan, Zhirinovskii moved to Russia in the 1960s. Although his obnoxious communication style earned him the nicknames "clown" and "fascist," Zhirinovskii was not an outlier in Russian politics. His offensive rhetoric was not uncommon among some Russian nationalists, and in 1991 he came in third in the presidential election, with more than six million votes.

Russian nationalists' claims on Kazakh territory reverberated loudly inside the republic. Nazarbayev called the nationalists' tactics "not simply tactless" but "extremely dangerous and provocative."[27] When a deputy in the Russian parliament claimed that the Gur'yev (renamed Atyrau in 1991) and Tselinograd (renamed Akmola in 1992) regions of Kazakhstan were "ancient Russian territories," Nazarbayev pushed back:

> Any border claims on Kazakhstan (and indeed any other republic) mean inevitable bloodshed today. I want that to be heard. If some people think that Nazarbayev is behaving in a "friendly" way through fear and that he will allow part of Kazakhstan's territory to be removed, then they are profoundly mistaken.[28]

Deep down, Kazakh leaders worried that Russia could challenge the Soviet-era borders between the republics at any moment. Decades later, in 2014, Russia's annexation of Crimea and war in eastern Ukraine showed that such fears were not ungrounded.

From his vantage point in Moscow, the American ambassador to Russia, Robert Strauss, described the conflicting perspectives: "To Russian politicians, Central Asia represents either the collapse of imperial glory or a rathole down which Russia's resources were thrown for seventy-odd years. Central Asians are suspicious of Russian chauvinism and divide-and-rule tactics."[29]

China presented its own set of territorial anxieties to Kazakhstan. For one, after the Soviet collapse Kazakhstan inherited unresolved Soviet-Chinese border disputes. Kazakhstan and China did not have a fully demarcated border, and Chinese textbooks included maps that showed parts of historically Kazakh land as belonging to China. Another problem was population. While

Kazakhstan's relatively small population of 16 million meant that large swaths of its vast land remained largely uninhabited, China's was increasing by more than 13 million people per year, creating land shortages and demand for more natural resources and food. Not surprisingly, some feared that China might look to Kazakhstan to satisfy those needs. Kazakh officials preferred not to talk openly about the Chinese threat, but Kazakh nationalists and Kazakhstan's analytical community did not shy away from the topic.

These combined external threats hung over discussions about the nuclear arsenal and, to some, made the continued presence of nuclear weapons on Kazakhstan's territory appealing. But the internal situation tipped the scale in the opposite direction.

POLITICS AT HOME

The defining feature of Kazakh domestic politics in the early 1990s was its Soviet-era legacy of centralized decision-making. Elsewhere in the world, political leaders, the nuclear industry, the military, and other groups had a stake in their countries' nuclear policy and a chance to influence policy-making. In Kazakhstan, however, Nazarbayev in consultation with political elites could make decisions.

The voices that were missing in Kazakhstan were the "pronuclear" ones. There were no organized political interest groups that might seek to convince the Kazakh leadership to keep Soviet nuclear weapons or develop a nuclear weapons program with the nuclear material and expertise available. Nor was there a pronuclear scientific or technical establishment. The Soviet-era nuclear sector lost influence following the USSR's disintegration. The disruption of industrial supply-chain ties with other Soviet republics led to the stoppage or the bankruptcy of Kazakhstan's nuclear facilities, including sites that mined uranium, produced nuclear material, and manufactured nuclear fuel components. The industry would remain in critical condition until the mid-1990s. And while Kazakhstan's nuclear facilities were a critical part of the Soviet weapons complex and experts in Kazakhstan knew a lot about nuclear material, they lacked the facilities and technical expertise to maintain, design, or produce nuclear weapons.

As the history of other nuclear states shows, the military usually plays a decisive role in the discourse about nuclear weapons. But in Kazakhstan at that time, the military did not even exist as an independent structure. After the Soviet breakup, Soviet military divisions based in Kazakhstan disbanded or relocated to Russia, and military officers from other Soviet republics left for home.

The lonely voices in support of a nuclear Kazakhstan came from Kazakh nationalist movements and some individual public figures. Those voices may not have been numerous or influential, but they were loud. For example, Kazakh historian Burkitbai Aiaganov strongly subscribed to the pronuclear view. He criticized the lack of clarity on the management and control of nuclear weapons in the framework of the Commonwealth of Independent States (CIS), the loose confederation of post-Soviet republics. He said Russia's future policies were not predictable, and he expressed concern about discussions surrounding the return of Crimea that were underway in the Russian parliament. Given these circumstances, Aiaganov argued, "in order not to squander arsenals" and to guarantee its security, "Kazakhstan should join the nuclear club in the nearest future."[30]

Aiganov reasoned that keeping nuclear weapons would "enable [Kazakhstan] to be equal among other sovereign states." Rebutting arguments that Kazakhstan would undermine its image as a peace-loving and responsible state if it kept nuclear weapons, Aiaganov wrote: "Nuclear weapons do not stop France or the UK from being considered civilized . . . other countries do not respect them less."[31]

He also saw economic and social benefits to keeping the weapons. With the republic's empty coffers, he argued, "It would be the ultimate profligacy to spend money on relocating the weapons. It is easier and more economically sound to keep them where they are." Regarding personnel involved in uranium production, including their families, Aiaganov further asked, "Where would they go?"[32]

Most Kazakh-language media did not shy away from publishing these and other pronuclear sentiments, but this perspective was nowhere near so powerful as in other states, including Ukraine. As Larry Napper, the US official in charge of post-Soviet affairs at the State Department at the time, put it: "Nazarbayev was in control of the internal situation in Kazakhstan in a way that Kravchuk [the president of Ukraine] was not."[33]

Popular opinion was even more important than the absence of political groups in rendering Kazakhstan antinuclear. The psychological scars from forty years of nuclear tests, with their environmental and health devastation, ran deep among the public. The nuclear weapons remaining in Kazakhstan served as painful reminders of decades of radioactive contamination, earthquakes caused by underground nuclear tests, many induced illnesses, and excessive death.

A NEWCOMER TO THE WORLD

Aside from security and domestic issues, Kazakh leaders also considered Kazakhstan's international reputation as they mulled the nuclear question. Tulegen Zhukeev described the general sentiment in Kazakhstan at the time: "We did not want to be a pariah state."[34]

For seven decades under Soviet rule, Kazakhstan had been largely invisible. To use the phrase of British historian Christopher Robbins, Kazakhstan had become "the land that disappeared."[35] The Silk Road, which for centuries had connected trade routes from the Korean Peninsula to the Mediterranean Sea, vanished during the Ottoman Empire. From the Bolshevik revolution to 1991, Central Asian republics were swallowed up by the Soviet government. Because of extensive test ranges and other military facilities, much of Kazakhstan was off-limits to foreign travelers.

Kazakhstan's access to the outside world lay only through Moscow, both literally and figuratively. No international flights left from or landed in Alma-Ata, Kazakhstan's capital. On the rare occasions that people from Kazakhstan traveled abroad, they had to go to Moscow to board international flights. The revenue from natural resources mined in Kazakhstan went first to Moscow, which then decided how the profit would be spent and what small part of it would return to Kazakhstan.

Ethnically, Kazakhstan and the rest of Central Asia hardly existed for the outside world. Despite the official Soviet emphasis on interethnic harmony, non-Slavic ethnicities were often relegated to secondary roles both within Soviet society and in the country's international profile. Except for propaganda booklets, non-Slavic voices hardly featured in political and economic discourse, even though they constituted more than a third of the Soviet population. Quite tellingly, promotional materials for Aeroflot, the flagship of Soviet civil aviation, displayed only Slavic-looking pilots and flight attendants.

Once the walls separating it from the international community began to crumble, Kazakhstan sought access to or membership in key international institutions, including the United Nations, the World Bank, and the International Monetary Fund, among others. The impetus was to save and reform the Kazakh economy, which was in shambles after the Soviet collapse and the consequent rupture of all-union production and supply ties. Simply put, Kazakhstan needed direct foreign investment, foreign expertise, and access to advanced technologies.

To access and attract foreign resources, Kazakh leaders knew their republic had to be seen as a responsible player in the world community. And saying "no" to nuclear weapons would fit strongly into that image. The stakes were great. Kazakhstan was rich in oil, gas, and other materials, and it could earn foreign currency by selling them in world markets. But Kazakhstan would need foreign investors and expertise to take fuller advantage of its resource bounty.

Paramount among Kazakhstan's oil resources was Tengiz, the world's sixth-largest oil field with estimated reserves of 25 billion barrels. For several years, the Kremlin had been negotiating a potential deal with a US company to develop Tengiz. Now the newly independent Kazakhstan sought to reach a direct deal with Chevron, the US oil giant, to develop Tengiz and receive much-needed cash to boost the Kazakh economy.

Kazakhstan was blessed with other valuable natural resources, such as copper and uranium, which could be developed and exported, further helping to strengthen Kazakhstan's economy. But as with oil, prospects for these projects depended on whether the government could secure international investment, technology, and access to foreign markets. Kazakh leaders understood that Kazakhstan's integration into the world economy could only happen if the country did not cling to nuclear weapons.

GLOBAL NUCLEAR ORDER

Considerations beyond Kazakhstan's immediate interests also played a role in the government's decision-making. Kazakhstan's Center for Strategic Studies had carefully observed developments on the international nuclear scene and concluded that Kazakhstan's decision on the nuclear issue could have a profound effect on the Treaty of Non-Proliferation of Nuclear Weapons (NPT), the only international treaty that codified states' nuclear behavior.

The 1968 treaty, which had been drafted mainly by the United States and the Soviet Union, bifurcated the world into nuclear-weapon states and non-nuclear-weapon states. The treaty established that only countries which tested nuclear weapons before 1967—France, China, the Soviet Union, the United Kingdom, and the United States—could become nuclear-weapon states. The United States, the Soviet Union, and the United Kingdom joined the NPT at its inception. Two other countries that tested nuclear weapons before 1967—China and France—waited until 1992 to join the treaty. The vast majority of the rest of the world's countries joined the treaty as non-nuclear-weapon states.

The treaty was designed to prevent the spread of nuclear weapons by means of a grand bargain. The nuclear powers promised that they would help countries without nuclear weapons to develop peaceful nuclear technology and that they would eventually disarm. The countries without nuclear weapons, in return, promised never to seek a bomb.

In early 1992, when Kazakh experts analyzed Kazakhstan's nuclear options, they could not be certain whether the NPT would even continue to exist. At an NPT Review Conference scheduled for 1995 in New York, the treaty members were to decide whether the agreement would be extended indefinitely, extended for a limited period, or scrapped altogether. But analysts from the Center for Strategic Studies noted that the treaty was showing signs of unraveling before the conference took place. For example, before China and France had signed the NPT in 1992, they remained free of the constraints it imposed on nuclear powers. China was continuing to test nuclear weapons at the Lop Nor testing site, a mere 1,100 kilometers (700 miles) from Kazakhstan's capital. India and Pakistan, two of Kazakhstan's nuclear-armed wider regional neighbors, did not have any plans to give up their weapons and join the NPT as non-nuclear-weapon states. (Neither could join the NPT as nuclear states as they did not test nuclear weapons before 1967. India conducted what it called a "peaceful nuclear test" in 1974, and Pakistan had been working on a nuclear weapon only since the 1970s.)

Even if the NPT's future were to be secured at the Review Conference with a limited or unlimited extension, its fundamental weaknesses, acutely felt in Kazakhstan, would not go away. Besides the difficulties noted above, the treaty, which was purportedly designed to make a nonnuclear path attractive to countries, failed to provide legally binding "negative security guarantees" that could ensure the attractiveness of a nonnuclear path. That is, the NPT lacked provisions that bound the nuclear powers not to use or threaten to use nuclear force against non-nuclear-weapon states.[36]

Kazakh analysts agreed with another major criticism of the NPT. Many countries that committed to not seeking nuclear weapons saw the NPT as unfairly benefiting states that already had nuclear weapons. By the 1990s, more than two decades after the treaty's arrival, countries with nuclear weapons had made insufficient progress toward their promised disarmament. Meanwhile, countries without nuclear weapons felt growing international pressure to comply with nonproliferation obligations, such as by accepting increasingly strict controls on the flows of sensitive goods and technologies. These controls complicated access to nuclear technology for peaceful use.

Nevertheless, despite the weaknesses and inequities of the NPT, Kazakhstan did not want to undermine the treaty, particularly at the critical juncture when its extension was being considered. Oumirserik Kassenov of the Center for Strategic Studies warned that, should Kazakhstan become a nuclear-armed state, it would create a dangerous precedent for "nuclear threshold" countries—nations that possess sufficient nuclear technology to quickly develop nuclear weapons but that haven't built them yet—and could furnish them with an additional excuse to go nuclear. Also, he believed, a nuclear Kazakhstan would add one more member to the nuclear club, which would itself inevitably add to global nuclear instability.[37]

There was an additional practical reason Kazakhstan's decision-makers were keen for their country to join the NPT as a non-nuclear-weapon state. Kazakhstan, blessed with uranium and eager to develop its civilian nuclear program, could only expect to receive international assistance in the nuclear field if it became a non-nuclear-weapon state.

SCENARIOS FOR THE KAZAKH NUCLEAR FUTURE

It was in this atmosphere of uncertainty about sovereignty, of economic crisis, and of popular antinuclear sentiment that Kazakhs deliberated their options. Chapter 5 explored the scenarios developed by Harvard analysts for the possible nuclear outcomes in Russia and the three nuclear republics in the post-Soviet world. In an analogous effort, analysts at the Center for Strategic Studies performed a similar exercise with respect to Kazakhstan. They advised the Kazakh leadership on the advantages and disadvantages of the options available: keeping the nuclear weapons; sharing custody of the weapons with the Commonwealth of Independent States (CIS) or Russia; or becoming a nuclear-free state.[38]

Scenario 1: Keeping the Nuclear Weapons

Under this scenario, the analysts surmised, control over nuclear weapons deployed in Kazakhstan would be transferred to its government, and the country would become a nuclear-armed state. This option, however, was not so straightforward as simply retaining and deploying the Soviet Union's leftover nuclear weapons.

Kazakhstan did not have access to the command-and-control operations of the Soviet nuclear weapons, and Kazakh decision-makers and analysts understood that fact well.[39] Throughout the Cold War, predominantly ethnic-Slav military forces exercised full physical and command control over the nuclear weapons deployed in Kazakhstan. These troops guarded the weapons, and Moscow controlled the silos where weapons and delivery systems were kept. After the collapse, Russian troops continued to control the weapons, even if formally the weapons were now on the territory of an independent Kazakhstan. Any attempt by Kazakhstan to gain control of the weapons by force could have ended in military conflict between Kazakhstan and Russia—suicide for a young country with fragile statehood and no military of its own. Moreover, as home to more Russians than Kazakhs at the time, Kazakhstan could find itself in a civil war between its two main ethnic groups should relations with Russia turn violent.

Even if Kazakhstan somehow gained physical control over the weapons, it would be unable to launch or service them. The Kazakh government had no access to the Soviet-era nuclear command system, and it lacked expertise in the maintenance, repair, and overhaul of nuclear weapons. Ethnic Slavs, mostly from Russia and Ukraine, made up most of the Soviet nuclear weapons workforce.

Theoretically, both China and Russia could threaten Kazakhstan with a nuclear attack or at least with advanced conventional military weapons. Kazakhstan could not compete with either country in either mode of attack. The Soviet strategic nuclear weapons it now possessed were designed to be launched across the ocean and would be useless in the regional conflicts that Kazakhstan most feared.

Further, the policy analysts argued, controlling nuclear weapons could decrease Kazakhstan's security. Kassenov wrote that the international community, especially Kazakhstan's neighbors, would view a nuclear-armed Kazakhstan as a potential adversary.[40] He warned that "If drawn into a nuclear conflict of any sort, Kazakhstan faces a greater risk of being turned into ashes, being a nuclear state, than if it remains a non-nuclear one. There is absolutely no point in bringing the nuclear weapons into play even with purely defensive intentions in mind."[41]

There was only one security benefit that nuclear weapons could bring Kazakhstan, policy experts concluded. The physical presence of nuclear weapons in Kazakhstan provided what they described as existential deterrence—it would make other countries think twice before attempting to threaten Kazakhstan.

Scenario 2: Nuclear Weapons under CIS or Kazakh-Russian Control

The second scenario involved joint control of the nuclear arsenal, either by the CIS or by Russia and Kazakhstan. Since the CIS consisted of the former Soviet states, its control over nuclear weapons could provide Kazakhstan with the continuity of existing security arrangements. However, the creation of such a shared nuclear deterrent faced challenges due to the uncertain status of the CIS itself and the different positions of its participants.

The main challenge of a joint CIS command would be the establishment of a clear procedure and means for collective decision-making for launching a nuclear attack. In the first days of the Soviet collapse, all parties to the CIS agreed that the decision on the use of nuclear weapons would be taken by Russia's president in agreement with the presidents of Belarus, Kazakhstan, and Ukraine.[42] Technically speaking, however, there were no practical means for any of the three non-Russian presidents to prevent a launch. This meant that under this scenario, Kazakhstan would run the risk of being involved in an accidental or nonsanctioned nuclear war.

Kassenov concluded, "It was much easier to *declare* a united nuclear policy than to make it a reality."[43] He suggested that if the CIS collective security mechanism, which Kazakhstan initially preferred, did not stand the test of time, Kazakhstan would need to think of other ways of obtaining security guarantees. One option was a defense treaty with Russia. In such a scenario, the weapons would remain in Kazakhstan, and the Kazakh leadership would receive the technical means to prevent a nuclear launch against its interests. This arrangement could have been a viable option—if not for the loud, nationalist calls within Russia to revise borders. As Kassenov warned in a 1992 memo:

> There is a chance that during political and economic instability, supporters of Bolshevik empire could take power [which] could create a paradoxical situation. Kazakhstan [is] in a defense treaty with Russia, [but] Russia controls the weapons on Kazakhstan's territory and at the same time [makes] territorial claims using force or threat of force.[44]

As it would turn out, the idea of a combined CIS command was discussed between Kazakhstan and Russia but was deemed not feasible. Apparently, Yeltsin said that Russia could not agree to a joint command with Kazakhstan because it would violate its international commitments, including under the NPT, and it would cause serious negative resonance in the world. In 1994, Kazakhstan and Russia agreed that nuclear weapons on the territory of Kazakhstan were Russian.

Scenario 3: A Nuclear-Free Kazakhstan

From the very beginning of Kazakhstan's independence, its policy analysts viewed a nuclear-free state as the most attractive option both for the country and for the international community. But they also warned that should

Kazakhstan choose a nuclear-free path, its government would have to think well and hard about how to guarantee Kazakhstan's security. Obtaining security guarantees from nuclear powers—namely, commitments not to threaten Kazakhstan and to help it if it were threatened by a third country—would have to be a priority.

A more practical concern was technical expertise. Although keeping the weapons presented significant technical hurdles for Kazakhstan, dismantling or removing them presented an equally serious challenge. How would a country that had never handled nuclear weapons oversee these tasks, and perform them safely? (Safety was a major concern; the still-palpable trauma of radioactive contamination from nuclear testing intensified Kazakhs' fears of nuclear accidents.) Also, in times of severe economic crisis, how could Kazakhstan pay for such elaborate operations?

This was the menu that Kazakh analysts presented their government. What would Kazakhstan choose to do? For the next two years, Washington waited anxiously as US diplomats actively attempted to influence decision-making by the young Central Asian state. Meanwhile, Nazarbayev, Zhukeev, and a handful of advisors devised ways to build their country. The two-year courtship saw the emergence of William Courtney, the first US ambassador to Kazakhstan, as a key interlocutor in the negotiations, as well as a pivotal trip to Washington by Nazarbayev.

CHAPTER 7

A TEMPORARY NUCLEAR POWER

It's not clear what will happen in Russia. In China, some of their books show part of our territory as Chinese. To the south is fundamentalism. What are we to do? That is why we wish to be close to the US. This is why we wanted to remain temporarily a nuclear state.

—Nursultan Nazarbayev, 1992

"ARE YOU INTERESTED IN BEING AN AMBASSADOR?" Larry Napper made informal inquiries like this to colleagues and friends in his diplomatic circle. "I started looking for all my old friends who were in the foreign service and had experience in the former Soviet Union, who spoke Russian or one of the other post-Soviet languages. I called them wherever they were: 'Would you like to be an ambassador?' And they said: 'Well, sure. Where?'"[1]

Napper, who had been appointed Director of Soviet Affairs at the State Department a mere two weeks before the attempted coup in Moscow, watched the Soviet Union unravel before his eyes. Napper had placed his calls within a day of the Soviet Union's dissolution on Christmas Day of 1991, per Secretary Baker's instructions. The secretary had been clear:

> I want to establish an American embassy in all these places within ninety days. And by the way, we do not want to go to Congress and ask for the budget supplemental to do that. You have to find means within your own resources to do it.[2]

The disintegrating Soviet Union left fifteen new states in its wake. The State Department somehow had to find resources to establish fifteen new embassies and find fifteen new ambassadors. Napper and his staff drafted recommendations for these ambassadorial positions, which made their way up the chain of command at the State Department. The "D Committee," chaired by the deputy secretary, made recommendations and the State Department submitted them to the White House.[3]

After President Bush approved selections, the Director General of the Foreign Service informed the candidates that the President would nominate them to the Senate for advice and consent. In a break with standard diplomatic practice, Baker sent the nominees to post before the Senate acted on their nominations. Baker saw an urgent need to set up new embassies as a way to reinforce US support for the sovereingty and independence of the fifteen post-Soviet states. Days earlier, small advance parties had already been sent to capitals to begin preparations.

The Department of State dispatched its teams with cash and satellite phones. The cash was needed because checks and credit cards could not be used. The new posts in non-Russian republics had shoestring budgets because of Baker's directive not to seek additional funds for the embassies from Congress.[4] They received instructions to find the best hotels they could get and rent adjacent rooms: one for the chancery and others for a few American personnel.

Once the advance teams reached their destinations and secured hotel rooms, the US government dispatched a transport plane from Edwards Air Force Base in southern California to Central Asia, with a stopover at the US air base in Incirlik, Turkey.

The plane's cargo included several room-sized pallets for different countries. Each pallet contained an embassy start-up kit: communications equipment, a TacSat antenna, several laptop computers, a typewriter, State Department forms, a flag, a small supply of US military meals ready to eat (MREs), and a seal with the national symbol, the bald eagle. Napper described those early days of the American presence in Central Asia:

> We landed in Almaty, Dushanbe, Tashkent. We would push one of those pallets off, and US personnel would meet us at the airport with old Soviet trucks and some laborers. We would stay with them for a day, have a little opening, invite the media and cut the ribbon of the hotel room door and say: "American Embassy!"[5]

For Napper, an American embassy was a tangible place, as opposed to words written on a piece of paper about the US relationship with Kazakhstan. As he described it, putting an embassy on the ground was a concrete step with an important symbolic meaning: "This is an independent country which the United States recognizes by having American diplomats to conduct a relationship appropriate for two independent nations."[6]

When the Soviet Union dissolved, Washington was quick to position itself as a supporter of the former Soviet republics as they began their journey into sovereignty. The United States was the first country to recognize Kazakhstan's independence, for example, doing so in a letter from President Bush to President Nazarbayev just ten days after the independence declaration.[7]

The letter from Bush also reflected US anxiety about the fate of Soviet weapons. Bush asked Nazarbayev "to ensure safe, responsible, and reliable control over nuclear weapons under a single authority . . . during and after transition."[8] Two days later, Bush sent another letter to Nazarbayev, this one subtly suggesting a linkage between US humanitarian aid and Kazakhstan's military expenditures:

> We would like to stay in close touch as we seek to mobilize the international community to help meet your near-term requirements for food, medical supplies, energy, and shelter. As we move to cooperate on these issues, it is important that the resources you devote to your military establishment be kept at the lowest possible level. I believe it is in our mutual interest to have as much transparency as possible in the plans and budgets for your military forces, to a degree comparable to what the U.S. makes public annually.[9]

In early January 1992, US Treasury Secretary Nicholas Brady declared US support for Kazakhstan (and the other republics) to join the International Monetary Fund (IMF) and the World Bank.[10] This was a huge step for Central Asia's economies; US support was critical for gaining access to these major institutions.

The American embassy opened at the beginning of February, only a few weeks after Kazakhstan proclaimed its independence. The first ambassador was William Courtney, a career diplomat well versed in nuclear matters. The offer of the post took Courtney by surprise. He had spent the previous four years in US-Soviet nuclear and space arms talks in Geneva, and in January 1992 he had gone to Moscow as cochair of the US government team engaged in early negotiations with the Russians on the safety and security of nuclear weapons. On his first day back in the office in Washington, he received a call from Ambassador Ed Perkins, the top personnel officer at the State Department. "President Bush has approved you as the nominee for ambassador to Kazakhstan." Unlike some fellow nominees, Courtney had no inkling that such an offer was coming: "I was dumbfounded," he said.[11]

Courtney accepted and eight days later arrived in Alma-Ata. It was Kazakhstan's first winter of independence—a time of deep economic crisis amid the Soviet collapse. Government coffers across the former Soviet space were empty. People were not receiving their salaries; pension payments were delayed. Babushkas were selling personal possessions on the streets—old books, knickknacks—as well as *pirozhki* (fried pastries filled with mashed potatoes or cabbage), cigarettes, chewing gum, and chocolate bars—anything to make a little bit of income. One of the first things Courtney bought was a Snickers bar, from one of those babushkas. "It was completely frozen," he remembers.

The embassy occupied several rooms in Alma-Ata's tallest building—the twenty-six-story Hotel Kazakhstan. That structure, an achievement of Soviet modern architecture and engineering, towered above the city, looking royal with a crown-like roof. It was built on a special platform to keep it standing in case of earthquake—a possibility in the seismically unstable capital city.

Right next to the hotel was another architectural gem—the Palace of Culture, built in 1970. The architects decided on a unified structure of 10,000 square meters (107,000 square feet) under a single roof. The roof consisted of aluminum scales painted in gold. The roof rested not on the building's wall but on eight independently built reinforced cement columns, a trick that made the building more seismic-proof. The palace, which could fit up to 3,000 people, hosted two kinds of gatherings—Kazakh Communist Party congresses and huge concerts of Soviet pop stars. Also nearby, diagonally across from the hotel and situated at one of Alma-Ata's busiest intersections, sat Kazakhstan's first Western-style business school (now a university), known as KIMEP. It was housed in the former Higher Party School, where Communist leaders received continuing education.

One of the rented hotel rooms held the embassy's communications equipment, with the TacSat antenna mounted on the balcony. Courtney lived in a suite on the twenty-fifth floor, from which he could enjoy views of the city and of the snow-capped Tian Shan mountains, Central Asia's largest mountain range stretching along Kazakhstan, Kyrgyzstan, and China. The suite served both as residence and meeting room. The Iranian ambassador lived across the hall, but the two were not allowed to talk due to tensions in the bilateral relationship. Courtney called the hotel home for fourteen months.[12]

Because Courtney had participated in the US-Soviet arms control process, he had followed Kazakhstan from a distance. He was familiar with it as the locale of the Soviet nuclear test site, the missile test site at Baikonur, the anti-aircraft and antimissile test site at Sary-Shagan, and two fields of giant SS-18 intercontinental ballistic missiles (ICBMs).

When he arrived in Kazakhstan, he was struck by how welcoming everyone was: "In Moscow, Western diplomats were accustomed to cautious Russian officials who were less than communicative. In Kazakhstan, both Russians and Kazakhs were much more open and friendly, even excited to have foreigners opening up embassies." Ambassador Courtney recalled with warmth: "I was on TV a lot those days. Kazakhs invited me often, perhaps as a way to show that the newly independent country had gained international recognition, including from great power America."[13]

The Kazakh government was pleased to have an American embassy set up, but at first inertia followed the Soviet-style rules of engagement. In the Soviet era, American diplomats in Moscow had to file a note to the Ministry of Foreign Affairs before being allowed to venture beyond the city. The Kazakh Foreign Ministry initially planned to impose a similar rule but dropped it after learning that this was not standard diplomatic practice in most countries. It was one of many examples showing that "despite instinctive Soviet-style responses, Kazakhs were more flexible and open."[14]

To hire local employees, the newly established embassy ran an advertisement in the largest newspaper, *Kazakhstanskaia Pravda*. On seeing this advertising, a top old-school foreign ministry official called Ambassador Courtney to express his concern: "You will only get riff-raff. Why didn't you come to us for help with hiring?" Courtney explained: "That's not how we work."[15]

Most of the applicants for the embassy's office positions were women fluent in English, graduates of Alma-Ata's Institute of Foreign Languages. Men mostly applied for security jobs and other positions that did not require English fluency.

Courtney's Kazakh counterpart, State Counselor Tulegen Zhukeev, described him as "the strongest, most effective American ambassador of all we had." In praising Courtney, Zhukeev said: "He had a good role—to be the first ambassador. Energetic, fluent in Russian, hard-working. He understood the problems very well. I would go as far as to say, among many factors that contributed to the US position to support Kazakhstan's independence, Courtney personally contributed a lot."[16] With an embassy in place, the United States moved quickly to establish direct links with the new Kazakhstan.

From the beginning, obtaining security guarantees from the United States and other major powers—a promise not to threaten Kazakhstan with nuclear weapons and to help it if it found itself threatened by others—was the number one item on Kazakhstan's agenda. In every interaction with Americans,

Nazarbayev and his advisors described their sense of insecurity, stemming from their complicated geopolitical situation.

Early on, Kazakh officials hoped they could get all-encompassing security guarantees from the United States—a commitment similar to what it was ready to do if a fellow NATO member faced an external threat. An attack on one is an attack on all, in NATO parlance. For Americans, this expectation was a non-starter, and the negotiations focused on a narrower promise—a commitment not to use (or threaten to use) nuclear weapons against countries that do not have them and a promise of consultation in case of an external attack.

Also important to Nazarbayev and his government was direct foreign investment. They knew Kazakhstan had rich oil resources that foreign investors and companies could help develop. Oil promised Kazakhstan wealth, but the country did not have the technology to retrieve it. At Tengiz, for example, oil was deep underground under a salt dome, and was mixed with a substantial sulfurous compound which was not easy to separate. Soviet technology had been unable to exploit the Tengiz reserve of valuable light oil.

More broadly, the entire economic future of this new republic partially depended on whether a range of foreign companies with modern technology, especially but not just oil firms, would invest in Kazakhstan. For Kazakhs, American investment also bought security. With business interests in Kazakhstan, the American government would be more invested in the country's political and economic future.

Before committing to a nonnuclear path, Kazakhs sought security guarantees from nuclear powers, American economic investment, and American recognition and support for Kazakh independence. For their part, the Americans were ready to help the newly independent nation with its immediate needs, but with conditions attached. In return for investments and political support, they expected the Kazakhs to renounce Soviet nuclear weapons.

However, the Kazakh president and his team were sending mixed messages about their intentions regarding the nuclear inheritance. Their public strategy boiled down to "do not rush." Outsiders struggled to discern whether Nazarbayev was ready to commit his country to a nonnuclear status, and Washington was worried.

The nuclear question was perhaps the most challenging and complicated that Nazarbayev's fledgling country had to confront. Not only was it geographically surrounded by nuclear powers Russia and China, but there was also the question of what might be Kazakhstan's relationship to the whole raft of nuclear-related treaties—the US-Soviet strategic arms reduction pact known as START, the Treaty on the Non-Proliferation of Nuclear Weapons (NPT), a collective security treaty among the former Soviet nations, and more. Barely a few months old, Kazakhstan had to joust with the major powers over these agreements, all the while seeking foreign investors to put the resource-rich nation on a firm economic footing.

MIXED SIGNALS

In one of his first cables to Washington, Ambassador Courtney warned that if nuclear weapons were still in Kazakhstan during any conflict, be it ethnic, internal, or regional, their presence would increase the danger to US friends and US interests in the region.[17]

Initially, Courtney believed there was a lack of consensus in Kazakhstan on the nuclear question:

> Some in Kazakhstan express the view that nuclear weapons could enhance the country's security or status, e.g., by deterring Russia from using intimidation or coercion to reacquire predominantly Russian areas, by giving Kazakhstan a regional or Muslim leadership role it would not otherwise have, and by ensuring greater powers will deal with Kazakhstan as something more than an isolated, less-developed, third-world state. But others acknowledge that nuclear weapons will have no usable military value for Kazakhstan.[18]

In reality, Nazarbayev and his inner circle understood earlier than they manifested to their interlocutors that they would not want and, more critically, would not be able to hold onto their nuclear weapons. Their strategy was to obtain maximum benefit from the United States in return for eventual denuclearization, including commitment to Kazakhstan's security. To achieve that, Nazarbayev played hard to get. Offering to denuclearize upfront might have made Washington stingier with its offers of aid and less attentive to Kazakhstan's security needs.

Nazarbayev kept external observers guessing with statements that Washington scrutinized for clues and that Moscow frowned upon. In February 1992, for example, Nazarbayev announced that Kazakhstan would eliminate its weapons only if Russia and other powers would do so.[19] That month Russia's foreign minister, Andrei Kozyrev, complained that "Kazakhstan's position on the NPT [was] still unclear." Kozyrev argued that Kazakhstan, as well as Belarus and Ukraine, could not be called "nuclear states."[20]

When Nazarbayev met with Courtney in March 1992 to discuss nuclear issues, he again sent a mixed signal. The Kazakh leader assured him that Kazakhstan would not help any foreign country to acquire nuclear weapons: "I give you my guarantee that we will not transfer any nuclear weapons, technology, or materials."[21] Nazarbayev made it clear that Kazakhstan did not plan to remain a nuclear power over the long term. But, at the same time, he told the American ambassador that security concerns weighed heavily on his mind, mentioning both ascendant China and the Islamic fundamentalist groups on Kazakhstan's southern borders.

Nazarbayev also reassured Courtney that Kazakhstan would reduce the number of nuclear weapons on its territory in accordance with the arms control treaties that the Soviet Union had signed with the United States. But here too Nazarbayev added a serious caveat—any reductions would have to be mirrored by Russia, Belarus, and Ukraine. Nazarbayev estimated it would take his country fifteen to twenty years to eliminate nuclear weapons from its territory. Dismantling each missile silo would cost up to a billion rubles, Nazarbayev estimated, roughly $12.5 million at the time.

He asked Courtney: "Where will the money come from?"

"Would you still need 15 to 20 years if you received international [security] guarantees?" Courtney responded, with a question of his own.

"There would be no need to wait that long," Nazarbayev replied.[22]

On the issue that most preoccupied the US government—whether Kazakhstan would formally commit to the NPT—Nazarbayev had a disappointing answer for Courtney. According to Nazarbayev's reading of the NPT, Kazakhstan could not sign onto the treaty as a non-nuclear-weapon state.[23] Why? Because nuclear tests were carried out on its territory before 1968, Nazarbayev explained.[24] He and his advisors argued that this testing put Kazakhstan in the same category as the five NPT-recognized nuclear powers–the Soviet Union, the United States, China, France, and the United Kingdom.[25]

This Kazakh position was essentially a legal argument supporting the notion that Kazakhstan had every right to the weapons stored on its territory. "We did not want to come across as spoiled brats who brandish deadly weapons and insist for no reason that they have a full stake in the nuclear debate," Zhukeev explained. "We tried to use all legal, political, and moral justifications to prove it. It was verbal tightrope walking if you will."[26]

A few days after his conversation with Courtney, Nazarbayev gave an interview to an Italian newspaper, *La Stampa*, that caused a stir in Washington. He stated, "Kazakhstan did not become an atomic power by its own will. . . . We want to become a denuclearized state and we have closed Semipalatinsk. But as regards the strategic missiles, we have asked for the status quo." Still hopeful that the former Soviet republics would have a common defense policy, Nazarbayev added, "Common sense requires that the reduction in strategic nuclear forces should be in line with the defensive needs of the Commonwealth [of Independent States], notions which unfortunately do not for the moment exist."[27]

Closely watching developments in Kazakhstan was Susan Koch, Director for Defense Policy and Arms Control at the National Security Council in Washington. On learning about the *La Stampa* interview, she wrote a memorandum to her colleagues with the title, "Kazakhstan as [a] Nuclear State?" She included a handwritten note: "In case you thought that things weren't out of control."[28] This memorandum reflected Washington's uncertainty around Kazakhstan's mixed messages.

Ambassador Courtney also was alarmed, sending cables to Washington reporting that Kazakhstan's leaders had insisted on the country's right to join the NPT as a nuclear-weapon state. Courtney wrote that "various officials have stated or implied this intention since the Embassy opened."[29] He cited as an example a recent NATO defense meeting in Brussels in which Kazakhstan had participated as an observer: "We suspected that Kazakhstan chose [observer] status to avoid dissenting from the meeting's agreed public statement on NPT that would have noted [the] intention of the (former Soviet) states to join the NPT as non-nuclear states."[30] Courtney also described an expert symposium in Alma-Ata at which he "witnessed a spirited exchange on the nuclear issue," with Kazakh participants arguing that Kazakhstan had a right to keep Soviet nuclear weapons:

> Arguments by Western participants that the Kazakhs neither controlled the weapons nor had a technical or economic base to support them did not seem to make a dent. Kazakh speakers retorted that the U.S., U.K., and France retained numerous weapons even though they were not threatened by anyone. By contrast, Kazakhstan faced serious threats from its neighbors. . . . These exchanges were the most controversial, with neither side giving any ground.[31]

Three weeks before President Bush welcomed Nazarbayev to Washington, the Kazakh president continued transmitting his mixed signals both in private conversations with US officials and in the press. The Kazakh leader told the *Christian Science Monitor* that he had written a letter to the American president expressing Kazakhstan's intention to become a non-nuclear-weapon state, but also proposing that Kazakhstan be considered a "temporary nuclear power" until its nuclear warheads were removed. He also reflected on Kazakhstan's security concerns:

> We do not know today what will happen to the Commonwealth of Independent States. . . . We don't have a normal state-to-state treaty with Russia. Nobody knows what will happen to the leadership of Russia in the future. Seventy kilometers [43 miles] from this place, China is testing her nuclear weapons. . . . We are prepared to proceed with the [total] reduction of nuclear weapons, but we want to be a participant in the negotiating process.[32]

Nazarbayev could not hide his irritation at the US focus on Kazakhstan's NPT status:

> I just don't understand why there is such pressure on Kazakhstan. Why doesn't the U.S. demand that China join this treaty [NPT] or force India to join it?[33]

In the *Monitor* article, the Kazakh president also reiterated Kazakhstan's quest for security guarantees and how receiving them would make its leadership feel differently about giving up nuclear weapons:

> Kazakhstan would feel better about this question . . . if it . . . had a guarantee of the inviolability of its territorial integrity, that it won't come under nuclear attack from the U.S., Russia, or China. Baker told me that according to the 1968 [NPT] treaty, the U.S. could take upon itself responsibility for this.[34]

Kazakhstan's leading newspaper, *Kazakhstanskaia Pravda*,[35] and Russia's major newspaper, *Izvestiia*, republished the *Monitor* interview. The interview and its reprints in the Kazakh press took Ambassador Courtney by surprise, mainly because he had not seen the letter Nazarbayev wrote to Bush. It might be that the letter was going through the Kazakh foreign policy bureaucracy and had not reached Courtney yet. He wrote to Washington: "After incubating largely out of public eye, Kazakhstan's nuclear policy burst forth today, April 29, in the nation's controlled press."[36] Courtney did not have a good feeling about it:

> It is a bad omen that Nazarbayev has publicly expressed Kazakhstan's position before offering the U.S. the courtesy of a private reply [to questions from Americans about Kazakhstan's intentions]. It is unlikely that Nazarbayev has

left enough of an opening to enable quiet diplomacy to get Kazakhstan to come off of its "temporary nuclear power" tack by the time of his visit to Washington in May.[37]

Earlier that day, Courtney had gone to Alma-Ata's international airport to meet Turkey's prime minister, Suleyman Demirel, who was making an official visit to Kazakhstan. Nazarbayev, who was also at the airport to greet the Turkish guest, asked Courtney: "Did you receive the letter [for President Bush]?" Courtney responded that he had not seen it, and Kazakh foreign minister Tuleitai Suleimenov promised that Courtney would get the letter the next day. Courtney recorded in his cable for Washington, "I told Suleimenov, and the Prime Minister with whom I had been speaking, that we hoped the letter would put aside the nuclear issue by pledging Kazakh willingness to adhere to the NPT as a non-nuclear-weapon state. Of course, the letter will say no such thing."[38]

That evening, at a reception for Demirel, Courtney confessed to Nazarbayev's chief of staff, Nurtai Abykaev, that he was puzzled by Nazarbayev's position, which was "revealed so fully in the press today." Courtney asked Abykaev whether Kazakhs actually thought Russia would leave behind missiles that could be pointed at Russia. That night Courtney relayed to Washington that "I noted that even if nuclear weapons were left behind, without technical support from Russia, they would become a safety risk in a matter of months. Had Kazakh officials thought about this? Walking out of the dinner with the defense minister, I made the same points to him."[39] Although the answers Courtney got are unknown, both Nazarbayev and Zhukeev had thought about all this but were reluctant to rush giving up their "nuclear card."

During those months, Nazarbayev and Zhukeev got to know Courtney well. Zhukeev and Courtney especially interacted a lot and developed respect for each other and appreciated that each promoted his country's national interests with conviction. Zhukeev described how important it was for newly independent Kazakhstan to assert its interests: "We always tried to prove to everyone that we had our own position, that we were guided by our national interests, not Russian, not American, only ours." Courtney remembers those interactions as "very direct," diplomat-speak for what Zhukeev described more bluntly as "we fought a lot." Courtney recounted that "Kazakhstan's leadership wondered, did they really have to give up nuclear weapons, whether the United States would mind if they did not. And we said, 'Yes, we would really mind,' and that was absolutely critical."[40]

Kazakh leaders knew that Moscow and Washington shared the view that Kazakhstan could have only a non-nuclear-weapon state status and should join the NPT as such, and Alma-Ata was under no illusions that those opinions would ever change. Kazakhstan's Foreign Minister Suleimenov wrote in his memos to President Nazarbayev, "Americans let us know they would not hesitate to use political and economic measures to put pressure on Kazakhstan."[41]

Nazarbayev continued to send his mixed, worrisome signals to Washington. In a May 1992 interview with the Russian newspaper *Nezavisimaia Gazeta*, he repeated his claim that the pre-1968 nuclear tests in Kazakhstan and its role in the Soviet weapons program meant it could not be considered an NPT non-nuclear-weapon state. He also recalled the Agreement on Strategic Nuclear Forces that the post-Soviet republics signed in 1991, which committed Ukraine and Belarus to become non-nuclear-weapon states while leaving the door open for Kazakhstan to keep nuclear weapons. Nazarbayev was correct to note that the agreement mentioned only Ukraine and Belarus in provisions related to weapons dismantlement, but incorrect in that the agreement did not explicitly say that Kazakhstan would keep nuclear weapons.

Nazarbayev explained his reasoning:

> Even if all would agree on full dismantlement of nuclear weapons, we would need ten to fifteen years to implement it. During all these years, the missiles will be present on the territory of these states. Why lie to people, telling them we are a non-nuclear-weapon state? Kazakhstan can change its position if there is a negotiating process with neighboring nuclear states and the U.S. that could guarantee our security.[42]

START I TREATY

In parallel to the nuclear negotiations between Alma-Ata and Washington, the United States and the four post-Soviet nuclear republics bargained over the US-Soviet Strategic Arms Reduction Treaty—START for short (a few years later, Russia and the United States would sign START II and the initial START agreement would be referred to as START I from then on). Mikhail Gorbachev and George H. W. Bush had signed START I in July 1991, five months before the Soviet collapse. This breakthrough agreement called for drastic reductions in the US and Soviet nuclear arsenals. It set a limit on the number of weapons each side could have as well as limits for certain types of weapons, to be reached within seven years from the moment of the treaty's entry into force. The treaty called for reducing nuclear arsenals to 1,600 missiles and 6,000 warheads for each side (a halving of the 10,000–12,000 warheads each side possessed prior to START I). Within these limits, the Soviet Union and the United States agreed that each side could have only 154 intercontinental ballistic missiles and no more than 4,900 warheads for intercontinental and submarine-launched ballistic missiles. Some nuclear delivery vehicles that exceeded START I limits were located in Belarus, Kazakhstan, and Ukraine and would have to be destroyed. The treaty would enter into force only after both countries ratified it and exchanged ratification notes. But the Soviet Union dissolved before Moscow and Washington had a chance to do so.

Even before START I's signature by both countries, US policymakers had worried about the risks of Soviet disintegration. Would the sovereign republics have any obligation to a treaty signed by the now nonexistent Soviet Union? Not necessarily.[43]

With the Soviet Union defunct, Washington viewed Russia as the legal successor state and hence as the inheritor of Soviet arms control obligations. But since Soviet nuclear weapons were located in the newly independent republics that had inherited everything that was on their territory (be it material, facilities, or equipment), the United States asserted that it and Russia had to bring Belarus, Ukraine, and Kazakhstan on board and secure their commitment to START I. In addition, Washington sought a specific promise from these three republics to remove all strategic delivery vehicles from their territories within a seven-year period. In other words, what Washington aimed for, and what Russia supported, was for START I cuts to include all strategic nuclear delivery vehicles that were located in Belarus, Kazakhstan, and Ukraine.

What Russia cared about was not letting three non-Russian republics deal with Washington directly. So its diplomats suggested a two-tier ratification process: Minsk, Kyiv, and Alma-Ata, the capitals of the republics with nuclear weapons, would ratify START and send their ratification notes to Moscow, and Moscow would present these three notes plus its own to Washington. Washington, in return, would present its ratification note to Moscow. Belarus, Kazakhstan, and Ukraine balked at Russia's insistence on taking the driver's seat and demanded equal treatment in the START I ratification process. They wanted their parliaments to ratify START and their capitals to transfer the ratification documents directly to Washington. What could be seen as a mere procedural issue was a matter of principle to the newly independent states. The three republics and Moscow negotiated. Russia put on pressure, but the republics stood firm, and several meetings in 1992 ended without agreement.

Washington also initially insisted that only one party–Russia—could ratify START I on behalf of the former Soviet Union. That was the sentiment James Baker expressed in his letter to Nazarbayev in March of 1992.[44] Nazarbayev asked Zhukeev and the foreign ministry to prepare a response: "explain our position on START in a manner acceptable for the U.S." The response to Baker said that Kazakhstan supported START I but "we prefer for the Supreme Soviet to ratify the agreement as appropriate for a sovereign state." Kazakh leaders added that "as realists and taking into consideration your position, we propose [that] after the Supreme Soviet ratifies the agreement, Kazakhstan could designate Russia as one of the legal inheritors of the USSR, act as a party to the agreement." And, the Kazakhs added, they would prefer to pass the ratification document directly to the United States.[45]

By late April 1992, it seemed that it was now agreed that Alma-Ata, along with Minsk and Kyiv, could exchange its START I ratification documents directly with Washington, and, together with Russia and the United States, it would sign the protocol to START I (later to be known as the Lisbon Protocol). Washington felt relieved since the United States' priority was to ensure the ratification of START I. However, the fate of the protocol would remain in limbo for another month; despite the earlier hopeful indications, the presidents of Ukraine and Kazakhstan were not yet ready to fully commit to it.

In addition to ratification notes, Washington requested so-called side letters from the republics on commitment to START I in which they were to commit that all nuclear weapons would be removed from their territories within seven years (the timeframe agreed on under START I). American diplomats also came up with what they called "the most elegant solution" in which all four post-Soviet states—Russia, Belarus, Kazakhstan, and Ukraine—would sign a protocol to START I that would make Russia the successor state to the Soviet Union and commit the three other republics to non-nuclear status under the NPT.[46]

The Americans focused on getting the Ukrainians to agree to the protocol and the text of a side letter to be submitted to Washington as part of the commitment to START. Washington calculated that the Kazakhs would have no choice but to follow if Kyiv was onboard. Ukraine had two concerns: first, it did not want to commit to a set deadline for the elimination of the weapons on its territory that fell under START I limits; second, it demanded security guarantees and international control over weapons elimination.[47]

The Americans agreed to let Belarus, Kazakhstan, and Ukraine join the NPT at the "earliest possible time" without a set date but insisted on START

I's original implementation period of seven years. As to the second point, Washington made it clear to Kyiv that it was out of the question to impose international control over a process that was designed (at least originally) as a two-party agreement. Ukraine's president Leonid Kravchuk visited Washington in early May of 1992, two weeks before Nazarbayev's scheduled trip. After some back-and-forth and creative wordsmithing, Kravchuk finally agreed to the protocol and the substance of the side letter.[48] Now, Washington could focus on Nazarbayev, who remained uncommitted to the START I protocol.

Nazarbayev's reluctance to embrace START I stemmed from his basic strategy of holding onto his "nuclear card" as leverage until he got a formal commitment from the United States on security guarantees. The mixed signals he was sending to Washington in his ongoing bilateral talks on nuclear issues were likely part of the same strategy.

Moreover, at the same time that Nazarbayev was involved in these two sets of nuclear negotiations, he and his immediate circle of advisors sought to improve the long-term security of their country in the other major way they could: by attracting foreign investment to Kazakhstan. They especially longed to develop their oil riches, and in that lucrative area US oil giant Chevron was their biggest hope.

CHEVRON'S LONG ROAD TO KAZAKH OIL

Both Alma-Ata and Chevron had long yearned to reach an oil agreement. In the spring of 1992, the matter became more urgent. They wanted to seal a deal in time for Nazarbayev's visit to Washington, and it was fast approaching.

The Chevron story began in 1979, when Soviet geologists discovered a promising oil field in the Caspian Sea in Kazakhstan. Stretching across 500 square kilometers (50,000 hectares), the field promised 60,000 barrels of oil per day.[49] The field's name, Tengiz, is Kazakh for "sea."

By the mid-1980s, Chevron had felt the pinch of collapsed oil prices and a lack of new fields to develop. Accessing a new major oil field would considerably brighten the company's future. Then, after years of exploration, Chevron decided that Tengiz was worth the investment. The company launched negotiations with the Soviet government, the government of Kazakhstan, and the local authorities of the Gur'yev (now Atyrau) region. Chevron aggressively pursued Soviet officials and succeeded in making its competitor, British Petroleum, drop out of the race for Tengiz.

But the downhill trajectory of the Soviet Union, with its republics vying for more economic autonomy from Moscow, stalled approval of a joint Soviet-American oil venture. By the summer of 1991, the Americans' impatience with the Soviet chaos was palpable. The bleak mood is clear in this memo from Commerce Secretary Robert Mosbacher to National Security Advisor Brent Scowcroft: "The business environment is highly unstable. The Center [Moscow], the republics, and the localities all argue over the division of authority and control over national assets. Laws contradict each other and constantly change. Nobody is willing to make decisions and stick by them."[50]

Officially, Washington did not lobby for Chevron; however, President Bush and Secretary of State Baker both had close ties to the oil industry and monitored Chevron's battle to enter the lucrative Soviet oil market. In July 1991, Chevron's chairman, Kenneth Derr, visited Bush for a fifteen-minute chat. The president spontaneously invited Derr to stay for lunch, which turned into an hour-and-a-half discussion of Chevron's progress in securing the deal.[51]

Nazarbayev involved himself in the Tengiz negotiations even before the Soviet Union collapsed and Kazakhstan became the main negotiator. He easily absorbed and analyzed the numbers and minutiae. In the summer of 1991, when Nazarbayev was invited to join a meeting with President Bush and President Gorbachev in Moscow, he did not shy away from skillfully arguing that Chevron was obtaining too sweet a deal:

> First, the rate of return is 27.9 percent, while Chevron gets 22 percent world-wide. Second, there is the issue of royalties. President Bush and Secretary Baker know the oil industry—7.5 percent royalties are too low. Third, the Soviet Union has spent $850 million developing the Tengiz oil field. The U.S. owes us 50 percent of that sum. Chevron has agreed to that. Fourth, this is a rich, complex oil field.[52]

The Kazakh president summed up the stakes for American leaders in the room: "This is a huge deal. . . . Over the first 40 years, the total revenues will be $169 billion, from an investment of $86 billion, with a new profit of $65 billion."[53]

With the Soviet Union falling apart, the Kazakh government had launched its own negotiations with Chevron and was driving a harder bargain. The Kazakhs discovered that the Soviet government had failed to invite a single lawyer to its team to negotiate with Chevron. Worried that the more experienced American negotiators would take advantage, the Kazakh team proceeded cautiously, recruiting the Oman Ministry of Petroleum and Minerals to help with negotiating the deal. International heavy-hitters—J. P. Morgan and the UK's Slaughter & May—were hired for investment banking and legal advice, respectively.[54] As Ambassador Courtney informed his colleagues in Washington: "Kazakhstan's leaders seem hesitant about taking risks with foreign investors."[55]

At one point, the negotiations almost broke down. The Kazakh government threatened to walk out of the negotiating room, call an open tender, and invite bids to develop Tengiz from other international companies. Nazarbayev sought 87 percent of the income from the field, significantly higher than the 72 percent the Soviet Union had earlier negotiated with Chevron. And Chevron did not want to budge.[56]

When Kazakhstan started engaging with Western companies, one particular American businessman, James Giffen, became a notable fixture. A former executive with the US-Soviet Trade and Economic Council, Giffen had developed wide networks in Russia during the Soviet period and used them to help Western companies enter the Soviet market. Then, when the Soviet Union was collapsing, Giffen inserted himself into the Kazakh scene and became a trusted advisor to Nazarbayev on the Chevron negotiations and other major foreign business deals. He even held a Kazakh diplomatic passport. Western companies appreciated Giffen's role ("He made sure Kazakhs knew how American business worked," said one former oil executive), but over time they bridled at his role as gatekeeper to the top Kazakh leadership.

As Kazakh leaders hammered out an agreement with Chevron, they continued to negotiate with Washington on the fate of Kazakhstan's nuclear inheritance—they knew some kind of resolution on the issue was necessary before Nazarbayev met Bush in Washington. A lot hinged on that trip for both nations. Kazakhs saw it as their chance to sign cooperative agreements with the United States that would help the fledgling economy. And Americans hoped they could make the Kazakhs commit to a nonnuclear future.

PREPARATIONS FOR NAZARBAYEV'S VISIT TO WASHINGTON

In March 1992, Ambassador Courtney liaised with Nazarbayev's advisor on foreign affairs, Gani Kassymov, on the substance and logistics of Nazarbayev's Washington trip. Kassymov, an ethnic Kazakh, had trained for the diplomatic service in the prestigious Moscow State Institute of International Relations and had served in the Kazakh foreign ministry before joining Nazarbayev's presidential team in February 1992. Courtney and Kassymov discussed such trip details as Nazarbayev's meetings with senior American officials, with members of Congress, and with business leaders in Washington and New York.

One issue that Kassymov needed to broach carefully with Courtney was the "delicate and serious concern" that Kazakhstan did not have hard currency to pay for travel expenses; it was also still using Russian rubles and had no currency of its own. Kassymov told Courtney with a smile that Kazakhstan would overcome this "temporary problem" once Chevron began developing Kazakh oil and paid Kazakhstan its share.[57] This exchange was the essence of Kazakhstan's situation at the time—vulnerable and poor but with great potential.

Courtney made clear to Kassymov that the Americans hoped to seal Nazarbayev's commitment to a nonnuclear path during the visit. They wanted assurance of Kazakhstan's adherence to START and its agreement to join the NPT as a non-nuclear-weapon state.[58] In return, they were ready to offer support for economic reforms, sign trade and investment treaties, and establish a business development committee to promote trade and investment.[59] The US government upgraded Nazarbayev's trip from a private visit to a more significant official working visit.[60]

Nazarbayev's advance team, led by his chief of staff, Nurtai Abykaev, and Kassymov, flew to Washington a month beforehand. Kazakhstan did not have an embassy in the American capital, the Russian embassy would not provide help, and the Kazakhs were unfamiliar with the United States, making it challenging for both sides to hash out the logistical details.[61]

Despite the difficulties, the two sides worked out the trip's fine points. The US government offered Andrews Air Force Base for the arrival and departure of the Kazakh delegation as well as a US presidential helicopter to ferry Nazarbayev and his delegation to downtown Washington. The Kazakh delegation was also given limousines and a sedan for Nazarbayev's wife.[62]

In Alma-Ata, the US embassy stayed in close touch with Kazakh officials. As arrangements were finalized, even the usually aloof foreign minister, Tuleitai Suleimenov, could not hide his excitement. Ambassador Courtney reported: "[Suleimenov], an old thinker who is normally cool toward us, gushed with warmth today as he described hopes for President Nazarbayev's official working visit to Washington."[63]

But there was still serious work to do. Nazarbayev was keen to sign investment and trade agreements during his visit, for instance, so Suleimenov asked Washington to send its experts to Alma-Ata so that the agreement texts could be polished and completed.[64]

Kazakhstan's currency problems remained unresolved with only a few weeks left before the trip. The unofficial part of Nazarbayev's trip would require a private sponsor given the shortage of money, but Nazarbayev was apparently optimistic about Chevron taking care of those expenses. Although, reacting to the Chevron hope, one wit at the National Security Council quipped that "historically [Nazarbayev] was more optimistic than appropriate," it turned out the joke was on the NSC official.[65] Still, Giffen was a master facilitator. When the Kazakh government and Chevron reached an agreement on Tengiz, it was not Chevron who picked up Nazarbayev's New York tab. But Giffen, who orchestrated the interaction between Nazarbayev and the Western companies, arranged to foot that bill.[66]

Nazarbayev wanted to raise the possibility during his visit of issuing with Bush a joint political statement, a high-profile document similar to what Bush and Yeltsin had signed, to indicate the importance of the bilateral relationship. Kazakhstan was seeking to be seen and treated as equal to Russia. But Courtney discouraged Nazarbayev from doing so, to avoid a situation in which the Kazakhs might be formally rejected.[67] Courtney thought it was too early. Nevertheless, just before Nazarbayev arrived in Washington, Kazakhstan's deputy foreign minister, Kassym-Jomart Tokayev, passed to Courtney a proposed text for a joint statement. Courtney promised to forward it to Washington but warned that his government would be unlikely to agree. Courtney said he understood that Kazakhstan wanted equal treatment with Russia.[68]

For Kazakhs, having something formal and tangible like such a statement would carry great symbolism. "But we simply did not have enough time to push Americans for a political document before Nazarbayev's visit," Zhukeev recalled. "We were a country of a few months of age but had all those high ambitions and dreams, and a degree of arrogance." If too early, though, apparently the Kazakhs' ambitions were not too high: just two years later, during Nazarbayev's February 1994 visit to Washington, Kazakhstan would sign an important Charter on Democratic Partnership with the United States, the kind of joint political statement Kazakhstan had so wanted.

As Nazarbayev's May 1992 US visit approached, Courtney sent an optimistic telegram to Washington:

> In the early months of relations with Kazakhstan, America has two urgent objectives—the Chevron deal and denuclearization. On both scores, things are going much better than expected. Two months ago the Chevron contract

seemed on the rocks. Now, it will be signed during Nazarbayev's visit. One month ago Kazakhstan claimed the status of a "temporary nuclear weapon state." Now it hints it will agree to denuclearize in return for U.S. security ties.[69]

Following intensive talks with Nazarbayev and Zhukeev, Courtney changed his interpretation of the internal Kazakh discourse on nuclear weapons from his views a few months earlier. Then, he had sounded alarmed; now, he exuded confidence that Alma-Ata would choose a nonnuclear path:

> The recent flirtation by political figures with the idea of holding onto nuclear weapons is not deeply rooted. This is not Pakistan or India. Despite concerns about instability in Moscow and intentions in Beijing, Kazakhstan seems unwilling to risk political isolation in order to cling to nuclear weapons which it does not (and never will) control. Rather, ethnic Kazakh politicians seem to perceive nuclear weapons as offering leverage against [Russia], and a means to attract pledges from America and the West.[70]

And on Chevron, Courtney wrote: "The Chevron oil deal—to be the largest foreign venture in the former USSR, and in one of the richest oil fields in the world—offers economic gain. Like the Marshall Plan, it also offers hope."[71]

THE TURNING POINT

Even though it may seem the Kazakh leadership had its hands full with START, NPT, the Chevron deal, and its bilateral negotiations with the United States, there was another major security-related pact on which it also focused during this busy time. On May 15, 1992, two days before Nazarbayev flew to Washington, Kazakhstan, Russia, Armenia, Kyrgyzstan, Tajikistan, and Uzbekistan signed the Collective Security Treaty, also known as the Tashkent Treaty after the Uzbek capital where it was signed. The treaty committed its parties not to use force against each other and to consider an attack against one as an attack against all.[72] This collective security mechanism, especially given Russia's participation, alleviated some of Kazakhstan's security concerns. With the Tashkent Treaty, Nazarbayev said, "Russia is now Kazakhstan's political and military ally."[73] Just before signing the Tashkent Treaty, Kazakhstan formed its own, independent armed forces.

In addition to mitigating potential security risks from Russia thanks to the Tashkent Treaty, Kazakhstan received a reassuring signal from its other neighbor—China. China's Foreign Ministry made a statement that it did not have territorial claims against Kazakhstan.[74]

Although Kazakhstan artfully deployed mixed signals to maximize its leverage with the United States and others, it faced push-and-pull from opposing
circumstances. As Zhukeev described it: On the one hand, many countries considered the NPT inadequate for a changed world order. Further, nuclear weapons
had been tested in Kazakhstan for years before the NPT, and nuclear weapons
were to remain on Kazakhstan territory for the next few years, making it a simple
reality that Kazakhstan was *not* a nuclear-free country. On the other hand, Zhukeev explained, Kazakh leaders had never considered nuclear weapons to be the
main component of Kazakhstan's security and knew that any attempt to flex its
nuclear muscles would not be wise. As Zhukeev put it, "Economy-wise, it made
more sense to spend billions we would otherwise waste on maintaining nuclear
weapons on the economic revival of our country, on helping its citizens."[75]

The Tashkent Treaty and security assurances from international partners
made Kazakhstan more comfortable. Zhukeev summarized the denouement
this way: "The final clarity to our position on nuclear weapons was added a few
days before the trip to Washington. . . . Once we received firm guarantees of our
security, we could not allow ourselves to continue with a dual position."[76] This
meant that Alma-Ata was ready to move forward with signing the START I
protocol that so preoccupied Washington. After receiving a "yes" from Ukraine
on the protocol, James Baker had a good feeling:

> Nazarbayev had nowhere to go, so I felt fairly confident when I wrote him on
> May 13, outlining our approach to START and reiterating our 1968 NPT com-
> mitment. He called me back on May 16, two days before he was due to arrive in
> Washington to see President Bush. He told me that Kazakhstan had received a
> collective security guarantee from Russia [under the Tashkent Collective Secu-
> rity Treaty] and combined with our NPT commitment, he felt secure in signing
> the START Protocol and joining the NPT as a non-nuclear weapons state.[77]

NAZARBAYEV GOES TO WASHINGTON

On May 18, Nazarbayev and his delegation touched down at Andrews Air Force
Base. There, the Kazakhs boarded helicopters to fly to the Washington Mall.
Blair House, a nineteenth-century residence within walking distance of the
White House, would be home away from home for the Kazakh delegation, as it
had been for many visiting dignitaries.

On that first day, two hours after landing, Nazarbayev and Chevron Chairman Kenneth Derr signed the Foundation Agreement for the development
of Tengiz. After five years of negotiations, first with Moscow and then with

Alma-Ata, Chevron had secured access to one of the world's most promising oil fields, and Kazakhstan had completed its first major international deal, opening the spigot for cash to flow into its fledgling economy.

The initial agreement promised a vast expansion of Tengiz. The number of operating wells was to increase from sixty to six hundred, with oil production to rise from 60,000 barrels a day eventually to 700,000.[78] Chevron's initial commitment was to invest up to $20 billion over forty years. Espy Price, the vice president of Chevron Overseas from 1992 to 1996, would later describe Tengiz as "the kind of opportunity that drains all your energy. . . . It tests your patience . . . and it sometimes makes you even question your sanity. But at the same time, it pumps you back up . . . [b]ecause it is a chance to be a part of something almost bigger than life."[79]

For Kazakhstan, the Chevron agreement and the possibility of similar deals represented a major source of security. Nazarbayev noted that a "powerful US business presence in Kazakhstan and our economic and diplomatic contacts are the best guarantee of our independence."[80] Over the next few days, Nazarbayev stayed busy with back-to-back meetings. On May 19, he had breakfast with James Baker at Blair House, where the two discussed security issues and opportunities for foreign private investment in Kazakhstan's economy.[81]

The highlight of the official program was Nazarbayev's meeting with President Bush. American and Kazakh journalists flooded the Oval Office for a photo op with the two presidents. Nazarbayev, confident and polished, made small talk and joked with Bush about how well Kazakhs got along with Secretary Baker. When Nazarbayev told Bush that he had signed an agreement with Chevron the day before, Bush nodded approvingly and said: "They will do what they say."[82]

Once the media left, Bush, Nazarbayev, and a small group of top officials got to the formal part of the meeting. Nazarbayev handed Bush a letter confirming Kazakhstan's adherence to START I. In that meeting, Nazarbayev did not hide his disappointment with the state of the CIS:

> At the moment the CIS is not working. Meetings like a President's Club. . . . We sign documents and they are meaningless. Russians exert pressure on many areas. I have told Yeltsin what I am telling you. . . . The CIS is collapsing. I am working hard to preserve it, but it is useless.[83]

Nazarbayev emphatically painted a picture of crisis in the former Soviet Union and hinted that if the West wouldn't help, Arab states would:

PHOTO 14   Official visit of the delegation of Kazakhstan, with President Nursultan Nazarbayev, to Washington, DC, 1992. Photograph by I. Budnevich.
SOURCE: Central State Archive of Film and Photo Documents and Sound Recordings, Kazakhstan. Image #2–114524.

Crisis is reaching an apex. We can't afford to be late. We could have a catastrophe. There is total disintegration in the Russian countryside. Now Kazakhstan is OK. We have a choice. Representatives of all Arab states have visited, including Iran. They have promised to provide what we need. But that would put Kazakhstan under their influence.[84]

Nazarbayev tried to make Bush empathize with Kazakhstan's sense of insecurity to make a case for security guarantees from the United States:

It's not clear what will happen in Russia. In China, some of their books show part of our territory as Chinese. To the south is fundamentalism. What are we to do? That is why we wish to be close to the U.S. This is why we wanted to remain temporarily a nuclear state.[85]

After making his point about security, Nazarbayev turned to another item on his country's wish list: economic deals. As the Kazakh president—his country's PR-man-in-chief—put it, "I will hand out a book in New York with 135 opportunities, with all the economic details, legislation on market economy, our achievements. . . . I am not coming empty-handed. I come with projects and opportunity!" After describing Kazakhstan's immense mineral wealth, Nazarbayev added, "Kazakhstan exports $5 billion annually. Gold and diamonds. We will put gold in Swiss banks as security."[86] Kazakh legislation offered foreign investors three years of tax-free profit-making.[87]

A working lunch in the Old Family Dining Room at the White House followed the meeting. After lunch, both presidents proceeded to the Roosevelt Room for the ceremonial signing of agreements. The bilateral investment agreement provided legal protection for investors of one country in the territory of the other.[88] The Overseas Private Investment Corporation (OPIC) agreement provided investment insurance, project financing, and other investor services to US investors in Kazakhstan.[89] The bilateral trade agreement allowed for reciprocal allocation of most favored nation status, which meant that, with respect to tariffs, quotas, and other trade-related matters, Kazakh goods exported to the United States and American goods exported to Kazakhstan would receive nondiscriminatory treatment.[90] Washington also offered a wide range of assistance programs on business training, agriculture, energy efficiency, judicial and legal training, and in other areas.

Under the Special American Business Internship (SABIT) program, which was run by the US Department of Commerce, groups of managers and technical experts from Kazakhstan could spend three to six months in the United States to receive training in their specific fields. For American companies, SABIT offered an opportunity to promote their products and services to a new market.

Another initiative, the farmer-to-farmer program, allowed American farmers to share hands-on expertise in Western agricultural methods with farmers in Kazakhstan. Earlier, the United States had sent a team of energy-efficiency experts to Alma-Ata to make an audit of the city's centralized heating system. Now they were ready to install equipment to make that system more efficient.

In the legal sphere, the US government funded an American Bar Association technical assistance program so that its legal experts could help Kazakhs draft laws. Washington offered assistance in such democracy-promoting areas as civic education, public administration, and the development of independent media.

Humanitarian assistance was on its way. Under Operation Provide Hope I, the United States announced during Nazarbayev's visit that it would supply Kazakhstan with more than 170 tons of food and more than 50 tons of medicine and medical supplies. Earlier, in February of 1992, the first cargo planes filled with American goods had landed in cities across Kazakhstan. Under another humanitarian project, Operation Provide Hope II, NATO shipped 74 tons of medical supplies and 500 tons of food.[91] Some of these donated Western goods were exotic for locals—fizzy medications that dissolved in water, disposable syringes, ready-to-eat meals produced for the US Army, and breakfast cereal. Americans helped equip hospitals in big cities and even drove "hospitals on wheels" to remote, rural areas. "I remember when I was a young boy, such a truck came to our village," one Kazakh man said. "They fixed my teeth and did the same for my friends!"

Private donations poured in as well. Mercy Corps International was ready to provide 80,000 pounds of granola to the Aral region, which had suffered environmental devastation due to the mismanagement of water resources during the Soviet period. Waukesha, a city of 70,000 in Wisconsin, collected 40,000 pounds of medications, food, and clothes for its sister city of Kokchetav in the northern part of Kazakhstan. The Northern California Ecumenical Council, International Services of San Francisco, donated 12 tons of medicine to a children's charity organization in Alma-Ata.[92]

After meeting with President Bush, Nazarbayev spoke at the National Press Club, where he reflected on how Kazakhstan's position on its nuclear weapons had evolved. He described Kazakhstan's initial caution when the USSR had collapsed, as it was unknown what would become of Russia or Kazakhstan's other neighbors.[93] The Kazakh president mentioned how the Tashkent Treaty helped Kazakhstan feel more secure in changed geopolitical circumstances. The armies of the Tashkent signatories will never be used against each other, Nazarbayev said, and as any threat of aggression or direct aggression against any of those nations would be regarded as an attack on all, it altered radically the situation pertaining to Kazakhstan's security.[94]

He added a hopeful note about the future:

Deployment or non-deployment of nuclear weapons on the territory of the states [which are] parties to the agreement will depend on the political situation. . . . I hope that we will continue moving ahead on issues of disarmament and full liquidation of nuclear weapons. Then the problem itself will disappear.[95]

Nazarbayev's long day continued into the afternoon, with senior US officials visiting him at Blair House. Treasury Secretary Nicholas Brady, for example, described to him the multilateral economic assistance package for Kazakhstan as well as US bilateral credit programs that the new nation could access. And when Defense Secretary Dick Cheney paid a visit, Nazarbayev shared with him Kazakhstan's security concerns and described his plans for building Kazakhstan's own armed forces. That night, the Citizens Democracy Corps hosted a dinner at Blair House with ten senior American CEOs who were interested in investment opportunities in Kazakhstan in oil, gas, gold, manufacturing, and food processing.[96]

Over the next couple of days Nazarbayev and his delegation continued to meet with various officials in Washington, including Vice President Dan Quayle, members of Congress, and representatives of the press.

After an eventful stay in Washington, Nazarbayev and his delegation traveled to New York. They arrived at the luxurious Waldorf-Astoria Hotel on Park Avenue on the evening of May 21. That night, J. P. Morgan hosted a reception for the Kazakh delegation in true New York style—on the fifty-sixth floor of the Pan Am Building (now the MetLife Building). About twenty CEOs came to meet the Kazakh president and learn about business opportunities in this Central Asian country that was newly opened to the world. The Kazakhs distributed a shiny briefing book with the 135 opportunities for future investors that Nazarbayev had spoken of in Washington.[97]

While in New York, Nazarbayev met with UN Secretary General Boutros Boutros-Ghali. Just before departing, Nazarbayev made a brief visit to the United States Military Academy at West Point, where he was promised US help with training the Kazakh military.[98]

Not surprisingly, Nazarbayev felt extremely pleased with the visit. At 8:15 p.m. on May 23, just a few hours after he left, Nazarbayev sent a message to Bush from an Aeroflot plane:

> As I depart your wonderful country, I wish to express my satisfaction with my visit. The warmest hospitality and the very positive results in our negotiations lead me to express my gratitude and appreciation to you and your country. This visit and the results achieved will serve well the establishment and future development of good relations between our two peoples.[99]

The Kazakh media celebrated Nazarbayev's first official trip to the United States with enthusiasm. All the major newspapers published detailed reports on each day of his stay. In particular, the photos of Nazarbayev and Bush together in the White House carried a lot of symbolism for a young republic: Just a year ago, Kazakhstan had been an invisible part of the Soviet Union. Now, its leader was received at the White House by the leader of the world's only superpower.

While Nazarbayev was en route to Kazakhstan from New York, his right-hand man, Tulegen Zhukeev, was traveling to Portugal. In Lisbon, Baker, Zhukeev, and the representatives of Belarus, Ukraine, and Russia signed a document that became known as the Lisbon Protocol to START I. The protocol stipulated that the three republics would reach the agreements necessary to implement the weapons reductions mandated by START I. It also proclaimed that Kazakhstan, as well as Belarus and Ukraine, would join the NPT as a non-nuclear-weapon state "in the shortest possible time."[100]

Washington thought it could finally exhale. Nazarbayev had personally promised to President Bush, and the Lisbon Protocol had codified that promise, that Kazakhstan would join the NPT as a non-nuclear-weapon state and that all nuclear weapons would be removed from Kazakhstan within the seven-year period set out in START I.

But as the next two years would show, it was too early for Washington to celebrate. Kazakhstan would hold off with officially committing to a nonnuclear path while waiting for Washington to formally guarantee Kazakhstan's security. Now that a handful of US and Kazakh negotiators knew each other, their interactions became even more interesting—as a good share of mutual respect now mixed with political bluffing.

CHAPTER 8

THE FINAL PUSH

We must not be distracted from the threat posed to the United States and its close allies by the thousands of nuclear warheads still mounted on intercontinental missiles in Russia, Belarus, Kazakhstan and Ukraine, still aimed at the United States, still capable of being launched without warning in massive numbers at our cities and our citizens.

—US Senators Sam Nunn and Richard Lugar,
"Still a Soviet Threat," *Washington Post*, December 22, 1992

"YOU CAN HIRE A HUNDRED LEGAL COMPANIES, even in America, but you will never be able to prove your right to keep the weapons," Nazarbayev's advisor Tulegen Zhukeev remembers US Ambassador William Courtney warning him. "Under no circumstances will the number of nuclear powers become higher than it is now." Zhukeev was quick to retort: "We get your message but no need for such tone. Do not push your schedule on us. We have our own."[1]

This heated exchange was one of many between Kazakhs and Americans as they negotiated over when Kazakhstan would join the Treaty on the Non-Proliferation of Nuclear Weapons (NPT).

After Belarus, Kazakhstan, and Ukraine had committed to START I under the Lisbon Protocol and to sign the NPT as non-nuclear-weapon states, Washington had waited anxiously for them to act on their promises and remove Soviet nuclear weapons from their territories. Soon, however, Washington realized that a bumpy road lay ahead. Among the many obstacles: strong sentiment in Ukraine to retain its arsenal, which in turn steeled Kazakhstan in its own US negotiations; questions over who would profit from the highly valuable uranium recovered in the warhead dismantlement process; and the difficulty of drafting security guarantees solid enough to convince Kazakhstan, sandwiched between two nuclear superpowers, to shed its nuclear weapons.

Ukraine, whose political climate varied sharply from Kazakhstan's, presented a particular challenge to the Americans. By early 1993, the United States, Russia, Belarus, and Kazakhstan had ratified START I, but Ukraine had stalled, not only on ratifying START I but also on joining the NPT. Kazakhstan remained cautious while carefully watching Ukraine's moves and the US response to them.

The Kazakhs believed that Washington viewed Ukraine as more important than Kazakhstan. Among the former Soviet republics, Ukraine was home to 50 million people strategically located in the heart of Eastern Europe. It was second only to Russia in significance to the United States and Europe. An advanced industrialized republic hosting nuclear power reactors, Ukraine possessed substantially more nuclear expertise than Kazakhstan. Critically, it was also home to the Yuzhnoe facility, which produced intercontinental ballistic missiles. As Zhukeev reflected, "We did not have as many trump cards as Ukraine, but we had oil and gas, and uranium."[2] The Kazakh negotiators wanted to avoid giving up their nuclear weapons if Washington allowed Ukraine to keep them.

In Ukraine, nationalist political groups enjoyed greater say in their country's politics than in Kazakhstan. They were well represented in Ukraine's parliament, which was more independent of the executive branch than was its Kazakh counterpart, and media freedoms allowed a more open and robust public debate on nuclear matters. While the nascent Kazakh military followed Nazarbayev's lead, the Ukrainian military was divided on the nuclear issue. Pronuclear elements pressured the Ukrainian leadership to hold onto the nuclear weapons, prompting the nation's president to press Washington over the same issues that Kazakhstan had raised—security guarantees and financial compensation for nuclear dismantlement.[3]

Kazakh nationalists admired Kyiv's firm position and argued that Alma-Ata should stop caving to Russia and the United States and drive a tougher bargain. Partly because Nazarbayev had to take into account the view of Kazakh nationalists, Courtney reasoned, he made several "aggressive" public statements and delayed his parliament's vote on joining the NPT. A step-by-step approach to the NPT, Nazarbayev believed, would prove to the nationalists that he would not quickly succumb to demands from the United States and Russia.[4]

Kazakhstan's negotiating position on nuclear matters reflected genuine strategic interests mixed with a healthy dose of political bluff and audacity. While Kazakh officials had said all the right things and appeared content with US promises on security guarantees prior to Nazarbayev's trip to Washington in

May 1992, they sought legally binding commitments from the United States and other nuclear powers, specifically in the form of a written document. After Nazarbayev's visit to Washington and the signing of the Lisbon Protocol, Kazakhs continued to seek maximum benefits from Americans in exchange for denuclearization.[5]

One major stumbling block was compensation for the highly enriched uranium (HEU) to be extracted from dismantled Soviet nuclear warheads. In August 1992, the United States and Russia reached agreement in principle on the sale of excess HEU from dismantled former Soviet warheads.[6] Under the Highly Enriched Uranium Purchase Agreement, finalized in 1993 and dubbed the HEU Deal, Russia would downblend to low enriched uranium (LEU) 500 metric tons of HEU from dismantled warheads and sell it to the United States for civil reactor fuel over a period of twenty years.[7] For the United States, the HEU Deal was a good way to reduce the volume of nuclear material in Russia and minimize the risk that it could fall into the wrong hands—such as those of terrorists. Under the slogan "megatons to megawatts," the HEU Deal would become a poster child of US-Russian cooperation. Nuclear fuel that might have powered Soviet nuclear bombs would end up providing electricity to American homes. The HEU Deal provided 10 percent of US electric power for fifteen years.[8]

In Kazakhstan, officials believed that part of the revenue generated from the HEU Deal should be shared with their country. Kazakhstan had provided uranium for nuclear material for Soviet nuclear weapons and it hosted some of them. The Kazakh government argued that it should receive compensation for the material coming out of the weapons to be removed from its territory. But opinions on how much Kazakhstan was owed varied.

Kazakhstan's Atomic Energy Commission estimated that roughly 20–30 metric tons of HEU would be removed from weapons stored in Kazakhstan, compensation for which could reach $400–600 million.[9] Tulegen Zhukeev thought the sum should be closer to $2 billion because of the HEU's value.[10]

From the start of negotiations, Washington's position with Moscow was that Kazakhstan, Belarus, and Ukraine had every right to benefit from the sale of the HEU from the weapons removed from their territories. The United States encouraged the former Soviet republics to resolve the issue of profit-sharing among themselves. However, Russia wasn't keen to share the profit with anyone and stalled negotiations with the republics.[11]

BARGAINING WITH WASHINGTON OVER THE NPT

For a year and a half following the signature of the Lisbon Protocol, Nazarbayev remained reluctant to sign the NPT. During that period, high-ranking American diplomats regularly visited Alma-Ata, now renamed Almaty to reflect the Kazakh form of the city's name, and top Kazakh officials led by Zhukeev in turn traveled to Washington. Security guarantees and compensation for highly enriched uranium remained at the top of the Kazakh agenda throughout the bilateral negotiations that took place between the summer of 1992 and winter of 1993.

Almaty's talking points for Washington reflected its genuine concerns about Kazakhstan's security, both political and economic. To maximize their return in terms of security guarantees, financial compensation, and economic investment, Kazakh leaders exploited every such concern and dramatized them for American ears.

One concern was the fate of the Commonwealth of Independent States (CIS), the loose union of eleven former Soviet republics, and the idea of a CIS collective defense. Nazarbayev had proposed such a defense union and was disappointed when the other republics failed to embrace it.[12] As months passed, Nazarbayev's frustration with the CIS and the uncertain future of its collective security apparatus intensified. He worried that the Soviet collapse had disrupted the global balance of power: "In these circumstances," he proposed, "the historic task of the CIS is to provide a power balance and constant reduction of strategic offensive weapons until reasonably sufficient levels."[13] Gradually, however, Nazarbayev accepted that the CIS was an amorphous structure, and that Kazakhstan was on its own when it came to security.

Meanwhile, the Kazakh government was waiting for Russia to do its part on the Lisbon Protocol. Under it, Russia was to collaborate with Kazakhstan in establishing a process for removing and dismantling nuclear weapons in compliance with START I. However, Almaty did not have the technical expertise and depended on Moscow to draft the implementation agreements. Through the spring of 1993, while negotiations with the US were ongoing, Kazakhstan continued to wrestle with Russia over the details of START I implementation as codified in the protocol. On the first anniversary of its signing, in May 1993, Nazarbayev lamented in an interview with a Russian military newspaper, *Krasnaia Zvezda*, that

> There is still no worked-out plan of how to develop and implement a joint nuclear policy. There is still no work plan and no scope of authority [determined]

for an established and, it seems, forgotten, Joint Consultative Commission on Disarmament. No agreement reached on START I implementation . . . The dismantlement and liquidation of ICBMs is a labor-intensive process requiring complex solutions and significant financial resources, which our republic does not yet have. This explains the behind-the-schedule withdrawal of nuclear weapons from Kazakhstan.[14]

In June 1993, Strobe Talbott, Special Advisor to the US Secretary of State on the Newly Independent States, arrived in Kazakhstan for talks. Nazarbayev did not mince words about Russia's behavior since the signing of the Lisbon Protocol, which had prevented Russia, Kazakhstan, Belarus, and Ukraine from reaching agreements on the process of weapons dismantlement and on profit-sharing from the sale of nuclear material. Nazarbayev complained to Talbott:

> Russia has expertise to prepare such documents but it doesn't demonstrate any willingness to deal with this. Russia directly violates the Lisbon Protocol. . . . Everyone, including the United States, accepted single control over nuclear weapons transferred to CIS Joint Military Forces. But now Russia demonstrates full departure from these agreements. A question arises: why then the other parties cannot depart from their obligations? How are we supposed to explain to our people Russia's attempts to throw Kazakhstan and Ukraine out of Lisbon Protocol? Not to mention the moral side of it—even from a purely formalist side, such a position is not legitimate and threatens the viability of the Lisbon Protocol.[15]

Nazarbayev told Talbott that the US government had to put pressure on Russia to resolve the outstanding issues.[16] Further, as in every meeting with US officials, Nazarbayev raised the issue of security guarantees with Talbott:

> We need security guarantees. Let's not discuss from where the threat might emanate. Kazakhstan's environment is complicated. We do not have claims against anyone, neither territorial nor political and expect the same from others. . . . We need these guarantees against the threat of nuclear use and against the threat to our territorial integrity. These guarantees should be in the form of an agreement.[17]

When Ambassador Courtney visited Nazarbayev a few weeks later, Nazarbayev again implored Washington to provide formal security guarantees:

> The US president should know that Kazakhstan needs security guarantees. It is important for domestic/internal calm—the people of Kazakhstan should be

confident of their security; without this, it would be difficult to rely on their support.[18]

Nazarbayev repeatedly explained to his American interlocutors the many reasons why Kazakhstan did not feel secure. China carried on with nuclear tests, Russia remained unstable, and clashes in neighboring Afghanistan continued. Nazarbayev told Courtney that his government did not expect any material contributions from the United States, such as military forces or equipment. A formal statement on security guarantees would be sufficient.[19]

The security guarantees were still not forthcoming and the US-Kazakh wrangle over the future of the nuclear weapons on Kazakhstan's territory continued.

STROBE TALBOTT RETURNS TO ALMATY

By late summer 1993, the US government continued to seek clarity from Kazakhstan on when it would adhere to the NPT. Washington planned to send Strobe Talbott to Almaty again in September. On instructions from the State Department, Ambassador Courtney wrote to the Kazakh foreign ministry, "We hope that by Ambassador Talbott's visit the Kazakhstan government will be able to advise him regarding a firm schedule of NPT consideration and ratification by the Supreme Soviet."[20] Critically for Kazakhstan, Courtney also relayed to the Kazakh government Washington's position on the issue of reimbursement for nuclear material:

> The major remaining obstacle is to work out an acceptable way [to] reimburse Kazakhstan, Belarus, and Ukraine for the value of the HEU in the warheads located on their soil. We are working with Russia on this, and expect to be in a position to discuss this subject with Kazakhstan soon.[21]

On September 12, 1993, Talbott landed in Almaty. To entice Nazarbayev to ratify the NPT, the US diplomat raised the possibility of a post-ratification summit with President Clinton.[22] Talbott even suggested that Clinton might consider a trip to Kazakhstan in January 1994 (the visit never materialized). He also indicated that US Secretary of State Warren Christopher planned to visit Almaty in October and that Vice President Al Gore could pay a visit in November (the visit took place in December).

The conversation between the Kazakh government and Talbott's delegation began with nuclear matters. The Americans promised to help Kazakhstan dismantle Soviet rocket launchers, strengthen nuclear material export controls, and convert the military industrial infrastructure to civilian use.

Talbott and his delegation also raised some broader aspects of the US-Kazakh relationship, including potential US assistance with privatization, environmental protection, and humanitarian aid for environmental disaster zones. Specifically, Talbott offered American help to decontaminate the former Semipalatinsk Polygon and revive the dying Aral Sea, which was losing water due to Soviet-era mismanagement. Americans were also keen to pursue business opportunities in what to them was a new market—beginning with Boeing airplanes and pipeline construction.[23] Economic cooperation between the two countries was exactly what the Kazakhs had hoped for.

THE VISIT OF WARREN CHRISTOPHER

In October 1993 Secretary of State Warren Christopher arrived in Almaty, accompanied by Strobe Talbott. During preparatory meetings with his Kazakh counterparts, Ambassador Courtney informed the foreign ministry that Christopher, America's top diplomat, would not discuss Kazakhstan joining the NPT during his visit to the Kazakh parliament to avoid being seen as putting pressure on the legislature. Instead, Christopher would focus on US economic assistance to Kazakhstan, and in so doing prepare favorable ground for NPT discussion.[24]

When Christopher's motorcade drove through Almaty, billboards with the image of Hashemi Rafsanjani, the president of Iran, adorned the city's streets.[25] Rafsanjani was scheduled to visit Almaty in a couple of days, and so Christopher was greeted with "Welcome President Rafsanjani"—an unintentional reminder to Americans that Iran, a country keen to develop a nuclear program, sought a close relationship with its neighbor.

A footnote to this visit by the top US diplomat revolved around Kazakhs' pride in their reputation as one of the most hospitable nations on earth. In line with this tradition, Kazakhs take feeding their guests very seriously, and the highlight of special dinners is the serving of a boiled sheep's head. The eldest person present or a special guest has the honor of cutting and distributing pieces of the head to the diners, starting with the elders and revered guests, followed by children and then relatives in order of closeness to the host.

By default, Christopher would have been chosen for this honor, but prior to Christopher's arrival Courtney asked Zhukeev to forgo this ritual. "He has delicate health," Courtney explained.[26] Although Christopher was saved from the sheep's head, he was not able to avoid a more disagreeable matter—Kazakhstan's indecision on adherence to the NPT.

Christopher had hoped that during his visit to Almaty, the parliament would vote in favor of Kazakhstan joining the NPT as a non-nuclear-weapon state. He knew that if he secured Kazakhstan's adherence, Washington would have leverage in its negotiations with Ukraine, which had been stalled on this same issue. Besides his speech on economic assistance to the Kazakh parliament, Christopher tried to reach his goal by directly persuading Nazarbayev of the benefits of the NPT.

But although Nazarbayev and his team received Christopher warmly, the Secretary of State's efforts to persuade Nazarbayev to ratify the NPT during his visit failed. "Those were difficult negotiations, not going anywhere," Zhukeev remembers. "We paused for lunch and then resumed."[27]

After lunch, growing more anxious, Christopher asked to meet in a smaller group. Zhukeev described that meeting: "It was Nazarbayev, myself, Talbott, and Christopher. Christopher said he promised Clinton [that Kazakhstan would join the NPT]. We explained to him: 'We are in a very difficult situation, the security guarantees had to be more clearly spelled out.'" Christopher then met with Nazarbayev one-on-one, but even this private meeting did not help.[28]

Washington had expected that the NPT would be ratified before or during Christopher's visit, and that he would sign an agreement on US assistance for removing and dismantling nuclear forces and associated infrastructure under the Nunn-Lugar Cooperative Threat Reduction Program.[29] James Goodby, chief US negotiator for the safe and secure dismantlement of Soviet nuclear weapons, summed up the visit:

> Secretary Christopher had been rebuffed by Nazarbayev in Almaty when he arrived there ready to sign a Nunn-Lugar umbrella agreement and some implementing agreements that I had negotiated with the Kazakhstanis. Nazarbayev insisted on meeting with President Clinton in Washington and delayed the signing ceremony.[30]

Kazakh participants in the meeting observed that Christopher left disappointed. Zhukeev recounted that "[Christopher] thought we would agree to sign the NPT. We refused. It was impossible to accept that; we did not have real security guarantees. They told us: 'Trust us. We will always be there for you.' But Nazarbayev and myself would not relent. . . . They understood we needed to survive."[31] From Almaty, Christopher and his delegation went to Kyiv, wishing for better luck there.

Toward their goal of getting satisfactory security guarantees before signing the NPT, Kazakh leaders waited for a higher-ranking American, Vice President Al Gore, to visit Almaty later that year. Ambassador Courtney reasoned: "I don't think the Kazakhs saw Christopher nearly so influential as Gore. They were trying to save it [NPT ratification] for his visit. . . . They were looking for political stagecraft if you will."[32]

A few days after Christopher's frustrating but important visit, Ambassador Courtney called Zhukeev to request a meeting with Nazarbayev. The three men met and discussed for an hour and a half Kazakhstan's nuclear policy. A couple of days after that meeting, Courtney called Zhukeev again and suggested that Zhukeev fly to the United States. Within three months, Zhukeev would visit Washington twice, later describing the ensuing talks as "exceptionally dramatic negotiations."[33]

THE DECISIVE TRIP TO DC

The trip that sealed the deal on Kazakhstan joining the NPT happened just before Thanksgiving in 1993. "That is when we made the main decision," Zhukeev recalled. On November 23, Zhukeev traveled to Washington with Alibek Kassymov, chief of the general staff, and Bolat Nurgaliev, a representative of the foreign ministry. They planned to discuss two main subjects: a package of documents related to START I implementation, and the memoranda between the United States and Kazakhstan on assistance under the Nunn-Lugar program.

Due to the Thanksgiving holiday, some of Washington's bureaucrats had already left town. Still, the Kazakh delegation tried hard to obtain a formal commitment on security guarantees from their American hosts. Zhukeev and his team spent hours at the State Department arguing with their American counterparts over the semantics of security guarantees.

The Kazakhs first met with Larry Napper and a few other State Department staffers. When they could not arrive at an agreement, Zhukeev and his entourage went to Strobe Talbott. Zhukeev described the encounter: "We argued for another hour. I used every argument I had and Talbott met each with a counterargument."[34]

Zhukeev pressed for language on security guarantees to include not only "consultation" in case of a security threat against Kazakhstan but also "measures," pushing the United States to act in case of aggression. "He wouldn't agree," Zhukeev recalled.

"We won't sign the NPT otherwise," Zhukeev declared.

"Are you sure? Would Nazarbayev approve?" Talbott responded.

"If I am telling you this now, this is how it will be," Zhukeev replied. "You will be Kazakhstan's hero one day, they will erect a golden monument in your honor, if you agree. This historic decision belongs to you."[35]

Zhukeev remembers that day in vivid detail:

> Christopher was not there and so I could not call on him. Clinton seemed to
> have left the White House to go somewhere. It was already evening and next
> morning I had to fly back. I insisted we resolve that dilemma. I told Talbott:
> "Call Christopher, ask him to come back, or we can fly anywhere necessary—
> anywhere . . ."[36]

Zhukeev tried to persuade Talbott: "Take responsibility. Then, when Gore comes in twelve or thirteen days, we will sign the NPT. If not, we will sign nothing, the pressure from you or Gore's visit won't matter."[37]

It was now dark; the clock showed that it was past 9 p.m. Zhukeev and his team, and Talbott, Napper, and a few other State Department staff continued to argue over language. "We fought, we made up," Zhukeev said, admitting he "engaged in demagogy" that night, suggesting to Americans that the Kazakh parliament would not ratify the NPT without solid security guarantees.[38] In fact, the Kazakh parliament wasn't that independent, and Nazarbayev was the sole decision-maker. Talbott used the same argument about the Congress— that the language on security guarantees that Kazakhs wanted would not be approved by American lawmakers.

Finally, close to 10 p.m., the Kazakh and American negotiators agreed on the wording of a statement on security guarantees that satisfied both parties. It would be included in the Charter on Democratic Partnership to be signed during a Nazarbayev-Clinton summit in early 1994. Washington would pledge that, should Kazakhstan come under attack or the threat of an attack from a nuclear power, the United States would seek immediate action from the UN Security Council. The United States would also reiterate its commitment to Kazakhstan under the NPT not to attack or threaten to attack it with nuclear weapons. Zhukeev was elated: "In excellent mood, we returned to the hotel and flew back to Kazakhstan the next morning."[39]

AL GORE'S VISIT

In December 1993, two weeks after the Kazakh delegation returned from
Washington, Almaty prepared to welcome Vice President Al Gore. However, the Kazakh winter did not cooperate, and Gore's plane could not land
at Almaty airport after two attempts due to heavy fog. Kazakh air traffic control diverted Gore's aircraft which was running low on fuel to a neighboring
republic—Kyrgyzstan.

Once refueled in Bishkek, the pilot offered to make a third attempt to get to
Almaty. That night, Kazakh officials had laid a state dinner for Gore, his wife
Tipper, and the delegation. A *New York Times* correspondent in Gore's traveling
pool described the conundrum:

> Through a slit curtain [at the front of the cabin], I could see and hear arguments
> presented: Oil-rich Kazakhstan which could be wooed further away from Rus-
> sia, might be put off by American queasiness about landing. Diplomats fretted.
> The gutsy pilot thought he could make it on another try. Gore glanced toward
> Tipper: Arms folded, she almost imperceptibly shook her head. I thought: Sen-
> sible woman.[40]

Gore and his entourage stayed in Kyrgyzstan's capital, Bishkek, that night.
Calling from Bishkek, the American vice president told Nazarbayev that he
hoped Kazakhstan would vote to join the NPT.[41] The Americans landed safely
at Almaty the next day.

On December 13, 1993, two years after the Soviet Union's collapse had left
Kazakhstan in possession of a nuclear legacy, its government was finally ready
to join the NPT as a non-nuclear-weapon state. Nazarbayev arrived at the parliament to give a reassuring speech in support of joining the NPT:

> Would our external security and defense needs continue to be met after we sign
> the NPT? The answer is a categorical Yes. Our security and our defense would
> not only not suffer but, to the contrary, they would be qualitatively different.[42]

Nazarbayev described the efforts his government had taken to negotiate
with the United States, China, and Russia in order to obtain security guarantees
for Kazakhstan. He also explained why it was not in Kazakhstan's best interests
to keep the weapons:

> Further presence of nuclear weapons on our territory cannot be justified either
> politically, economically, or militarily. We are not in a position to maintain a

technical level of safety of nuclear weapons on our own, and this is a constant complicating factor in our relationship with Russia. Moreover, the presence of such weapons in Kazakhstan, without complete and comprehensive control over them, is fraught with an enormous security threat, [and] makes us practically a hostage of the military-strategic decisions of others.[43]

Nazarbayev emphasized that keeping nuclear weapons would put "an unbearable financial burden on a young state."[44] Having been so promised by the Americans, he told the parliament that Kazakhstan would receive financial compensation from the sale of highly enriched uranium from the dismantled warheads.[45] He estimated that the amount would be "roughly one billion dollars," noting that the sum would become a major contribution to Kazakhstan's currency reserves.[46] Nazarbayev's figure of a billion dollars was higher than the estimate of the Kazakh Atomic Energy Commission ($400–600 million) but lower than what Zhukeev insisted Kazakhstan should get ($2 billion). In fact, it would take many years for Kazakhstan and Russia to sort through the specifics of profit-sharing.

The parliament voted 238 to 1 in favor of joining the NPT. At last, Kazakhstan had officially committed never to seek the bomb, paving the way for the removal of all nuclear weapons from its land.

During Gore's visit, he and President Nazarbayev signed an umbrella agreement on the Nunn-Lugar Cooperative Threat Reduction (CTR) program—a novel initiative under which the United States would, among other things, pay for dismantlement of nuclear forces and associated infrastructure in Kazakhstan. Defense officials signed initial CTR implementing agreements which would, among other things, support this activity. Kazakhstan and the United States also signed a number of other agreements on military cooperation, science and technology projects, and other matters.[47]

With plenty to celebrate, the Kazakh government hosted an official reception that night. Afterward, Nazarbayev invited the Gores to a post-dinner party at his home. Zhukeev, Gore, Prime Minister Sergei Tereshchenko, Talbott, Courtney, and Gore's senior staff were there. That night, Gore and Nazarbayev talked for an hour in Nazarbayev's study.

Afterward, Nazarbayev's family treated their American guests to an impromptu concert of Kazakh songs. Everyone in the family seemed to have a musical talent. Nazarbayev and his wife sang multiple songs after which they turned to their American guests. "We were embarrassed and humbled," Ambassador Courtney recalls. Unlike their Kazakh hosts, who easily sang numerous songs in Kazakh and in Russian, the only lyrics all Americans knew were for "Home on the Range," the unofficial hymn of the American West.[48]

With Kazakhstan now firmly committed to a nonnuclear future and the Nunn-Lugar Cooperative Threat Reduction agreement in place, the two countries could focus on freeing Kazakhstan from its nuclear inheritance. Nuclear adventures and secret operations, worthy of James Bond movies, awaited them.

CHAPTER 9

PROJECT SAPPHIRE AND THE NUNN-LUGAR COOPERATIVE THREAT REDUCTION PROGRAM

BEFORE THE FIRST RAYS OF SUNLIGHT emerged on that chill November day in 1994, trucks loaded with steel containers of highly enriched uranium made their way to the airport of the industrial town of Ust-Kamenogorsk, in eastern Kazakhstan. The trucks, facing black ice and pounding, freezing rain, had departed from the Ulba Metallurgical Plant, previously one of the Soviet Union's leading suppliers of nuclear fuel. Due to the facility's sensitive mission, even the names of the nearby bus stops were misleading and had nothing to do with the plant. The entire town was "closed" during Soviet times, known only under the code name Mailbox Number 10.

Danger stalked the convoy as it approached the airport. At any moment, the trucks might slide on the sleet and overturn, spilling their extraordinary cargo—enough HEU to build more than twenty nuclear bombs. Or a well-informed terrorist group might attack the trucks and steal the uranium.

This precarious drive was part of an ultra-secret Kazakh-American operation known as Project Sapphire. Its goal was to airlift Kazakh HEU to a safe location in the United States.

Project Sapphire opened a years-long effort by these two nations, sometimes with the help of Russia, to destroy the silos where missiles used to sit, seal the tunnels and boreholes where underground nuclear tests were conducted, and secure nuclear material. Most of these efforts were possible thanks to an innovative project—the Cooperative Threat Reduction program established thanks to Senators Sam Nunn and Richard Lugar and sponsored by the United States.

Kazakhstan's journey from the decision to give up its nuclear inheritance to actually becoming nuclear-free required diplomatic tightrope-walking between two superpowers—the United States and Russia. Both nations possessed elements vital for the success of Kazakhstan's plan: the United States had the money that would pay for Kazakhstan's denuclearization, while Russia held all the sensitive information on Kazakhstan's nuclear infrastructure.

PROJECT SAPPHIRE

In 1993, Kazakhstan prepared to join the NPT as a non-nuclear-weapon state. As part of its obligations under the NPT, it was required to put all nuclear material on its territory under the safeguards of the International Atomic Energy Agency (IAEA). Nuclear facilities had to conduct internal housekeeping before opening up to the international inspectors. As a soon-to-be non-nuclear-weapon state with no plans and ambitions to build a nuclear weapon, Kazakhstan would have to demonstrate that whatever nuclear material it possessed was necessary for peaceful nuclear purposes, such as nuclear science or a civilian nuclear program. Moreover, for any material that Kazakhstan kept, it had to ensure that the material was safely and securely stored.

Meanwhile, the Ulba Metallurgical Plant, Kazakhstan's main nuclear industrial facility inherited from the Soviet Union, was struggling financially to keep afloat. In its heyday, Ulba had been a flagship facility of the Soviet nuclear program. In the 1970s and 1980s, it produced almost half of all fuel pellets used in Soviet-type nuclear power reactors. It also fabricated HEU fuel pellets for the secret nuclear submarine project Alfa. At its peak Ulba was the world's second-largest producer of beryllium and fourth-largest producer of tantalum, two metals with rare characteristics and widespread usefulness.

Beryllium is a rare metal of gray color. Due to its unusual properties, such as having a melting point of more than 1200° C (2300° F), beryllium is used in the aerospace industry, typically in missiles and satellites. As such, it is a dual-use material—equally useful for peaceful and military purposes. International export controls regulate products containing beryllium and require suppliers to seek permission from their governments before exporting them. Tantalum, another rare metal, is blue-gray in color and has a melting point of more than 3000° C (5400° F). It is resistant to corrosion and has high endurance in severe conditions. Like beryllium, its export is controlled because it is valuable for both military and peaceful applications, in space and missile programs, advanced electronics, and video systems.

During the early 1990s, the Ulba plant had fallen on hard times. With the collapse of the Soviet economy, the plant lost most of its orders from formerly powerful Soviet ministries. As a result, its production had to be reduced by ten to fifteen times, with Ulba managers mothballing most product lines except for those using uranium.[1] Plant employees' paychecks were delayed as well.[2]

Although production at Ulba had nosedived, a warehouse still stored something of great value and extreme danger—highly enriched uranium. The material was a leftover from the secret Soviet Alfa-class nuclear submarine projects. The fuel assemblies produced for Alfa submarines contained beryllium and HEU enriched to 90 percent. The project ended in the 1980s, leaving behind more than two metric tons of fuel elements containing more than 600 kilograms of HEU.

Kazakhstan wrestled with many questions surrounding this trove of uranium. The major ones were: What about the risk of theft? Did it want to keep this material? If not, to whom to give it?

And many outside Kazakhstan had their eyes on Ulba. Vladimir Bozhko, the national security official responsible for the East Kazakhstan region at the time, hinted that foreign powers were interested in Ulba and what it stored. In the early 1990s, intelligence agents from foreign embassies had become quite active in collecting information about Ulba. "Even taking a photo of Ulba from a bridge [across the river] was [considered to be] pre-intelligence [gathering]," he said.[3]

According to Kazakh officials, foreign countries were curious not only about Ulba but about Kazakhstan's entire nuclear inheritance—nuclear weapons and nuclear material. The foreign minister at the time, Tuleitai Suleimenov, has described how emissaries from "several Arab countries" had tried to persuade Kazakhstan to keep the arsenal. "We will help you," they allegedly promised. Suleimenov even named names, asserting that Libya's leader Muammar Qaddafi had penned a letter to Kazakh leaders offering a billion dollars to help build "the first Muslim nuclear bomb."[4]

With all this in mind, the few people in Kazakhstan who knew about the nuclear material—Ulba's leadership and the highest government officials—hatched an ingenious plan. Kazakhstan should sell HEU to a safe buyer—the United States. That way, Kazakhstan would eliminate the risk that bad actors would acquire the material and the country could join the IAEA without having to declare an enormous amount of nuclear material it didn't need and would have to struggle to protect. As a cherry on top, Kazakhstan would receive the financial infusion it so badly needed in those times of economic crisis. Vitalii Mette, Ulba's entrepreneurial leader, was the best person to start the wheels rolling on this ambitious idea.

Mette, in his forties at the time, was charismatic and soft-spoken with blue eyes, wavy hair, and a bearing acquired in his time as a navy officer. Mette was born in a village in Kazakhstan not far from the Russian border and received training in naval engineering in Russia. In the 1970s, he served in the Soviet navy and manned a nuclear reactor on a nuclear submarine, so he knew well the origins of the HEU left behind by the Soviets at his plant.[5] He became Ulba's director at a young age and led Ulba through the tough years of transition from the Soviet system to independent Kazakhstan.

The interaction between Kazakhstan and the United States on the Ulba HEU would turn into one of the century's most impressive transfers of sensitive nuclear material. But it started very informally.

The authorization for Mette to disclose sensitive information to Americans came from the very top—Kazakhstan's president. Still, for a few months, the contact between Mette and the US embassy in Almaty remained clandestine. It was only in September of 1993 that Mette found a way to tell diplomats from the US embassy about Ulba's stash of uranium.

The first American that Mette told was Andy Weber, First Secretary, Chief of the Political Military Section at the US embassy in Kazakhstan, and Mette approached him through an intermediary. Weber had expertise in weapons of mass destruction (WMD) from his previous assignment in Bonn, where he worked against Qaddafi's WMD program. Weber had asked to be posted to Kazakhstan after he read a *Wall Street Journal* profile of the US embassy and Ambassador Courtney.[6] The piece was titled "Kazakhstan Is Best for Diplomats Who Find Paris a Bore." Weber was intrigued.

The first meeting between Mette and Weber took place discreetly in the office of a company that sold hunting equipment. The men chatted briefly. Weber, who had studied Russian before his posting to Almaty, did not need an interpreter. That evening, Weber, now joined by Ambassador Courtney, met with Mette again. Mette revealed that there was uranium at his facility but said nothing about the amount or its level of enrichment. An avid hunter, Mette then invited Weber to join him on one of his hunting expeditions in the picturesque Altai region of eastern Kazakhstan. Weber accepted.

It was October, and the first snow was falling. The two men, accompanied by a few others, spent a weekend bonding in typical Soviet male style—hunting, drinking beer and vodka, eating dried salted fish, and sweating in a steamy Russian sauna. The Kazakh national security service sent one of its men to accompany Mette and Weber. That special agent's shooting skills—he put down a moose with a Makarov revolver—made Weber joke that no enemy should take on Kazakhstan if its men could kill moose with a revolver.[7] The time they spent together built trust between Mette and Weber. Weber would later describe Mette as "a natural leader, very confident, and very smart, with a wry sense of humor."[8]

On the return trip from the hunt, Mette drove with Weber around the Ulba plant grounds for a windshield survey but did not offer to show the sensitive material. Even though Weber was Mette's guest, and the powers above him had authorized his communication with Weber, the Kazakh Committee on National Security was on alert. With an American official visiting sensitive nuclear facilities, special agents followed Weber's every move.[9]

By December of that year, the US embassy staff, including Weber, were busy preparing for Vice President Al Gore's visit to Almaty. After two years of negotiations with Washington, Kazakhstan was finally ready to move ahead and join the Treaty on the Non-Proliferation of Nuclear Weapons as a non-nuclear-weapon state. As we have seen, the Kazakhs timed their NPT ratification to coincide with Gore's visit. The two countries also sealed the umbrella Nunn-Lugar Cooperative Threat Reduction (CTR) agreement, which permitted US assistance for nonproliferation work, along with several implementing agreements. Against the backdrop of this new high in US-Kazakhstan relations, Mette arranged through his intermediary to meet Weber again.

This time Mette was ready to disclose to Weber the real value—and danger—of the material sitting at his plant. During the encounter, Mette's messenger, without saying it aloud, passed Weber a small piece of paper that read "U235, 90 percent, 600 kilos." This tiny note set off big alarms for the Americans. Uranium enriched to 90 percent, in that quantity, is enough to fill twenty weapons. And it sat at a facility in Kazakhstan with little protection. Any number of determined groups might try to get their hands on the material.

Weber immediately fired off a cable to Washington. A few days later, as Gore left Almaty, the US embassy staff woke Weber up in the middle of the night: "We received a Night Action cable from Washington," he was told. In diplomat-speak, a Night Action cable meant that the matter could not wait till

morning. Weber immediately drove to the embassy to read the cable and respond to "the thousand questions" it contained.[10]

But after the initial urgency, there was no movement on the issue for an entire month. Washington was preoccupied with other urgent nuclear matters—
Ukraine's resistance to giving up nuclear weapons and North Korea's reluctance
to let IAEA nuclear inspectors visit its sites.[11] Washington's lack of immediate
action could have also been because it had never dealt with anything similar
before—that is, the removal of highly sensitive nuclear material from another
country. No template existed on how to proceed. After a month of inaction,
Ashton Carter, one of the authors of Harvard's *Soviet Nuclear Fission* report on
nuclear risks in the disintegrating Soviet Union and then the Assistant Secretary of Defense for International Security Policy, volunteered to lead.

In February 1994, President Nazarbayev flew to Washington to meet with
President Clinton. As during his first official visit in 1992 to meet with President Bush senior, Nazarbayev stayed in the residence for foreign dignitaries,
Blair House. There Ambassador Courtney and Weber talked in confidence with
Nazarbayev and asked if the United States could send an expert to the Ulba facility to check out the uranium.[12] Nazarbayev agreed. With that, the Americans
received the official green light to proceed.

Meanwhile, senior US officials from several agencies met and discussed
how to move forward. The United States preferred that Russia take back the
material since it had secure storage facilities and the material originated in
Soviet facilities now in Russia. This would have been the quickest solution,
and lowest cost from the US perspective. According to media reports, some
officials, especially at the Department of Energy, wanted Russia to take the
material back "because of the legal, financial, and logistical headaches." Some
at the State Department worried about Russia's reaction if the United States
were to take the material.[13]

Ashton Carter from the Pentagon, Robert Gallucci from the State Department, and Daniel Poneman from the National Security Council decided that
the Pentagon would lead a secret operation to remove the HEU from Kazakhstan. Jeffrey Starr, the principal director for threat reduction policy in the Office
of the Secretary of Defense, would assemble an interagency "Tiger Team."

The pace of the mission then quickened. The following month, Elwood
Gift, a nuclear materials expert from the Oak Ridge National Lab in Tennessee, flew to Kazakhstan. From Almaty, Gift, accompanied by Weber and a lieu-
tenant colonel from Kazakhstan's Committee on National Security, traveled to

Ust-Kamenogorsk. Gift's and Weber's air tickets were in false names to maintain secrecy.[14]

What Gift and Weber saw at Ulba sent chills down their spines. Highly enriched uranium—two-thirds of which did not require any processing to be used in a nuclear weapon—was stored in a building protected with only a padlock.[15]

Gift conducted material analysis on site and confirmed that the uranium was enriched to 90 percent. He carefully packaged samples of the dangerous material in glass vials 1 centimeter in diameter by 4 centimeters long (0.4 inches diameter by 1.5 inches long) to be shipped to the Oak Ridge lab for further analysis. The samples, 15 grams (0.53 ounces) in total, were in different forms—metal chips or filings, four powders, and three small chunks of metal. When Oak Ridge specialists analyzed the samples, they determined that the average enrichment level hovered at 89.6 percent.[16]

In March 1994, Rose Gottemoeller of the US National Security Council chaired an interagency group in which American officials struggled with how to approach Russia about this matter. Would Russia want to take the material in? Would Russia be upset if Americans stepped in and removed material that was produced as part of the Soviet nuclear program? The representatives of the Department of Energy preferred that Russia take the Soviet HEU back. They worried that US environmental groups would protest transporting Soviet nuclear material to the United States. Pentagon officials preferred the opposite. They did not want Russia to increase its stock of nuclear material by more than half a ton.

It remains unclear whether the HEU at Ulba was forgotten by top Russian nuclear officials, or if information was so compartmentalized in Russia that the few people who were aware of it had moved on and were no longer in a position to shed light. The Soviet paper-based system of tracking material likely didn't help. The Russian Minister of Atomic Energy, Viktor Mikhailov, initially referred to the material as "waste." After some back and forth, Russia's vice president, Viktor Chernomyrdin, told Vice President Al Gore that the Americans could have the HEU.[17]

Nazarbayev also reached out directly to Yeltsin. "Yeltsin was indifferent," Nazarbayev later said. Yeltsin told Nazarbayev that, on the one hand, Kazakhstan could keep the HEU, but, on the other, "Why would you need it?"

The bottom line, according to Nazarbayev, was that "we were left alone with the United States [to deal with it]."[18]

Once it became clear that the matter was between only the Kazakhs and the Americans, planning started in earnest—but quietly. Nazarbayev was aware that other countries and their intelligence operatives were interested in the highly enriched uranium. "That is why we agreed with the US leadership that we would carry everything out in secret," Nazarbayev explained.[19] For the same reason, only a small number of people in the United States and Kazakhstan knew about the operation.

The mission received a code name—Project Sapphire—as a nod to the material's value. The story goes that one of the Oak Ridge lab scientists coined the name after seeing officials walking around with manila envelopes labeled "Kazakh HEU"—announcing to everyone the presence of weapons-grade material in a Central Asian state.[20]

In August 1994, a team from the Department of Energy traveled to Ust-Kamenogorsk to assess the situation. Two military personnel from the US embassy in Almaty accompanied them. One of them carried highly classified material back to Washington.[21]

THE SECRET OPERATION

By October 1994, after some bureaucratic delays in Washington, a US technical team descended on Ust-Kamenogorsk. The team consisted of twenty-nine men and two women, including twenty-five technical contractors of the Department of Energy (DOE), a communications technician, and a medical doctor also from the Department of Energy. The remaining four were staff members of the On-Site Inspection Agency (OSIA), a Pentagon group that conducted on-site inspections to verify nuclear forces' destruction under the US-Soviet agreement on intermediate-range nuclear weapons.[22] The final approval from President Clinton came at the last minute. The OSIA team left Washington for Knoxville, Tennessee, on October 6, 1994, to meet the rest of the group. The next day, on the eve of the team's scheduled departure, Clinton authorized the plan.

Over the next two days, three US military cargo planes carrying the technical team and their equipment departed Knoxville for Ust-Kamenogorsk. The planes, Lockheed Galaxy C-5s, were a model that the United States deployed in all major military operations and were outfitted for refueling in midair. The airport of Ust-Kamenogorsk had never received planes like these. The city's air traffic controllers described the scene: "We didn't know what kind of aircraft would arrive . . . and the Americans only had approximate data on the airport. . . . They almost landed on a nearby highway [instead of the landing strip]."[23]

While it was a secret operation, there was no way to hide the landing of gigantic aircraft at a small provincial airport. Locals heard the C-5s' roar on their approach, and the word spread around town: "The Americans are here." But the public didn't learn the real purpose of the visit until much later.

The team planned for complete self-sufficiency while in Kazakhstan. They carried their own heaters, generators, and supplies.[24] Within four days of arrival, with no time for acclimatization or rest, the team set up all the equipment and started packaging the Ulba HEU for transport.[25]

As if a few hundred tons of HEU was not enough to worry about, during the packing of the HEU the Americans saw a stack of wooden crates with beryllium postmarked to an Iranian address. As Mette told Weber, the middlemen transacting the deal on behalf of the Iranians had put in an order but disappeared as soon as the Ulba personnel requested their end-use certificate.[26] This document certifies that an imported dual-use good will not be used in a military program.

Iran's top nuclear official, Reza Amrollahi, denied a US charge that Iran had tried to buy enriched uranium from Kazakhstan in 1992 or that Iran had sent a purchasing team to Kazakhstan and come back empty-handed: "We didn't send any team . . . Definitely not. What is the use of enriched uranium for? The Russians do have many, many nuclear weapons but they couldn't use them. I think the bomb age is over. We don't think we need a nuclear weapon."[27]

The technical team worked six days a week, with only one day to rest. To save time during their long twelve-hour shifts, they ate ready-to-eat military meals on site.[28] The bus brought them to the Ulba plant from their hotel before daylight and returned them after nightfall, all to minimize exposure and avoid publicity.[29]

The Ulba staff, which had never before interacted with Westerners, and the American visitors, some of whom had never before traveled abroad, got along well. "They treated us to coffee," a woman in charge of the warehouses at Ulba recalls. Local employees, in turn, introduced their American guests to local specialties. They cooked fish soup, which the Americans relished. They also brought homemade pickled cucumbers and tomatoes, a staple in Soviet families. Each summer, families would pickle vegetables to enjoy them in wintertime when no fresh vegetables were available. The warehouse manager laughed as she recalled how confused their American guests were when they were asked to return their empty glass pickle jars.[30] Even such simple things as glass jars were scarce in Kazakhstan at the time.

There were some glitches in the operation. In its after-action report, the military complained that DOE members of the team "were poorly prepared for the mission" and "failed to grasp the gravity of their situation." Thrown into hard conditions in a strange land and with less rigorous security training than the military, the technical personnel sometimes disclosed sensitive information during health and welfare phone calls home on unsecured lines or chatted too freely about classified details at the hotel. Some were not physically fit for the demanding task, the military also claimed. But, as the same report acknowledged, "the composition, technical competency, and ingenuity of the DOE technical team was perfect for the nature of the project: there were no technical problems that could not be handled by the team."[31]

It took the team four weeks to handle 2,200 kilograms (4,850 pounds) of material rendered into various shapes. All in all, there were roughly 600 kilograms (1,322 pounds) of HEU. Handling and packing were difficult because the material was toxic and corrosive. The team packed the HEU into 448 shipping containers, each 6 meters (19.7 feet) in length; then eight containers were packed together into one cargo restraint transporter (CRT), for fifty-six CRTs in total.[32] By November 16, everything and everyone were ready to go, but it would take another few days before the operation would be complete.

The C-5s that brought the team to Ust-Kamenogorsk were back at Incirlik in Turkey, and their return to pick up the team and the material was delayed due to a combination of mechanical problems with the aircraft and erroneous weather reporting.

The weather reporting for the trip was outdated, which baffled Weber, who provided current weather reports to the Air Operations Center: "C-5s were staged at Incirlik. I remember looking at blue skies in Ust-Kamenogorsk and being told by the US Air Force that they couldn't fly due to bad weather. It was very frustrating."[33] A few days were lost in waiting for the C-5s. When the planes did arrive, the weather also had its customary plans. It was now late fall, and conditions deteriorated with each day. When the trucks loaded with the dangerous cargo finally left the Ulba facility for the airport at 3 a.m. on that grim November day, they slid on black ice.

Police and security officers accompanied the trucks. Weber rode in the lead vehicle with General Bozhko from Kazakhstan's National Security Committee. By then, the two men had gotten to know each other well as they had worked closely to coordinate security for the secret operation. Bozhko, who was organized and possessed a command presence, was gregarious and had a good sense of humor. But that night, both Bozhko and Weber were on edge. Bozhko summed up the finale of the operation with a Russian proverb: "A spoonful of tar spoils a barrel of honey." He described the treacherous conditions that night: "It started raining heavily, and temperatures dropped below freezing. The road turned into a skating rink. And those were huge trailer trucks with containers full of uranium. You can imagine, if one of the containers dropped or a trailer overturned, what would happen."[34] Weber, sitting next to Bozhko as they drove, was equally terrified of a potential disaster: "I just couldn't imagine having to report to Washington that one [of the trucks] slid off right into the Irtysh River."[35]

Luckily, people in Kazakhstan know how to drive on ice, joked Weber.[36]

Similar harrowing conditions awaited the convoy at the airfield: sleet, ice, and rain. When the first C-5 from Incirlik arrived, the team loaded it with half the HEU cargo. It lifted off on November 20. The next day, two more C-5 cargo planes were loaded with the rest of HEU, the technical team and its equipment, and departed from Ust-Kamenogorsk.[37] The planes flew 9,000 kilometers (almost 6,000 miles) nonstop to Dover Air Force base in Delaware. Several refuelings were done in the air. Lt. Colonel Mike Foster, in charge of the airlift, said, "we were sitting there in the cockpit, writing Tom Clancy novels in our heads about what would happen if we had to go down."[38] All went well, and the planes landed safely. The Kazakh HEU was loaded onto "safe and secure transports" (SSTs), which looked like truck trailers but were, as Ashton Carter and William Perry described, "a veritable funhouse of violent tricks that immobilize, stun, or kill anyone who tries to hijack them or tamper with them."[39] The heavily protected SSTs were tracked with radio beacons throughout their drive to Oak Ridge.

Despite the best efforts to keep the operation secret, someone in the US media learned about it about fifteen hours before completion—after the planes landed at Dover but before the cargo arrived at Oak Ridge. The White House, citing national security, asked the journalist not to disclose the story before material was safety in the Oak Ridge facility. The journalist agreed.[40]

After the trucks arrived at Y-12, the heads of the three agencies which spearheaded the operation—William Perry of the Department of Defense, Warren Christopher of the State Department, and Hazel O'Leary of the Department of Energy—held a press conference in Washington. US Ambassador Bill Courtney and Kazakh Ambassador Tuleitai Suleimenov (formerly the foreign minister) joined the high-level officials.

Defense Secretary Perry, who was highly respected in Kazakhstan and described as "an extremely competent, thoughtful negotiator,"[41] opened the press conference and summed up the security value of Project Sapphire: "By removing [HEU] from the Ulba Metallurgical Facility in Kazakhstan where it was stored, and placing it at the [Oak Ridge] plant, we have put this bomb-grade nuclear material forever out of the reach of potential black marketeers, terrorists, or a new nuclear regime."[42] Perry also wanted to make sure that nobody blamed the Kazakh government for the conditions of storage at the Ulba plant:

> I want to emphasize, [the Kazakhs] were guarding this material properly. The statement that it was poorly guarded is not correct. But it was a great drain on their resources to do it. They do not have the facilities that enable them to do that routinely, as we do. It's much more effective and efficient for this to be included in the large supply of similar material that we have at the [Oak Ridge] plant.[43]

Shortly after the US press conference, the Russian media published a commentary from a representative of the Russian Ministry of Atomic Energy. This official implied that the United States had exaggerated the security risk involved:

> Any nuclear physics undergraduate knows that beryllium-alloyed uranium, even if highly enriched, is suitable only for power plants (for instance, nuclear submarines or icebreakers). Experts believe that only Russia or the United States can produce a bomb from $U235$ alloyed with beryllium. Only these countries possess a technology for refining uranium from beryllium isotopes which the USSR used deliberately to "tarnish" uranium in order to prevent its further use for military purposes.[44]

The Russian nuclear establishment appeared irritated that the United States had pulled off this high-profile project. Another controversy, this time about the actual amount of material, hit the news two years later thanks to a story in the *Washington Times*, a conservative daily newspaper. The story implied that almost 50 pounds (22 kilograms) of HEU had gone missing during the operation.

On October 24, 1996, at a press briefing at the Pentagon, journalists alerted by the story wanted to know where the "missing" Kazakh HEU had gone. The Pentagon official responded that an accounting error was likely responsible and advised the media to inquire at the Department of Energy, which was "looking into it." The Department of Energy called the claim of missing HEU "completely false" and further stated that the containers were sealed in Kazakhstan and under protection at all times.

Bolat Nurgaliev, who participated in Project Sapphire and who succeeded Suleimenov as the Kazakh ambassador to the United States, met with the Department of Energy's representatives and the *Washington Times* journalist who wrote the story. It transpired that an internal DOE memo mentioning a revised amount of HEU (down by 49 pounds [22 kilograms] from the initially publicized amount) had been leaked.[45] That leaked memo was the basis of the journalist's story.

A couple of days after the Pentagon briefing, the US government explained in a statement what had happened:

> At the time the U.S. crew packaged this material for transport to the United States, much of it was not well characterized, and the quantities of HEU were not well defined. Both governments clearly understood that the quantities of HEU were imprecise. The point was to secure the material first and perform accurate characterization of material later. The fact that DOE analysis of the materials imported is now resulting in a different total quantity of highly enriched uranium than the original estimate is not a surprise. Nor does it indicate that some of the original material was diverted.[46]

Paying for the secret operation "took a village" on the US side. Kim Savit, who was instrumental in identifying the funds authorized and appropriated from multiple agencies, said: "It was not a single effort—there were multiple agencies, multiple programmatic ways. It was not something the United States had done before. We were learning as we went how to develop new programs and how to coordinate among all those different agencies. Nobody wanted to use their appropriations, but everyone wanted to participate. It is always easier to do programs with someone's else money."[47] In the end, the Department of Energy paid for its involvement, the Department of Defense for its, and the Department of State reimbursed Ulba for the SWU value of the HEU (SWU is a separative work unit, a standard measure of the effort required to separate isotopes of uranium during an enrichment process).

The actual compensation for Kazakh HEU was another sensitive hurdle to overcome. In April of 1994, Vladimir Shkolnik, then head of Kazakhstan's Agency on Nuclear Energy, was invited to DC to negotiate this point. At that time, he was in Monterey, California, where he was a guest of the Monterey Institute of International Studies. At a meeting at the State Department, Shkolnik found himself to be the lone representative of Kazakhstan in a group of many US officials. His American counterparts told Shkolnik that the uranium in question was worth $3 million. Shkolnik told the Americans, "I cannot accept or refuse. I just do not know the market." According to Shkolnik, in the end, Kazakhstan received the equivalent of $30 million.[48]

Some of these resources came in the form of in-kind assistance for medical facilities in the Semipalatinsk region, which had suffered greatly from the Soviet nuclear tests; for the cities of Semipalatinsk and Kurchatov, and for the Ulba facility, which had stored the HEU. As described by her colleagues, it was Kim Savit who "literally got on the phone to U.S. medical supply companies, asking what could be donated."[49]

Five hospitals in the Semipalatinsk region, including one that specialized in cancer treatment, received equipment worth $1.74 million. The medical supplies that went to the cities of Semipalatinsk and Kurchatov ranged from durable medical equipment down to syringes. The Ulba nuclear plant received $2.2 million worth of medical equipment for patient monitoring, ultrasound, anesthesia, and other services for a medical facility catering to its employees. Americans also supplied the Ulba facility with specialized equipment for protecting, accounting, and controlling nuclear material, including an alarm system for material storage areas.[50]

In addition, the Project Sapphire money paid for the computers supplied to several Kazakh government agencies. The tax agency received computers worth $1.15 million. The agencies involved in implementing export controls received computers worth $2 million. Additionally, the US Department of Energy helped its partners from the Kazakh Committee on Atomic Energy with a half-million dollars for conducting inspections at its nuclear facilities.[51]

Thanks to Project Sapphire, the International Science and Technology Center (which was headquartered in Moscow with funding from the United States, European Union, Japan, and other countries) financed seven scientific projects in Kazakhstan. The projects focused on helping the country with its immediate nuclear challenges, such as analyzing the scope of radioactive contamination at the Semipalatinsk Polygon, and devising better controls for nuclear material. Under one of the ISTC-funded projects, for example, scientists modeled the migration of radionuclides through the soil and underground water.[52]

Under Project Sapphire, Kazakhstan's National Nuclear Center received eight pursuit vehicles equipped with radios and patrol lights, five minivans, eight pickup trucks, four buses, twenty Nikon cameras, more than a hundred computers, eighty printers, ten scanners, ten photocopiers, computer software, and medical supplies.[53]

Behind the Hollywood-style dazzle of the secret operation—with its secret meetings, technical team deployment, and C-5 nonstop flights between the continents—what remains most important is the quiet trust between Kazakhstan and the United States that allowed for the operation to happen. As Carter and Perry would later marvel, it was extraordinary that when Nazarbayev, "Kazakhstan's former Communist party boss and its first president after the Soviet Union disintegrated—discovered that there was a huge quantity of bomb-grade highly enriched uranium on the territory of his new Central Asian state, he called the president of the United States half a world away and asked to have it taken away for safekeeping."[54] The communication on Project Sapphire went all the way to the top—to the level of Presidents Clinton and Nazarbayev.[55]

Project Sapphire was the first major US-Kazakh joint operation in the nuclear field. "We passed the audition," American officials joked. After Project Sapphire, Kazakhs were ready to tell the Americans about other sensitive security challenges they faced. Those problems included tons of spent fuel that contained plutonium, unprotected sample collections of rare infectious diseases such as bubonic plague and tularemia left from the Soviet bioweapons program, plutonium vulnerable to theft, and tunnels and boreholes at the Polygon with radioactive material inside. Project Sapphire was just the beginning for more joint activity. The trust built during the operation opened the door to a wide range of projects in Kazakhstan funded by the Nunn-Lugar Cooperative Threat Reduction program.

THE ORIGINS OF THE NUNN-LUGAR PROGRAM

These projects all had their origins in late 1991, when the Soviet Union hung by a thread. Two US senators—Sam Nunn and Richard Lugar—proposed a radical idea: US taxpayers should pay to dismantle Soviet nuclear weapons infrastructure in the non-Russian republics, to help reduce Russian nuclear forces and to strengthen the security of sensitive Soviet nuclear material.

Right after the attempted coup against Soviet President Gorbachev in 1991, Senator Nunn traveled to Moscow. Gorbachev admitted to him that during the three days of the coup, it was not clear who was in command and control of Soviet nuclear weapons. Nunn reflected on what he heard: "I concluded that the Soviet Union was in great peril. In particular, I believed that we needed to do everything we could to help the Soviet authorities gain control and keep control over their nuclear weapons."[56]

Senator Nunn joined efforts with Les Aspin, the chair of the House Armed Services Committee, to pass a bill that would authorize humanitarian and security assistance to the Soviet Union. The bill failed. A few days later in Washington, Senator Nunn met for breakfast with two prominent Soviet military experts, Andrei Kokoshin and Sergei Rogov. They confirmed Nunn's fears that unless the Soviet Union received immediate assistance, the world would face a serious security problem.

Soon after, Nunn, a Democrat, joined with a Republican colleague, Senator Richard Lugar, to host a breakfast briefing for twenty key senators. They asked Ashton Carter, one of the authors of *Soviet Nuclear Fission*, to brief the senators on potentially dangerous scenarios that a collapsing nuclear power represented.[57] A few days after this briefing, Nunn and Lugar, with the help of twenty-four cosponsors, introduced a new bill that would address Soviet nuclear risks.

Nunn and Lugar sought support from the George H. W. Bush administration for their bill, but Secretary of Defense Dick Cheney opposed taking $400 million out of the defense budget for this purpose. So the Bush administration's National Security Council staff informed the senators that the administration neither supported nor opposed the bill. William Courtney, who now cochaired the interagency Safety, Security, and Dismantlement of Nuclear Weapons Working Group, reinforced this position in a meeting with senior staffers for Nunn and Lugar. But, as Courtney later reflected, "Congress saved us."[58]

Congress approved the Soviet Nuclear Threat Reduction Act, and on December 12, 1991, two weeks before the Soviet Union officially ceased to exist, President Bush signed it into law.[59] The program of assistance became known as the Nunn-Lugar Cooperative Threat Reduction (CTR) Program.

In those times of political and economic crisis in the former Soviet Union, fears ran high in the West that Soviet nuclear weapons, sensitive nuclear material, and the expertise of its weapons scientists could end up in the wrong hands. In Washington, policymakers knew that they'd rather help Belarus, Kazakhstan, Russia, and Ukraine to deal with those challenges than to see nuclear weapons fall into the hands of a terrorist group or some other countries keen on getting them. The United States wanted to prevent both Soviet nuclear material from showing up on the black market and Soviet weapons scientists, with no jobs or income, being forced to sell their expertise abroad.

By August 1992, Washington had informed the Kazakh capital that it could rely on CTR funds to pay for the dismantlement and elimination of former

Soviet nuclear weapons infrastructure on Kazakh territory. At that point, the Kazakh government was open to general discussions of US aid. However, it wasn't ready to go into specifics because it was still negotiating with the Russians about how weapons could be moved to Russia.[60]

Amid the heavy traffic of US officials visiting Kazakhstan during 1992–94, conversations about nonproliferation assistance under the Nunn-Lugar CTR program featured prominently. Senators Nunn and Lugar themselves traveled to Russia and the other "nuclear republics"—Belarus, Kazakhstan, and Ukraine—to talk about the availability of funding. During a meeting in November 1992, the senators told Nazarbayev that about $100–200 million could be made available to Kazakhstan for the destruction of silos and missiles. The visit happened days after Clinton won the presidency. Nazarbayev told the senators his government wasn't ready to talk substance but would be prepared to "begin negotiations and talk with the new administration on the full complex of questions."[61]

That same month, General William Burns, the first US special envoy for denuclearization negotiations with former Soviet countries under Nunn-Lugar, went to Kazakhstan to discuss potential cooperation. The US government offered specifics on potential areas for assistance: it could help with accident response during dismantlement and transfer activities, with building a control and accounting system for sensitive nuclear material, with designing an export control system to prevent the illegal transfer of sensitive goods, and with establishing a special government-to-government communication link between the two capitals.[62]

A few months later, in March 1993, Burns retired. The responsibility for negotiating the CTR agreements with Kazakhstan, Russia, Belarus, and Ukraine devolved upon Ambassador Jim Goodby, a seasoned US arms control negotiator who had joined the US Foreign Service in the 1950s.

Almost immediately after taking the new assignment, Goodby and his colleague Gloria Duffy from the Department of Defense embarked on their first visit to Kazakhstan. It was Goodby's first time anywhere in Central Asia and he liked Almaty from the start: "[It was] a pretty place with snow-covered Tian Shan mountains. We visited Medeu [an ice-skating rink up in the mountains outside of Almaty]. I also liked the food."[63]

Goodby's task was to secure Nazarbayev's commitment to the CTR program, but since Kazakhstan was still playing a waiting game and had not yet joined NPT as a non-nuclear-weapon state, the Kazakh president did not rush to say yes. Goodby described those first fruitless interactions: "Nazarbayev did not want to give way. There was nothing much I could do."[64]

Goodby's next trip, in September 1993, was more productive. He and his counterpart—Deputy Foreign Minister Bolat Nurgaliev—successfully negotiated the main provisions of the CTR umbrella agreement. With this framework for cooperation in the nuclear field in place, things started moving rapidly. Soon the agreement was ready for signature. "Seemed like Nazarbayev gave the green light," Goodby recalled.[65]

Still, when US Secretary of State Warren Christopher arrived in Almaty in October 1993, the Kazakhs refused to sign the $85 million CTR umbrella agreement because they were not ready to commit to the NPT. They said they needed a couple more months before they would be ready to take the plunge. Soon after Christopher's visit, Tulegen Zhukeev, Kazakhstan's state counselor, went to Washington to finalize the US security guarantees to Kazakhstan that sealed Kazakhstan's decision to join the NPT and to finalize details on the CTR umbrella agreement. Optics were another reason Kazakhs resisted signing agreements. To elevate the big moment, they preferred to wait for US Vice President Al Gore's visit to Almaty.

In December 1993, when Gore arrived, the Kazakh parliament finally voted for Kazakhstan to join the NPT as a non-nuclear-weapon state. Now that Kazakhstan was officially committed to a nonnuclear path, it was time to get down to business. CTR funds were to pay for most of the dismantlement and removal activities and for bolstering the security of nuclear material. It was against this backdrop that Gore and Nazarbayev signed the CTR umbrella agreement. Susan Koch from the Pentagon and General Alibek Kassymov from the Kazakh Defense Ministry signed five additional CTR implementing agreements that went into specifics on each area of cooperation. Separately, Gore announced that the United States would provide an aid package worth $140 million for civilian purposes.

The bulk of the CTR program focused on Russia, where it would pay to secure facilities containing nuclear weapons and material, install nuclear tracking and control systems, and create nonmilitary research opportunities for former weapons scientists. In Kazakhstan, Belarus, and Ukraine, the first and foremost goal for the US government and the CTR program was to dismantle and eliminate nuclear infrastructure. In addition, but on a smaller scale than in Russia, CTR funds would pay for removing or securing sensitive nuclear material, designing better systems to keep track of such material, and creating opportunities for scientists to work on civilian projects.

Cooperation under the CTR umbrella in Russia was more fraught than in the other republics because of mutual distrust. It was harder for the parties to cooperate on technical matters that went to the core of Russia's nuclear program, especially given that, as with the United States, nuclear weapons remained at the heart of Russia's national security strategy. Nonetheless, substantial cooperation took place over time, including to augment secure nuclear storage capacity and to strengthen the security of naval nuclear weapons.

In Kazakhstan, Belarus, and Ukraine, the CTR dynamic was different. Once these three countries had decided on the nonnuclear path, their governments were eager to cooperate with Americans. "In Kazakhstan, there was no sense of drawing boundaries in terms of what information to share. The geopolitical instinct was extremely different compared to Russia," said Pentagon official Laura Holgate.[66] Although cooperation was smoother, it wasn't without its challenges, which made its overall success even more notable.

When Congress approved the Nunn-Lugar legislation in 1991, it did so under a transfer authority. That meant the Pentagon was tasked to do the job and could transfer funds from any existing appropriations in its budget, but no new money was offered in the first year. The Pentagon had to report to Congress before every single transfer of funds from one of its lines of budget to a CTR project. "That made it very difficult to obligate the funds, and the Congress was upset that funds were not getting out of the door" shared Kim Savit, responsible for reporting to Congress on behalf of the Pentagon. A year later, Congress had appropriated direct funding to the CTR program, and it became easier to move funds for CTR projects.[67]

To persuade US lawmakers to spend US tax dollars on nonproliferation assistance, CTR champions in Congress attached a "Buy American" clause to the legislation. All equipment and many services for nonproliferation assistance for the former Soviet republics had to come from the United States whenever possible. For example, if project managers needed excavators to dig soil, they had to buy them from US suppliers, pay prices much higher than those charged for local equipment, wait for these items to be delivered, and, if they broke, wait for ages for spare parts to arrive. In addition, the US-made equipment was sometimes simply unsuitable for local conditions. Some machinery would break in the middle of Kazakhstan's harsh winters, for example. An anecdote from Holgate illustrates how little sense the "Buy American" rule made in some circumstances: "We wanted to provide radios for the fast boats that were going to patrol Kazakhstan's coastline, and guess what? American radios don't talk with Kazakhstan's base stations."[68] In addition, during the earlier years of the program, all projects were contracted to US companies. Kazakh subcontractors were left to carry out only low-tech activities, harming the spirit of international cooperation.

Nor did the priorities of the program fully align between the United States and Kazakhstan. The US government's highest goals were for the removal of nuclear weapons, the securing or removal of nuclear material, and the dismantlement and elimination of WMD infrastructure. While the Kazakh government shared those goals, it was also keen on preserving the country's scientific and technological foundations: where possible, it wanted to convert infrastructure to produce conventional weapons to equip Kazakhstan's young military or to set up production lines for civilian goods. After all, Kazakhstan's own resources—its materials and its labor—had gone into building those facilities and equipment. Razing what had been painstakingly built through the decades didn't appeal to Kazakhs. Attempts at defense conversion under the CTR program didn't succeed except for a handful of cases, one of them a former torpedo factory, Gidromash, that was transformed into the Byelkamit facility which produced cryogenic tanks for the oil and gas industry. A final blow for conversion hopes came in 1996 when the US Congress banned using CTR funds for any defense conversions in the former Soviet Union.[69]

The Americans pushed to shut down the few defense-related facilities that the Kazakhs had planned to keep. In the eyes of one former Kazakh official, "Americans sometimes would go too far. They proposed that the facility that produced torpedoes in Almaty should stop producing them. The United States was keen to buy up all the stock because, 'What if Iranians would want to buy them?'" Similarly, US officials pushed for the closure of the Uralsk Metallurgical Plant, which manufactured tanks. Kazakhs responded by reminding their American counterparts: "We are partners and friends. Partners should not be totally weak. We have plans for army modernization."[70]

Personnel shifts in both governments further complicated bilateral projects. As Holgate phrased it, the constant rotation of people on both sides "did not allow the human trust to develop." She added, "We underestimated how much stability would be important." Not surprisingly, for Kazakh participants who had never before worked with Western companies, the CTR project presented a steep learning curve. Holgate called it a "CTR MBA."[71]

Another novelty for former Soviet officials was the fact that four women— Laura Holgate, Susan Koch, Elizabeth Sherwood, and Gloria Duffy—led CTR efforts on behalf of the Pentagon: "It took a while before the disbelieving gener-als in Moscow, Kyiv, Minsk, and Almaty realized that these women really did carry the authority of the Secretary of Defense."[72] Holgate added that out of all post-Soviet states, "it was least an issue in Kazakhstan." She added: "I do not know how much this was due to the traditional Kazakh notion of being a good host, or their sense of their own equality coming out of the Slavic domination" of the Soviet era.[73]

Despite the challenges associated with cooperation in a sensitive field, the cultural and language obstacles, and the limitations introduced by the "Buy American" clause, the collaboration between Kazakhstan and the United States under Nunn-Lugar was an achievement of which both countries could be proud. Not only did they meet their own goals (shedding its nuclear burden for Kazakhstan, minimizing nuclear risk for the United States), but the experience fostered numerous personal friendships between Kazakhs and Americans and laid a foundation for bilateral cooperation in other areas.

Moreover, thanks to the CTR projects, many Americans visited Kazakhstan for the first time. Kazakhstan, a mixture of Soviet and Asian cultures, surprised and fascinated them. Americans enjoyed the warm hospitality and friendliness of their hosts. Still, at the same time, they saw telling signs of the economic crisis and the dilapidated infrastructure that plagued that new country in the early 1990s.

On arrival at Almaty airport, there wasn't even a baggage carousel. Instead, airport employees passed suitcases out through a tiny window. Passengers lined up and tossed up the luggage, much like a human conveyor belt. The people waiting for their luggage in those early days were a mix of foreigners from the oil and gas industry and missionaries eager to proselytize in the newly opened society. Indeed, adventurous foreigners swiftly filled up the few decent hotels in Almaty. On one trip, a Pentagon delegation struggled to secure rooms. But the good hotels were all fully booked because that week Almaty was hosting a trade show which had attracted many foreign entrepreneurs.

Roy Gardner, a US government lawyer who helped negotiate the CTR agreements, diplomatically described the hotel they eventually landed in as one "of lesser quality." In fact, its first floor was flooded and the rooms were not clean. When their colleagues at the Kazakh Defense Ministry realized where their American guests had found rooms, they told them: "You cannot stay there." "They put us in a nice hotel," Gardner said.[74]

American participants of CTR projects remember their first impressions of Almaty and Kazakhstan vividly. Seeing the Tian Shan mountains on landing in Almaty and their hosts' warmth and tremendous hospitality—the qualities that Kazakhs pride themselves on—top the list of most vivid first impressions.

Less formal interactions, the human elements of the first exposure of Americans and Kazakhs to each other, were no less important than the technical negotiations on safely and securely dismantling WMD infrastructure. Holgate was fascinated with Almaty architecture—typical Soviet buildings with a very distinct Central Asian twist thanks to their interesting surface decorations reflecting traditional Kazakh motifs. And to add to the exotic flavor of her first trip, she observed a camel walking in the snow down a major road.[75] It is not uncommon to see a colorfully decorated camel in Almaty's largest city parks—much to the joy of the kids who ride them.

On one of his trips to Kazakhstan, once the day's work was done, Gardner and his colleagues went for a stroll in a pedestrian square in central Almaty. There, local artists sold their work. One painting caught Gardner's eye, and he bought it on the spot. The artist then invited these total strangers to his apartment to see more of his paintings. It was a tiny apartment, with one room stacked with paintings from top to bottom. As any Kazakh would do, the artist invited his guests to stay for dinner. His wife prepared the most traditional Kazakh dish—*beshparmak*, made of mutton and layers of pasta. More than two decades later, Gardner still remembers this encounter with warmth: "It was the best dinner I had in Kazakhstan."[76]

James Turner, the associate director for nuclear weapons safety at the Department of Energy and another key American negotiator, described his first impressions of the country: "I never realized how big Kazakhstan was!" When Turner and his colleagues went to Aktau, the site of the fast-breeder plutonium reactor BN-350 in western Kazakhstan, they were fascinated by the sight of camels running loose in the steppe with the equivalent of dog tags around their necks.

Turner described meetings with his Kazakh counterparts as very cordial, productive, and professional: "They were well prepared, and I really enjoyed it," he said. He also offered a telling observation. During his initial visits to Kazakhstan, the senior officials he and his colleagues met with were often ethnic Russians. That pattern was a legacy of the Soviet practice of placing ethnic Russians in charge as directors of the factories, top officials in the regions, and heads of institutions, and Kazakhs or members of other non-Russian ethnicities as their subordinates. As Kazakhstan settled more and more into its independence, this ethnic division of power in the republic shifted. "Every time," Turner noticed, "[ethnic] Kazakhs were more and more in control."[77]

Turner, like many others in the 1990s who worked on nonproliferation assistance projects in Kazakhstan, keeps warm memories of his visits. In accordance with their traditions, Kazakh hosts gave him a long, embroidered coat, called a *chapan*, and a traditional embroidered cap, pointed on top and with a split upturned brim reminiscent of a ship. When Turner donned his ornate Kazakh outfit at home in the States, his cat was startled by the unusual hat.[78]

Weber stayed involved with Kazakhstan for decades after Project Sapphire and participated in many more cooperative threat reduction projects. He remembers that period with warm nostalgia, calling them "the best years" of his life when they "played hard" and "worked hard." Weber describes hunting and hiking in the "heavenly" Tian Shan mountains.[79]

Laura Holgate continued to work with Kazakhstan on nuclear matters for decades in and outside of the US government.

The twenty years of cooperative threat reduction that followed Project Sapphire created many good memories. Above all, they made the world safer.

CHAPTER 10

FAREWELL TO BOMBS

THE SEMIPALATINSK POLYGON, once a secret and highly guarded place in the Soviet Union, was now wide open to humans and animals. The Polygon operated no longer, but its immense infrastructure—hundreds of structures above and below the ground, tunnels and boreholes for nuclear tests, and kilometers of cables made of high-quality copper—remained. Given the socioeconomic crisis that engulfed Kazakhstan, the now-open Polygon became a target. Metal scavengers—both locals who struggled to feed their families and organized groups eager to profit from an abandoned site—started showing up every day in search of valuable metal. Not knowing or not caring about radioactive contamination, they dug out cable and took what they wanted with no safeguards.

But the Polygon's tunnels and boreholes were laced with unvaporized nuclear material, and buried underground were containers with plutonium that had been abandoned by the military. In addition to nuclear tests, hydronuclear and hydrodynamic experiments (tests that produce a low yield, comparable to conventional explosions) left behind radioactive contamination. Above ground, in some parts of the Polygon, the soil contained enough radiological material to make a "dirty" bomb. It turned out that in addition to testing nuclear devices, the Soviet military had experimented with dispersing radiological material to see if it would work in combat.

Behind all this lay a dark fear: What if not just entrepreneurial scavengers but determined terrorist groups or state agents were hunting for nuclear or radiological material at the Polygon? Moreover, what about other Kazakh nuclear facilities that had nuclear material and could be appealing to terrorist groups?

The Kazakh government thus faced daunting nuclear-security risks. In the early 1990s, Kazakhstan still hosted the fourth largest nuclear arsenal in the world—intercontinental ballistic missiles, nuclear warheads, heavy bombers, and the military bases that supported them. Now that the Kazakh government had committed to a nonnuclear future, it wanted to get rid of these nuclear hazards as quickly and as safely as possible.

Nuclear security was just one concern. Repairing the environment and shielding public health were vital as well. How to clean up and secure the vast territory of the Polygon? And how to do it without knowing what had been left behind? In addition to nuclear tests and experiments with nuclear and radiological material at the Polygon, the Soviet nuclear-industrial complex had experimented with peaceful nuclear explosions at smaller testing grounds across the country. They required cleanup as well.

Nor was the environmental and technological damage limited to the Polygon and other testing grounds. As the Russian military withdrew, it left behind missile silos, military bases, and storage facilities full of toxic missile fuel.

And Kazakhstan had to continue balancing its superpower relations. It could not afford to antagonize its former patron Russia. Kazakhstan still depended on it for the needed information about the nuclear sites, so it engaged Russia to the fullest extent possible in denuclearization projects. As for Kazakhstan's relations with the United States, fortunately they were not so tense and distrustful as those between Russia and the United States. Kazakhstan did not carry the baggage of a defeated superpower, nor did it see the United States as a former archenemy. Instead, Kazakhstan perceived the United States as a powerful conduit that could help it grow its economy and enter the international community. Thanks to the ingenuity of Senators Nunn and Lugar and their Cooperative Threat Reduction Program, Kazakhstan had access to practical help from the United States in removing and eliminating nuclear weapons infrastructure and materials and securing its nuclear facilities.

But even more important than political will at the highest level was the uniting power of science. Scientists, engineers, and technical experts from Kazakhstan, the United States, and Russia, not burdened by ideological differences, were at the forefront of efforts. They often saved the day by finding ways to break through bureaucratic processes and overcome technical obstacles and

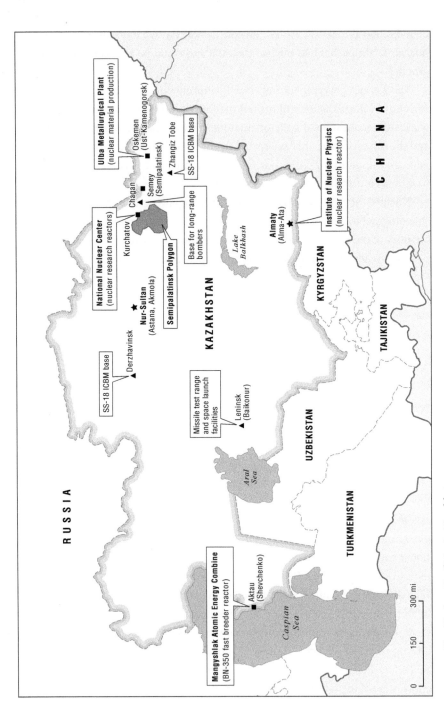

MAP 2   Key Nuclear Facilities in Kazakhstan.

political barriers. These unsung heroes played a significant part in moving along denuclearization projects on the ground.

A DIFFICULT CHANGING OF THE GUARD AT THE POLYGON

After the Soviet Union collapsed in December 1991, the Russian military remained in the satellite town of Kurchatov and controlled the Polygon until December 1993. During that time, the status of the military divisions stationed in Kazakhstan and the future of the Polygon remained unclear. In fact, the Polygon staff and the military found themselves between three jurisdictions—the now dissolved Soviet Union, the Russian Federation, and the newly independent Kazakhstan.

In late 1992, the Polygon's head—General Yuri Konovalenko—described in a letter to President Nazarbayev the Polygon staff's precarious position. In 1991–92, not a single young specialist arrived at the Polygon, while many of the best specialists left the Polygon because of its uncertain future. With no new equipment and ties to Russia's scientific institutions disappearing, the Polygon's staff could not carry out serious scientific research. But despite the hardships, in 1992, the remaining Polygon staff did what it could within the limits of the circumstances. For example, they conducted retrospective research on radiation doses received by the population living near the Polygon. They carried out other projects in and around the Polygon, which now stood silent.[1]

Not surprisingly, Polygon specialists felt betrayed by both the Kazakh and Russian governments. The Kazakh government was not keen on trying to keep the Polygon specialists, and the Russian government was preoccupied with more immediate challenges. "They did not come and protect us"—from an increasingly hostile political and social environment around the Polygon—was a prevalent sentiment.

The law guiding the Soviet "divorce" stated that all property present in each newly independent republic at the time of the collapse remained that republic's property. Nevertheless, the Kazakh government struggled to control when, how, and with what the formerly Soviet (and now Russian) military departed from its territory during the 1991–93 period when many practical matters yet remained to be worked out between Russia and Kazakhstan. For Kazakhstan, this lack of control over its sovereign territory manifested visibly and painfully at the Polygon and Kurchatov.

More specifically, as the Russian troops were leaving the Polygon, Kazakhstan's customs officials could not inspect the cargo flown out on airplanes
and taken by trains from Kurchatov to Russia. Even two years after becoming an independent country, in 1993, Kazakh authorities were denied access
to both the Polygon and Kurchatov. The Russian military still operated the
checkpoints.

In September 1993, in an internal document, the deputy governor of the
Semipalatinsk region, Akezhan Kazhegeldin, lamented the situation: "This in
no way can help Kazakhstan to retain its property located at the former Semipalatinsk Polygon and Kurchatov." Kazhegeldin urged the national government
to take urgent measures to preserve the town to make sure that the newly created National Nuclear Center in Kurchatov could function.[2] The Kazakh government had established the National Nuclear Center to preserve scientific and
technical knowledge for peaceful nuclear research and to study and deal with
the consequences of nuclear testing at the Polygon.

Moreover, in 1993, when the Kazakh government commission assigned to
oversee the property transfer arrived at Kurchatov to make an inventory of the
property, documents, and materials, the Polygon's leadership initially did not
even allow commission members in and refused to allow troops from the Ministry of Internal Affairs of Kazakhstan to replace the Russian soldiers who were
guarding the Polygon and the town. In his refusal General Konovalenko cited
orders from the Russian Defense Ministry.[3]

Shortly afterward, Kazakhstan's military prosecutor accused Konovalenko
of illegally selling cable and equipment to commercial enterprises. The cable
in question, with a total length of 1,000 kilometers (625 miles), came from the
Polygon, and Konovalenko had authorized its sale at dumping prices. Commercial buyers then exported it abroad. In his defense, Konovalenko said he
was "sure he was selling property of Russia, not Kazakhstan, because even if
there [was] an agreement between Russia and Kazakhstan proclaiming testing
grounds [in general] to be a property of Kazakhstan, there was no separate
agreement on the Semipalatinsk Polygon. It wasn't transferred to Kazakhstan,
and that mean[t] the cable belong[ed] to Russia."[4] If this argument was accepted at face value, it meant that the Russian military rushed to sell off as
much as it could before the formal transfer of the town of Kurchatov and the
Polygon to Kazakhstan.

In addition to selling cable, Konovalenko authorized used cables to
be converted into high-grade scrap metal, valuable because it contained

electronics-grade copper. The Polygon's leadership was also busy selling the buildings—hotels, army canteens, army barracks—to be converted to commercial use, as well as equipment and automobiles at below-market prices. According to an investigation document from Kazakhstan's military prosecutor, the funds received from those sales were sent to Russia to pay for the construction of summer houses for high-ranking Russian military officials. Konovalenko never denied any of this. Instead, he said that as a Russian military officer, he followed the orders of his superiors in Moscow.[5]

In December 1993, the Russian Defense Ministry disbanded divisions stationed at the Polygon and brought its troops back to Russia. Kazakhstan's government was now in charge of the Polygon and Kurchatov, on its own to deal with the remaining problems, the extent of which it didn't yet fully grasp.

Over the next few years, whether on the issue of the Polygon or on their broader relationship, Kazakhstan worked to assert itself with Russia. This often required delicacy. Kazakhstan wanted to maintain a friendly relationship with its powerful neighbor while reclaiming its sovereignty.

And what about Kazakhstan's dealings with the United States, its other most crucial international relationship? Kazakhstan was doing well. As Nazarbayev prepared for his meeting with President Clinton in Washington in February 1994, Clinton's advisors were busy writing memos for the American president on how he should respond to Nazarbayev's concerns about Russia. Beyond that, the visit promised to be a good occasion to celebrate the progress in the US-Kazakhstan relationship.

FEBRUARY 1994: NAZARBAYEV MEETS CLINTON

"I remember it as being a joyous trip," said Ambassador Thomas Simons, who then oversaw US economic and social (non-CTR) assistance to the former Soviet Union.[6] His assessment is not surprising; by early 1994 Kazakhstan and the United States had untied some difficult knots. For one, the United States had achieved its main goal of Kazakhstan's full commitment to a nonnuclear path. To cap this off, Nazarbayev was bringing Kazakhstan's NPT ratification documents to Washington to present to Clinton. US-Kazakhstan agreements on trade and investment began to bear fruit. Foreign investment started flowing into Kazakhstan, and US commercial interests in Kazakhstan were on the rise. In Washington, National Security Advisor Anthony Lake in his memo to Clinton described Nazarbayev as "one of the region's most capable leaders" who "has proven himself a savvy political player," able to implement both political and economic reforms more effectively than Yeltsin in Russia or Kravchuk in Ukraine.[7]

It was a crisp and clear February day when Nazarbayev's motorcade pulled into the White House driveway lined with the US military cordon. The US chief of protocol led Nazarbayev and his party to the Roosevelt Room, often used as a holding room for guests before meetings with the US president. There, the Kazakh president signed a guest book before proceeding to the Oval Office for his first encounter with President Clinton.

After a brief photo op, the meeting began. Several men from both sides had met in the past; some even knew each other well. In addition to Vice President Al Gore, who had visited Kazakhstan just a couple of months earlier, the US party also included the US ambassador to Kazakhstan, Bill Courtney, who by then was on a first-name basis with all the key Kazakh officials. Nazarbayev brought with him Tulegen Zhukeev, the state counselor who had led negotiations on nuclear matters on behalf of Kazakhstan, and Foreign Minister Tuleitai Suleimenov, who regularly communicated with American officials on various matters.

After a working lunch at the Old Family Dining Room, the White House space for smaller private meals, the American hosts and their Kazakh guests proceeded to the opulent East Room with its large crystal chandeliers, the White House's largest room. There, Nazarbayev formally presented Clinton with Kazakhstan's NPT ratification documents. Interestingly, the Kazakh government could have presented the ratification document to any of the NPT's three founding members—the United States, the United Kingdom, or Russia. But Nazarbayev, eager to break with the Soviet tradition of "everything goes through Moscow" and to fortify his relationship with Washington, chose the United States. Clinton remarked, "We are pleased and honored he chose the United States."[8]

Clinton praised Kazakhstan for adhering to the NPT and announced that his government would increase economic assistance to the new state from $91 million in 1993 to more than $300 million in 1994—directly linking this increase to Kazakhstan's nonnuclear choice.[9]

For the United States, Kazakhstan's ratification of the NPT and the deposit of the ratification documents was an important bookend to more than two years of active diplomacy. Most of the time, the US government relied on carrots—economic assistance and support for independence—but there were

PHOTO 15 President Nursultan Nazarbayev (center) during a meeting with the business community in the United States; behind him, to his right, is Tulegen Zhukeev, 1994. Photograph by I. Budnevich.

SOURCE: Central State Archive of Film and Photo Documents and Sound Recordings, Kazakhstan. Image #2–110582.

also occasional hints of sticks, such as pressure on Kazakh leaders behind closed doors.

For the Kazakhs, the most anticipated part of the visit was the signing of the Charter on Democratic Partnership. From the early days of its independence, the Kazakh leadership had hoped for a high-level political agreement with the United States to codify the relationship. Finally, it became possible.

The charter's emphasis on the US commitment to Kazakhstan's future and its language on security guarantees, which Kazakhstan had sought from the very beginning, meant a lot to the young republic: "The United States of America recognizes the security, independence, sovereignty, territorial integrity, and democratic development of the Republic of Kazakhstan as matters of the highest importance."[10]

The charter added a vow of US protection of Kazakhstan:

If, in the future, an external threat to the territorial integrity, political independence or security of the Republic of Kazakhstan should arise, the United States
of America and the Republic of Kazakhstan intend to consult and to undertake
steps as appropriate to achieve a peaceful resolution consistent with international law and the principles of the CSCE [Commission on Security and Cooperation in Europe], as well as with the principles of the Partnership for Peace of
the North Atlantic Treaty Organization (NATO).[11]

The charter reiterated the commitments that nuclear-weapon states offer to
non-nuclear-weapon states within the NPT context. Importantly, it said that
the United States would seek immediate UN Security Council action to provide
assistance to Kazakhstan if it should become "a victim of an act of aggression or
an object of a threat of aggression with nuclear weapons."[12]

On close reading, the United States' promises to Kazakhstan in the charter did not go much beyond what the United States had already committed to
under the NPT, CSCE, and other international instruments. But the fact that
the US government offered Kazakhstan-specific security guarantees meant
more to the Kazakh leaders than the American officials appreciated. Decades
later, in interviews, Kazakh decision-makers still underscored the importance
of specific security guarantees from the United States, while American policymakers mention them less often.

Another landmark agreement with direct implications for Kazakhstan's
security was reached several months after the Washington visit. In late 1994,
three nuclear powers—the United States, Russia, and the United Kingdom—
formalized their security commitments to Belarus, Kazakhstan, and Ukraine.
They did so in the Budapest Memorandum on Security Assurances, signed in
Hungary's capital on the margins of a summit meeting of the Organization for
Security and Cooperation in Europe (OSCE, formerly the CSCE but renamed
at the meeting). The memorandum codified the commitment of the three nuclear powers not to use or threaten to use force against the territorial integrity
of Belarus, Kazakhstan, or Ukraine.[13]

Washington, likely relieved that, after an intense back-and-forth, Ukraine
had finally committed to give up its nuclear arsenal, wanted to honor Kyiv by
beginning the signing ceremony with Ukraine's president, Leonid Kuchma. The
Kazakh diplomatic establishment balked at the unusual suggestion and insisted
that the signing should follow the standard alphabetical order—Belarus, Kazakhstan, Ukraine. Similarly, the Kazakh Foreign Ministry resisted the US plan

to invite Ukraine to join the United Kingdom and Russia in authoring the Dec-laration on European Security, to be announced at the memorandum signing ceremony. Kazakh diplomats believed that Kazakhstan and Belarus had to be invited to join, or the announcement of the declaration should be done outside the ceremony.[14] Both these Kazakh efforts succeeded, and they underscore Ka-zakhstan's desire to be treated equally with Ukraine, which Washington consid-ered more consequential.

Nevertheless, just as with the Charter on Democratic Partnership signed in Washington, Kazakhstan was generally much pleased with the Budapest Mem-orandum. Nazarbayev called its signing "a genuinely historic event for Kazakh-stan." He added, "We consider these [security] guarantees to be an adequate response to Kazakhstan's responsible policy in the area of disarmament."[15]

During the Washington visit, there was one other piece of important busi-ness besides the signing of the charter and Kazakhstan's presentation of its NPT documents. This was a meeting between Nazarbayev and Vice President Gore to discuss cooperation on science and technology, space research, and other areas. The science and technology agreement addressed cooperation in all science fields and the protection of intellectual property resulting from such cooperation. Home to the Baikonur Cosmodrome from which Yuri Gagarin set out to become the first man to travel to space, Kazakhstan was a natural partner for space-related projects. As Nazarbayev and Gore looked on, the rep-resentatives of their governments and Russia signed a trilateral agreement on launching a US-manufactured satellite, INMARSAT-3, on a Russian Proton ve-hicle from Baikonur.[16]

Senior US government officials generously praised Kazakhstan, noting that it was "further along in economic reform than just about any country in the former Soviet Union" and had done "just about everything right in trying to promote Western trade and investment." They added that the amount of US investment in Kazakhstan was unprecedented:

> There may not even be a country that comes really close to what Kazakhstan has been able to do in attracting significant Western, and particularly Ameri-can, trade and investment. The single largest American investment project in all the former Soviet Union is in Kazakhstan, Chevron's $20 billion Tengiz oil field project.[17]

By the time of Nazarbayev's visit in early 1994, seventy American com-panies worked in Kazakhstan. Chevron paved the way for multinational oil companies; after its pioneering deal, a consortium consisting of Mobil Oil, British Petroleum, Agip, and Total arrived to develop Kazakh oil fields.

Once Kazakhstan and the United States had assembled all the main pieces for cooperation in the political, economic, and nuclear spheres, the time was ripe to start the elimination of nuclear weapons infrastructure in Kazakhstan. Before the Kazakhs and Americans could get down to business, though, Russia had to remove the nuclear weapons.

REMOVAL OF NUCLEAR ARSENALS
Intercontinental Missiles, Bombers, and Warheads
Ambiguity about the status of the nuclear arsenal as well as about Russia's military units stationed in Kazakhstan to support it were discomfiting to the Kazakhs. On the one hand, the weapons were located on sovereign Kazakh territory. On the other, the commanders of missile divisions in Zhangiz Tobe and Derzhavinsk retained their allegiance to the Strategic Rocket Forces in Moscow.[18] This was in contrast to the situation in Ukraine, where some military commanders were ethnic Ukrainians who pledged allegiance to Kyiv.

Even before Kazakhstan formally committed to joining the NPT as a non-nuclear-weapon state in December 1993, and before the legal status of nuclear weapons in Kazakhstan was resolved in March 1994 giving Russia full custody, Russian pilots began flying heavy bombers out of Kazakhstan to Russia. Similarly, at missile bases Russian military personnel drained fuel from missiles and put it in special containers for rail shipment to Russia. By late 1993, the Russian military had already moved 120 out of 1,040 strategic nuclear warheads, and all intercontinental missiles sat deactivated, waiting to be moved to Russia.[19] By early 1994, all forty heavy bombers stationed in Kazakhstan had been flown to Russia. The Russians' great desire to grab the nuclear arsenal in Kazakhstan was in sharp contrast to its indifference in dealing with the highly enriched uranium located at Ulba, as discussed in chapter 9.

For its part, Kazakhstan was eager to get rid of nuclear missiles and warheads but was concerned about safety and security. The scars of radioactive contamination from forty years of nuclear tests ran deep. Its government sought three things from Russia: detailed information on nuclear and radioactive waste left behind, the status of nuclear arsenals and military divisions present in Kazakhstan, and guarantees that Moscow would compensate Almaty for nuclear material from the warheads removed from Kazakhstan.

In March 1994, during a meeting between Nazarbayev and Yeltsin in Moscow, Russia and Kazakhstan signed twenty-three agreements, two of which decided two critical issues about the nuclear arsenal: who was in charge of weapons and their removal, and whether Kazakhstan could expect to be compensated for nuclear material from dismantled warheads, as Kazakhstan had contributed material and resources into building these weapons and Russia was now set to sell enriched uranium from dismantled warheads to the United States. The agreements—On Strategic Nuclear Forces Temporarily Located on the Territory of the Republic of Kazakhstan and On Military Cooperation—unequivocally decided that the nuclear arsenal belonged to Russian strategic nuclear forces.

As for compensation, the agreements provided that Russia would pay Kazakhstan in cash or in goods for the nuclear material inside the warheads removed to Russia. The deal hinged in part on the HEU Deal reached by Russia and the United States a year earlier, in which Russia would downblend HEU from dismantled warheads into LEU, which the United States would then buy for use in US power reactors. In other words, Russia expected to receive US currency for material derived from the warheads. To increase the value of the Russian-Kazakh agreement to Russia, it stipulated that Russia could deduct from its payment to Kazakhstan its expenses for maintenance, transportation, and dismantlement of the warheads.[20] Only years later would Kazakhstan and Russia finalize the details of compensation.[21]

The Kazakh parliament ratified the 1994 bilateral agreements despite serious reservations. The prevailing sentiment at the time was that Russia behaved like an overbearing big brother.[22] At that time, Moscow still treated newly independent Kazakhstan as a satellite republic.

But removing the intercontinental missiles from their silos and transporting them to Russia was not an easy feat. Each missile weighed more than 200 tons and had to be defueled, lifted from an underground silo, and put in special rail transporters.

By April 1995, all intercontinental nuclear ballistic missiles and nuclear warheads had been removed—except one.

An Orphan Nuclear Device

As Kazakhs, Russians, and Americans negotiated the fate of nuclear weapons in Kazakhstan, an unaccounted-for nuclear device sat deep underground at the Semipalatinsk Polygon.

Where did the device come from? It turned out that in May 1991, the Soviet military placed the device in one of the tunnels at the Polygon, planning to use it in an experiment to study the effects of radiation. Their plans were overtaken by events, as just a few months later, in August, Kazakhstan's president signed a decree to close the Polygon. In October, Gorbachev announced a unilateral moratorium on Soviet nuclear testing. And just like that, a nuclear charge was left buried and unexploded.

For a country that had shut down the nuclear testing site, banned nuclear tests, and was on its way to becoming a non-nuclear-weapon state, this nuclear device was more than a minor inconvenience. How could Kazakhstan be considered nuclear-free if there was a nuclear device buried in its soil?

While not a bomb but rather a device with a nuclear charge inside, its presence did not look good. A US diplomat in Washington telegraphed the US embassy in Almaty in October 1992:

> The permanent presence of any such device(s) on Kazakhstan's territory would
> be inconsistent with President Nazarbayev's letter to President Bush that prom-
> ised to eliminate all nuclear weapons from Kazakhstan's territory. Further, any
> implication that such a device was not under the control of the strategic forces
> of the CIS and that Kazakhstan eventually would retrieve such a device would
> raise significant non-proliferation concerns.[23]

Since it was 1992, and Kazakhstan and Russia were still negotiating the agreements on nuclear weapons and the Polygon, when US Ambassador Courtney asked State Counselor Zhukeev how his government planned to deal with it, Zhukeev had no more information to offer.[24]

Kazakh officials wanted to get rid of the emplaced device, not least because if left indefinitely it could contaminate underground waters. But they couldn't do it on their own. They were adamant about not allowing anything that would even remotely resemble a nuclear test, but in internal deliberations they wondered if it was even possible to remove the device without a nuclear explosion.[25] Kazakh officials appealed to the Russian defense ministry and the Russian ministry of atomic energy, asking them how the device could be destroyed, how soon, and how to prevent doing any damage to people and the environment.

Antinuclear activists from the Nevada-Semipalatinsk movement kept Polygon officials on the hook and regularly inquired about the device's fate. The deputy head of the Polygon—Russian General Fedor Safonov—could not hide his irritation with higher-ups in both Russia and Kazakhstan who were taking too long to agree on how to proceed: "The politicians delay the process, they have created a whole working group to negotiate five lines of an agreement!"[26]

The negotiations between Kazakhstan and Russia on the orphan device dragged on until March 1994, when both countries finalized the bilateral agreements on nuclear weapons. Russia agreed to fund the dismantlement of the device and, more importantly, promised that if the engineers could not extract it, they would use a chemical explosive to detonate it to avoid a nuclear explosion.[27]

It would take another year for the last nuclear device to be destroyed. When the engineers opened the tunnel and reached the device, they saw that, during the four years the device had sat underground, water had seeped inside. Their task became even harder, but they succeeded. On May 30, 1995, a month after all nuclear weapons were removed from Kazakhstan to Russia, a chemical explosive obliterated that last remaining nuclear device.[28] Both Russian and Kazakh governments honored the project participants with awards.[29]

DESTRUCTION OF MISSILE SILOS

Once the Russian military removed its warheads and missiles from Kazakhstan, it was time to destroy the missiles' "homes"—the silo launchers.

Ready-to-launch intercontinental ballistic missiles known in NATO classification as SS-18s had sat in 122 silo launchers in two locations—Derzhavinsk and Zhangiz Tobe. Both towns, home to Soviet strategic rocket forces divisions, were secret and not identified on any maps. Another fourteen test silo launchers were located at the Balapan site at the Semipalatinsk Polygon, with twelve more in Leninsk near the space launching site at Baikonur.

Silos for the intercontinental ballistic missiles looked like gigantic coffee tumblers built out of steel and cement, inserted about 130 feet (40 meters) underground. Built to be indestructible, each silo weighed 187 tons. The silo door (a lid) alone weighed 120 tons and was 6 meters (almost 20 feet) in diameter. In the event of nuclear war, the silo lid would open, and a missile outfitted with nuclear warheads would be launched on its deadly trajectory. The silos were connected to underground bunkers up to 100 meters (300 feet) away. A complex network of underground and above-ground structures hosting electricity, cooling, and other support systems ensured proper functioning of the silos.

These intercontinental missiles and their silos fell under the provisions of the START agreement that put limits on the nuclear arsenals of Russia and the United States. That meant that the destruction of the silos had to meet START requirements—they had to be either exploded to a depth of 6 meters (20 feet) or excavated to a depth of 8 meters (26 feet). Before withdrawing, the Russian military had removed the missiles, equipment, and supplies and blasted the top part of the silos to the required 6-meter (20-foot)-deep crater, leaving the blown-off 120-ton silo doors and the rest of the semidestroyed silos behind.[30] But the Russian military withdrew from the missile bases in Derzhavinsk and Zhangiz Tobe in haste. An American who participated in US-Kazakh projects to clean up the former missile bases observed, "[The] Russians knew how they treated [the] Kazakhs. They just wanted to get out. They wanted to get their nukes out."[31]

So it was Kazakhstan's government that was left to deal with the half-destroyed missile silos. It wanted to reclaim the land. Its number one concern was potential environmental damage. Kazakh defense officials sought insight from their American counterparts, eager to learn from the US Air Force's experience in dismantling silos.[32]

The CTR program furnished aid for the silo destruction. Out of the first $85 million allocated to Kazakhstan under the CTR program, $70 million was earmarked for the destruction of all 148 missile silos and their supporting infrastructure.[33]

Jim Reid, a senior US Air Force colonel, was on the American team that helped with the former missile bases. He arrived in Kazakhstan in January 1994. A native of Michigan, Reid was used to snow, but even for him, the amount of snow and the cold temperatures of the Kazakh winter left an impression. Reid also recalled another regular feature of Kazakhstan, or at least of its international relations: its light touch in dealing with Russia. Nazarbayev "was very interested in not creating any schism between Russia and Kazakhstan," Reid said, "and didn't want Kazakh military [at the former missile bases before the Russians withdrew]."[34]

The project on silo destruction officially began in 1994. Still, the real work started only in early 1996, when the Pentagon awarded the CTR contract to the Swedish-Swiss industrial group ABB and a Houston-based construction company, Brown and Root.[35]

Two factors contributed to the delay. First, Kazakhstan had to coordinate everything with Russia since anything related to strategic nuclear forces involved highly sensitive information that Russia was eager to protect from the Americans.[36] Second, the "Buy American" provisions that added to the project's high expense did not contribute to enthusiasm on the Kazakh side. Writing in the mid-1990s, foreign policy advisors at the Kazakhstan Institute of Strategic Studies lamented:

> Use of mostly American labor is unjustified considering its relatively high cost. Enterprises in Kazakhstan are particularly interested in working with American firms in significant stages of the project, which would give them desperately needed work as well as opportunities to develop contacts with U.S. technical experts and industrial managers. Instead, Kazakhstani specialists have been limited to participating in only the low-technology and low-skill aspects of silo destruction.[37]

Once work got underway, each silo was first evaluated for environmental and radiation hazards. After any hazards were abated, the team demolished the silos. Because silos were built to withstand attack, destroying them was an arduous task. More than six tons of explosives were required to blow up one silo. Metal that could be salvaged was given to the local communities. Any openings were filled with debris and a concrete cap was put over the silo tube. The crater surrounding the silo was then also filled with debris. As a final step, the site was graded to match the topography.[38]

In the process, large pieces had to be blasted and cut. A Kazakh company—*Almatypromstroi*—contracted to do the work used antitank mines. Aboveground structures were demolished by a bulldozer or wrecking ball, and some buildings were exploded with dynamite.[39]

All ICBM silos were destroyed by the year 2000, and, to an untrained eye, the newly regraded landscape looked natural. In fact, just a meter and a half (5 feet) below the ground, debris remained. The rubble was removed from the top meter and a half in three locations (Derzhavinsk, Zhangiz Tobe, and Leninsk) to allow a return to farming. The Balapan site did not have arable land because it was too rocky, and debris was removed from only the top half-meter.[40] But in all the locations, Kazakh land will bear the remnants of the Soviet military presence for a long time to come.

POLYGON CLEANUP

By late 1993, Kazakhstan's government was in charge of the Polygon and Kurchatov, but it still did not have a full picture of what had transpired at the Polygon for forty years and what was left on its territory. The Russian military and scientists did not leave much data or documents behind. Over the next two decades, Kazakhstan would gradually learn and deal with the presence of more than just that orphan nuclear device dismantled in 1995.

The Kazakh government faced two main problems: first, how to make sure its nuclear or radiological material did not become the makings of someone else's nuclear or radiological device; second, how to clean up radioactive contamination at the former Polygon. Plus, the government, seeking to increase economic activity, was eager to grant permission for mining of gold and other natural resources in the vicinity of the Polygon but was concerned with radioactive contamination. Additionally, the US government wanted to make sure nobody, including Russia and Kazakhstan, would be able to use the weapons infrastructure. Like their Kazakh counterparts, they also wanted to prevent the loss of any residual nuclear and radiological material to a terrorist group or a third country.

For security reasons, one urgent task was the sealing of the Polygon's extensive network of tunnels and boreholes for underground nuclear testing. Anyone could access the 181 tunnels at Degelen used for nuclear tests or the thirteen unused boreholes at Balapan. If there was nuclear material in those abandoned installations, someone could use it in a nuclear device. If the soil at the Polygon was contaminated with enough radiological material, someone could turn it into a dirty bomb. But Kazakh officials and even the staff at the National Nuclear Center, the facility created in Kurchatov as the inheritor of the Polygon operations, were initially flying blind. They had no idea if, how much, and where such material remained.

Terrorists were not the only issue. There were health dangers, too, with animals grazing on grass, some of which was contaminated. Metal scavengers faced such risks, too, and the fact that scavengers could so easily access abandoned infrastructure and equipment presented a glaring security threat.

To start answering pressing questions on conditions at the former Polygon, Kazakhstan sought help from the international community. The International Atomic Energy Agency (IAEA) conducted two preliminary radiological surveys, in 1993 and 1994. They determined that most of the expansive territory assigned to the Polygon had little or no residual radioactivity, with important exceptions—some areas where tests were conducted, such as the Ground Zero and Lake Balapan areas, were heavily contaminated with relatively high concentrations of cesium-137 and strontium-90, and, to a lesser extent, with plutonium and americium-241.[41]

Similarly, in November 1993 a joint team of Kazakh and US scientists conducted a radiation survey of the Polygon, led by Don Linger from the Defense Nuclear Agency (later renamed the Defense Threat Reduction Agency [DTRA], part of the US Department of Defense), who had a PhD in civil engineering and designed tunnels for US nuclear tests. Linger and his team performed an initial survey and then briefed their findings to scientists from Kazakhstan, the United States, and Russia who had gathered at Kurchatov for an international conference. Kurchatov, once a thriving military-scientific town, by then looked like a ghost version of itself. As one American participant at the conference described it, "Hotel rooms were cold, meeting rooms frigid and pipes frozen. The city was isolated and abandoned."[42] The struggling town reflected the kind of hardships Kazakhstan's government and technical experts faced, and it was in these conditions that they also somehow had to deal with the challenges that the Polygon presented.

That first interaction between the scientists and technical experts from the United States, Kazakhstan, and Russia would plant seeds for long-term productive cooperation. In their meeting in Washington in 1994, Nazarbayev and Clinton had signed a joint statement laying the groundwork for US assistance in assessing the consequences of nuclear tests at the Polygon. The next year, in Almaty, the two nations had also signed a formal agreement titled "The Elimination of Nuclear Weapons Infrastructure." Under this agreement, in a provision funded by the Cooperative Threat Reduction program, the United States paid to seal tunnels and boreholes at the Polygon.

By then, the US government had softened its "Buy American" approach to Kazakhstan's weapons infrastructure dismantlement. More flexible solutions, such as awarding contracts to a Western integrating contractor that hired local subcontractors, or giving a lead role to Kazakh entities, were proving to work well. Kazakhstan's National Nuclear Center, for example, oversaw the radiation survey of the Polygon's tunnels and boreholes, which was carried out by local contractors. On the American side, DTRA provided technical expertise.

Over 1995 and 1996, the National Nuclear Center team surveyed the tunnels and boreholes and assessed the radioactive contamination of each. In some areas, the team discovered radionuclides, including strontium-90, cesium-137, and plutonium.[43] Each tunnel and borehole required a tailored approach— some of them collected water and required special handling.[44] This painstaking process required the labor of almost two hundred local experts over three years. The sealing of tunnels previously used for nuclear tests helped to reduce the Polygon's overall radioactive contamination. With time, some animals and birds came back to the region, including the rare species listed in Kazakhstan's *Red Book of Protected Species*.[45]

As the work plugging tunnels and boreholes proceeded, more information emerged on what was still hidden underneath the Polygon's surface. In addition to nuclear tests at the Semipalatinsk Polygon, the Soviet military had conducted all kinds of experiments involving radiological and nuclear material.

With the radiological materials, the Soviets tested the utility of dirty bombs on the battlefield. As one study would later detail, the Soviet military sought to determine if it could form a "radiological alternative to a minefield." As part of those experiments, the Soviet military dispersed a cocktail of radioactive isotopes code-named R-904. They applied R-904 in liquid form from bombers, by mortar fire, and within artillery shells. They also brought in large lead containers filled with R-904 and exploded them with TNT at the ground level.[46]

The experiments with nuclear material focused on how conventional explosives interacted with HEU and plutonium, and on the effects of fire on nuclear weapons. Some of these tests were conducted in giant steel containers known as *Kolbas*. The word means "laboratory flask" in Russian and was a nod to its use for mixing nuclear material and explosives. But unlike a fragile glass laboratory flask, a *Kolba* weighed 30 tons and could hold the equivalent of 200 kilograms (440 pounds) of dynamite.

Information on more nuclear material at the Polygon kept on trickling in. When, in 1995, the National Nuclear Center staff confided to their American counterparts from Los Alamos National Lab that nuclear material still remained at the Polygon, Americans knew what they were talking about. Like the Soviet scientists, American scientists had conducted enough experiments at the Nevada Test Site to know that material could be left behind. In some experiments, such as when studying plutonium's behavior ("equation-of-state"), entire chunks of plutonium could be left in shallow boreholes.[47] Los Alamos National Lab scientists Danny Stillman and Harry (Mac) Forehand visited the Polygon and estimated that the amount of nuclear material left behind could be enough to produce several nuclear devices.[48]

As with any Polygon-related work, Kazakhs could not proceed without conferring with Russians first. Only the Russians knew where the *Kolbas* were buried. As it turned out, some *Kolbas* remained in tunnels and some outside the tunnels. In 1997, Kazakhstan and Russia signed an agreement titled *On Kolbas*. At the same time, Kazakhstan and the United States were cooperating under a bilateral agreement on eliminating the nuclear weapons testing infrastructure signed in 1995.[49]

The Kazakh-Russian agreement on *Kolbas* was an example of the parallel bilateral tracks on which the Polygon cleanup was based, Kazakhstan dealing with Russia on some issues, such as the *Kolbas*, and dealing separately with the Americans on other issues. But those bilateral arrangements were soon to change to a fully trilateral one, in a move prompted by the security fears of an American scientist, Siegfried Hecker.

Hecker, a metallurgist and perhaps the world's leading expert on plutonium, had just stepped down from directing the Los Alamos National Lab, the birthplace of the American atomic bomb. Scientists in Russia and Kazakhstan respected and trusted him. When a delegation from Kazakhstan visited Los Alamos in 1998, they met with Hecker to discuss scientific cooperation. By then, Hecker had already given thought to the possibility that nuclear material could have been left behind at the Polygon: "If Nevada became an independent country, would I be worried? The answer was Yes."[50] Kairat Kadyrzhanov, director of the Institute of Nuclear Physics near Almaty and later director of the National Nuclear Center in Kurchatov (which incorporated the Institute of Nuclear Physics), described his conversations with Hecker, Stillman, and others on that trip: "We were amazed that the Americans knew everything or almost everything about the Polygon,"[51] a nod to the impressive work of US intelligence. Among other things that the scientists discussed, Kadyrzhanov told Hecker about the copper-cable thieves who frequented the Polygon.

Kadyrzhanov then invited Hecker to visit Kazakhstan, and Hecker acted on the invitation the same year. American visitors, such as Hecker and Linger, expressed to Kadyrzhanov that while they "knew every stone" at the Polygon, they could never have imagined visiting it. Hecker, an avid runner, described his runs in Kurchatov: "It was one of the most surreal moments of my life. All these abandoned buildings. Ravens all over the place. It was like running on Mars—all this territory! Birds and wild horses. That was an interesting experience."[52]

As Kadyrzhanov was showing Hecker the Polygon, they came across two old men boiling tea at the Degelen Mountain tunnel. The elders' sons were busy cutting cables inside the tunnel. Kadyrzhanov describes the effect the scene had on the American: "Hecker was nothing but shocked. Such an episode would not be possible in Nevada [Nuclear Testing Site], nor would it have been possible at our site in the Soviet era."[53]

But it wasn't just locals trying to get metal with rudimentary tools. When Kadyrzhanov first mentioned "copper-cable thieves" to Hecker during their chat at Los Alamos, Hecker expected to see thieves on camelback. Instead, as he described, "it was a highly industrialized operation" involving heavy machinery. Hecker was worried about what could be at the end of those copper cables. Even before visiting the Polygon, Hecker, who was very concerned that material from the Polygon could go astray, had talked with his Russian colleagues a year earlier. As someone who intimately knew the US nuclear testing program, he understood that not all tests worked. When they didn't, nuclear material was not fully used up and stayed behind in the tunnels of the Nevada Test Site. Hecker was sure that nuclear material stayed in the Semipalatinsk tunnels as well. He tried to persuade his Russian counterparts to go back to the Polygon but received a firm "we are not going back."[54]

After his trip to the Polygon and seeing with his own eyes how unprotected it was, Hecker went back to Russia, now armed with the photos. He personally lobbied key Russian scientists, such as Radii Ilkaev, who led one of Russia's main nuclear labs in Sarov.[55] The lab, known by the abbreviation of its long name in Russia—VNIIEF—conducted testing experiments at the Polygon during Soviet times and its experts would be indispensable in guiding where material remained at the Polygon. Hecker knew that persuading Ilkaev and his lab to join the material cleanup efforts at the Polygon was critical. As Hecker described it:

> Director Ilkaev said that he would much prefer not to do this project. He said he saw very little good that could come out of this for Russia. He and Minatom officials [Russian ministry for the nuclear sector] were concerned that any work at Semipalatinsk would paint them as irresponsible with respect to environmental problems that had been left behind. He drew an analogy to the British situation at Maralinga [Britain conducted nuclear tests in Maralinga in South Australia]. He said that unlike the U.K., Russia could not afford to pay. However, since he knew we were going to do this project with Kazakhstan anyway, they might as well be there to protect their own interests. He also said that in the end, it was the right thing to do.[56]

Ilkaev and the Russian scientists, including several who participated in the Soviet experiments with radioactive and nuclear material at the Polygon, knew better than the Americans that large amounts of material were left behind. They persuaded the Russian government to get involved. Hecker would later describe conscientious Russian scientists, such as Yuri Styazhkin, Viktor Stepanyuk, and others, who felt it was their moral obligation to help with the cleanup of the Polygon.[57]

The next year Hecker went back to Kazakhstan, now with Ilkaev. The agreement that Hecker, Ilkaev, and Kadyrzhanov signed in 1999 would be the starting point for many years of trilateral cooperation between the United States, Russia, and Kazakhstan to make the Polygon safer.[58] With time, experts from another Russian nuclear lab from Snezhinsk, known as VNIITF in Russian and led by Evgenii Avronin, also joined the effort. These scientists and technical experts from three countries—Russia, the United States, and Kazakhstan—were the driving force for trilateral cooperation. Scientists pushed their countries to cooperate in sensitive fields, something that the politicians would have been much more cautious about.

Disclosing to Americans sensitive information about the location of material at the Polygon understandably did not come naturally to the Russians. What if they disclosed the whereabouts of material, but for some reason the Americans did not keep their promises and secure it? This would increase, not decrease, proliferation risks, the Russian scientists worried. To keep information on the whereabouts of material as protected as possible, it was agreed that the exact sites would not be identified in preliminary documents, and "only fictitious names of the sites containing radioactive waste would be allowed in engineering and field documentation."[59]

The ability of scientists to agree on the urgency of the effort to secure the Polygon set the stage for the governments themselves to discuss trilateral cooperation. At the political level, support of Vladimir Shkolnik, Kazakhstan's Minister for Energy, Industry, and Trade; Rose Gottemoeller, the US Assistant Secretary of Energy; and Lev Ryabev, Russia's Deputy Minister of Atomic Energy, and the meeting they held in 2000, helped to move the process forward.[60]

Meanwhile, by 2000, the United States and Kazakhstan had completed the work they started in 1996 on the closure of tunnels and thirteen unused boreholes.

With trilateral cooperation in place, the scientific teams tackled what they considered the most immediate security risk—remaining boreholes. The best protection would be to build a sarcophagus to cover them all. The idea of a sarcophagus was inspired by the experience of securing the remnants of the Chernobyl nuclear reactor. But the harsh Kazakh winters, with temperatures dropping below -40° C (-40° F), caused delays. The sarcophagus construction finally began in August 2000, only to be interrupted by politics in Washington. At the time, the new George W. Bush administration requested a review of all CTR programs. On the Kazakh side, the original CTR umbrella agreement lapsed in 2000 and a new agreement was pending ratification in the Kazakh parliament. All CTR projects stalled. The half-constructed sarcophagus at the Polygon made things worse—the visible dome made it clear to scavengers that something of value was at the site.[61]

Meanwhile, the 9/11 attacks and al-Qaeda's overt interest in acquiring weapons of mass destruction gave Washington a new sense of urgency over confronting nuclear security risks, especially at places like the former Semipalatinsk Polygon. In late 2002, Kazakhstan's National Nuclear Center notified its American partners that many previously closed tunnels had been breached. In 2003, a piece in *Science* magazine made this information public—it described that previously sealed tunnels had been reopened by scavengers.[62] Alarm bells rang loudly. The quick sealing of tunnels and boreholes, described by a former American official as "plugging on the cheap," had failed to stop metal scavengers. They had opened around 70 percent of them in the years that followed.[63] In a worrying development, those scavengers appeared to be not run-of-the-mill entrepreneurial locals from nearby villages but organized operations that used mining equipment.

After the delay, by 2003, the sarcophagus, more than 70 meters (76 yards) in length, finally rose above the boreholes. It was an impressive engineering feat; now, no one could gain access. The engineers used more than a thousand plates made of cement and weighing 4 tons each as a foundation. The dome was made of steel, with cement poured on top.[64] In its completed state, it was camouflaged to blend into the environment as a hill.

In 2004, a US-Russian-Kazakh team secured three *Kolbas* stored above the ground in a bunker. The engineers filled the *Kolbas* with a mixture of cement and sand to make it very hard for anyone to retrieve nuclear material from inside them.[65]

In another instance of scientists driving policy, Russian scientists took it upon themselves to persuade their government to continue releasing information about the remaining material at the Polygon:

> Of course, we were not completely confident about the security of these tunnels. Understanding that sooner or later we would have to return to the problem of radioactive waste in the tunnels, we proposed that Minatom agree to conduct a project on further securing the remaining three contaminated *Kolba* containers inside one of the tunnels.[66]

Making these three contaminated *Kolbas* safe was a difficult engineering task because they were buried in the mountain. They could be taken out of the tunnels and filled with cement, but then they would be too heavy to move back into the tunnels. And the Americans were not keen on reopening the previously sealed tunnels.

The scientists devised an ingenious solution. The Russians agreed to provide the exact location of those *Kolbas*, which allowed the engineers to drill into the tunnels at those precise points. They punctured one *Kolba* and filled it with sand and cement. With the other two, they were forced to use a slightly different method—filling the space around the *Kolbas* with the same mixture of sand and cement to prevent access.[67]

Once the work on *Kolbas* was completed in 2005, the Russian government, under pressure from Russian scientists, disclosed another piece of rather shocking information. Almost 100 kilograms (220 pounds) of plutonium sat underground in so-called end-boxes—containers that were less secure than *Kolbas*. As one of the US project managers described: "You could still go back to the end-box and scrape plutonium from the walls. With a few 20-liter buckets, you could have enough plutonium which you could reprocess in your garage if you were not concerned about safety."[68]

Among the disclosed sites, three were referred to as Special Projects X, Y, and Z and categorized as high risk. At one of those sites, someone had dug out a manhole, indicating an attempt to get inside the tunnel. Other sites may have been tampered with as well. As always, the team had to work around difficult and sometimes dangerous conditions. When they opened one of the tunnels, for example, they saw that rock formations had been encased in ice. Apparently, nuclear tests conducted inside the mountain broke off large rock pieces, creating fissures into which rain poured, then froze to ice inside. Mountain rescuers had to be called in to cut through a passage.[69] Getting metal out of the frozen rocks was arduous and had to be done manually. But the hard work paid off, and the team collected dangerous material inside and improved the site's physical security. Debris removed from two of the tunnels, referred to as "special technical equipment," was taken back to Russia.[70]

Over the next few years, the trilateral team continued to work at the Polygon to properly and permanently seal all the tunnels. By 2012, it had secured additional sites there, previously identified as low risk, and eliminated all manholes. Overall security at the Degelen Mountain area improved significantly. Signs warned about the site's special status, with the word "radiation" written in all capital letters and warnings to trespassers to stay away. Fences, wires, and trenches surrounded the site. Hidden detectors, video cameras, and drones helped with surveillance. The first electrical system, supplied by the United States back in 2009, did not withstand the harsh Kazakh winters. By the time the trilateral effort neared completion, engineers had constructed an autonomous electricity system powered by solar batteries.[71]

Seventeen years after trilateral cooperation started in 1996 and over 100 kilograms (220 pounds) of secured plutonium later, the leaders of Kazakhstan, the United States, and Russia told the world that the Polygon was safer. They announced it at the Nuclear Security Summit in Seoul in March of 2012, a gathering of almost fifty world leaders.[72] President Obama had launched the Nuclear Security Summits in 2010, with an ambitious goal to secure vulnerable nuclear material around the world. Every two years between 2010 and 2016, world leaders met to report on efforts to secure nuclear material in their countries. Nazarbayev was by then nearing the end of his almost three decades at the helm of Kazakhstan. The summit furnished him with an opportunity to remind the world how far Kazakhstan had come—from a source of global nuclear anxiety to a country that diligently promoted nuclear disarmament and nonproliferation.

On the ground at the Polygon, the National Nuclear Center, which had led the work for all these years under the leadership of its consecutive directors (Gadlet Batyrbekov, Yuri Cherepnin, Shamil Tukhvatulin, Kairat Kadyrzhanov, Erlan Batyrbekov), hosted a picnic for the trilateral team at Degelen Mountain. It was a bittersweet moment—a chance to celebrate the achievements and pay tribute to some members of the team who had passed away without seeing the end result of their important work. A simple plaque installed that day under the flags of Kazakhstan, Russia, and the United States read: "1996–2012. The world has become safer." As Byron Ristvet, one of the key participants in the trilateral projects, summed up, "without the close cooperation of all three countries, any work at the Polygon would be doomed."[73]

Whether the Polygon will ever be fully secure is an open question. Plutonium's half-life is more than 24,000 years. Most Kazakh, Russian, and American scientists who know the Polygon agree its story will not be over any time soon.

SECURING NUCLEAR MATERIAL OUTSIDE THE POLYGON

When it came to nuclear material it was not only the Polygon that worried Kazakhs and Americans. In addition to the Ulba Metallurgical Plant, from which roughly 600 kilograms (1,322 pounds) of HEU were airlifted during Project Sapphire, three other nuclear facilities in Kazakhstan—the Mangyshlak Atomic

Energy Combine (MAEK) in Aktau, the Institute of Atomic Energy in Kurchatov, and the Institute of Nuclear Physics near Almaty—had varying quantities
of nuclear material. If stolen, it could easily end up in a nuclear device.

All four facilities suffered from the shortcomings of the Soviet approach
to nuclear management. Its pen-and-paper inventory methods, for instance,
meant that no facility knew the exact amounts of nuclear material it stored.
Soviet managers also didn't worry much about insiders stealing nuclear material; they focused more on protecting facilities from foreign threats. In a time of
economic crisis, with nuclear and other workers struggling to stay afloat, these
failings might prove disastrous. Nuclear custodians might feel less motivated to
carry out their duties properly or be tempted to help divert material to interested parties in exchange for money. The imprecise inventory methods made
detecting any missing material impossible.

In December 1993, Kazakhstan and the United States signed the Material
Protection, Control, and Accounting (MPC&A) implementing agreement to
carry out nuclear material security work. Until 1996, the US Department of Defense funded MPC&A efforts; after that, the US Department of Energy sought
and received its own congressional funding for MPC&A projects.

The MPC&A program paid for many security improvements at all Kazakh
nuclear facilities—the building of fences, installation of alarms, and establishment of computerized accounting systems for nuclear material. Other DOE-
administered programs paid for removing spent fuel to safe storage and for
downblending HEU fuel to the less dangerous LEU fuel.

Mangyshlak Atomic Energy Combine (MAEK) in Aktau

More than three metric tons of plutonium in spent reactor fuel remained at the
BN-350 nuclear reactor at the Mangyshlak Atomic Energy Combine in Aktau,
on the shore of the Caspian Sea.

Starting in 1973, the BN-350 reactor provided heat, electricity, and fresh
water to nearby towns. Daily it desalinated up to 120,000 cubic meters (over
4 million cubic feet) of water from the Caspian Sea. The reactor ran on HEU
fuel and could breed more than 100 kilograms (220 pounds) of high-quality
plutonium per year, which meant it could produce nuclear material easily usable in a nuclear weapon.[74] These multiple-purpose features made it a unique
installation.

The Soviet, and later Kazakh, nuclear industry was proud of the MAEK's
BN-350 reactor, one of the world's first fast neutron breeder reactors. But in the

1990s, MAEK managers faced two serious problems: First, what to do with the spent reactor fuel that contained plutonium? Second, how to ensure a safe end of operations for a reactor that was nearing the end of its operational lifespan?

Policymakers in Washington worried about MAEK and Iran's interest in it. Iran, just across the Caspian Sea from Aktau, had its eyes on MAEK for the weapons-grade plutonium it produced and stored. When Andy Weber of Project Sapphire visited MAEK in 1995, his hosts served him Iranian pistachios that Iranian guests who had visited the facility the day before had given them.[75]

John Ordway, the US Ambassador to Kazakhstan from 2004 to 2008, described how Washington viewed the cache of spent fuel at MAEK: "I went to Aktau, saw all the stuff sitting at the [spent fuel] pool. We had access. We understood what was going on. At that point, we did not have immediate concerns. The fear was longer-term. A more stable solution was needed."[76]

Spent fuel stored at MAEK contained enough plutonium to build hundreds of nuclear weapons. Similar to the Ulba plant in Ust-Kamenogorsk, MAEK used to be a flagship facility of the Soviet nuclear industry. In the 1990s, like Ulba and other nuclear facilities, it housed material that could be used in weapons but now didn't have the resources to protect it. As with Ulba, foreign powers watched MAEK closely. Some, such as the United States, worried about the potential diversion of material from MAEK; others, like Iran, were interested in the nuclear fuel assemblies and the plutonium they contained for their own nuclear programs.

In 1995, the MPC&A program was ready to help. That year, MAEK managers invited experts from the US Department of Energy for their first MPC&A visit during which the United States learned about the plutonium remaining at the facility. Dr. Pete Planchon, a technical expert on this type of reactor from Argonne National Laboratory, did some quick nuclear physics calculations during the visit. It became clear to the team that the quantity of "ivory-grade" plutonium was three metric tons. The term "ivory-grade" refers to plutonium in which the amount of less desirable isotopes is extremely low, making it exceptionally attractive for use in a weapon. As a result, the US government offered assistance and initiated a study on available options to secure it.

Technical experts from the United States and Kazakhstan began regular visits and meetings. In 1996, Argonne National Lab hosted technical experts from Kazakhstan for a three-week stay. In addition to Argonne specialists, the bilateral team included experts from other US national labs—Los Alamos, Sandia, and Pacific Northwest. The team developed a Joint Action Team study that evaluated dry storage technologies, spent fuel storage sites, and transportation methods.[77]

The first efforts at MAEK focused on MPC&A upgrades. Under MPC&A efforts, the joint team worked on material characterization and accounting. With inventory work complete, the material was declared to the IAEA and placed under international safeguards. Material characterization was necessary to understand, for example, if the fuel assemblies had already failed or if they were too brittle to safely handle or transport. If a canister filled with fuel assemblies experienced a bump, would the assemblies fail?[78]

So the technical experts needed to know which fuel assemblies had failed or were about to fail. A fuel assembly is comprised of fuel pins which look like a thin tube (imagine a magic wand) filled with small fuel pellets. A failed fuel assembly has fuel pins that did not stay intact. In the earliest type of fuel assemblies developed for the BN-350 reactor (Type 1 fuel) in Soviet times, the cap at the ends of the fuel pins were too small. When the air inside a fuel pin expanded due to the high temperature inside the reactor core, the fuel pin would rupture, leaking radioactive contamination. With the next generation of fuel assemblies (Type 2), this problem was mostly solved. The newest generation of fuel assemblies for this type of reactor (Modern) eliminated failures.[79]

Since the BN-350 reactor in Aktau was one of the world's earliest fast breeder reactors, it used its share of earlier type fuel assemblies, which meant that quite a few failed assemblies had to be packaged in special failure fuel stabilization canisters. In addition, the reactor systems had to be cleaned from radioactively contaminated sodium (a problem that the US-Kazakh team would later solve as well).

As the team worked on packaging the assemblies, it resolved technical problems and came up with engineering solutions as it went. For example, before putting fuel assemblies in long-term storage, they had to be dried. The Argonne specialists designed a closure-drying station, which they then built and tested in Idaho before shipping it to MAEK for installation in a shielded hot cell. The team loaded the fuel assemblies into canisters and then placed them into the closure-drying station. This process involved heating the assemblies to boil off the moisture while evacuating the moist air from each canister, replacing it with dry helium gas, and then welding the canister closed for long-term storage.[80]

The joint Kazakhstan-United States team worked together to improve material inventory systems as well. A universal challenge for all facilities working with nuclear material is the inevitable loss of some material during technological processes. US experts helped their MAEK colleagues improve their capability to measure this legitimate loss. In so doing, it made them better able to detect any illegitimate losses—namely, thefts.[81]

The MPC&A program also helped to computerize nuclear material accounting at MAEK and move it away from the paper-based system of Soviet times. Paper-based accounting presented problems, not least because sometimes handwriting was illegible. In addition, while each fuel assembly was supposed to have a unique number, the team members that worked on developing the inventory noticed that a few assemblies had the same number.[82]

When the work was done, all fuel assemblies had been analyzed, categorized, accounted for, and packaged into 480 stainless steel canisters.

In addition to work involving the nuclear material itself, the US-Kazakh team worked on physical security upgrades at MAEK, starting with the spent fuel pool area, as it contained the most sensitive material. After a thorough survey of MAEK's security needs, the team developed a long-term plan for security upgrades.

The MAEK facility sprawled across a large territory surrounded by a concrete fence that stretched for miles. The security experts decided to start at the core of the facility—the BN-350 reactor. The engineers hardened the exterior doors, windows, and entrances to the reactor building, the spent fuel storage pool, and the building that stored fresh fuel. The upgrades included installing a modern alarm system, lights, outside cameras, and intrusion sensors. The portal through which personnel entered and left the facility was improved to help control their comings and goings. The MPC&A program enhanced communication capabilities between MAEK and Kazakh law enforcement.[83]

Meanwhile, spent nuclear fuel could not be stored at MAEK indefinitely. For the BN-350 reactor to be decommissioned, it had to be moved to a secure long-term storage location—the site selected was the Baikal-1 reactor complex, a secluded area of the Semipalatinsk Polygon and the site of two nuclear research reactors.

Moving the spent fuel from the BN-350 site required financial resources and innovative thinking. The money came from the US Department of Energy. On the practical side, the experts had to choose the kind of casks to use to transport the fuel. They could use smaller casks that were already designed and available or design and build new heavier casks. Heavier casks were chosen for counterterrorism reasons—it was simply much harder to steal and move the heavy casks.[84]

Next, the MAEK staff carefully packaged the fuel into sixty of the newly designed and fabricated casks. Each cask weighed 100 tons (110 tons when filled)
and served a dual purpose—transport and storage.[85] Procuring two cranes—one
for MAEK and one for the storage site at Baikal-1—that could lift up to 150 tons
was another challenge the project team had to solve. After a contractor in Russia
took too long to fulfill the order, the project team turned its eyes to China. After
a careful search that included team members going to China to check three potential manufacturers, one Chinese company was entrusted with the task.

The company worked day and night to build the first crane and ship its
parts to the MAEK facility on time. Project managers faced a new challenge—
putting the crane together would take months. Eric Howden, the US Project
Manager, describes how a solution was found:

> We needed to have the crane operational to meet an important deadline, but it
> would take months. My exceptional colleague, Alexander Baldov [Kazakhstan Proj-
> ect Manager from KATEP, Kazakhstan's state corporation for nuclear power and
> industry] and I were having tea with Valerii Marchenko, who joked that the only
> way we could make it happen was to have hundreds of Chinese workers [from the
> manufacturing company] come to Kazakhstan. What started as a joke turned out to
> be the best solution. The Chinese manufacturer sent dozens of its workers to Aktau
> who knew the crane and set it up within weeks to successfully meet our deadline.[86]

By 2010, the operation to transport the spent fuel to the Polygon storage
site had begun. The crane hoisted the full casks and placed them on special
railcars. Harsh winter weather sometimes interfered with the mission: when
temperatures dropped to -40° C (-40° F), it was simply impossible to operate
the equipment.

The casks were to travel by rail from Aktau to Kurchatov in five special
railcars accompanied by two security railcars, and from Kurchatov by road to
the Baikal-1 complex at the Polygon. Ministry of Internal Affairs special forces
troops received specific training for the mission. The entire route was also
checked for bombs or any other security vulnerabilities.

To account for all eventualities, the US-Kazakh team conducted a dry run
in 2009—transporting an empty cask from MAEK to Baikal-1. Howden, who
participated in the dry run, remembers this milestone in vivid detail:

> It was a three-day rail trip across the steppe. I remember how bright the stars
> were. It was very cold, -40 Celsius [-40 F], the coldest weather I had ever

PHOTO 16 Transport overpack being removed from a cask using 150-metric-ton crane with hydraulic lifting yoke at the Baikal-1 Cask Storage Facility. US team photo, provided by Eric Howden.

experienced. In the railcar bunk, one wall was next to coal heating and was very hot. The other wall—all iced up, from the outside cold. At night, my feet were sweating, and my head was freezing. I would switch back and forth. When I woke up, my hair was frozen to the iced wall.[87]

Howden, the rest of the team, and the cask made it to Kurchatov where, as planned, the cask was transferred onto a heavy-haul truck. It was in the middle of winter, and a sand truck ahead scattered sand so that the truck with the special cargo didn't slide off the road and overturn. As the convoy neared the Baikal-1 facility, the sand truck turned to the side at the last bend, as its driver knew he would not be able to enter the secure facility. The heavy-haul truck with the 110-ton cask on its trailer suddenly did not have sand to help it drive on snow and ice, and it started sliding and then crashed into concrete barriers.

A Kazakh law enforcement official—Colonel Sadykov from the Kazakh Ministry of Internal Affairs—saved the day. Sadykov, who oversaw the security of the operation, barked some orders "and two military vehicles pulled our truck by chains through the fenced gate and onto the secure Baikal-1 site," as Howden described. And just as planned, the cask reached its destination before midnight. Colonel Sadykov, whom Howden remembers as "a wonderful man, a class act and someone who knew how to get things done," remained a feature of the removal operation until its successful completion.

After the test run, twelve trips would follow, with five casks of spent fuel conveyed during each. Hundreds of troops were involved in ensuring the safe and secure transfer of spent fuel. Guards with automatic weapons accompanied each run. Images of the casks *en route* were beamed to Kurchatov and to the military unit responsible for the security of special cargo. Law enforcement stopped all traffic along the train route as the casks moved slowly from the Caspian shore to the Polygon in the middle of the Kazakh steppe. On average, each trip took twenty-one days.[88]

The last cask reached its destination in November 2010. When it reached the concrete platform at Baikal-1, the site was hooked up to the IAEA safeguards monitoring system. Material enough to make hundreds of nuclear weapons was now secure, in casks that could not be moved, in a protected facility, and under the watchful eye of the IAEA.

After that last cask made it safely to Baikal-1, Kazakh and American project participants celebrated with an impromptu vodka toast in the middle of the steppe. As they left the Baikal-1 facility and started driving to Kurchatov, Colonel Sadykov made the cars stop and then got a bottle of vodka from the trunk of his car so that everyone could toast to the successful completion of the operation. More formal celebrations followed at the MAEK facility, at the National Nuclear Center, and in Kazakhstan's new capital, Astana.[89]

The fuel can be safely stored at the Polygon for fifty years.[90] The operation cost the United States $219 million, and, as US officials said at the time, the price was a bargain, considering spent fuel that could have been fashioned into hundreds of weapons was secured.[91]

In addition to the spent fuel at MAEK, there was also fresh HEU fuel at MAEK that had not yet been used in a reactor. As far as potential use in a weapon was concerned, the fresh fuel also presented a security risk. The Nuclear Threat Initiative (NTI), a nongovernmental organization funded by US millionaire Ted Turner and co-led by Senator Nunn, worked out an arrangement with the Kazakh authorities to move almost three metric tons (6,400 pounds) of fresh HEU fuel from MAEK to Ulba. At Ulba, the HEU fuel was mixed with LEU powder to lower its enrichment level.[92] On completion of the $2 million project in 2007, the NTI chartered a plane and took its board members to Ulba, where a huge party awaited them. President Nazarbayev flew in from Astana to participate in the festivities.[93]

Another big challenge for the MAEK managers was shutting down the BN-350 reactor safely. In 1992, it reached the end of its original twenty-year operating license, and from 1992 onward the Kazakh government extended its operating license one year at a time. In 1998, however, the Kazakh nuclear regulator refused to extend the operating license.[94] In the same year, the International Atomic Energy Agency conducted a safety survey of the reactor and determined that it needed major upgrades. Shortly after, in 1999, the government of Kazakhstan announced that it would shut down the reactor permanently. It asked the United States and the IAEA for technical assistance.[95] The US Department of Energy and its technical experts from the Idaho National Lab stepped in to help the MAEK team.

The first task in the decommissioning of the reactor was to decontaminate the sodium coolant—the liquid used to cool the reactor core—as it had accumulated high levels of radioactive cesium due to failed fuel assemblies that had leaked radioactive contamination into the coolant loops. In addition to radioactivity, the sodium could ignite spontaneously in moist air. Decontamination of sodium coolant required design and production of cesium traps—devices with special filters—which, when placed into the coolant system, "trapped" cesium. In yet another example of an international scientific effort, Argonne National Lab experts worked with the MAEK team to design the traps. After the Kazakh nuclear regulatory body approved the design, a local company—the Byelkamit facility—produced seven cesium traps.[96] As noted earlier, the Byelkamit facility was a case of successful defense conversion—a repurposed former military plant that, with assistance from the US Defense Conversion and Enterprise Fund, switched from producing torpedoes to producing cryogenic tanks for the oil and gas industry.[97] The careful draining of the 950 cubic meters (250,000 gallons) of sodium coolant followed.

As of 2021, Kazakh experts continue to cooperate with the international community, the IAEA, and the United States on putting the reactor into a SAF-STOR condition—a safe state in which long-lived radioactive material cools down and buys time before the full reactor dismantlement, which requires large expenditures.[98] A reactor can stay in a SAFSTOR condition for fifty years.

Over two decades, scientists from Kazakhstan and the United States tackled complex technological tasks often without speaking each other's language. Joyce Connery, who participated in BN-350 projects in the early 2000s as Argonne West National Lab's on-site project manager, described their interaction: "It was fascinating to watch Idaho folks talk to scientists at BN-350. They were speaking technical to each other. They got each other."[99]

The Institute of Atomic Energy and the Institute of Nuclear Physics

Another of the four Kazakh nuclear facilities was the Institute of Atomic Energy in the town of Kurchatov, near the Polygon. The institute was home to three nuclear research reactors and contained both fresh and spent HEU fuel. Two reactors at the Baikal-1 complex at Kurchatov—referred to as IVG-1M and R.A.—ran on HEU fuel. Under the MPC&A program, the facility's physical security was enhanced with metal and nuclear detectors, hardened portal and access points, and alarms and communication systems. An electronic system of material accounting and control was installed as well.[100] From 1996 to 1998, 138 kilograms (304 pounds) of spent HEU fuel from Baikal-1 were moved to Russia.[101] By 1998, the R.A. reactor core with 10 kilograms (22 pounds) of HEU fuel was shipped to Russia and the reactor ceased operation.[102] By 2023, after more than a decade of collaboration, the IVG-1M reactor will be operating on LEU fuel.

The third nuclear research reactor in Kurchatov—the IGR—also ran on HEU fuel. MPC&A upgrades were implemented by 1997.[103] Over the years, the United States helped to move fresh HEU fuel from the IGR reactor to Ulba for downblending into LEU. The final 2.9 kilograms (6.3 pounds) of fresh HEU fuel were transported by truck to Ulba and converted there to LEU in 2020.[104]

The Institute of Nuclear Physics, located in the settlement of Alatau near Almaty, used HEU fuel in its research reactor. During the Soviet period, the reactor was used for experiments ordered by the Soviet Ministry of Defense. Kairat Kadyrzhanov, a former director of the Institute of Nuclear Physics, described security at the institute that was typical of any civilian nuclear facility across the former Soviet Union: "The staff made sad jokes that the reactor (a nuclear installation!) was guarded by a lone *babka* [old woman] who secured the door to the reactor room with a mop. That was all the security! . . . Police posts were expensive, and we did not have money for that."[105]

The MPC&A security efforts at the Institute of Nuclear Physics began in 1995. As at the Institute of Atomic Energy at Kurchatov, metal and nuclear material detectors were installed, portals and access points were hardened, and alarm and communication systems were improved.[106] The MPC&A program also funded the installation of electronic scales, a gamma spectroscopy system, computer equipment, and the electronic system of material accounting and control to help the institute keep track of the material.[107] Necessary upgrades were completed by 1998.

In an effort to minimize the number of facilities and countries that possess HEU, in 2014 the United States funded the removal of 158 kilograms (348 pounds) of spent HEU fuel from the Institute of Nuclear Physics to Russia.[108] Almost 50 kilograms (110 pounds) of fresh HEU fuel from the institute was downblended into LEU fuel at Ulba.[109] By 2017, following a 2006 agreement, Kazakhstan and the United States had converted the research reactor to run on low enriched uranium instead of highly enriched uranium and completed the removal of HEU from the reactor.[110]

Although freeing itself of its nuclear inheritance was politically sensitive and technologically challenging, it was doable for Kazakhstan thanks to its careful balancing of relations with Russia and the United States, the availability of US technical and financial assistance for denuclearization, and the stamina, creativity, and flexibility of policymakers, scientists, and technical experts from Kazakhstan, Russia, and the United States.

In the last quarter-century, Kazakhstan has been transformed from a nuclear wasteland and source of severe international nuclear anxiety to a country free of nuclear weapons, nuclear weapons infrastructure, and vulnerable plutonium and highly enriched uranium. But not for many decades will the nuclear story of Kazakhstan be over. Remnants of military installations are forever buried in its vast landscape. Kazakhstan's future generations must deal with dismantling the obsolete nuclear power reactor at Aktau and finding a permanent solution for spent nuclear fuel now temporarily stored in casks. The Polygon can never be left unguarded.

EPILOGUE

REIMAGINING THE ATOMIC STEPPE

Restrained pulse of moaning steppe—
With waves of pain and grief.
The drops of rain? Crushing seas?
Those're mothers' trembling tears . . .

Here's a place of whispering spell—
Abai. Earth's bleeding chest.
Death's stealing lives—time multiplies.
Submission never justifies.

—Alimzhan Akhmetov, Kazakh poet, Semipalatinsk region, 2019

IT IS SUMMER 2019, and our small plane with fifty passengers lands at Semipalatinsk, now known by its new Kazakh name, Semey. At the airport I am met by Dmitrii—a forty-four-year-old victim of nuclear tests whose primary source of income is working for the local equivalent of Uber. Dmitrii is friendly and cheery, his physical appearance only subtly suggesting his severe health issues. We chat about his story on the way to my hotel. His mother, an ethnic Kazakh, is a native of Semipalatinsk. She met his father, an ethnic Russian, in the Siberian city of Novosibirsk, famous for its high-quality education, where she studied at university. His parents moved to Semipalatinsk, where they had several children. Dmitrii was born in 1976, thirteen years after the last atmospheric nuclear test but during the period of underground nuclear testing, promoted by the Soviet military as "safe."

Dmitrii, diagnosed with a genetic mutation, is officially recognized as a victim of nuclear testing, a determination made by a special government commission in Kazakhstan established after the Polygon's closure. His rare mutation resulted in altered skull bones and missing collarbones. "My arms are not connected to my shoulders," he tells me matter-of-factly. What it means in practical terms is that he has trouble doing anything with his arms when his ailment flares up. Every couple of months, sharp pain debilitates him for a week at a time, and he cannot lift a spoon during such episodes.

Despite these severe health issues, during the entire ride Dmitrii exudes a positive vibe and tells me with a smile that he accepts his fate: "It is okay that Nature decided to take a day off on me." His only complaints are the outdated and, on occasion, illogical rules on assistance for nuclear test victims. Kazakhstan passed a law aiding victims in 1992, a measure good for its time but desperately out of date nearly thirty years later. As a result, although Dmitrii is officially recognized as a victim, the government does not recognize him as disabled because he can still take care of himself despite losing use of his arms every couple of months. Unlike victims who suffer from cancer or blood diseases, Dmitrii does not qualify for subsidies for his medical treatment because his rare disease is not on the list of diseases associated with the law on victims. The only benefit he receives is fourteen days of additional paid leave per year. He is worried that once he can no longer work and has to retire, he will lose his only source of income. He adds wryly: "But let's face it, the chances I will make it to retirement age are small anyway."

It is only when I am ready to leave his car near my hotel that he stops me: "There is something I wanted to add," he said. "The saddest thing for me is that I decided not to have children. Nobody can guarantee my children will not have my genetic disorder. I do not want to inflict this pain on anyone."[1]

The story of Dmitrii is the story of thousands of victims in Kazakhstan. It is a story of the lingering legacy of Soviet nuclear testing and Kazakhstan's imperfect attempts to help its victims. But above all, it is a story of resilience.

Besides the struggles of Dmitrii and his fellow nuclear victims, other stories have spiraled forth from Kazakhstan's nuclear heritage. The nation has become determined to turn its military heritage to new purposes and foster a domestic peacetime nuclear industry that bolsters the economy. On the international arena, Kazakhstan has taken on the task of curbing the spread of nuclear weapons and pursues active nonproliferation diplomacy.

As Kazakhstan is building its new identity in this field, it is doing so in a complicated global context.

NUCLEAR DIPLOMACY: FROM
SWORDS TO PLOUGHSHARES
Nuclear Order at the Dawn of the 2020s

As of this writing, the global nuclear order is at an inflection point. Nuclear risks, while less than during the Cold War, remain troubling. Arsenals comprising more than 14,000 nuclear weapons, enough to destroy the planet many times over, are eating up the nuclear powers' national budgets with money that could be invested in education, health care, and climate change solutions. Nine countries—the United States, Russia, France, the United Kingdom, China, India, Pakistan, North Korea, and Israel—choose to keep their nuclear weapons programs.

The United States and Russia possess more than 90 percent of all nuclear weapons in the world, with more than 6,000 each. Yet only one bilateral treaty now curbs these giants—New START. It came dangerously close to expiring in 2021 when the Trump administration refused to extend it, but within days of taking office President Biden extended it for five years.

Nuclear dangers of a different kind brew in Kazakhstan's neighboring region of South Asia, where any conflict between India and Pakistan could potentially escalate into a nuclear conflagration. Together, New Delhi and Islamabad have more than three hundred nuclear warheads.

North Korea remains a major nuclear hot spot. Despite UN sanctions that stretch from a ban on buying nuclear technology to a ban on selling seafood, North Korea still finds a way to skirt these deterrents and augment its nuclear abilities. The North Korean regime raises an impressive amount of money from illicit activities such as producing and selling drugs and weapons and dispatching its people to work overseas. North Korea then uses the cash raised to build up its nuclear and missile programs. Pyongyang has approximately thirty to forty nuclear warheads and enough nuclear material to build a few more. It also has missiles that can reach the US mainland.

China, France, and the United Kingdom collectively add another eight-hundred-plus nuclear weapons to the mix. None has plans to part with its nuclear weapons. Israel does not confirm or deny its nuclear weapons program but is believed to possess about ninety devices.

As the nuclear-weapon states party to the Treaty on the Non-Proliferation of Nuclear Weapons (NPT), Russia, the United States, the United Kingdom, France, and China have committed themselves to work toward eventual disarmament. There has been progress, with a significant reduction in the numbers of US and Russian warheads from Cold War peaks. But none of the five seems interested in pursuing total nuclear disarmament. Further, four nuclear powers outside the international nuclear regime—India, Pakistan, North Korea, and Israel—show no signs of abandoning or reducing their nuclear arsenals. Policymakers and officials in these countries continue to discuss nuclear weapons as something abstract. This notion feels especially out of touch in places like Kazakhstan, the Marshall Islands, or states near the former Nevada Test Site where people continue to suffer from past nuclear tests—or in Japan, whose people experienced the nuclear attack. People in these and other places know the all-too-real suffering these "abstractions" can inflict.

The chasm between nuclear "haves" and "have nots" is getting worse. Many countries, especially in the developing world, see the global nuclear order as unjust. Some countries get to keep their nuclear weapons. Other countries that gave up the right to nuclear weapons when they signed the NPT as non-nuclear-weapon states still face obstacles when attempting to develop peaceful nuclear programs due to controls on dual-use nuclear goods and technology.

In 2017, the frustration among some non-nuclear-weapon states about the nuclear powers' broken promises on disarmament gave birth to a treaty that would ban all nuclear weapons—the Treaty on the Prohibition of Nuclear Weapons (TPNW).[2] Not surprisingly, not a single nuclear power has expressed a desire to join the treaty. The United States, during the Trump administration, even put pressure on countries to withdraw from the TPNW.[3] But by January 2021, fifty countries had signed and ratified it, enough for the new treaty to enter into force.

The practical implications of this treaty for disarmament are unclear. Japan's ambassador to the UN once said: "A ban treaty, if it does not lead to an actual reduction of a single nuclear warhead, would be of little significance."[4] The naysayers' skepticism notwithstanding, the treaty is disrupting the status quo and, in some places, strengthening sentiment against nuclear weapons. Kazakhstan was among the first fifty countries to sign and ratify the treaty. Symbolically, it ratified the pact on August 29, 2019—the seventieth anniversary of the first Soviet nuclear test on the Kazakh steppe.[5] This step followed Kazakhstan's commitment thirteen years earlier to a treaty banning nuclear weapons from Central Asia.

The Central Asian Nuclear-Weapon-Free Zone

In 2006, Kazakhstan and its four Central Asian neighbors—Kyrgyzstan, Tajikistan, Turkmenistan, and Uzbekistan—signed a treaty to establish a nuclear-weapon-free zone in Central Asia. Significantly, the signing took place in Semipalatinsk, a city in direct proximity to nuclear weapons during the Soviet era. By joining a treaty that banned all nuclear weapons from the region, Kazakhstan came full circle—from hosting the world's fourth-largest nuclear arsenal to a country that would never allow nuclear weapons on its territory.

The idea of nuclear-weapon-free zones dates back to the 1950s, when the hope was to establish one in Central and Eastern Europe. This European zone never came to fruition, but in some areas of the world political momentum for regional nuclear-weapon-free zones has continued or increased. A treaty for the world's first nuclear-weapon-free zone, in Latin America and the Caribbean, opened for signature in 1967. Nuclear-weapon-free zones followed in the South Pacific, Southeast Asia, and Africa. Mongolia is a one-state nuclear-weapon-free zone. Countries that join nuclear-weapon-free zones take on additional obligations never to acquire nuclear weapons. The existing nuclear-weapon-free zones cover 116 countries, comprising more than half the land on Earth.[6]

When conversations began about establishing a nuclear-weapon-free zone in Central Asia, Kazakhstan still hosted Soviet nuclear weapons. In 1993, the president of Uzbekistan, Islam Karimov, put forward a proposal for such a zone at the 48th Session of the UN General Assembly. Kyrgyzstan soon formally supported its neighbor.

Meanwhile, in Kazakhstan, in 1994, the head of Kazakhstan's Institute of Strategic Studies, Oumirserik Kassenov, my father, also proposed the idea in an internal memo addressed to State Counselor Tulegen Zhukeev and the Ministry of Foreign Affairs. But Kazakh officialdom was not ready for such a step. "Too early," was their response to the memo.[7]

In 1995, Uzbekistan and Kyrgyzstan again put forward the idea. And when Kazakhstan became nuclear-free in mid-1995, its government was finally ready to join its neighbors. In 1997, at a meeting intended to focus on environmental issues in the region, the five Central Asian states adopted the Almaty Declaration, which called for establishing a nuclear-weapon-free zone. In a few months, the foreign ministries of all five states signed a statement to that effect. Then the long work of drafting the treaty began.[8]

An important part of treaties establishing nuclear-weapon-free zones is a protocol to which the five nuclear-weapon states under the NPT—China, France, Russia, the United Kingdom, and the United States—are supposed to adhere. This would legally bind them to respect the status of a zone and not use or threaten to use force against treaty-state parties. But adherence to this protocol by the five NPT nuclear-weapon states has been mixed depending on their own strategic interests. The five Central Asian governments, wary of this lukewarm support from the five nuclear-weapon states, made sure to involve them in consultations long before a treaty text was finalized.

China and Russia, two nuclear powers bordering Central Asia, offered their support as the new zone would not interfere with their interests. But the United States, United Kingdom, and France opposed two provisions in the draft treaty. Their first complaint was that the provisions governing the transportation of nuclear weapons and materials through the zone were not clear enough.

Their second concern centered around the collective defense treaty that several former Soviet republics, including four of the five Central Asian states, had signed in 1992. The agreement, informally referred to as the Tashkent Treaty, established that Kazakhstan, Kyrgyzstan, Tajikistan, Uzbekistan, Armenia, Belarus, and Russia will offer all "necessary assistance, including military [assistance]" if one of them comes under attack. As noted earlier, this treaty positively contributed to Kazakhstan's decision to join the NPT as a non-nuclear-weapon state. Russia's commitment to collective security provided Kazakhstan with extra confidence back in the early days of its independence. But the US, French, and British governments now argued that the term "military assistance" might be interpreted to imply that Russia could station its nuclear weapons in Central Asia.[9] This posed a predicament for the Central Asian states: They could not afford to jeopardize the most important security arrangement they had with Russia, yet they were committed to a nuclear-weapon-free zone in their region.

Central Asian diplomats came up with a clever solution, inserting careful language into the nuclear-free-zone treaty. One paragraph said that the new treaty did not "affect the rights and obligations" of the parties under other international treaties, but another paragraph, hedging that assertion, added that the parties should "take all necessary measures" to effectively implement the new treaty in accordance with its "main principles." Translated from diplomat-speak, this rather elegant solution allowed Central Asian states to keep the Tashkent Treaty intact while delineating a line: nuclear weapons should not be present in their region.

The United States, the United Kingdom, and France—not burdened with Central Asia's geopolitical complexities and proximity to Russia—strongly opposed the language. They considered it vague and watered down, as it did not spell out in black and white that Russia could never deploy nuclear weapons in Central Asia.[10] Nevertheless, all five NPT nuclear-weapon states eventually signed the protocol, and all but the United States have ratified it.

The Central Asian Nuclear-Weapon-Free Zone is the first one in the northern hemisphere. It creates a disarmament pocket in a nuclear-heavy region. Russia, China, Pakistan, and India, all nuclear powers, are the signatories' next-door neighbors. Then, just across the Caspian Sea, there is Iran, with its nuclear aspirations that worry the international community.

The Soviet WMD program used all the Central Asian republics in one way or another, and each Central Asian country inherited facilities that could be turned to military use. By creating the Central Asian Nuclear-Weapon-Free Zone, the Central Asian states decided not only to get rid of the WMD legacy but to assume obligations beyond those under the NPT and other signed treaties. The Central Asian countries committed to allow international inspectors from the International Atomic Energy Agency (IAEA) to monitor not just declared nuclear facilities and material, as in most nuclear-weapon-free zones, but to check for undeclared activity too.[11] They also committed not to export nuclear material to non-nuclear-weapon states that do not allow international inspectors to check on their nuclear activities, and they have pledged to ensure that nuclear material is not stolen or misused, committing to the Convention for the Physical Security of Nuclear Material.

The possibility of international assistance to deal with nuclear-related environmental problems was a strong incentive for Central Asian republics to pursue the zone. The treaty includes important language about environmental rehabilitation of territories contaminated as a result of past activities related to the development, production, or storage of nuclear weapons or other nuclear explosive devices. And it specifically referred to uranium tailings storage sites and nuclear test sites.

Global Ban on Nuclear Tests

The Central Asian states also committed to ban nuclear testing, signing on to the Comprehensive Test Ban Treaty, a provision especially important for Kazakhstan. The Comprehensive Test Ban Treaty, which would ban all nuclear tests, opened for signature in 1996. Signed by 184 countries, the treaty would enter into force if and when all countries with substantial nuclear capacity joined. North Korea, India, and Pakistan have yet to sign the treaty, and the United States, China, Israel, Egypt, and Iran have yet to ratify it.[12]

Once in force, the treaty would rely on the International Monitoring System—a network of 321 monitoring stations and sixteen labs around the world. These facilities can detect signs of a nuclear explosion. They include hydroacoustic stations which detect sounds from the oceans, infrasound stations which observe the atmosphere, and seismic stations which detect shaking of the earth—and can distinguish between natural events like earthquakes and nuclear explosions.[13]

The Semipalatinsk tragedy remains an open wound for Kazakhstan. But in its quest to ban nuclear testing forever, the nation is orchestrating a remarkable turnaround, with the former test site poised to make a unique contribution to the verification regime of the Comprehensive Test Ban Treaty.

In this symbolic "swords to plowshares" change, the Polygon's infrastructure is now deployed to make the world safer. Kazakhstan hosts several seismic stations and one infrasound stations, and the former Polygon is uniquely suited for conducting explosions (with conventional explosives) to calibrate this important detection equipment. In 1999–2000, as an international team worked hard on sealing tunnels and boreholes, it used the opportunity also to conduct calibration experiments for the monitoring stations.

In each of three exercises, dubbed Omega, Omega-2, and Omega-3, 100 metric tons of chemical conventional explosive were exploded inside Degelen Mountain tunnels.[14] The exercises not only helped to calibrate the monitoring equipment and confirmed that monitoring stations accurately picked up the location and the power of the explosions but also carried symbolic meaning. The Omega tests opened a new chapter in the Polygon's history—one in which it is dedicated to peace, not war.

Since then, Kazakhstan has hosted several field experiments at the former Polygon in support of the Comprehensive Test Ban Treaty Organization Preparatory Commission, a Vienna-based international organization set up to build the monitoring and verification system.

Most notably, in 2008 Kazakhstan hosted the largest ever on-site inspection simulation exercise for the commission. The exercise called for an investigation into a suspected nuclear test conducted by the fictitious country of Arkania. The scale of the exercise was impressive—forty tons of equipment was shipped to the Kazakh steppe to support simulated inspections carried out by forty inspectors.[15] Commission inspectors had the chance to test all stages of the inspection regime in conditions that resembled real-life ones as closely as

PHOTO 17   CTBTO Preparatory Commission Integrated Field Exercise IFE08 at the Semipalatinsk Polygon, 2008.
SOURCE: CTBTO Public Information, http://www.ctbto.org.

possible. And few places in the world could provide more realistic conditions than the former Polygon.

The IAEA Nuclear Fuel Bank

Another notable nuclear diplomacy initiative was Kazakhstan's decision to host an internationally controlled depository for nuclear fuel. In 2006, the US NGO Nuclear Threat Initiative (NTI, funded by Ted Turner) developed a way to weaken the temptation for countries to develop their own nuclear fuel production facilities. The idea was important because nuclear fuel technology is inherently dual-use; nuclear fuel production for nuclear power plants can provide a foundation for a military program. The fewer countries possessing this technology, the lower the proliferation risk.

The problem was that countries have a right to build nuclear power plants to provide heat and electricity to their population, and they need nuclear fuel to power them. Although countries can buy nuclear fuel on the commercial market, there is no guarantee of access. For political and other reasons, a nation may not be able to obtain the fuel. This fear could drive nations' demands for self-sufficiency in nuclear fuel production.

NTI's idea was to add a third option to the existing ones of either buying nuclear fuel or producing one's own—a "nuclear fuel bank" controlled by the IAEA. An IAEA-owned stock of nuclear fuel would provide an extra sense of security for any country deliberating whether to develop domestic capacity to produce nuclear fuel. The IAEA describes the fuel bank as "an assurance-of-supply mechanism of last resort" available to eligible IAEA member states when fuel supply for a nuclear power plant is disrupted "due to exceptional circumstances."[16]

Laura Holgate, then an NTI senior employee who promoted the fuel bank strategy, explained another potential benefit. She and her colleagues thought that Russia, attracted by the prospect of a large new buyer for nuclear fuel, would speed up its conversion of highly enriched uranium (HEU) from dismantled Soviet warheads into the low enriched uranium (LEU) fuel that a nuclear fuel bank would seek to purchase. At the time, Russia was selling LEU to the United States under an agreement informally known as the HEU Deal. When NTI approached Russia with the idea of a fuel bank, it was too late to incentivize Russia, as it was close to meeting its quantitative obligations under the HEU Deal. Although this Russia angle did not pan out, the concept of a global nuclear fuel bank remained.

When in 2006 Ted Turner offered NTI $50 million toward a nuclear fuel bank, Kazakhstan was the only country to offer to host it, and it was well suited to the purpose. Kazakhstan's Ulba Metallurgical Plant had facilities capable of handling nuclear fuel as well as the necessary technical expertise. As a developing non-Western country, Kazakhstan was also potentially more appealing as a host to other developing countries, many of which were potential customers for fuel bank services. For Kazakhstan, hosting the IAEA fuel bank was politically, diplomatically, and technically attractive. It underscored Kazakhstan's credentials as a country with an advanced nuclear industry as well as a desire to contribute to the global nonproliferation regime. The fuel bank would also push Kazakhstan to improve management and security at Ulba further to meet the high IAEA standards. The only downside to Kazakhstan's location was its landlocked status and the lack of a seaport for easy transport.

President Nazarbayev announced Kazakhstan's offer to host the fuel bank in 2009 at a joint press conference with Iran's President Mahmoud Ahmadinejad, who was visiting Kazakhstan. In a perfect world, Iran would be an ideal fuel-bank customer. In the 2000s, the international community grew more and more concerned about Iran's nuclear capability, including its uranium enrichment technology, fearing that Iran might use it for a weapons program. Iran, which runs a nuclear power reactor and a nuclear research reactor that produces medical radioisotopes, argues that its program is peaceful. Persuading Iran to abandon indigenous fuel-making would minimize the perceived proliferation risk. Ahmadinejad said he supported Kazakhstan's proposal to host the fuel bank, but he did not indicate whether Iran would be interested in its services.[17]

The fuel bank became operational in 2019 when it received cylinders with LEU from France and Kazakhstan's own Ulba plant.[18] It will not provide a panacea from nuclear-related worries. As Iran's lukewarm response demonstrated, countries set on being independent of the whims of the international nuclear fuel markets may continue to prefer their own domestic fuel-production capacity. Nonetheless, the IAEA nuclear fuel bank offers an additional tool to the international community to promote nuclear nonproliferation. Kazakhstan, as the bank's host, plays an important part.

NUCLEAR POLITICS AT HOME:
A PEACEFUL NUCLEAR PROGRAM

While pushing for a global ban on nuclear weapons, Kazakhstan is keen on nuclear technology for peaceful use. Its Soviet nuclear inheritance not only left deep scars but also laid the foundation for a civilian nuclear sector. Building up from that foundation was hardly easy. Although Kazakhstan inherited a massive nuclear industry that was an integral part of the Soviet nuclear megaproject, that industry collapsed together with the Soviet Union. Networks of industrial ties between the republics were disrupted. Transforming that bankrupt nuclear sector into one of the world's main players on the international nuclear market has been successful, but it did not happen overnight.

In the early 1990s, nuclear facilities involved in uranium mining and nuclear fuel production, such as the Ulba Metallurgical Plant in Ust-Kamenogorsk, were bankrupt. Orders for their products from enterprises across the former Soviet Union dried up amid an all-engulfing economic crisis. Starting gradually in the mid-1990s, Kazakhstan's nuclear sector began to revive. Kazatomprom, a state-owned company tasked with the import and export of uranium, rare metals, and nuclear fuel production for nuclear power plants, became a notable player in the commercial nuclear market, not least thanks to Mukhtar Dzhakishev, who led the company during its rapid growth in the 2000s. Kazakhstan became the world's largest producer of uranium ore. The Ulba plant, now part of Kazatomprom, regained its footing and restarted production of uranium, tantalum, beryllium, and niobium products.

Kazatomprom's strategy has been to move from exporting raw natural uranium to producing more value-added products. The multistage process of producing nuclear fuel, known as the nuclear fuel cycle, includes uranium mining and milling, conversion, enrichment, production of fuel pellets and fuel assemblies, and spent fuel reprocessing.

Kazakhstan is well positioned when it comes to the first stage—uranium mining and milling. With twenty-six uranium deposits, the country contributes 24 percent of the total world supply and is the world's largest producer of raw uranium (yellowcake).[19] But Kazakhstan does not currently have the capacity for the second stage, uranium conversion, which creates uranium hexafluoride suitable for enrichment. To solve that problem, Kazatomprom is seeking to obtain the necessary technology from foreign partners.

Kazakhstan approaches the third stage, enrichment, differently than do some other nations. The issue is that uranium enrichment technology is dual-use—it can be used to produce fuel for nuclear power plants, but it can also be used to produce HEU for nuclear weapons. Iran, Brazil, and a few other nations place considerable value on developing a domestic enrichment capability, citing their goals of self-sufficiency and technological independence. But Kazakhstan, making decisions based on economic feasibility (the international commercial market offers enough enrichment services), does not seek to possess sensitive enrichment know-how for itself. Kazakhstan's decision contributes to the nonproliferation regime since the fewer nations that are familiar with this know-how, the better. Instead, Kazakhstan has secured access to Russian uranium enrichment services, a "black box" arrangement that gives it the benefits of enrichment while the technology itself remains invisible.

The fourth stage in the production of nuclear fuel is bundling uranium fuel pellets into fuel assemblies or rods. Kazatomprom produces pellets at Ulba and is building a plant with Chinese partners to produce fuel assemblies for Chinese power reactors.

At this point, Kazakhstan does not have plans for engaging in the final stage of the nuclear fuel cycle, spent fuel reprocessing. Like the enrichment stage, spent fuel reprocessing presents a potential proliferation risk because in this process plutonium can be separated from highly radioactive waste and become potentially suitable for a weapon. Kazakhstan, like other countries with power reactors, faces the steep challenge of arranging permanent disposal of spent fuel.

Kazakhstan's policy and choices regarding its peaceful nuclear program are a good example of how a country can utilize its potential, such as Kazakhstan's vast uranium resources and nuclear fuel technology, without raising proliferation concerns.

Like the mining and processing of uranium, nuclear power is seen as promising by at least some in Kazakhstan. In 2012, the government adopted a draft master plan for power generation through 2030, directing that the share of nuclear power in electricity generation should reach about 4.5 percent. Proponents of nuclear energy note that the industry could stimulate a green economy and, by producing cleaner energy, fulfill Kazakhstan's international obligations on the environmental front. Currently, 80 percent of Kazakhstan's electrical energy comes from burning coal.

But the 2012 master plan and several other earlier attempts to jumpstart a nuclear power program in Kazakhstan have not succeeded. In a 2016 effort, it appeared as though Kazakhstan would start building two nuclear power plants. Potential sites for a nuclear power plant included Aktau (the town that hosts the now shuttered BN-350 reactor), the village of Ulken near Balkhash Lake, and the town of Kurchatov. Aktau was soon dropped—if built there, a power station would produce more energy than the locality needs with no cost-effective way to export the rest. In addition, the city's government was opposed to a nuclear power plant. Ulken, with its need for electricity and favorable attitude toward a potential plant not least because of the jobs it could create, and Kurchatov, a town unafraid of nuclear technology, remained.

Every few years, the news of Russian, Japanese, or other foreign partners ready to build medium-size nuclear reactors for Kazakhstan surface. But as of this writing, the government of Kazakhstan has not made a decision. Reasons may include negative public sentiment toward nuclear energy and the question of whether Kazakhstan's economy needs the addition of nuclear energy. Some observers also hint at the role of the coal lobby.

A STUDY OF CONTRASTING NUCLEAR TOWNS

Kazakhstan is trying to promote nuclear power, science, and technology for peaceful purposes, while simultaneously dealing with its military nuclear legacy. In that sense, the fate of two nuclear towns near the Polygon—Chagan and

Kurchatov—and their divergent paths—Chagan as a ghost town, Kurchatov as a functioning scientific center—show the possibilities, negative and positive, for Kazakhstan's reimagined nuclear future.

Chagan

During the era of Soviet nuclear might, the Soviet military stationed heavy bombers near the Semipalatinsk Polygon at a specially built airfield called Chagan. The facility was impressive. There was a landing strip 4 kilometers (2.4 miles) long, and it was built with concrete plates more than a meter (3.2 feet) in depth so that it could withstand the world's heaviest aircraft.

The pilots from the 79th Heavy Bomber Air Division, their families, and other military and support personnel lived in a military town built about 9 kilometers (5.5 miles) from the airfield. The first officers started arriving in the town, also called Chagan, in 1958.

The pilots stationed in Chagan carried out various military and civilian missions. They explored the North Polar basin as a potential theater for military action, including the use of tundra airports for training in takeoffs and landings. In addition to war training, crews from the Chagan airbase participated in nuclear tests at the Semipalatinsk Polygon when those experiments involved dropping nuclear devices from planes. Chagan airmen would sometimes be called for nonmilitary missions as well. For example, they dropped bombs in Siberia to prospect for oil and gas fields.

The military town of Chagan, with 17,000 residents in its heyday, was much like other Soviet military towns that dotted the steppe: from its early days of no heating and canalization and personnel living in barracks, it grew into an oasis of comfortable life. Chagan's stores were well-stocked with food and consumer products not easily available elsewhere. It was a cozy town with freshly baked bread and desserts that its former residents remember decades later. The town offered its closely knit community of military families regular concerts featuring well-known performers, weekend dance parties, and cinema. Chagan also had its own kindergartens and school.

The location of the airfield was not accidental. Military planners chose the spot for its proximity to the Polygon and access to a railway. The closed military town and the airfield coexisted with a tiny local village servicing the railway station of Chagan.

In 2021, the now-abandoned military town, the nearby struggling railway village of Chagan with its six hundred residents, and the stories and memories that its residents share, constitute a bittersweet tale of what happens when a nuclear superpower falls.

Present-day Chagan is an empty shell. Just a few buildings remain, their windows gaping and the apartments within completely stripped of anything valuable, including metal and brick. Most structures are simply ruins. The former airfield, now eerily empty, survives only thanks to the very thick concrete plates on the landing strip, which cannot be removed. There are ditches everywhere—a reminder of the search for long-since-removed cables and piping sold as scrap metal. Only six simple houses remain on the edge of the former military town, and only a dozen residents choose to stay.

One of that dozen is the pilot Gennadii Bartashevich, who retired in 1990 just before the Soviet collapse. Through his eyes, the former glory of Chagan comes to life, but so does the pain of its crumbling. Born in Chagan to a military family, Gennadii followed in his father's footsteps and joined the Chagan military division. Today Gennadii recalls the generations of powerful aircraft he flew. From 1980 to 1990, he flew the heavy bomber Tu-95. When the new Tu-95MS arrived at Chagan, Gennadii was chosen to join the first squadron to pilot it. The new Tu-95MS, a powerful model that could fly nonstop for thirty hours and refuel in midair, "smelled like a new car," Gennadii recalled.[20] Also stationed at Chagan were the Tu-160 (which NATO calls the Blackjack), the world's heaviest supersonic military aircraft with a maximum takeoff weight of 275 metric tons.[21]

In the early 1990s, the military families stationed in Chagan found themselves on their own. The Russian military establishment in Moscow gave Chagan officers paid leave to look for work in Russia. But that did not diminish the difficulties. Some who had served in the Soviet military for years, but had not reached retirement age, found themselves without an income or a place to live and with nowhere to go. "People were crying as they left Chagan," Gennadii recalled. "Many turned to alcohol. Families fell apart." Like the Russian government, the Kazakh government, in the throes of early independence, didn't see much use for this once-Soviet military town. By 1993, all military personnel had departed, and the town was left to decay.

While nostalgic for the past, Gennadii admits to the fear with which he and his fellow military officers had to live during the Cold War: "We were very scared. Okay, we would have flown our bombers to retaliate in case of an attack. But our [airfield] and our town would be the immediate targets. And there were so many children here . . ."[22] With the end of the Cold War and

PHOTO 18   Abandoned military town of Chagan, 2020. Photograph by Togzhan Kassenova.

the abandonment of the military town of Chagan, this area is no longer a US nuclear target. But it clearly faces challenges of another kind.

The locals in the nearby village of Chagan—a mix of ethnic Kazakhs, Russians, and others—regret that the military left, and that the town's infrastructure wasn't put to good use. A local woman from the village recalls with warmth how, as kids, they attended the school in the military town, shopped for freshly baked bread, and drank "the most delicious lemonade." With the large military presence, there were more jobs for the locals both at the rail station and in the military town. The railway continues to operate, and the trains on their way to larger towns make brief stops at Chagan. Thanks to the railway, at least, some villagers have a job looking after the rail tracks. But otherwise, there are no jobs and no entertainment. Kazakhstan's government has some programs in place to help rural areas, but their implementation is lacking.

Despite all these past and present troubles, local attitude toward the Soviet nuclear program is not straightforward. "It was big politics that we wouldn't be

able to understand," one local said. As children, those villagers regularly encountered two-headed animals and did not think much of it. Now, as adults
who choose to stay in the village, they joke when asked about the global CO-
VID-19 pandemic: "We are from the Polygon, nothing can kill us."

Kurchatov

As Chagan was being left to disintegrate, the town of Kurchatov, one of the
most consequential places for the Soviet nuclear weapons program built to service the Semipalatinsk Polygon, also went into crisis in the 1990s. Yet its fate
was different.

Kurchatov's prospects seemed bleak initially. In the first years of Kazakhstan's independence, the Polygon staff—the scientists and the military—hoped
that somehow the Polygon could continue to function for the sake of defense,
science, and technology. For its part, Russia was busy with numerous crises
raging in the aftermath of the Soviet collapse. Plus, with the end of the nuclear
testing program, it saw no point in negotiating the fate of the Polygon with
now-independent Kazakhstan, especially against the backdrop of public outcry
against nuclear testing. This was different from the other Soviet-era military
testing grounds in Kazakhstan, which Russia continues to lease to this day. As
for Kazakhstan, as we have seen, it shut down the Polygon in August 1991, keen
not to keep it going but to dismantle its weapons infrastructure and rehabilitate
the land.

Some of Kazakhstan's nuclear experts, interviewed decades later, tell stories
of dedicated Polygon scientific staff who offered to stay but were not formally
offered such an opportunity during the painful transition from Soviet military
to civilian oversight of the Polygon. One of those who offered to stay was Russian general Fedor Safonov, deputy head of the Polygon responsible for the scientific work. Safonov, warmly nicknamed by those who knew him as "general
with a humane face," hoped to use the unique expertise of his team to establish
a university in Kurchatov. His offer was not taken up and he returned to Russia.

The strong antinuclear sentiment in Kazakhstan hurt the workers of the
Polygon, who felt they had devoted their lives to a critical national security
project. As someone privy to the mood of the Polygon's personnel at the time
said: "They felt abandoned by both Russia and Kazakhstan. They felt forgotten. They felt angry. That is why when they were leaving, they destroyed things
behind them. Even the bathroom sinks."[23] A witness recalled how the military
burned, ripped, or stuffed documents into bags to be taken to Russia.[24]

Kurchatov soon plunged into crisis. A place of 50,000 residents at its height turned into nearly a ghost town. About 17,000 people left between 1993 and 1996, and by 2003 only 10,000 remained. The Kurchatov of the 1990s will be remembered for no heat, no hot water, no funding, and empty buildings. The rates of premature death from heart attacks, alcoholism, suicide, and other stress-induced illnesses spiked[25]—a tendency shared with the rest of the former Soviet Union, but especially striking in a formerly gilded town.

Kazakhstan's government had other plans for Kurchatov. It wanted to detach the town from its nuclear-testing legacy but preserve its scientific status and install oversight for the Polygon there. This led to the ambitious initiative that created the National Nuclear Center in Kurchatov, established in 1992 and given its scope of work in 1993.

The National Nuclear Center, the leading entity for nuclear science and technology in the country, was charged with a wide range of tasks that included studying and eliminating the consequences of nuclear testing, developing methods to dispose of and store radioactive waste, strengthening the safety of nuclear energy installations, developing nuclear technologies to benefit science and the economy, performing basic and applied research in nuclear physics and nuclear energy, and training a new generation of nuclear science specialists.[26] Several Kazakh institutions, such as the Institute of Atomic Energy, the Institute of Radiation Safety and Ecology (an entity created from the Polygon's radiological safety service), the Institute of Geophysical Research (which hosted seismic stations capable of detecting nuclear tests worldwide), and the Institute of Nuclear Physics in Alatau became part of the National Nuclear Center.

When the first National Nuclear Center director, Gadlet Batyrbekov, arrived at Kurchatov in 1993, he and his team faced a dire situation. In Soviet times, soldiers carried out all town-related duties—from baking bread to running the boiler facility that heated the town. Once the military left, there was no one to perform these tasks.

The first winters were especially hard. The National Nuclear Center team struggled with a lack of diesel fuel and technicians who could man the boiler facility. Gradually, the town started coming back to life. Sergey Lukashenko, the former director of the Institute of Radiation Safety and Ecology, described how the atmosphere changed: "[In the late 1990s] many did not know whether they would leave or stay." But in the 2000s, Lukashenko said, the mood turned positive. Those who chose to live in Kurchatov did it deliberately. Residents of modern Kurchatov hope to make their town a prominent scientific hub.[27]

Over the years, the National Nuclear Center and its dedicated staff continued to work on peaceful nuclear science projects, making the most of the remaining unique facilities such as the nuclear research reactors.

In 2004, the Kazakh government established a state-owned Park of Nuclear Technologies in Kurchatov to develop commercially viable nuclear and radiation technologies. The enterprise developed a few interesting products, including super-absorbents—gel capsules that can retain water in dry soil to help plants grow, a useful innovation for Kazakhstan's arid areas. Another service developed under the park's umbrella is the sterilization of products using high-energy electrons. The products inside hermetically sealed packages remain sterile for a long time.[28] But despite some successes, the Park of Nuclear Technologies faces challenges. Kazakhstan's economy, still oriented toward export of raw resources, generates only limited demand for the high-technology products that the park can produce. Plus, as a state-owned enterprise, it must comply with strict procurement rules and buy everything by public bid. Several attempts to sell the enterprise to a private investor have so far not succeeded.[29]

Although the Kurchatov of the early 2020s is in better shape than the Kurchatov of the 1990s, it still confronts obstacles. A town in the middle of the steppe, far removed from major cities, it struggles to attract a younger generation, although some young scientists come, attracted by the unique infrastructure of the National Nuclear Center. The town's population has stabilized and now hovers around 10,000. The abandoned apartment buildings for which there are not enough dwellers are reminders of the town's lost prosperous past, while the National Nuclear Center's newly renovated buildings symbolize resilience and hope for the future.

The center has put to good use facilities inherited from the Soviet nuclear program. It uses the Tokamak device for plasma physics experiments.[30] The Baikal-1 complex at the Polygon hosts two research reactors—the IVG.1M and R.A. reactors. (The R.A. reactor stopped operating.) The reactor complex has an interesting history. Between 1962 and 1970, it was used to model a nuclear rocket engine prototype.[31] The IGR nuclear research reactor there allows for modeling serious nuclear reactor accidents, which provides important data on how to prevent them.[32]

The reputation and self-image of modern Kurchatov and its current residents are complex. The awe and pride for the cutting-edge science that happened here and respect for those who built the country's nuclear shield coexist with the public's negative view of the Polygon and the government's attempts to rebrand the town of Kurchatov. Echoing the staffers at the Polygon in the early 1990s hurt by local anti-Polygon sentiment, some Kurchatov nuclear experts express frustration with what they describe as nuclear phobia. After years of assessments, specialists confidently say most of the former Polygon territory—aside from specific hot spots with radioactive contamination—does not now present a radiation risk.[33] Kairat Kadyrzhanov, the former director of the National Nuclear Center, expressed frustration that "uranium phobia" makes people see the former Semipalatinsk Nuclear Testing Site as a curse, and to reject out of hand the idea "that it is also a genuine national treasure, a unique object of international importance."[34]

By 2011, the National Nuclear Center had developed a program of returning some of the Polygon's uncontaminated land to industrial use, offering its expertise on the radioecological assessment and leaving the final decision on releasing the land to the government. The technical experts recommended redrawing the Polygon's boundaries to demarcate "red zones" to be forever protected and other areas to be freed up for use.[35] Kadyrzhanov described potential benefits of the plan:

> The entire gigantic territory is not required for scientific purposes now. Much of the "clean" land that is completely safe can be transferred for use with a safety guarantee. You can mine coal here—of good quality, by the way. There is gold, molybdenum, magnesium, fluorites, possibly—rare earth elements. You can mine them in a controlled fashion, with safety measures in place. The former military Polygon has a civilian future.[36]

This proposal for transfer of some of the Polygon's land to civilian use proved controversial. As of 2021, ten years later, the Kazakh government has not ruled on the recommendation, but there are signs that the government is looking at the issue closely. In 2021, the government submitted a draft law, *On Semipalatinsk Nuclear Safety Zone,* to the parliament. One of the draft law's components deals with potential changes in the Polygon's boundaries.[37]

Technical studies point out two important phenomena. First, large areas of the former Polygon are safe, but some hot spots with radioactive contamination remain. Second, the overall levels of contamination of the environment and locally produced food products have been decreasing.

According to data from the Institute of Radiation Safety and Ecology of the National Nuclear Center, most radioactive contamination occurred as a result of atmospheric nuclear tests. Contaminated areas at the main testing field stretch

TABLE 2. EFFECTS OF RADIONUCLIDES

RADIONUCLIDE	HALF-LIFE	HEALTH HAZARDS
Americium-241	432.2 years	Americium-241 is primarily an alpha emitter but also emits some gamma rays. It poses a more significant risk if ingested (swallowed) or inhaled. Once in the body, it tends to concentrate in the bone, liver, and muscle. It can stay in the body for decades and continue to expose the surrounding tissues to radiation, increasing the risk of cancer.
Iodine-131	8 days	External exposure to large amounts of iodine can cause burns to the eyes and skin. Internal exposure can affect the thyroid gland. The thyroid gland uses iodine to produce thyroid hormones and cannot distinguish between radioactive iodine and stable (nonradioactive) iodine. If iodine is released into the atmosphere, people can ingest it in food or water, or breathe it in. If dairy animals consume grass contaminated with iodine, the radioactive iodine will be incorporated into their milk. People can receive internal exposure from drinking the milk or eating dairy products made from contaminated milk. Once inside the body, radioactive iodine will be absorbed by the thyroid gland, potentially increasing the risk for thyroid cancer or other thyroid problems.
Cesium-137	30.17 years	External exposure to large amounts of cesium-137 can cause burns, acute radiation sickness, and even death; it can also increase the risk for cancer because of the presence of high-energy gamma radiation. Internal exposure

		to cesium-137 through ingestion or inhalation allows the radioactive material to be distributed in soft tissues, especially muscle tissue, which increases cancer risk.
Cobalt-60	5.27 years	Because it decays by gamma radiation, external exposure to cobalt-60 can increase cancer risk. Most cobalt-60 that is ingested is excreted in feces; however, a small amount is absorbed by the liver, kidneys, and bones, which can cause cancer from internal exposure to gamma radiation.
Strontium-90	29 years	Strontium-90 can be inhaled, but ingestion in food and water is the greatest health concern. Once in the body, strontium-90 acts like calcium and is readily incorporated into bones and teeth, where it can cause cancers of the bone, bone marrow, and soft tissues around the bone.
Plutonium-239 Plutonium-240	24,400 years 6,564 years	Most forms of plutonium emit alpha particles, which can be very damaging when inhaled. The alpha particles can kill cells, which causes scarring of the lungs, leading to further lung disease and cancer. Plutonium can enter the blood stream from the lungs and travel to the kidneys, meaning that the blood and the kidneys will be exposed to alpha particles. Once plutonium circulates through the body, it concentrates in the bones, liver, and spleen, exposing these organs to alpha particles.
Tritium	12.3 years	Tritium emits a very weak beta particle. Tritium primarily enters the body when people swallow tritiated water, inhale tritium as a gas in the air, or absorb it

through their skin. Once tritium
enters the body, it disperses quickly and
is uniformly distributed throughout
the body. Tritium is excreted through
the urine within a month or so after
ingestion. Organically bound tritium
(tritium that is incorporated in organic
compounds) can remain in body for a
longer period.

SOURCE: Adapted from "Radionuclides," US Environmental Protection
Agency, https://www.epa.gov/radiation/radionuclides.

across hundreds of meters and contain radioisotopes of cesium-137, americium-
241, cobalt-60, europium-152, europium-154, strontium-90, plutonium-239, and
plutonium-240. In addition, the areas used for hydronuclear experiments, underground nuclear tests, and other experiments remain contaminated. The further
from the test sites, the lower the levels of contamination. However, in the case of
the Atomic Lake, artificially created with the help of a nuclear explosion, the area
of contamination stretches for 3–4 kilometers (1.8–2.4 miles) around the water.[38]

In 2012–14, specialists of the Institute of Radiation Safety and Ecology conducted the most comprehensive study of the Polygon's Experimental Field to
date with the help of gamma spectroscopy. The Experimental Field is an area
of approximately 300 square kilometers (30,000 hectares) where atmospheric
tests were conducted during the 1949–62 period. For three years, during the
warm months, these scientists worked from 6 a.m. late into the night to collect
a total of 2.5 million spectrum samples. This provided the institute with a detailed understanding of the radioecological situation at the Experimental Field,
including the location of hot spots with elevated radioactive contamination.[39]

These "red zones" will remain at the Polygon forever. In addition, as nuclear
experts warn, some isotopes, such as tritium, tend to migrate. Tritium is not
so harmful as plutonium, americium, or cesium, but it has dangers, traveling
through water to get into plant and animal cells and destroy them. Isotopic
migration will need to be monitored.[40]

The former Polygon continues to be a focal point of attention for the National Nuclear Center staff, and study of the area will continue into the foresee-
able future.

PHOTO 19   An educational trip to the Semipalatinsk Polygon organized by the Center for International Security and Policy for young foreign diplomats and interns, 2019. Photograph by Oleg Butenko.

LIVING WITH THE NUCLEAR LEGACY

As Kazakhstan makes strides as a leader in nuclear diplomacy and builds back up the scientific standing of Kurchatov, the nuclear legacy continues to take a toll on its people.

In attempting to reconstruct and understand the impact of Soviet nuclear tests on the population, Kazakh authorities faced serious challenges. These included a lack of data on what transpired at the Polygon and imperfect systems for measuring radiation, especially during the early years of tests. Perhaps the biggest hindrance was the unavailability of the comprehensive health data collected by the Soviet military and health institutions.

The Kazakh Institute of Radiation Medicine and Ecology in Semey, for example, was heir to Soviet-era Dispensary No. 4 (then disguised as an antibrucellosis clinic) which studied the effects of radiation on people. But most of Dispensary No. 4's critical health data was removed to Russia. Similarly, the Soviet military hospital in Kurchatov, which treated not only military officers and their families but also civilians who lived in Kurchatov and nearby, amassed valuable archival health data. That documentation too was transferred to Russia.

Early on, Kazakhstan energetically sought this critical but missing information. In the first years of independence, it repeatedly pleaded with Russian authorities to provide its data on nuclear tests, radioactive fallout and its path, and health data from Dispensary No. 4 and, especially, medical histories of civilian patients at the hospital in Kurchatov. Many of these entreaties failed.[41]

Today, more than thirty years after the last nuclear test, Kazakh scientists have a better understanding of the effect of Soviet nuclear tests on the environment and people's health. Still, questions remain about the long-term impact on future generations.

According to the experts from the Institute of Radiation Medicine and Ecology who studied radioactive contamination in areas adjacent to the Polygon from 1953 to 1996, after the 1962 ban on atmospheric nuclear tests, there was a systematic decrease in fallout, radionuclides in environment and food products, and soil contamination. Decades after the end of atmospheric nuclear testing, short- and medium-lived radioactive elements have decayed. Long-lived elements, such as strontium-90 and cesium-137, have only partly decayed and have migrated to deeper levels of soil. Thanks to decreasing amounts of radioactive elements in food, locals' annual internal exposure to ionizing radiation has gone down.[42]

When Kazakhstan gained independence, the Institute of Radiation Medicine and Ecology received a mandate to assess nuclear tests' impact on locals' health and to treat the victims. This was a departure from its predecessor's role; Dispensary No. 4 had studied but not treated locals. The institute's scientists, in cooperation with international colleagues, most notably from Japan, conducted various studies on the health impact of ionizing radiation on the people in the Semipalatinsk region. The studies sorted the people into the first generation (those born before 1963, the year after atmospheric nuclear tests were banned); the second generation (those born between January 1963 and December 1981); and the third generation (people born between January 1982 and December 2000). The studies resulted in a relatively good understanding of the health impacts of the tests.[43]

One study reassessed the cases of almost 10,000 people who were examined by Dispensary No. 4 starting in the 1960s. The locals chosen for the study were born before 1960 and lived in close vicinity to the Polygon during the period of atmospheric tests. Almost 10,000 people from a region several hundred kilometers away from the Polygon were studied as a control group. In this retrospective analysis, the institute's experts concluded that people directly exposed to ionizing radiation faced significantly higher risks of general and cancer-related mortality. The most common cancers for that group were esophageal, stomach, lung, and breast (among women).

Various other studies further confirmed that those exposed to radiation with a dose of 250 millisieverts (mSv) and above had higher risks of developing serious illnesses than people from other Kazakhstan regions. For comparison, an average person is exposed to 2.4 mSv a year of typical background radiation, depending on location.[44] Worryingly, elevated risks of serious illness persist for the next two generations—the children and grandchildren of those exposed— including diseases ranging from cancer to mental illness to infectious disease.

Additional DNA studies carried out at the Institute of Radiation Medicine and Ecology demonstrated a significant increase of chromosome aberrations among the children and grandchildren of locals exposed to doses of 250 mSv or higher. The studies confirm that they have a higher risk of developing many forms of leukemia. The children of victims have a higher risk of developing lung and breast cancers, high blood pressure, and diseases brought on by narrowed heart arteries. The grandchildren have a higher risk of developing malign tumors in the eyes, brain, and other organs of the central nervous system as well as malign tumors in lymphoid and blood cell-producing tissues.[45]

The director of the Institute of Radiation Medicine and Ecology, Talgat Muldagaliev, says the institute's priority at the moment is the study of risks for the third and fourth generations of victims.[46]

HUMANS OF THE POLYGON: RESILIENCE AND LOVE FOR THE NATIVE LAND

Behind statistics and studies are people, and life for many of them, especially those in the rural areas near the former Polygon, is not easy. Most villages lack central water systems and modern sewage. People continue to live in simple houses, in some cases with no running water. Except for new buildings, there are no restrooms inside dwellings, just outhouses. There is no internet in smaller villages, a shortcoming felt especially acutely during the COVID-19 pandemic. In fact, village mayors found it easier to travel to the city to get status updates on the COVID-19 situation than to try to get them via a limited cellphone connection. Schools in some villages were left with no choice but to operate in person during the pandemic as online learning is not an option. There are few jobs other than to raise livestock or work at one of the gold or coal mines nearby. Locals know that mining operations can be detrimental to health. Harmful methane emissions and other toxic substances get released into the air, water supplies get contaminated, and land gets disturbed. Living in close proximity to mines is bad enough. Working in them makes it worse.

PHOTO 20   An artist from Kazakhstan, Pasha Kas, painting a rendition of Munch's *Scream* at the Semipalatinsk Polygon, 2016. Photograph by Timur Nusimbekov.

Young people do not stay in the villages as there are no local colleges and no education beyond high school. There is "simply nothing to do," the villagers say. These struggles are universal for all rural areas of Kazakhstan, but in the Semipalatinsk region, the locals bear an additional burden—the aftermath of the Soviet nuclear tests. Thirty years after the last test rocked the Kazakh steppe, people continue to live under its shadow.

Dmitrii, the driver and nuclear testing victim who picked me up at the airport in Semey, is unfortunately far from alone. Too many people, including children, continue to get sick—cancers, blood diseases, and gastrointestinal tract illnesses. Local doctors say that rates of cancer, blood, and other diseases are high, and people get sick at a younger age. These are now the fourth and fifth generations of Soviet nuclear test victims.

It is hard to paint an accurate picture of the Polygon's direct impact on the population's health since Russia refuses to hand over its data, no comprehensive health surveys were conducted in independent Kazakhstan, and multiple difficult conditions in the villages contribute to the health problems. But there are far too many sick people in villages not far from the former Polygon, too many stories of cancer and people dying too young. Here are some of the stories I heard when I visited the vicinity of the Polygon in 2019 and 2020.

In Karaul, a village so close to the former Polygon that its residents could see nuclear mushroom clouds during the atmospheric tests, the youngest victim I met was a six-month-old boy. He is named Nursultan after Kazakhstan's first president. He has a large bright red spot on his head—a benign tumor. He also has six fingers on his left hand—an extra pinky finger attached to the palm. His mom, a young woman in her twenties, tells me how at the hospital where she delivered her son, she met a baby with seven toes on one of his feet: "The big toe is in the middle; there is nothing they can do about it." She heard that Nursultan's extra finger could be removed with a laser; she worries that, if his hand is left as it is, her boy will be teased later in life. When I research this idea, I could not find any references to laser treatment. Instead, traditional surgery is recommended within the first month of birth. Nursultan smiles at us with his happy toothless smile, unaware of his predicament. The condition, known by the scientific name polydactyly, is caused by a genetic mutation.

The next victim I met in Karaul was a six-year-old girl named Kuralai, who is missing four fingers on her left hand.[47] She has a genetic disease similar to Nursultan's. Her parents, Baian and Muratkali, have lived in the area all their lives. Baian is an ambulance nurse and Muratkali is a security guard. The couple say their grandparents and parents never discussed nuclear tests at home: "Everything was forbidden," said Baian. "Everyone was scared of repercussions. They took what they knew [about the tests] to the grave."

Baian's grandfather was among the few people left behind in Karaul when the military evacuated the town during the first Soviet thermonuclear test in 1953. "My father told me that it would be the fourth generation that would suffer," she said sadly. "He was right." Her children are the fourth generation.

While Kuralai was born with missing fingers, her older sister, Nargiz, developed cancer on the bones of her face at age three and endured two years of chemotherapy. Now eleven, Nargiz is free of cancer but has a benign tumor on her bone that needs regular checkups. The checkups can be done only in larger cities such as Semey, and those trips require financial resources that the family does not have. The law on victim assistance provides for certain types of medical help but not for related costs. The charitable organization this family approached could not help because Nargiz is officially cancer-free. Despite these difficulties, her parents vow to continue with her required checkups.

Baian and Muratkali lost their other daughter at age six. "She just died suddenly from pneumonia," Baian said.

Nargiz and Kuralai are bright, friendly, beautiful, and full of life. They love singing and dancing. They have long black shiny hair—it is a tradition for Kazakh girls to have long hair that can be braided. I try not to think about how traumatic it must have been for parents to see Nargiz lose her hair when she was undergoing chemotherapy.

Another village that bears the scars of the Polygon is Sarzhal, which has about 2,000 people and is 20 kilometers (12 miles) away. Historically, Sarzhal was famous for its fertile land, livestock, and dairy production, especially fermented mare's milk—a Kazakh traditional specialty and an important source of nutrition for nomads. In the past, more than 5,000 people lived in Sarzhal, but the economic decline of the post-Soviet period and the lack of higher education and jobs have pushed people out to larger cities.

In Sarzhal, I meet a sixty-year-old high school teacher, Bolatbek Baltabek.[48] Bolatbek has worked in the local school for decades, teaching kids drawing and technology. He was a toddler when, in 1961–62, the Soviet military conducted its highest number of atmospheric tests in the run-up to the ban on such tests. Young Bolatbek and his siblings were eagerly awaiting a new brother or sister in 1962, but, he said, "Our Mum gave birth to a stillborn baby." It was only many years later, Bolatbek added, that "I started thinking that she lost the baby because there were too many tests that year."

Stillbirths, of course, result from many causes, not just nuclear tests, so the reason for that stillbirth is not clear. But it was indisputable that the tests were behind the next tragedy that struck the family five years later. One day, two of his sisters did not wake up for school. It turned out that they were poisoned with carbon monoxide. Shaking from an underground nuclear test had damaged the chimney, and a brick fell inside it and prevented the venting of the poisonous gas. One of the girls died.

In a calm voice, Bolatbek tells other stories about friends, neighbors, and former classmates he lost and continues to lose. A first-grade classmate, Marzhan, went blind and then died from leukemia. Another classmate, Zukhra, succumbed to leukemia when she was eighteen. There were many similar cases in his youth. "We were kids," Bolatbek said. "Who will defend our rights as children? I wish I knew where I could seek justice."

This was not all. Bolatbek's father had stomach cancer; his mother had brain cancer. His brother died at the age of fifty-seven from heart disease. His grandchildren have dysplasia, a scientific term for the abnormal development of cells within tissues and organs.

The darkest side of life under a nuclear cloud was suicide. For reasons not fully studied or understood, nuclear tests seem to trigger mental illnesses that result in a rise in suicides. The deadly increase persisted in the aftermath of the tests; suicides continued in the 1990s after the Polygon was shut down. Bolatbek recounts cases of suicide in Sarzhal—mostly young men, but also young girls and adults.

Bolatbek also explained that initially those who died of suicides were not buried with their relatives, as suicide was considered to violate Islamic tradition. But with time, he said, there were too many suicides to continue that practice. "We started calling it a Polygon disease and burying them like everyone else." Then, without pausing or changing his voice, he added: "My son hung himself when he was in the ninth grade." I fall silent, stunned by this tragedy related in so matter-of-fact a manner. Shortly after his son's suicide, Bolatbek continued, his son's friend became mentally disturbed, at one point telling Bolatbek: "I saw your son. We had a conversation." Three days later, the young man was found hanging in his family's shed. "They found him because of the smell. The neighbor smelled it."

The number of suicides went down after nuclear tests stopped, but people continued to die. In Sarzhal alone, a village of about 2,000 people, forty locals chose to end their lives. Bolatbek describes: "I had a neighbor next door. His daughter hung herself in the yard. Her parents moved out and the house now stands empty for twenty-five years. My other neighbor Askhat, a carpenter— kids adored him, and he liked kids. He hung himself when he was thirty-one."[49]

In judging the Soviet government's decision to test nuclear bombs in the middle of the Kazakh steppe, Bolatbek does not hide his frustration: "Couldn't they choose a desert or a taiga?" he asked. "Why do experiments on humans? We were lab rats for them."

In 1989, when Olzhas Suleimenov launched the Nevada-Semipalatinsk antinuclear movement, Bolatbek joined and became an active participant, marching in antinuclear protests. Later, he mailed the banner he used during the protests to Suleimenov.

Bolatbek has not even reached retirement age, but he hardly has any surviving contemporaries. He receives a small benefit each month, the equivalent of $8. This meager benefit is extended to people who meet the dual criteria of being victims of nuclear tests *and* employees of the state education or health care system. As a teacher, Bolatbek has seventy days of vacation. Each summer, he spends about forty of those days on medical checkups. Free health care is available to him due to his status but requires a three-to-four month wait for medical procedures—time he does not have. He has no choice but to pay for his health checkups in order to fit them into his school calendar. He travels to big cities—Semey and Nur-Sultan (formerly Astana)—to get treatment and buy medications. One comprehensive blood test costs four times more than the monthly benefit he receives as a victim of nuclear testing.

Bolatbek is not alone in lacking support to deal with the suffering left behind. The Kazakh law to aid Soviet nuclear test victims, passed in 1992, carried both moral and practical meaning as it recognized those who suffered from nuclear tests and created legal and regulatory mechanisms to help them. But it is now woefully out of date and victim assistance is inadequate. For example, the law provides benefits for victims who continue to live in the region. But if they move to another region, they lose the benefits. Health experts say victims should be classified by the dose of ionizing radiation they received because the already acquired radiation dose remains with a person forever, even if he or she moves far away from the Polygon.[50] Talgat Muldagaliev, the director of the Institute of Radiation Medicine and Ecology, describes this provision as unfair:

> It doesn't matter whether the person moves to Almaty, Israel, or Germany. Their acquired dose of radiation will remain with them. The inherent risks will not go anywhere. They will still need to have an annual checkup to make sure no diseases associated with the ionizing radiation develop. And it is not only about the person: it is about their children and grandchildren.[51]

Bolatbek and other fellow victims of Soviet nuclear tests say their number one request is early retirement. Current legislation allows only a specific subcategory of victims to retire early. This benefit applies to victims who lived in the zone of extreme or maximum radiation risk for five years during the period of August 29, 1949, to July 5, 1963. Others must work till they reach the age of sixty-three for men and sixty for women. "Many of us simply do not live to that age," several of the people I met told me.

Many nuclear victims, like Bolatbek, and their descendants live in rural areas that desperately need infrastructure improvement, including local medical services. Kazakh villages, including those near the Polygon, continue to feed the cities with their farm products. These villages are a lifeline of the country and support for them is crucial. The villages near the Polygon, with so many nuclear victims, require extra attention as they carry an additional burden.

Local medics confirm the villagers' claims of illness and scarce medical care. Tiny village clinics, staffed with only one doctor and a few support staff, offer only emergency help. For a multitude of other medical assistance—to consult with a specialist, get checked for cancer, get lab tests or cancer treatment, see a dentist, or even have an X-ray—the villagers must travel to Semey. A village physician tells of persistent issues with miscarriages and pregnancies. With better prenatal screening, doctors can identify pregnancies involving deformed children and allow mothers not to continue with the pregnancy. "If there is a pathology, the decision on how to proceed is made in 'the city,'" referring to Semey. Such pregnancies end in abortions in most cases.

The people who live close to the former Polygon share the burden of a tragic past. But, strikingly, they also share a quiet resilience in the face of hardship, an ability to find joy and pride in their native lands.

As I visited the villages of Znamenka (Kokentau), Karaul, Sarzhal, Dolon, and Chagan, every person I met had experienced serious illnesses or the early deaths of loved ones. But somehow they find strength to go on with their lives, building families and raising children. They shared their astounding stories unadorned by dramatic trappings. The calm voices in which they recounted their harrowing tragedies pierced me more deeply than any scream ever could.

So does their strength in adversity. Bolatbek, who lost his son to suicide and numerous classmates, neighbors, and friends to illness, is recording names and stories so that they are never forgotten. Yet although locals like Bolatbek want their pain to be acknowledged and remembered, they don't want to be defined only by the tragedy unleashed in the Kazakh steppe.

Dmitrii, who picked me up at the Semey airport and shared his story, continues to earn his living and take care of his mother. He tells me that he wants to contribute to science and would agree to any lab tests if he were asked by scientists interested in studying the effect of ionizing radiation.

Baian and Muratkali's daughters are doing well in school. They flourish in extracurricular activities, and have a strong following on Tik-Tok for which they rope their parents into choreographed family dancing videos.

The Semipalatinsk region is not just the site of Soviet nuclear tests and its attendant human suffering and ecological damage. It is also the ancestral home of some of Kazakhstan's most revered poets and writers, such as Abai, Shakarim, and Mukhtar Auezov. So it is perhaps not surprising that here there is an almost mystical feeling of sacred space. People of the Semipalatinsk region are proud to share their roots with these great luminaries and talk with much love about their land. I often heard them describe their home as their "Tugan zher," Kazakh for "place of birth." The harsh beauty of the endless steppe carries pain and joy, memories of ancestors and hopes for the future. And it is mesmerizing.

NOTES

CHAPTER 1: THE STEPPE

Abai, "Summertime," bridge translation by Rose Kudabayeva, in *Abai*, published by Public Foundation National Bureau of Translations in partnership with Cambridge University Press (2020), 74–76. *Auyl* originally referred to a community of Kazakh nomads that, through the eighteenth century, led a mobile life moving along pasture routes. When Kazakhs adopted a settled mode of life in the nineteenth and twentieth centuries, *auyl* started to refer to a permanent rural settlement.

1. A. D. Shevchenko, "Vzryvaem zemnye zvezdy" [Exploding earth stars], in *Istoriia atomnogo proekta* [History of atomic project], ed. Sergei Davydov (Moscow: Kurchatovskii Institut, 1995), part 3, issue 4, 262.

2. I. A. Akchurin, *Semipalatinskii iadernyi poligon: Sozdanie, stanovlenie, deiatel'nost'* [Semipalatinsk Nuclear Polygon: Creation, development, activity] (Moscow: Ministry of Defense of the Russian Federation, 2007), 12.

3. A. Kh. Margulan et al., *Drevniaia kul'tura Tscentral'nogo Kazakhstana* [Ancient culture of central Kazakhstan] (Alma-Ata: Nauka, 1966), 11, 228.

4. Abai Center, https://abaicenter.com.

5. Zharkyn Shakarimov, *Amre v Parizhe* [Amre in Paris] (N.p.: Signet Press, 2016).

6. Altynbek Kumyrzakuly, "Mikhaelis—a Spiritual Mate of Abai," *Qazaqstan Tarihy* (October 1, 2016), https://e-history.kz/en/news/show/6930/.

7. Dulat Moldabaev, "Nash Dostoevskii" [Our Dostoevskii], *Kazakhstanskaia Pravda*, June 9, 2017.

8. For an account of Russia's conquest of Kazakhstan in English-language literature, see, e.g., Martha Brill Olcott, *The Kazakhs*, 2nd ed. (Stanford, CA: Hoover Institution Press, 1995), 28–53; for Kazakhstan's history, see, e.g., N. E. Massanov et al., *Istoriia Kazakhstana: Narody i kul'tury* [History of Kazakhstan: People and culture] (Almaty: Dike Press, 2000).

9. V. N. Kashliak, *Semipalatinskie arabeski* [Semipalatinsk arabesques] (Semey, 2010), 1:7–50.

10. N. Martynenko, ed., *Alash Orda* (Alma-Ata: Aikap, 1992).

11. Alash database (in Russian), Universal Library of East Kazakhstan Oblast, Semey, http://alash.semeylib.kz/?lang=ru; Z. Saktaganova et al., "Alash Party: The Historiography of the Movement," *Space and Culture, India* 7, no. 4 (2020): 208–18.

12. Akhmet Baitursynov, "Revoliutsiia i kirgizy" [Revolution and Kyrgyz people], cited in K. A. Sagadiev, "Akhmet Baitusynov i ekonomicheskie vzgliady liderov Alash Ordy" [Akhmet Baitursynov and Alash Orda leaders' views on economy], *Otechestvennaia Istoriia* (Almaty: Institute of History and Ethnology named after Chokan Valikhanov, 1998), 29–33.

13. See, e.g., Sarah Cameron, *The Hungry Steppe: Famine, Violence, and the Making of the Kazakh Steppe* (Ithaca, NY: Cornell University Press, 2018); Robert Kindler, *Stalin's Nomads: Power and Famine in Kazakhstan* (Pittsburgh: University of Pittsburgh Press, 2018).

14. For a detailed history of Stalin's efforts, see David Holloway, *Stalin and the Bomb: The Soviet Union and Atomic Energy 1939–1956* (New Haven, CT: Yale University Press, 1994).

15. Helen Rappaport, *Joseph Stalin: A Biographical Companion* (Santa Barbara, CA: ABC-CLIO, 1999), 12.

16. Yuli Khariton and Yuri Smirnov, "The Khariton Version," *Bulletin of the Atomic Scientists* 49, no. 4 (1993): 20–31; Yuli Khariton and Yuri Smirnov, *Mify i real'nost' sovetskogo atomnogo proekta* [Myths and realities of the Soviet Atom Project] (Arzamas-16: VNIIEF, 1994), 40–41.

17. I. A. Ryzhikov, "Na stroitel'stve poligona" [At the Polygon's construction], in *Istoriia atomnogo proekta*, ed. Davydov, 1995, issue 2, 75.

18. Ryzhikov, "Na stroitel'stve Poligona," 74.

19. M. A. Sadovskii, "Institut khimicheskoi fiziki" [Institute of Chemical Physics], in *Istoriia atomnogo proekta*, ed. Davydov, 1997, issue 11, 52.

20. A. I. Khovanovich, "RDS-1 i vsia zhizn'" [RDS1 and the entire life] in *Istoriia atomnogo proekta*, ed. Davydov, 1995, issue 3, 109.

21. F. A. Kholin, "Radost' truda i bol' veterana" [Joy of labor and pain of a veteran], in *Istoriia atomnogo proekta*, ed. Davydov, 1995, issue 4, 52.

22. I. A. Akchurin, *Semipalatinskii iadernyi poligon*, 23.

23. Kholin, "Radost' truda i bol' veterana," 52.

24. S. L. Davydov, "Zadacha, stavshaia delom zhizni" [Task of a lifetime], in *Istoriia atomnogo proekta*, ed. Davydov, 1995, issue 1, 199.

25. Davydov, "Zadacha, stavshaia delom zhizni," 199.

26. Davydov, "Zadacha, stavshaia delom zhizni," 87.

27. Thomas B. Cochran and Robert S. Norris, *Making the Russian Bomb: From Stalin to Yeltsin* (Boulder, CO: Westview, 1995), 12; Veniamin Tsukerman and Zinaida Azarkh, *Arzamas-16: Soviet Scientists in the Nuclear Age: A Memoir* (Nottingham: Bramcote Press, 1999), 75.

28. Tsukerman and Azarkh, *Arzamas-16*, 75.

29. Cochran and Norris, *Making the Russian Bomb*, 12.

30. V. P. Zhuchkov, "Na strazhe atomnoi [On nuclear guard]," in *Istoriia atomnogo proekta*, ed. Davydov, 1995, issue 2, 151–52.

31. A. N. Viukov, "Na grani osobogo riska" [On the brink of special risk], in *Istoriia atomnogo proekta*, ed. Davydov, 1995, issue 4, 94.

32. "Doklad L. P. Beriia i I. V. Kurchatova I. V. Stalinu o predvaritel'nyh dannyh, po-luchennyh pri ispytanii atomnoi bomby. 30 avgusta 1949 g." [Report from L. P. Beria and I. V. Kurchatov to I. V. Stalin on Preliminary Data Obtained during the Atomic Bomb Test. August 30, 1949], *Atomnyi proekt SSSR*, vol. 2: *Atomnaia bomba, 1945–1954* [USSR atomic project: Documents and materials, vol. 2: Atomic bomb, 1945–1954] (Sarov: RFNC and VNIIEF, 1999), 639–43.

33. Tsukerman and Azarkh, *Arzamas-16*, 77.

34. Tsukerman and Azarkh, *Arzamas-16*, 76.

35. Arkadii Kruglov, *The History of the Soviet Atomic Industry* (London: Taylor and Francis, 2002), 123.

36. Michael Gordin, *Red Cloud at Dawn* (New York: Farrar, Straus and Giroux, 2009), 176.

37. Khovanovich, "RDS-1 i vsia zhizn'," 115.

38. Kholin, "Radost' truda i bol' veterana," 64.

39. Holloway, *Stalin and the Bomb*, 217.

40. Shevchenko, "Vzryvaem zemnye zvezdy," 262.

41. Khovanovich, "RDS-1 i vsia zhizn'," 115, 116.

42. Roentgen (R) is a unit of exposure to ionizing radiation. "Roentgen-R," U.S. Nuclear Regulatory Commission, https://www.nrc.gov/reading-rm/basic-rf/glossry/roentgen-r.html.

43. V. M. Nerushenko, "Esche odin porazhaiushchii faktor" [One more striking fac-tor], in *Istoriia atomnogo proekta*, ed. Davydov, 1995, issue 4, 278.

44. Mutan Aimakov, *Iz togo, shto ia videl* [What I saw], 49–57, cited in Medeu Sarseke, *Semipalatinskaia tragedia* [Semipalatinsk tragedy] (Astana: Foliant, 2016), 134.

45. Aimakov, *Iz togo, shto ia videl*, 49–57, cited in Sarseke, *Semipalatinskaia tragedia*, 134.

46. B. I. Gusev, "Radiatsionno-giginiecheskaia kharakteristika raionov, prilegaiush-chih k Semipalatinskomu ispytatel'nomu poligonu" [Radiation-hygienic characteristics of the districts adjacent to the Semipalatinsk Polygon], in *Mediko-biologicheskie posled-stviia iadernyh ispytanii na Semipalatinskom poligone* [Medical-biological consequences of nuclear tests at the Semipalatinsk Polygon], collection of papers, vol. 5, Ministry of Health of the Republic of Kazakhstan, Semipalatinsk, 1994.

47. Tsukerman and Azarkh, *Arzamas-16*, 77–78.

48. Khariton and Smirnov, *Mify i real'nost' Sovetskogo atomnogo proekta*, 45.

49. Nikita Khrushchev revoked it after Stalin's death. Khariton and Smirnov, *Mify i real'nost' Sovetskogo atomnogo proekta*, 45.

50. Sergey Lukashenko, introduction, *Aktual'nye voprosy radioekologii Kazakhstana* [Topical issues of radioecology of Kazakhstan], issue 3, vol. 1, 2011 (Kurchatov: Institute of Radiation Safety and Ecology), 8.

CHAPTER 2: FORTY YEARS OF NUCLEAR TESTS

1. A test means a detonation of one nuclear device or several nearly simultaneous detonations of several devices.

2. L. P. Viukova, "Byt' vmeste liuboi tsenoi," [To be together at any price], in *Istoriia atomnogo proekta* [History of atomic project], ed. Sergei Davydov (Moscow: Kurchatovskii Institut, 1995), issue 4, 133, 137.

3. A. I. Khovanovich, "RDS-1 i vsia zhizn'" [RDS-1 and the entire life], in *Istoriia atomnogo proekta*, ed. Davydov, 1995, issue 3, 111.

4. Khovanovich, "RDS-1 i vsia zhizn'," 112.

5. Viukova, "Byt' vmeste liuboi tsenoi," 148.

6. I. A. Akchurin, *Semipalatinskii iadernyi poligon: Sozdanie, stanovlenie, deiatel'nost' [Semipalatinsk Nuclear Polygon: Creation, development, activity]* (Moscow: Ministry of Defense of the Russian Federation, 2007), 50.

7. F. A. Kholin, "Radost' truda i bol' veterana" [Joy of labor and veteran's pain], in *Istoriia atomnogo proekta*, ed. Davydov, 1995, issue 4, 67.

8. "Thermonuclear Bomb," Britannica, https://www.britannica.com/technology/thermonuclear-bomb.

9. "1 November 1952—Ivy Mike," CTBTO, https://www.ctbto.org/specials/testing-times/1-november-1952-ivy-mike.

10. Yuli Khariton, Viktor Adamskii, and Yuri Smirnov, "The Way It Was," *Bulletin of the Atomic Scientists* 52, no. 6 (November/December 1996): 55.

11. "Lavrentii Beria Executed," *History Today* 53, no. 12 (December 12, 2003), http://www.historytoday.com/richard-cavendish/lavrenti-beria-executed.

12. I. S. Ipatkin, "Metodika KT" [CT methodology], in *Istoriia atomnogo proekta*, ed. Davydov, 1997, issue 11, 153.

13. Alex Wellerstein and Edward Geist, "The Secret of the Soviet Hydrogen Bomb," *Physics Today* 4, no. 40 (April 2017): 44.

14. "Ispytaniia pervyh termoiadernyh vzryvov RDS-6s i RDS-37" [First tests of thermonuclear RDS-6s and RDS-37s], chap. 5 in *Iadernye ispytaniia SSSR*, ed. V. N. Mikhailov (Sarov: Russian Federal Nuclear Center, 1997), 1:218.

15. Andrei Sakharov, *Memoirs* (New York: Knopf, 1990), 171.

16. Sakharov, *Memoirs*, 172.

17. Sakharov, *Memoirs*, 170; Akchurin, *Semipalatinskii Poligon*, 116.

18. "Ispytaniia pervyh termoiadernyh vzryvov RDS-6s i RDS-37," 219.

19. Kairat Kabdrakhmanov, *470 bomb v serdtse Kazakhstana [470 bombs in the heart of Kazakhstan]* (Almaty, 1994), 97.

20. Sakharov, *Memoirs*, 172–73.

21. "Ispytaniia pervyh termoiadernyh vzryvov RDS-6s i RDS-37," 216.

22. I. A. Ryzhikov, "Na stroitel'stve poligona" [Building the Polygon], in *Istoriia atomnogo proekta*, ed. Davydov, 1995, issue 2, 92.

23. "Ispytaniia pervyh termoiadernyh vzryvov RDS-6s i RDS-37," 215.

24. A. N. Viukov, "Na grani osobogo riska" [On the brink of special risk], in *Istoriia atomnogo proekta*, ed. Davydov, 1995, issue 4, 128.

25. N. A. Kozlov, "Koe-shto o sebe i sluzhbe bezopasnosti" [A bit about myself and the safety service], in *Istoriia atomnogo proekta*, ed. Davydov, 1995, issue 5, 156.

26. Information from the Kurchatov museum of nuclear testing; V. V. Alekseev, "Vo imia iadernogo shchita strany" [In the name of the country's nuclear shield], in *Istoriia atomnogo proekta*, ed. Davydov, 1995, issue 3, 87; Viukov, "Na grani osobogo riska," 128.

27. Khovanovich, "RDS-1 i vsia zhizn," 126.

28. V. N. Sakharov, "Nevidomoe porazhaiuschee izluchenie" [Invisible ionizing radiation], in *Istoriia atomnogo proekta*, ed. Davydov, 1997, issue 11, 125.

29. Kabdrakhmanov, *470 bomb v serdtse Kazakhstana*, 105.

30. Evgenii Gusliarov, "Shto zhe eto bylo togda v poselke Karaul?" [What happened back then in Karaul Village?] *Prostor*, no. 11 (1989): 130–31.

31. "Iz zaiavleniia zhitelia sela Karaul Abaiskogo raiona T. Sliambekova invalida Velikoi Otechestvennoi Voiny sekretariu Semipalatinskogo obkoma kompartii Kazakhstana K. B. Boztaevu o provedenii iadernyh vzryvov na SIIaP" [From a letter of the resident of Karaul of Abaiskii raion T. Sliambekov—World War II veteran—to the Secretary of the Semipalatinsk Oblast Executive Committee of Kazakhstan's Communist Party Boztaev about the nuclear explosions at the Semipalatinsk Nuclear Testing Site], May 29, 1988, Center of Modern History Documentation of Eastern Kazakhstan Oblast,' f. 103, o. 21, d. 73, 31–35; Talgat Sliambekov, interview [in Russian] in documentary film *Polygon*, produced by Oraz Rymzhanov, codirected by Oraz Rymzhanov and Vladimir Rerikh, 1990.

32. Kabdrakhmanov, *470 bomb v serdtse Kazakhstana*, 105.

33. Kabdrakhmanov, *470 bomb v serdtse Kazakhstana*, 105.

34. "Iz zaiavleniia zhitelia sela Karaul," 31–35.

35. Kabdrakhmanov, *470 bomb v serdtse Kazakhstana*, 107.

36. Essengarin named his granddaughter Samantha—after Samantha Smith, an American girl who had become famous after sending a letter to the Soviet leader Yuri Andropov asking him about a possibility of a nuclear war. Samantha became a goodwill ambassador and even visited the Soviet Union on a personal invitation from Andropov before her tragic death in a plane crash at the age of thirteen. Kabdrakhmanov, *470 bomb v serdtse Kazakhstana*, 109.

37. Information from the Museum of Nuclear Testing, National Nuclear Center, Kurchatov. Roentgen is a legacy unit used to measure the exposure of X-rays and gamma rays in the air. The actual absorption dose by humans depends on many factors and, therefore, the "Roentgen" unit would be later retired and replaced with "roentgen equivalent man" (rem). Rem is a unit to measure the dose equivalent (or effective dose), which combines the amount of energy (from any ionizing radiation that is deposited in human tissue), along with the medical effects of the given type of radiation (source: US NRC Glossary, www.nrc.gov/reading- rm/basic-ref/glossary/rem-roentgen-equivalent-man.html).

38. Dr. H. Smith, "The International Commission on Radiological Protection: Historical Overview," IAEA, https://www.iaea.org/sites/default/files/30302094244.pdf.

39. "Ispytaniia pervyh termoiadernyh vzryvov RDS-6s i RDS-37," 221.

40. Boris Gusev, interview in documentary film *Where the Wind Blew*, directed by André Singer, 2017.

41. Sakharov, *Memoirs*, 179, 181, 184.

42. "22 November—RDS-37," CTBTO, https://www.ctbto.org/specials/testing-times/22-november-1955-rds-37.

43. Sakharov, *Memoirs*, 190.

44. Sakharov, *Memoirs*, 190.

45. Witness account by S. T. Shalaeva, in Keshrim Boztaev, *29 avgusta* [August 29] (Almaty: Atamura, 1998), 27.

46. "Ispytaniia pervyh termoiadernyh vzryvov RDS-6s i RDS-37," 226; V. A. Logachev, ed., *Iadernye ispytaniia SSSR: Sovremennoe radioekologicheskoe sostoianie poligonov* [Nuclear tests of the USSR: Current radioecological state of Polygons] (Moscow: Izdat, 2002), 61.

47. "Ispytaniia pervyh termoiadernyh vzryvov RDS-6s i RDS-37," 226–27.

48. "Alleged Nuclear Weapons Tests Near Semipalatinsk," Central Intelligence Agency, Information Report, April 1, 1957; secret, excised copy, National Security Archive, https://nsarchive2.gwu.edu//dc.html?doc=4430809-Document-03-Central-Intelligence-Agency.

49. G. I. Kniazev, "13 let na iadernom poligone" [13 years at the Nuclear Polygon], *Istoriia atomnogo proekta*, ed. Davydov, 1995, issue 2, 140.

50. G. F. Zorin, "I vse zhe . . . rabota i zhizn' byli interesnymi" [And still . . . work and life . . . were interesting], in *Istoriia atomnogo proekta*, ed. Davydov, 1995, issue 4, 216; Sakharov, *Memoirs*, 192.

51. Sakharov, *Memoirs*, 192; Logachev, *Iadernye ispytaniia SSSR*, 62.

52. Sakharov, *Memoirs*, 192.

53. Logachev, *Iadernye ispytaniia SSSR*, 62, 90, 250–51.

54. Sakharov, *Memoirs*, 192.

55. Logachev, *Iadernye ispytaniia SSSR*, 62.

56. Sakharov, *Memoirs*, 193.

57. Sakharov, *Memoirs*, 193–94.

58. Sakharov, *Memoirs*, 194–95.

59. Sakharov, *Memoirs*, 201.

60. Vladimir S. Shkolnik, ed., *The Semipalatinsk Test Site: Creation, Operation, and Conversion* (Albuquerque: Sandia National Laboratories, 2002), 49.

61. "Kak eto bylo. Perrvyi vzryv" [How it happened. The first explosion], witness account by Khamza Baibolatov, recorded by Kanat Kabdrakhmanov, *Izbiratel'* newspaper, October 6–19, 1990, no. 16, 6; Kabdrakhmanov, *470 bomb v serdtse Kazakhstana*, 104.

62. Jeff Kingston, "Blast from the Past: Lucky Dragon 60 Years On," *Japan Times*, February 8, 2014.

63. William Burr and Hector L. Montford, "The Making of the Limited Test Ban Treaty, 1958–1963," National Security Archive, http://nsarchive.gwu.edu/NSAEBB/NSAEBB94/index2.htm.

64. Shkolnik, *Semipalatinsk Test Site*, 26.

65. Robert Norris and William Arkin, "Soviet Nuclear Testing, August 29, 1949–October 24, 1990," *Bulletin of the Atomic Scientists* 54, no. 3 (May–June, 1998): 69–71.

66. "United States Nuclear Tests: July 1945 through September 1992," Federation of American Scientists, https://fas.org/nuke/guide/usa/nuclear/nv209nar.pdf.

67. Martin Sherwin, *Gambling with Armageddon: Nuclear Roulette from Hiroshima to the Cuban Missile Crisis* (New York: Knopf, 2020); Robert F. Kennedy, *Thirteen Days: A Memoir of the Cuban Missile Crisis* (New York: W. W. Norton, 1969).

68. Burr and Montford, "Making of the Limited Test Ban Treaty."

69. "Nuclear Test Ban Treaty," John F. Kennedy Presidential Library and Museum, https://www.jfklibrary.org/learn/about-jfk/jfk-in-history/nuclear-test-ban-treaty.

70. "Commencement Address at American University, June 10, 1963," John F. Kennedy Presidential Library and Museum, https://www.jfklibrary.org/Asset-Viewer/BW-C7I4C9QUmLG9J6I80y8w.aspx; Burr and Montford, "Making of the Limited Test Ban Treaty."

71. N. A. Nazarbayev et al., *Provedenie kompleksa nauchno-tekhnicheskih i inzhenernyh rabot po privedeniiu byvshego Semipalatinskogo ispytatel'nogo poligona v bezopasnoe sostoianie* [Scientific-technical measures and engineering work to transform the former Semipalatinsk Polygon into a safe state] (Kurchatov: National Nuclear Center, 2016), 1:25; Kazakhstan's government commission, Akt Proverki materialov o kolichestve iadernyh vzryvov, provedennyh na Semipalatinskom iadernom poligone, c 1949 g. po 1989 g. [A record of inspection of materials on the quantity of nuclear explosions conducted at the Semipalatinsk Nuclear Polygon, 1949–1989], February 28, 1992, Archive of the President of the Republic of Kazakhstan, Almaty, Kazakhstan, f. 5H, o. 1, d. 1020a.

72. Akchurin, *Semipalatinskii iadernyi poligon*, 37–41; Nazarbayev et al., *Provedenie kompleksa nauchno-tekhnicheskih i inzhenernyh rabot*, 1:24.

73. Shkolnik, *Semipalatinsk Test Site*, 22; Akchurin, *Semipalatinskii iadernyi poligon*, 41.

74. Anatolii Yegai, "Glazami ochevidtsa," *Kyzylordinskie Vesti*, n.d.

75. Logachev, *Iadernye ispytaniia SSSR*, 55.

76. On April 25, 1980, an underground test was equivalent to an earthquake registering 6.3 on the Richter scale. "USSR Conducts Siberian Nuclear Test," *Xinhua*, April 25, 1980.

77. "Poiasnitel'naia zapiska zamestitelia predsedatelia ispolkoma Zhanasemeiskogo raionnogo soveta narodnyh deputatov B. Golintseva v Semipalatinskii oblastnoi sovet narodnyh deputatov ob ushcherbe, nanesennom hoziaistvam i naseleniiu Zhanasemeiskogo raiona v rezul'tate ispytanii na SIIaP" [Explanatory note of the Deputy Chairman of the Executive Committee of Zhanasemei Raion Soviet of People's Deputies B. Golintsev to Semipalatinsk Oblast Soviet of People's Deputies on the damage from nuclear tests inflicted on households and population], June 7, 1990, f. 771, o. 8, d. 1075, 2–4, Center for Modern History Documentation of Eastern Kazakhstan.

78. Author's interview with Sergazy Diussembaev, Semey, 2017.

79. Author's interview with Anuarbek Suichinov, Semey, 2017.

80. "The United States' Nuclear Testing Programme," CTBTO, https://www.ctbto.org/nuclear-testing/the-effects-of-nuclear-testing/the-united-states-nuclear-testing-programme/.

81. Robert S. Norris and Thomas B. Cochran, "Nuclear Weapons Tests and Peaceful Nuclear Explosions by the Soviet Union," draft report, Natural Resource Defense Council, October 1996, 5.

82. I. D. Aseev, "Iadernyi vzryv v mirnyh tsceliah" [Peaceful nuclear explosion], in *Istoriia atomnogo proekta*, ed. Davydov, 1995, issue 4, 97.

83. Shkolnik, *Semipalatinsk Test Site*, 67.

84. Memorandum, Council of Ministers of the Kazakh SSR to the President of the Kazakh SSR Nazarbayev N. A., signed by the chairman of the Council U. Karamanov, July 27, 1990, f. 7, o. 1, d. 88, Archive of the President of the Republic of Kazakhstan.

85. "Radiation Thermometer," Centers for Disease Control and Prevention, https://www.cdc.gov/nceh/radiation/emergencies/radiationthermometertext.htm.

86. Memorandum, Council of Ministers of the Kazakh SSR.

87. "Informatsiia zaveduiushchei oblzdravotdelom Semipalatinskogo oblispolkoma F. Abdykhalykovoi sekretariu Semipalatinskogo obkoma KP Kazakhstana M. P. Karpenko ob obnaruzhenii povyshennogo gamma-fona i vypadeniia radioaktivnyh produktov vzryva" [Information from the head of the health unit of the Semipalatinsk Oblast Executive Committee of Kazakhstan's Communist Party F. Abdykhalykova to the Secretary of Semipalatinsk Oblast Committee of Kazakhstan's Communist Party M. P. Karpenko on the detection of elevated gamma- levels and post-explosion radioactive fallout], dated after January 21, 1965, f. 103, o. 73, d. 12, 44–45, Center for Modern History Documentation of Eastern Kazakhstan; V. Shepel', ed., with A. E. Assanbaeva, E. M. Gribanova, contributors, *Kazakhstan za bez'iadernyi mir: Sbornik dokumentov i materialov* [Kazakhstan for a nuclear-free world: A compilation of documents and materials] (Almaty: Archive of the President of the Republic of Kazakhstan, 2011), 52–53.

88. "Pis'mo rukovoditelei soiuznyh ministerstv A. I. Burnaziana i E. P. Slavskogo pervomu sekretariu TsK KP Kazakhstana D. A. Kunaevu o bezopasnosti dlia naseleniia posledstvii provedeniia eksperimental'nyh vzryvov" [Letter from the Soviet ministers A. I. Burnazyan and E. P. Slavskii to the First Secretary of Kazakhstan's Communist Party D. A. Kunaev on the population safety of experimental explosions], February 8–9, 1965, f. 708, o. 36/1, d. 3, 113–114, Archive of the President of the Republic of Kazakhstan; *Kazakhstan za bez'iadernyi mir*, ed. Shepel', 53–55.

89. Sakharov, *Memoirs*, 213.

90. M. D. Nordyke, *The Soviet Program for Peaceful Uses of Nuclear Explosions* (Livermore, CA: Lawrence Livermore National Laboratory, 2000), 8.

91. "Vblizi Atomnogo Ozera tiho uviadaet, bez pit'evoi vody, selo Sarzhal" [Sarzhal village near the Atomic Lake is quietly dying without fresh water], Azattyq, September 17, 2009, https://rus.azattyq.org/a/Saryzhal_village_at_nuclear_field/1823951.html.

92. "O voprosah v sviazi s vozobnovleniem Sovetskim Soiuzom iadernyh ispytanii i argumentatsii prichin etogo shaga" [On the resumption of nuclear tests by the Soviet Union and the argumentation in support of this development], Central Committee of

the USSR Communist Party, signed by L. Zaikov, E. Shevardnadze, V. Chebrikov, A. Yakovlev, V. Kataev, box 8, folder 9; Postanovlenie TsK KPSS, V. Kataev, box 8, folder 9, Hoover Institution Library and Archives.

93. Gregory E. van der Vink and Christopher E. Paine, "The Politics of Verification: Limiting the Testing of Nuclear Weapons," *Science and Global Security* 3 (1993): 261–88.

94. Memorandum on the Soviet-American Negotiations on Limiting and Banning Nuclear Tests, Hoover Institution Archives.

95. Mark A. Stein, "Nevada A-Blast Makes Arms Control History," *Los Angeles Times*, August 18, 1988.

96. "JVE Airlift Factsheet," April 14, 1988, https://lab2lab.stanford.edu/sites/g/files/sbiybj8331/f/jve_airlift_factsheet_04.14.1988.pdf.

97. Victor Alessi's diary. Copy in author's possession.

98. Alessi's diary.

99. Alessi's diary.

100. Alessi's diary.

101. "Treaty between the United States of America and the Union of Soviet Socialist Republics on the Limitation of Underground Nuclear Weapon Tests (and Protocol Thereto) (TTBT)," US State Department, http://www.state.gov/t/isn/5204.htm.

CHAPTER 3: THE HUMAN TOLL

1. "Hollywood and the Downwinders Still Grapple with Nuclear Fallout," *Guardian*, June 6, 2015.

2. "Estimation of the Baseline Number of Cancers among Marshallese and the Number of Cancers Attributable to Exposure to Fallout from Nuclear Weapons Testing Conducted in the Marshall Islands," Division of Cancer Epidemiology and Genetics, National Cancer Institute, National Institutes of Health, Department of Health and Human Services, 2004, http://marshall.csu.edu.au/Marshalls/html/Radiation/NCI-report.pdf.

3. "Marshall Islands: Status of the Nuclear Claims Trust Fund," Government Accountability Office, 2002, https://www.gao.gov/assets/220/216721.pdf.

4. V. M. Maliutov, "Tak my nachinali" [That is how we started], in *Istoriia atomnogo proekta* [History of atomic project], ed. Sergei Davydov (Moscow: Kurchatovskii Institut, 1995), issue 2, 113.

5. Maliutov, "Tak my nachinali," 114.

6. G. F. Zorin, "I vse zhe . . . rabota i zhizn' byli interesnymi" [And still . . . work and life . . . were interesting], in *Istoriia atomnogo proekta*, ed. Davydov, 1995, Issue 4, 234–36.

7. K. P. Kedrov, "Sluchai ostroi luchevoi bolezni na Semipalatinskom poligone" [A case of acute radiation sickness at Semipalatinsk Polygon], in *Istoriia atomnogo proekta*, ed. Davydov, 1996, issue 5, 226–30.

8. Robert Elegant, "Fallout: In Kazakhstan, the Human Wreckage of Soviet Nuclear Tests," *National Review* (September 16, 2002), 30–32.

9. Author's interview with Melgis Metov, Almaty, 2016.

10. Elegant, "Fallout," 30–32.

11. I. A. Akchurin, *Semipalatinskii iadernyi poligon: Sozdanie, stanovlenie, deiatel'nost'*

[Semipalatinsk Nuclear Polygon: Creation, development, activity] (Moscow: Ministry of Defense of the Russian Federation, 2007), 64; "Gosudarstvennaia sistema organizatsii iadernyh ispytanii v SSSR" [State system of nuclear tests in the USSR], vol. 1, chap. 2, in *Iadernye ispytaniia SSSR* [Nuclear tests of the USSR], ed. V. N. Mikhailov (Sarov: Russian Federal Nuclear Center, 1997), 79.

12. Vladimir S. Shkolnik, ed., *The Semipalatinsk Test Site: Creation, Operation, and Conversion* (Albuquerque: Sandia National Laboratories, 2002), 86.

13. Author's interview with a former resident of Kurchatov, Almaty, 2009.

14. G. I. Kniazev, "13 let na iadernom poligone" [13 years at the Nuclear Polygon], in *Istoriia atomnogo proekta*, ed. Davydov, 1995, issue 2, 158.

15. Author's interview with Gulsum Kakimzhanova, Almaty, 2009.

16. Author's interview with Kakimzhanova.

17. Saim B. Balmukhanov, "The Semipalatinsk Nuclear Test Site—Through My Own Eyes," DTRA Technical Report, July 2014, 18.

18. K. P. Kedrov, "Mediko-biologicheskie issledovaniia pri iadernyh vzryvah" [Medical-biological research during nuclear tests], in *Istoriia atomnogo proekta*, ed. Davydov, 1996, issue 5, 139.

19. *Population Health in Regions Adjacent to the Semipalatinsk Nuclear Test Site*, Institute of Biophysics, Physical Training Center, 1998, 3.

20. K. Gordeev et al., "Fallout from Nuclear Tests: Dosimetry in Kazakhstan," *Radiation and Environmental Biophysics* 41, no. 1 (March 2002): 61–67.

21. Shkolnik, *Semipalatinsk Test Site*, 78.

22. Fred Pearce, "Exposed: Soviet Cover-Up of Nuclear Fallout Worse Than Chernobyl," *New Scientist* (March 20, 2017), 16.

23. *Iadernye ispytaniia SSSR: Semipalatinskii poligon* [Nuclear tests in the USSR: Semipalatinsk Polygon] (Moscow: Midbioextrem, 1997), 44–45.

24. Shkolnik, *Semipalatinsk Test Site*, 100.

25. Keshrim Boztaev, *Sindrom Kainara* [Kainar syndrome] (Almaty, 1995), 156.

26. "Spravka o rabote gruppy nauchnyh sotrudnikov Instituta Biofiziki Akademii meditsinskih nauk SSSR po obsledovaniiu naseleniia Semipalatinskoi obl." [Memorandum on the work of the scientific staff of the Institute of Biophysics of the USSR Academy of Health Science on the examination of the population in Semipalatinsk Oblast], March 1, 1958, Semipalatinsk, top secret, f. 103, o. 73, d. 12, 13–17, Center for Modern History Documentation of Eastern Kazakhstan; V. Shepel', ed., with A. E. Assanbaeva and E. M. Gribanova, contributors, *Kazakhstan za bez'iadernyi mir: Sbornik dokumentov i materialov* [Kazakhstan for a nuclear-free world: Collection of documents and materials] (Almaty: Archive of the President of the Republic of Kazakhstan, 2011), 27–29.

27. "Spravka o rabote gruppy nauchnyh sotrudnikov Instituta Biofiziki Akademii meditsinskih nauk SSSR," f. 103, o. 73, d. 12, 13–17, Center for Modern History Documentation of Eastern Kazakhstan.

28. "Spravka o rabote gruppy nauchnyh sotrudnikov Instituta Biofiziki Akademii meditsinskih nauk SSSR," f. 103, o. 73, d. 12, 13–17, Center for Modern History Documentation of Eastern Kazakhstan.

29. "Spravka o rabote gruppy nauchnyh sotrudnikov Instituta Biofiziki Akademii meditsinskih nauk SSSR," f. 103, o. 73, d. 12, 13–17, Center for Modern History Documentation of Eastern Kazakhstan.

30. "Spravka kollektiva vrachei dispansera #4 sekretariu Semipalatinskogo obkoma KP Kazakhstana M. A. Suzhikovu o radiologicheskoi obstanovke oblasti i ee vliianiia na liudei" [Memorandum of the staff doctors of the Dispensary #4 for the Secretary of Semipalatinsk Oblast Committee of Kazakhstan's Communist Party M. A. Suzhikov on the radiological situation in the oblast and its impact on the population], top secret, February 24, 1958, f. 103, o. 73, d. 12, 2–12, Center for Modern History Information of Eastern Kazakhstan; *Kazakhstan za bez'iadernyi mir*, ed. Shepel', 21–27.

31. "Vysshaia otsenka—Pamiat' naroda" [Highest reward—People's memory], *Kyzylordinskie Vesti*, March 25, 2017.

32. "Spravka kollektiva vrachei dispansera #4," f. 103, o. 73, d. 12, 2–12, Center for Modern History Information of Eastern Kazakhstan; *Kazakhstan za bez'iadernyi mir*, ed. Shepel', 21–27.

33. "Spravka kollektiva vrachei dispansera #4," f. 103, o. 73, d. 12, 2–12, Center for Modern History Information of Eastern Kazakhstan; *Kazakhstan za bez'iadernyi mir*, ed. Shepel', 21–27.

34. "Vysshaia otscenka—pamiat' naroda."

35. "Zabytye stranitsy iz istorii zakrytiia Semipalatinskogo poligona" [Forgotten pages from the history of the Semipalatinsk Polygon shutdown], August 28, 2014, https://e-history.kz/ru/publications/view/715.

36. Medeu Sarseke, *Semipalatinskaia tragediia* [Semipalatinsk tragedy] (Astana: Foliant, 2016), 323–24; information available at the Auezov Museum, Borli village.

37. Sarseke, *Semipalatinskaia tragediia*, 327.

38. Letter from M. Karpenko to First Secretary of Kazakhstan's Communist Party D. A. Kunaev on supplying the population of Semipalatinsk with dwellings, August 18, 1962, f. 103, o. 12, d. 73, 45–47, Center for Modern History Documentation of Eastern Kazakhstan.

39. Letter from M. Karpenko to First Secretary of the Central Committee of Kazakhstan's Communist Party D. A. Kunaev, August 25, 1962, f. 103, o. 12, d. 73, 40–41, Center for Modern History Documentation of Eastern Kazakhstan.

40. Memorandum written by Fomichev, head of the special unit of the KGB, August 23, 1962, f. 103, o. 12, d. 73, 42, Center for Modern History Documentation of Eastern Kazakhstan; letter from B. N. Ledenev (Ministry of Medium Machine-Making), I. N. Gureev (commander of the military division 52605), M. I. Voskoboinikov (12th Main Directorate of the Soviet Ministry of Defense), Yu. P. Makshakov (3rd Main Directorate of the Soviet Ministry of Health) to the First Secretary of Semipalatinsk Oblast Committee of Kazakhstan's Communist Party M. P. Karpenko, August 23, 1962, f. 103, o. 12, d. 73, 43, Center for Modern History Documentation of Eastern Kazakhstan.

41. Letter to the First Secretary of Semipalatinsk Oblast, 43.

42. "Informatsciia nachal'nika UKGB pri Sovete Ministrov Kazakhskoi SSR po Semipalatinskoi obl. M. Dzhandil'dinova pervomu sekretariu Semipalatinskogo obkoma

KP Kazakhstana M. P. Karpenko ob otritsatel'noi reaktsii naseleniia na atomnye ispytania" [Information from the chief of the department of KGB at the Council of Minister
of Kazakh SSR M. Dzhandil'dinov on the Semipalatinsk Oblast for the First Secretary
of Semipalatinsk Oblast Executive Committee of Kazakhstan's Communist Party M. P.
Karpenko on the population's negative reaction to nuclear tests], August 19, 1966, Semipalatinsk, Secret, signed by Dzhandil'dinov, f. 708, o. 36/1, d. 4, 166–76, Archive of the
President of the Republic Kazakhstan; *Kazakhstan za bez'iadernyi mir*, ed. Shepel', 64.

    43. "Informatsciia nachal'nika UKGB," 65.

    44. E. L. Iakubovskaia, V. I. Nagibin, and V. P. Suslin, *Semipalatinskii iadernyi poli-
gon, 50 let* [Semipalatinsk Nuclear Polygon: 50 years] (Novosibirsk: Sovetskaia Sibir',
1998), 7.

    45. Zalikha Mezhekenova, presentation, panel sponsored by Global Women's As-
sociation against Nuclear Testing (GWANT), Astana, August 28, 2014.

    46. Kairat Kabdrakhmanov, *470 bomb v serdtse Kazakhstana* [470 bombs in the
heart of Kazakhstan] (Almaty, 1994), 97.

    47. Aliia Meshtybaeva, presentation, panel sponsored by Global Women's Associa-
tion against Nuclear Testing (GWANT), Astana, August 28, 2014.

    48. M. A. Makarov, L. M. Kisseleva, et al., "Stressovoe vozdeistvie faktorov okru-
zhaiushchei sredy na chastotu samoubiistv" [Stress impact of environmental factors on
suicide frequency] in *Zdorov'ye liudei, prozhivaiushchih v raione prilegaiushchem k Semipalatinskomu poligonu* [Health of residents in the vicinity of Semipalatinsk Polygon],
collection of articles, vol. 2, Semipalatinsk, 1994.

    49. Masatsugu Matsuo et al., "A Full-Text English Database of Testimonies of Those
Exposed to Radiation Near the Semipalatinsk Nuclear Test Site, Kazakhstan," *Hiroshima
Peace Science* 26 (2004): 86.

    50. M. A. Makarov, T. N. Sailibaev, et al., "Sravnitel'naia kharakteristika suicidov po
raionam s preimushchestvennym prozhivaniem kazakhskogo naseleniia v Semipalatinskom regione" [Comparative characteristics of suicides in the areas in the Semipalatinsk
Region with a predominantly Kazakh population] in *Zdorov'ye liudei, prozhivaiushchih v
raione prilegaiushchem k Semipalatinskomu poligonu.*

    51. Sarseke, *Semipalatinskaia tragediia*, 360–63.

    52. Sarseke, *Semipalatinskaia tragediia*, 365.

    53. B. A. Atchabarov, *Zabluzhdeniia, lozh' i istina po voprosu otsenki vliianiia na
zdorov'ye liudei ispytaniia atomnogo oruzhiia na Semipalatinskom iadernom poligone*
[Fallacies, lies, and truth in assessing impact of nuclear weapons testing at Semipalatinsk Nuclear Polygon on population's health] (Almaty: Karzhy-Karazhat, 2002), 10–11.

    54. The only Soviet-period study with findings fully available at the Kazakhstan's
Academy of Sciences.

    55. S. A. Peisakh, I. I. Velikanov, "Nevrologicheskie kharakteristiki obsledovannogo
naseleniia nekotoryh raionov Semipalatinskoi i Pavlodarskoi oblastei" [Neurological
characteristics of the studied populations in some areas of Semipalatinsk and Pavlodar
Oblasts], in *Radioaktivnost' vneshnei sredy i sostoianie zdorov'ia naseleniia i selskohoziaistvennyh zhivotnyh v Tsentral'nom Kazakhstane* [Radioactivity of environment and the

health of population and livestock in central Kazakhstan], ed. E. A. Khairushev and S. A. Peisakh, vol. 3 (Institute of Regional Pathology, Almaty, 1961), 3–112.

56. B. A. Atchabarov and S. A. Peisakh, "Khronicheskaia nedostatochnost' golovnogo mozga" [Chronic brain deficiency], in *Radioaktivnost' vneshnei sredy*, 3:113–28; E. A. Khairushev, "Rezul'taty issledovaniia taktil'no-bolevoi chuvstvitel'nosti kozhnogo analizatora" [Research findings of tactile-pain sensitivity of skin analyzer], in *Radioaktivnost' vneshnei sredy*, 3:129–67.

57. A. S. Sokolova, S. N. Nugmanov, and Kh. D. Abtieva, "Rezul'taty akushersko-geneticheskogo obsledovaniia nekotoryh raionov tsentral'nogo Kazakhstana" [Results of obstetric-genetic examinations in some areas of central Kazakhstan], in *Radioaktivnost' vneshnei sredy*, ed. A. S. Sokolova and V. S. Mashkevich, 4:3–41; A. S. Sokolova, S. N. Nugmanov, and Kh. D. Abtieva, "Kharakteristika ginekologicheskih zabolevanii u obsledovannyh zhenshchin" [Characteristics of gynecological diseases among examined women], in *Radioaktivnost' vneshnei sredy*, 4:60–109.

58. V. S. Moshkevich, "Kraevye osobennosti patologii v LOR organah u zhitelei Tsentral'nogo Kazakhstana" [Regional pathologies of respiratory organs among residents of central Kazakhstan], in *Radioaktivnost' vneshnei sredy*, 4:185–300.

59. B. A. Atchabarov, T. Kh. Aitbaev, Zh. A. Khairushev, and A. L.Pitiushin, "Opyt klinicheskogo izucheniia stareniia" [Experience in clinical study of aging], in *Radioaktivnost' vneshnei sredy*, 4:358–419.

60. A. T. Aldanazarov, A. N. Butorina, and V. V. Varganov, "Kartina perifiricheskoi krovi u sel'skohoziaistvennyh zhivotnyh (korov i ovets) v nekotoryh raionah Tsentral'nogo Kazakhstana (po dannym kompleksnoi ekspeditscii 1959 g.)" [An overview of periphery blood in livestock (cows and sheep) in some areas of central Kazakhstan (data from the 1959 expedition)], in *Radioaktivnost' vneshnei sredy*, 5:52–55; A. T. Aldanazarov, Yu. I. Toropkina, and V. V. Varganov, "Sostoianie soprotivliaemosti kozhnyh kapiliarov u ovets v otdel'nyh hoziaistvah Severo-Vostochnoi zony Kazakhstana" [Resistence of skin capillaries in sheep in some areas of north-east Kazakhstan], in *Radioaktivnost' vneshnei sredy*, 5:6–30; A. Murzamadiev, "Issledovanie tsentral'noi nervnoi sistemy ovets i sobak (po materialam ekspeditsii za 1959 g.)" [Study of central nervous system in sheep and dogs (data from the 1959 expedition)], in *Radioaktivnost' vneshnei sredy*, 5:87–142; Kh. M. Kadyrbayeva, "Gistologicheskie issledovaniia vnutrennih organov po materialu ekspeditsii 1959 g." [Histological study of internal organs based on the data from the 1959 expedition], in *Radioaktivnost' vneshnei sredy*, 5:56–68.

61. Ia. L. Bul'vakhter and A. A. Karpov, "Nekotorye dannye radiokhimicheskih issledovanii pochvy, rastenii i organov zhivotnyh" [Data on radiochemical studies of soil, vegetation, and animal organs], in *Radioaktivnost' vneshnei sredy*, ed. E. N. Alekseev and S. A. Akkerman, 1960, 1:149–51.

62. E. N. Alekseev, "Radioaktivnoe zagriaznenie rastitel'nosti v obsledovannyh raionah" [Radioactive contamination of vegetation in examined areas], in *Radioaktivnost' vneshnei sredy*, 1:118–19.

63. E. N. Alekseev, "Beta-aktivnost' zhilyh pomeshchenii v poselkah Shchadrinsk,

Tel'mana, Kainar i Abai" [Beta-activity of dwelling in the settlements of Shchadrinsk, Tel'mana, Kainar and Abai], in *Radioaktivnost' vneshnei sredy*, 1:126–32.

64. Sarseke, *Semipalatinskaia tragediia*, 429.

65. K. K. Makashev and A. S. Sokolov, "Materialy radiologicheskogo obsledovaniia nekotoryh raionov Kazakhstana" [Data of the radiological examination in some areas of Kazakhstan], in *Radioaktivnost' vneshnei sredy*, 1958, 2:20–47.

66. *Population Health in Regions Adjacent to the Semipalatinsk Nuclear Test Site*, 5.

67. Full expedition findings were declassified in Kazakhstan after the Soviet collapse.

68. Atchabarov, *Zabluzhdeniia, lozh' i istina*, 5.

69. Atchabarov, *Zabluzhdeniia, lozh' i istina*, 6–7.

70. Report of B. I. Gusev, Chief Physician of the USSR Ministry of Health's Radiological Clinic, to the USSR First Deputy Minister of Health Gennady V. Sergeev, "Overview of the Health Status of Persons Residing in the Territories of Abay, Beskaragay, and Zhana-Semey Districts, Semipalatinsk Region Previously Exposed to Ionizing Radiation at Various Dose Ranges," copy of original document in Shkolnik, *Semipalatinsk Test Site*, 324–28.

71. Radiation Emergency Preparedness and Response, US Department of Labor, https://www.osha.gov/emergency-preparedness/radiation/response.

72. "Informatsiia glavnogo vracha radiologicheskogo dispansera MZ SSSR, kandidata meditsinskih nauk B. I. Guseva o radiatsionno-gigienicheskoi obstanovke na territoriiah, prilegaiuschih k iadernomu poligonu, sostoianii zdorov'ia liudei, podvergavshihsia oblucheniiu ioniziruiushchih izluchenii v real'nyh usloviiah nazemnyh i vozdushnyh vzryvov (1949–1965 gg.)" [Information of the chief doctor of the USSR Ministry of Health's Radiological Clinic candidate of medical sciences, B. I. Gusev, on the radiological-hygienic situations on the territories in the vicinity of the Nuclear Polygon, health of the residents exposed to ionizing radiation during ground and air explosions], September 6, 1990, Center for Modern History Documentation of Eastern Kazakhstan.

73. Ian Mather and Paul Lowe, "Life and Death under a Cloud in Radiation City," *European*, weekend edition (June 1–3, 1990).

74. Ian MacWilliam, "Atom-Test Legacy Shadows Kazakh Prairie's Calm," *Los Angeles Times*, September 15, 1993.

75. Boztaev, *Sindrom Kainara*, 156.

CHAPTER 4: THE NATION RISES

1. Bagila Bukharbayeva, "Kazakhs Remembering Uprising of 1986," *Washington Post*, December 16, 2006.

2. Martha Brill Olcott, *Kazakhs* (Stanford, CA: Hoover Press, 1995), 90.

3. "Chernobyl Nuclear Accident," IAEA, https://www.iaea.org/newscenter/focus/chernobyl.

4. Memorandum from Yu. Sheiko, deputy head of the socioeconomic section of the Central Committee of the Kazakhstan Communist Party, March 1, 1989, Archive of the President of the Republic of Kazakhstan.

5. Author's interview with Olzhas Suleimenov, Almaty, 2018.

6. Open Statement to the USSR Supreme Soviet and Kazakhstan's Supreme Soviet, signed by O. Suleimenov, S. Muratbekov, D. Snegin, K. Myrzaliev, February 25, 1989, Archive of the President of the Republic of Kazakhstan.

7. Author's interview with Murat Auezov, Almaty, 2017.

8. *Nevada-Kazakhstan*, documentary directed by Sergei Shafir, Kazakhfilm, 1990.

9. *Nevada-Kazakhstan*, documentary.

10. A. Ustinov, "O mitinge obshchestvennosti g. Alma-Aty v konferents-zale Soiuza Pisatelei Kazakhstana 28 fevralia 1989 goda" [On the public rally in Alma-Ata in the conference hall of Kazakhstan's writers' union on February 28, 1989], internal memo, Central Committee of Kazakhstan's Communist Party, Archive of the President of the Republic of Kazakhstan.

11. Sergei Shafir, *Megapolis* newspaper, no date.

12. "Putniki" [Travelers], *Izbiratel'* newspaper, April 21–May 5, 1990, No. 5, 8.

13. "Tolegen Mukhamedzhanov: vozmozhno, ia utopist" [Tolegen Mukhamedzhanov: It is possible, I am a utopian], *Karavan*, November 9, 2012, https://www.caravan.kz/gazeta/tolegen-mukhamedzhanov-vozmozhno-ya-utopist-66406/.

14. Author's interview with Auezov.

15. Author's interview with Auezov.

16. Author's interview with Auezov.

17. Author's interview with Auezov.

18. Author's interview with Suleimenov.

19. Keshrim Boztaev, *29 avgusta* [August 29] (Almaty: Atamura, 1998), 30; Vladimir S. Shkolnik, ed., *The Semipalatinsk Test Site: Creation, Operation, and Conversion* (Albuquerque: Sandia National Laboratories, 2002), 169–70.

20. Boztaev, *29 avgusta*, 30–31, 33.

21. Memorandum from Yu. Sheiko; "Informatsiia sotsial'no-ekonomicheskogo otdela TsK KP Kazakhstana o vyvodah, sdelannyh pri vyezde na ispytatel'nyi poligon posle vzryva 12 fevralia 1989 g." [Information of the Social-Economic Section of the Central Committee of the Communist Party of Kazakhstan on the findings from the field visit to the Testing Polygon after the February 12, 1989 explosion], March 1, 1989, in V. Shepel', ed., with A. E. Assanbaeva, E. M. Gribanova, contributors, *Kazakhstan za bez'iadernyi mir: Sbornik dokumentov i materialov* [Kazakhstan for a nuclear-free world: Collection of documents and materials] (Almaty: Archive of the President of the Republic of Kazakhstan, 2011), 71–74.

22. "Rasporiazhenie Soveta Ministrov Kazakhskoi SSR ob udtverzhdenii Komissii po nabliudeniiu za sostoianiem ekologicheskoi obstanovki v Semipalatinskoi Obl." [Order of the Council of Ministers of the Kazakh SSR on establishing a commission to monitor the ecological situation in Semipalatinsk Oblast], March 1, 1989, in *Kazakhstan za bez'iadernyi mir*, ed. Shepel', 75.

23. Shkolnik, *Semipalatinsk Test Site*, 172.

24. "Iadernyi poligon: slukhi i fakty" [Nuclear Polygon: Rumors and facts], interview with V. A. Bukatov recorded by V. Ovcharov, *Kazakhstanskaia Pravda*, May 20, 1989.

25. "Informatsiia pervogo sekretaria Semipalatinskogo obkoma KP Kazakhstana K. B. Boztaeva pervomu sekretariu TsK KP Kazakhstana G. V. Kolbinu o rabote iadernogo poligona v raione Semipalatinska" [Information from the First Secretary of the Committee of Semipalatinsk Oblast of the Communist Party of Kazakhstan K. B. Boztaev for the First Secretary of the Central Committee of Kazakhstan's Communist Party G. V. Kolbin on the work of the Semipalatinsk Nuclear Polygon], March 29, 1989, in *Kazakhstan za bez'iadernyi mir*, ed. Shepel', 76–81.

26. "Informatsiia pervogo sekretaria Semipalatinskogo obkoma."

27. "Ob obstanovke v Kazakhskoi SSR v sviazi s podzemnymi iadernymi vzryvami na Semipalatinskon poligone" [On the situation in the Kazakh SSR in relation to underground nuclear explosions at the Semipalatinsk Polygon], signed by D. Yazov, O. Baklanov, I. Beloussov, G. Kolbin, L. Ryabev, N. Nazarbayev. Kataev's collection, 2335, Hoover Institution Archives, Stanford University.

28. Decree of the Central Committee of the Communist Party of the Soviet Union "On the Situation in Kazakh SSR in Regards to Underground Nuclear Tests at Semipalatinsk Polygon," Secretary of CCCPSU. Kataev's collection, 2335, Hoover Institution Archives, Stanford University.

29. "Millirentgeny Semipalatinska: kompetentnoe mnenie ob ekologicheskoi obstanovke bliz iadernogo poligona" [Milliroentgen of Semipalatinsk: A competent opinion on the ecological situation near the Nuclear Polygon], *Krasnaia Zvezda*, April 2, 1989.

30. Nazarbayev's statement at the Semipalatinsk Oblast Communist Party meeting, April 7, 1989, in Shepel', *Kazakhstan za bez'iadernyi mir*, 81–83.

31. Olcott, *Kazakhs*, 91.

32. Author's interview with Auezov.

33. A. Vodolazov, "Na poligone—bez otklonenii" [At the Polygon—Without deviations], *Ogni Alatau*, July 11, 1989.

34. Author's interview with Auezov.

35. Information from Kurchatov museum on testing; "Rekomendatsii nauchno-prakticheskoi konferentsii 'Zdorov'ye naseleniia i ekologicheskaia obstanovka v g. Semipalatinske i Semipalatinskoi obl. Kazakhskoi SSR'" [Recommendations from the scientific-practical conference "Population Health and Ecological Situation in Semipalatinsk and Semipalatinsk Oblast"], Semipalatinsk, July 17–19, 1989, f. 409, o. 12, d. 1807, 1–10, Center for Modern History Documentation of Eastern Kazakhstan; *Kazakhstan za bez'iadernyi mir*, ed. Shepel', 90–97.

36. "Vyvody mezhvedomstvennoi komissii, obrazovannoi Minzdravom SSSR v sootvetstvii s rasporiazheniem zamestitelia predsedatelia Soveta Ministrov SSSR" [Conclusions by the interagency commission created by the USSR Ministry of Health by the decree of the Deputy Chairman of the USSR Council of Ministers], signed by the correspondent member of the USSR Academy of Medical Scientists USSR Professor A. F. Tsyb, f. 708, o. 139, d. 1718, 41–44, Archive of the President of the Republic of Kazakhstan; Obraschenie vrachei Semipalatinskoi oblasti k ministru zdravoohraneniia SSSR E.

I. Chazovu o vliianii podzemnyh iadernyh ispytanii na zdorov'e liudei [Appeal of doctors from the Semipalatinsk Oblast to the USSR Minister of Health E. I. Chazov on the impact of underground nuclear tests on population health], May 1989, f. 387, o. 7, d. 941, 36–37, Center for Modern History Documentation of Eastern Kazakhstan.

37. "V otvete za nastoiashchee i budushchee" [Responsibility for present and future], *Irtysh*, July 20, 1989.

38. "V granitsah estestvennogo fona" [Within the limits of background radiation], *Irtysh*, July 19, 1989.

39. Bahiya Atchabarov, "Sindrom Kainara" [Kainar Syndrome], *Izbiratel'*, April 21-May 5, 1990, No. 5, 3.

40. "Soviet Union to Close Testing Site," *Arms Control Today*, April 1990, 31.

41. Author's interview with Auezov.

42. Shafir, *Megapolis* newspaper.

43. Maidan Abishev, "Dvizhenie Nevada-Semipalatinsk," *Prostor*, no date available, 13.

44. Kairat Kabdrakhmanov, *470 bomb v serdtse Kazakhstana* [470 bombs in the heart of Kazakhstan] (Almaty, 1994), 114–15.

45. Shkolnik, *Semipalatinsk Test Site*, 167, 178, 181.

46. Shkolnik, *Semipalatinsk Test Site*, 167.

47. Shkolnik, *Semipalatinsk Test Site*, 167.

48. Kabdrakhmanov, *470 bomb v serdtse Kazakhstana*, 113.

49. Information of the Council of Ministers of Kazakh SSR for the Central Committee of the Communist Party of Kazakhstan on cessation of testing, May 10, 1990, in *Kazakhstan za bez'iadernyi mir*, ed. Shepel', 117–19.

50. Boztaev, *29 avgusta*, 40–41.

51. Boztaev, *29 avgusta*, 40–41.

52. "A Minute of Silence at the World's End: The Last Interview of Academician Sakharov," translated into English, *Izbiratel'* newspaper, May 5–24, 1990, no. 8, 6–7.

53. Olzhas Suleimenov, "Deviatnadtsatogo oktiabria" [On October 19th], *Novaiia Gazeta* newspaper, October 15–22, 2020, no. 35, 17.

54. "Pi'smo pervogo sekretaria Semipalatinskogo obkoma KP Kazakhstana, narodnogo deputata SSSR K. B. Boztaeva Prezidentu Kazakhskoi SSR N. A. Nazarbayevu po voprosu Semipalatinskogo iadernogo poligona" [Letter from the First Secretary of the Semipalatinsk Oblast Committee of Kazakhstan's Communist Party, USSR People's Deputy K. B. Boztaev to the President of the Kazakh SSR N. A. Nazarbayev on the Semipalatinsk Nuclear Polygon], April 29, 1990, f. 708, o. 140, d. 78, 1–5, Archive of the President of the Republic of Kazakhstan; letter from Nazarbayev to Gorbachev, March 6, 1991, f. 5H, o. 140, d. 78, in *Kazakhstan za bez'iadernyi mir*, ed. Shepel', 113–15.

55. "Pi'smo pervogo sekretaria Semipalatinskogo obkoma, April 29, 1990; letter from Nazarbayev to Gorbachev, March 6, 1991.

56. Decree of the Supreme Soviet of Kazakh SSR, "On Cessation of Nuclear Testing

at Semipalatinsk and on Health and Environment Protection Measures," May 22, 1990, *Kazakhstanskaia Pravda*, May 29, 1990.

57. Proposal of the Communist Party of Kazakhstan to the USSR Supreme Council on Cessation of Nuclear Testing at Semipalatinsk, June 20, 1990, in *Kazakhstan za bez'iadernyi mir*, ed. Shepel', 126–27.

58. Author's interview with Suleimenov.

59. "Konichiwa, Hiroshima!" *Kazakhstanskaia Pravda*, no specific date available, 1990.

60. Daniel Young, "Thousands in Alma-Ata Demand Test Ban," Physicians for Social Responsibility, *PSR Reports* 11, no. 2 (Summer 1990); "Informatsiia o press-konferentsii, sostoiavsheisia pered otkrytiem mezhdunarodnogo kongressa 'Izbirateli mira protiv iadernogo oruzhiia,' sozdannogo po initsiative antiiadernogo dvizheniia 'Nevada-Semipalatinsk' i mezhdunarodnoi organizatsii 'Vrachi mira za predotvrashchenie iadernoi voiny'" [Information on the press conference held on the eve of the international congress "International Voters for the Prevention of Nuclear War" established on the initiative of the antinuclear movement Nevada-Semipalatinsk and the international organization "International Physicians for the Prevention of Nuclear War"], May 24, 1990, Archive of the President of the Republic of Kazakhstan, f. 7, o. 1, d. 156, 24–25.

61. *Rudnyi Altai*, July 19, 1990; *Leninskaia Smena*, May 24, 1990; Matthew Evangelista, "The Paradox of State Strength: Transnational Relations, Domestic Structures, and Security Policy in Russia and the Soviet Union." *International Organization* 49, no. 1 (1995): 1–38.

62. Some members of the Shoshone tribe lived in Nevada, Utah, and Idaho—areas that suffered from the radioactive fallout from the nuclear tests at the Nevada Test Site. Jacqueline Cabasso, "The Enduring Legacy of the Nevada-Semipalatinsk Movement," presentation at the international conference "Building a Nuclear-Weapon-Free World," Astana, Kazakhstan, August 29, 2016.

63. Young, "Thousands in Alma-Ata Demand Test Ban."

64. Mary-Wynne Ashford, "We Were the World," *Medical Post*, November 20, 1990.

65. Author's interview with Mary-Wynne Ashford, by phone, 2020.

66. Cabasso, "Enduring Legacy."

67. Young, "Thousands in Alma-Ata Demand Test Ban."

68. Decree of the Council of Ministers of the USSR on speeding up economic and social development in Semipalatinsk Oblast, July 10, 1990, in *Kazakhstan za bez'iadernyi mir*, ed. Shepel', 127–28.

69. Decree of the Council of Ministers of USSR on speeding up economic and social development in Semipalatinsk Oblast; from the Council of Ministers of the Kazakh SSR to the President of the Kazakh SSR Nazarbayev N. A., signed by the chairman of the Council U. Karamanov, July 27, 1990, f. 7, o. 1, d. 88, Archive of the President of the Republic of Kazakhstan.

70. "Informatsiia pervogo sekretaria Semipalatinskogo obkoma partii, narodnogo deputata SSSR K. B. Boztaeva v Verhovnyi Sovet SSSR A. I. Luk'ianovu o destabilizatsii politicheskoi obstanovki v Semipalatinskoi oblasti" [Information of the First Secretary

of the Semipalatinsk Oblast Committee of the Communist Party USSR People's Deputy K. B. Boztaev for the USSR Supreme Council A. I. Lu'kianov on the destabilization of political situation in Semipalatinsk Oblast], June 14, 1990, f. 103, o. 73, d. 21, 99–101, Center for Modern History Documentation of Eastern Kazakhstan.

71. Letter from medical professionals of Zharminskii raion of Semipalatinsk oblast, June 13, 1990, in *Kazakhstan za bez'iadernyi mir*, ed. Shepel', 125–26.

72. Letter from K. Mardanov, lecturer of the Ideology Section of the Central Committee of the Communist Party of Kazakhstan to K. Sultanov, head of the section (August 19, 1990) on the visit to Semipalatinsk testing site, in *Kazakhstan za bez'iadernyi mir*, ed. Shepel', 129–30.

73. "Nashe terpenie ne bespredel'no" [Our patience is not limitless], appeal from the participants of a city-wide rally in Semipalatinsk, *Rudnyi Altai*, July 19, 1990.

74. "Davaite sledovat' zdravomu smyslu" [Let's follow common sense], appeal from the scientists, testers, and residents of Kurchatov to labor collectives and residents of Leninogorsk, *Rudnyi Altai*, July 19, 1990.

75. "Davaite sledovat' zdravomu smyslu."

76. *Irtysh*, August 9, 1990.

77. "Net—iadernomu bezumiiu [No to nuclear madness], *Ogni Alatau*, September 12, 1990; author's interview with Mariiash Makisheva, Almaty, 2017.

78. Author's interview with Makisheva.

79. Author's interview with Makisheva.

80. L. Reznikov, "Radi mira na zemle" [For the sake of peace on Earth], unindentified newspaper, September 22, 1990.

81. Author's interview with Makisheva.

82. L. Reznikov, "Radi mira na zemle."

83. Moscow television, December 4, 1990, FBIS-SU, December 5, 1990.

84. Letter from Nazarbayev to Gorbachev, March 6, 1991, f. 5H, o. 1, d. 574, in *Kazakhstan za bez'iadernyi mir*, ed. Shepel', 152–53.

85. Boztaev, *29 avgusta*, 37.

86. Boztaev, *29 avgusta*, 37.

CHAPTER 5: THE SWAN SONG OF THE SOVIET UNION

1. Amelia Schonbek, "This Portentous Composition: Swan Lake's Place in Soviet Politics," March 26, 2015, https://hazlitt.net/feature/portentous-composition-swan-lakes-place-soviet-politics.

2. Mikhail Gorbachev, *The August Coup: The Truth and the Lessons* (New York: Harper Collins, 1991), 18.

3. Anatoly S. Chernyaev, *My Six Years with Gorbachev* (University Park: Pennsylvania University Press, 2000), 375.

4. "The 1991 Monetary Reform in the Soviet Union," *Sputnik*, February 2, 2011, https://sputniknews.com/business/20110202162419049/.

5. One day in April 1991, the Soviet people woke up to yet another shock—the prices

for all goods were suddenly three times higher. This was another "shock therapy" experiment of Soviet planners to resuscitate the economy.

6. New Union Treaty, *Sovetskaia Rossiia*, August 15, 1991.

7. Gorbachev, *August Coup*, 15.

8. Bridget Kendall, "New Light Shed on 1991 and Anti-Gorbachev Coup," BBC, August 18, 2011; Chernyaev, *My Six Years with Gorbachev*, 371.

9. Gorbachev, *August Coup*, 15.

10. "Chronology of the President's Warning to President Gorbachev Concerning a Possible Coup Attempt," Nick Burns for General Scowcroft, National Security Council, November 13, 1991, including a memorandum of telephone conversation between President Bush and Mikhail Gorbachev, President of the Soviet Union, June 21, 1991, the Oval Office, George H. W. Bush Presidential Library and Museum.

11. John Aitken, *Nazarbayev and the Making of Kazakhstan: From Communism to Capitalism* (London: Continuum, 2009), 95.

12. Boris Yeltsin, *The Struggle for Russia* (New York: Crown, 1994), 46.

13. Yeltsin, *Struggle for Russia*, 46–47; Lev Sukhanov, *Kak Yeltsin stal prezidentom: Zapiski pervogo pomoshchnika* [How Yeltsin became president: Notes of the first assistant] (Moscow: Eksmo-Algoritm, 2011), 6; Aitken, *Nazarbayev and the Making of Kazakhstan*, 95.

14. Chernyaev, *My Six Years with Gorbachev*, 375.

15. Anatoly Chernyaev's diary, 1991, excerpt "Three Days in Foros," trans. Anna Melyakov, ed. Svetlana Savranskaya, National Security Archive, 100; also in Chernyaev, *My Six Years with Gorbachev*, 408.

16. Chernyaev, *My Six Years with Gorbachev*, 416.

17. Yeltsin, *Struggle for Russia*, 54.

18. Yeltsin, *Struggle for Russia*, 69.

19. Victoria E. Bonnel, Ann Cooper, and Gregory Freidin, *Russia at the Barricades: Eyewitness Accounts of the August 1991 Coup* (Abingdon-on-Thames: Routledge, 2015), 14.

20. Aitken, *Nazarbayev and the Making of Kazakhstan*, 99; "Kak veli sebia vlast' i pressa Kazakhstana v dni putcha 1991 goda" [How politicians and press carried themselves during 1991 putsch], Azattyq, August 18, 2011, https://rus.azattyq.org/a/putsch_august_1991_moscow_nazarbaev_/24299598.html.

21. Aitken, *Nazarbayev and the Making of Kazakhstan*, 98–99.

22. Aitken, *Nazarbayev and the Making of Kazakhstan*, 99.

23. Valentin Stepankov and Evgenii Lisov, *Kremlyovskii Zagovor* (Moscow: Ogonek, 1992), 111.

24. Statement of Nursultan Nazarbayev, *Kazakhstanskaia Pravda*, August 19, 1991.

25. "Tri dnia avgusta 1991-go. V vospominaniiah kazakhstantsev" [Three days in August of 1991. In memories of people from Kazakhstan], *Vlast KZ*, https://vlast.kz/istorija/18863-tri-dna-avgusta-1991-go-v-vospominaniah-kazahstancev.html.

26. "Tri dnia avgusta 1991-go. V vospominaniiah kazakhstantsev."

27. "Tri dnia avgusta 1991-go. V vospominaniiah kazakhstantsev."

28. "Tri dnia avgusta 1991-go. V vospominaniiah kazakhstantsev."

29. Memorandum of telephone conversation with Prime Minister Brian Mulroney of Canada, Kennebunkport, Maine, August 19, 1991, George H. W. Bush Presidential Archives and Library.

30. Jack Matlock, *Autopsy for an Empire: The American Ambassador's Account of the Collapse of the Soviet Union* (New York: Random House, 1995), 587–88, 575.

31. "Chronology of the President's Warning to President Gorbachev Concerning a Possible Coup Attempt," Nick Burns for General Scowcroft, National Security Council, November 13, 1991, including a memorandum of telephone conversation between President Bush and Mikhail Gorbachev, President of the Soviet Union, June 21, 1991, the Oval Office, George H. W. Bush Presidential Library and Museum.

32. Andrei Zhdanov, "Avgustovskii putsch: kak ruhnul SSSR" [August putsch: How the USSR collapsed], *Vechernii Almaty*, August 12, 2016.

33. Chernyaev's diary, 1991, excerpt "Three Days in Foros," 108; Chernyaev, *My Six Years with Gorbachev*, 377.

34. Chernyaev, *My Six Years with Gorbachev*, 377.

35. Memorandum of telephone conversation, Telcon with President Boris Yeltsin of the Republic of Russia, August 20, 1991, the Oval Office, George H. W. Bush Presidential Library and Museum.

36. Zhdanov, "Avgustovskii putsch: kak ruhnul SSSR."

37. Zhdanov, "Avgustovskii putsch: kak ruhnul SSSR."

38. "Twenty-five Years On: The Failed Coup That Ended the Soviet Union," *RT*, August 20, 2016, https://www.rt.com/news/356579-ussr-coup-august-yeltsin/.

39. "Nazarbayev Resigns from the Politburo and the CPSU Central Committee, Accusing the Secretariat of Collaborating with the Leaders of the Putsch," Interfax News Agency, August 22, 1991, George H. W. Bush Presidential Library and Museum; Zhdanov, "Avgustovskii putsch: kak ruhnul SSSR."

40. "Twenty-five Years On."

41. Chernyaev's diary, 1991, excerpt "Three Days in Foros," 113.

42. Chernyaev, *My Six Years with Gorbachev*, 377.

43. Chernyaev, *My Six Years with Gorbachev*, 377.

44. Chernyaev, *My Six Years with Gorbachev*, 378.

45. Memorandum of telephone conversation, Telcon with President Mikhail Gorbachev of the USSR, August 21, 1991, Kennebunkport, Maine, George H. W. Bush Presidential Library and Museum.

46. Chernyaev's diary, 1991, excerpt "Three Days in Foros," 113.

47. Memorandum of telephone conversation, Telcon with President Mikhail Gorbachev August 21, 1991.

48. Chernyaev's diary, 1991, excerpt "Three Days in Foros," 115.

49. Gorbachev, *August Coup*, 17.

50. Gorbachev, *August Coup*, 50.

51. Chernyaev, *My Six Years with Gorbachev*, 386–91.

52. "The Coup Two Months Later," cable from the US embassy in Moscow, written by Robert Strauss, October 1991, George H. W. Bush Presidential Library and Museum.

53. Bruce Blair, *The Logic of Accidental Nuclear War* (Washington, DC: Brookings Institution Press, 2011), 72.

54. Chernyaev's diary, 1991, excerpt "1991," 60.

55. Chernyaev, *My Six Years with Gorbachev*, 375–76.

56. Nikolai Sokov, "Controlling Soviet-Russian Nuclear Weapons in Time of Instability," http://www.npolicy.org/article_file/Controlling_Soviet-Russian_Nuclear_Weapons_in_Time_of_Instability.pdf.

57. Sokov, "Controlling Soviet-Russian Nuclear Weapons."

58. Robert Norris and Hans Kristensen, "Global Nuclear Stockpiles, 1945–2006," *Bulletin of the Atomic Scientists* 62, no. 4 (2006): 64–67.

59. Amy F. Woolf, "91144: Nuclear Weapons in the Former Soviet Union: Location, Command, and Control," CRS Issue Brief, updated November 27, 1996, http://www.fas.org/spp/starwars/crs/91-144.htm.

60. Gulnaz Imamniiazova, "10 Let, kotorye ne triasli mir" [10 years that did not shake the world], *Ekspress-K*, August 29, 2001.

61. Imamniiazova, "10 Let, kotorye ne triasli mir."

62. Thomas K. Friedman, "Soviet Turmoil; Baker Eases Terms for Aid to Soviets," *New York Times*, September 11, 1991.

63. G. Ostrovskii, "Gospodin Baker shchitaet Kazakhstan odnoi iz vedushchih respublik v strane" [Mr. Baker considers Kazakhstan one of the leading republics in the country], *Express-K*, September 17, 1991.

64. Memorandum, National Security Council, June 21, 1991, George H. W. Bush Presidential Library and Museum.

65. James A. Baker, *The Politics of Diplomacy: Revolution, War, and Peace, 1989–1992* (New York: G. P. Putnam's Sons, 1995), 538.

66. Baker, *Politics of Diplomacy*, 538.

67. Baker, *Politics of Diplomacy*, 539.

68. Baker, *Politics of Diplomacy*, 539.

69. "Kazakhstan-SShA: Plodotvornyi dialog" [Kazakhstan-USA: Fruitful dialog], KazTAG, *Kazakhstanskaya Pravda*, September 17, 1991; "Key Points in Secretary Baker's Meetings in the USSR and the Baltics: September 11–16, 1991," National Security Council, no date, George H. W. Bush Presidential Library and Museum.

70. Russian Television Network (Moscow), September 16, 1991, in "Nazarbayev Confirms Nuclear Arms Stance," FBIS-SOV-91–180, September 17, 1991, 68 (Source: Mark D. Skootsky, "An Annotated Chronology of Post-Soviet Nuclear Disarmament 1991–1994," *Nonproliferation Review* (Spring–Summer, 1995): 65.

71. "Key Points in Secretary Baker's Meetings in the USSR and the Baltics: September 11–16, 1991."

72. "Baker Urges Kazakh Leader to Push Unity: Diplomacy: The Visit is Seen as an Effort to Boost the Prestige of a Man Who Has Fought the Breakup of the Soviet Republics," *Los Angeles Times*, September 16, 1991.

73. Kazakhstan would finally establish its own defense ministry in May of 1992 after all the republics went their separate ways. General Nurmagambetov became Kazakh-

stan's first defense minister. Interview with Sagadat Nurmagambetov, "Komitet Oborony Kazakhstana: iadernaya knopka respublike ne nuzhna" [Kazakhstan's defense committee: Republic does not need a nuclear button], recorded by P. Vitvitskii and A. Stulberg, *Kazakhstanskaia Pravda*, December 11, 1991.

74. Author's interview with Larry Napper, College Station, TX, 2008.

75. Ashton Carter, Kurt Campbell, Steven E. Miller, Charles E. Zraket, *Soviet Nuclear Fission: Control of the Nuclear Arsenal in a Disintegrating Soviet Union* (Cambridge, MA: Belfer Center for Science and International Affairs, Harvard University, 1991), 33.

76. Carter et al., *Soviet Nuclear Fission*, 62.

77. Carter et al., *Soviet Nuclear Fission*, 107–13.

78. "PNI: Nuclear Weapons, the Former Soviet Union, and Independent Republics," memorandum, National Security Council, December 6, 1991, George H. W. Bush Presidential Library and Museum.

79. Yeltsin, *Struggle for Russia*, 116.

80. Memorandum of telephone conversation, "Telcon with President Yeltsin of the Republic of Russia," the White House, December 8, 1991, George H. W. Bush Presidential Library and Museum.

81. Matlock, *Autopsy for an Empire*, 718.

82. "Ak Orda opublikovala istoricheskoe video vstrechi glav 11 gosudarstv v Alma-Ate" [Ak Orda published a historic video from the meeting of 11 heads of state in Almaty], *Kazakhstanskaia Pravda*, December 21, 2016, https://www.kazpravda.kz/multimedia/view/akorda-opublikovala-istoricheskoe-video-vstrechi-glav-11-gosudarstv-v-alma-ate.

83. "Baker-Yeltsin Meeting," memorandum from R. Nicholas Burns for Florence E. Gantt, Wilma G. Hall, Kristen K. Cicio, December 16, 1991, National Security Council, George H. W. Bush Presidential Library and Museum.

84. David Hoffman, "Kazakhstan Keeping Nuclear Arms, Republic's President Tells Baker," *Washington Post*, December 18, 1991.

85. Baker, *Politics of Diplomacy*, 581.

86. Baker, *Politics of Diplomacy*, 581.

87. Baker, *Politics of Diplomacy*, 585.

88. Memorandum of a telephone conversation between President Bush and President Yeltsin, the Oval Office, December 23, 1991, George H. W. Bush Presidential Library and Museum.

89. Author's interview with Tulegen Zhukeev, Almaty, 2018.

90. Maxim Sokolov, "Alma-Atinskaia vstrecha udel'nyh kniazei" [The Almaty meeting of the feudal princes], *Kommersant*, December 23, 1991.

91. Baker, *Politics of Diplomacy*, 585.

92. Memorandum of a telephone conversation between President Gorbachev and President Bush, December 25, 1991, George H. W. Bush Presidential Library and Museum.

93. NTI Nuclear Profiles: Ukraine, http://www.nti.org/learn/countries/ukraine/nuclear/.

94. Agreement on Strategic Forces, December 30, 1991, http://www.bits.de/NRA-NEU/START/documents/strategicforces91.htm.

95. Agreement on Strategic Forces.

CHAPTER 6: FEARS IN WASHINGTON AND ALMA-ATA

1. Marco de Andreis and Francesco Calogero, *The Soviet Nuclear Weapon Legacy*, SIPRI Research Report no. 10 (Oxford: Oxford University Press, 1995), 6; I. Akhtamzian, "Iadernyi faktor v Tsentral'noi Azii" [The nuclear factor in Central Asia], in M. Narinskii and A. Mal'gin, eds., *Iuzhnyi flang SNG. Tsentral'naia Aziia—Kaspii—Kavkaz: vozmozhnosti i vyzovy dlia Rossii* [CIS Southern Flank. Central Asia—Caspian—Caucasus: Opportunities and challenges for Russia] (Moscow: Navona, 2005), 197.

2. Background briefing by senior administration officials, the White House, February 1994, William J. Clinton Library and Museum.

3. "Geological Exploration," Kazatomprom, http://www.kazatomprom.kz/en/content/company/activity/geological-exploration.

4. This process includes several steps. Groundwater is injected into the ore, and the liquid with dissolved uranium comes out to the surface. Uranium concentrate extracted from the water is called yellowcake for its yellow color. Uranium mined in Kazakhstan is refined into yellowcake on the spot. Half of all uranium concentrate to meet Soviet needs came from Kazakhstan (William N. Szymanski, "The Uranium Industry of the Commonwealth of Independent States," *Uranium Industry Annual 1991* [October 1992] quoted in William C. Potter, "Nuclear Exports from the Former Soviet Union: What's New, What's True," *Arms Control Today* [January/February 1993]: 4–5). For the next step in the fuel cycle process, yellowcake is converted into gaseous form (uranium hexafluoride gas UF6) and then enriched to a higher concentration of U235 isotope. Natural uranium contains less than 1 percent of U235, the isotope that can sustain the fission reaction necessary for a nuclear explosion. The rest is mostly U238 isotope, which cannot sustain a fission reaction. To cause a sustained nuclear explosion in a bomb, natural uranium needs to be enriched, a technological process of increasing the concentration of the U235 isotope. To produce nuclear fuel for nuclear power plants, the concentration of the U235 has to be raised to about 3.5–5 percent. To produce nuclear fuel for bombs, the concentration of the U235 has to be raised to 90 percent or more. Plutonium, the other fuel for nuclear bombs, does not occur in nature in large quantities. Once nuclear fuel is burnt in a reactor, the resulting waste product—spent reactor fuel—includes plutonium among other substances. To obtain bomb-grade plutonium, spent fuel must be reprocessed, a method that separates plutonium from the waste ("The Physics of Nuclear Weapons," STS152, "Nuclear Weapons, Risk and Hope," Handout #2, AUT 2011–12, Stanford University, https://ee.stanford.edu/~hellman/sts152_02/handout02.pdf). Uranium enriched to a concentration of U235 more than 20 percent is called highly enriched uranium (HEU). There were no facilities in Kazakhstan for this part of the process—Kazakh yellowcake traveled to Russia for enrichment. Part of the enriched uranium came back to Kazakhstan where it was encased in fuel pellets at Ulba Metallurgical Plant in Ust-Kamenogorsk. The fuel pellets then traveled back to Russia where they were they put into fuel assemblies.

5. Jessica Eve Stern, "Cooperative Activities to Improve Fissile Material Production, Control, and Accounting," in John M. Shields and William C. Potter, eds., *Dismantling the Cold War: US and NIS Perspectives on the Nunn-Lugar Cooperative Threat Reduction Program* (Cambridge, MA: MIT Press, 1997), 314.

6. William C. Potter and Elena Sokova, "Illicit Nuclear Trafficking in the NIS: What's New? What's True?" *Nonproliferation Review* 9, no. 2 (Summer 2002): 113.

7. Interview with Leonid Smirnov, 1996, *PBS Frontline*: "Loose Nukes," http://www. pbs.org/wgbh/pages/frontline/shows/nukes/interviews/smirnov.html.

8. Interview with Smirnov.

9. Interview with Smirnov.

10. William Potter, "Nuclear Insecurity in the Post-Soviet States," Congressional testimony, *Nonproliferation Review* 1, no. 3 (Spring–Summer 1994): 62.

11. Steve Goldstein, "U.S. to Move Plutonium at Site Near Iran/The Weapons-Usable Cache Is from an Old Soviet Reactor in Kazakhstan/The Operation Will Be Complex," *Philadelphia Inquirer*, September 6, 1998.

12. John Deutch, "The Threat of Nuclear Diversion," statement for the record, March 20, 1996, *PBS Frontline*: "Loose Nukes," http://www.pbs.org/wgbh/pages/frontline/shows/nukes/readings/overview; Scott Parish and Tamara Robinson, "Efforts to Strengthen Export Controls and Combat Illicit Trafficking and Brain Drain," *Nonproliferation Review* 7, no. 1 (Spring 2000): 118; "Iran Says It Plans 10 Nuclear Plants But No Atom Arms," *New York Times*, May 14, 1995.

13. "America and the Collapse of the Soviet Empire: What Has to Be Done," Address by Secretary of State James A. Baker III at Princeton University, December 12, 1991, George H. W. Bush Presidential Library and Museum; emphasis added.

14. Mark Hibbs, "'Vulnerable' Soviet Nuclear Experts Could Aid Clandestine Weapons Aims," *Nuclear Fuel*, October 28, 1991.

15. Jennifer G. Mathers, *The Russian Nuclear Shield from Stalin to Yeltsin* (London: Palgrave Macmillan, 2000), 17.

16. "The Coup Two Months Later," cable from the US embassy in Moscow, written by Ambassador Strauss, October 1991, George H. W. Bush Presidential Library and Museum.

17. "The Coup Two Months Later"; memorandum "Baker-Yeltsin Meeting," written by R. Nicholas Burns for Florence E. Gantt, Wilma G. Hall, Kristen K. Cicio, National Security Council, December 16, 1991, George H. W. Bush Presidential Library and Museum.

18. "Sounding an Alarm: Soviet Disunion and Threats to American National Security," letter written by Graham Allison to Brent Scowcroft, September 6, 1991, 2, https://www2.jiia.or.jp/kokusaimondai_archive/2000/2006-09_007.pdf?noprint.

19. "Sounding an Alarm: Soviet Disunion and Threats to American National Security," 4.

20. Earlier notable publications on Kazakhstan's nuclear decision-making include Mitchel Reiss, *Bridled Ambition: Why Countries Constrain Their Nuclear Capabilities*

(Washington, DC: Woodrow Wilson Press, 1995); William Potter, *The Politics of Re-nunciation: The Case of Belarus, Kazakhstan, and Ukraine* (Henry L. Stimson Center, occasional paper no. 22, 1995); and Anuar Ayazbekov, "Kazakhstan's Nuclear Decision-Making, 1991–92," *Nonproliferation Review* 21, no. 2 (2014): 149–68.

21. Author's interview with Tulegen Zhukeev, Almaty, 2017.

22. Author's interview with William Courtney, Washington, DC, 2009.

23. Sebastien Peyrouse, "'The Imperial Minority': An Interpretative Framework of the Russians in Kazakhstan," *Nationalities Papers* 36, no. 1 (2008): 5.

24. Alexander Solzhenitsyn, *Rebuilding Russia: Reflections and Tentative Proposals* (New York: Farrar, Straus and Giroux, 1991), 13.

25. Solzhenitsyn, *Rebuilding Russia*, 8.

26. Samantha Brietich, "The Crimea Model: Will Russia Annex the Northern Region of Kazakhstan?" *Modern Diplomacy* (October 16, 2014).

27. "President Nazarbayev Interviewed," translation from Russian by FM FBIS, George H. W. Bush Presidential Library and Museum.

28. "President Nazarbayev Interviewed."

29. "Defining U.S. Interests in Central Asia," National Security Council memorandum, March 6, 1992, George H. W. Bush Library and Museum.

30. B. Aiaganov, "Kazakhstan i iadernoe oruzhie: novye podhody i otsenki" [Kazakhstan and nuclear weapons: New approaches and assessment], *Kazakhstanskaia Pravda*, February 2, 1992.

31. B. Aiaganov, "Kazakhstan i iadernoe oruzhie: novye podhody i otsenki."

32. B. Aiaganov, "Kazakhstan i iadernoe oruzhie: novye podhody i otsenki."

33. Author's interview with Larry Napper, College Station, TX, 2012.

34. Author's interview with Zhukeev.

35. British writer Christopher Robbins used that expression to describe Kazakhstan in his book *Apples Are from Kazakhstan: The Land That Disappeared* (London: Atlas, 2008).

36. In 1995 the NPT was extended indefinitely.

37. Oumirserik Kasenov, *The Fragile Future of the NPT*, memo, 1992, copy in author's possession; Oumirserik Kasenov, "Iadernoe oruzhie i bezopasnost' Kazakhstana," *Mysl'* no. 6 (1992), 25–28.

38. Kasenov, *The Fragile Future of the NPT*; Kasenov, "Iadernoe oruzhie i bezopasnost' Kazakhstana."

39. Kasenov, *The Fragile Future of the NPT*; Kasenov, "Iadernoe oruzhie i bezopasnost' Kazakhstana."

40. Kasenov, *The Fragile Future of the NPT*; Kasenov, "Iadernoe oruzhie i bezopasnost' Kazakhstana."

41. Kasenov, *The Fragile Future of the NPT*; Kasenov, "Iadernoe oruzhie i bezopasnost' Kazakhstana."

42. Agreement on Strategic Forces, December 30, 1991, http://www.bits.de/NRA-NEU/START/documents/strategicforces91.htm.

43. Kasenov, *The Fragile Future of the NPT*; Kasenov, "Iadernoe oruzhie i bezopasnost' Kazakhstana"; emphasis added.

44. Kasenov, *The Fragile Future of the NPT*.

CHAPTER 7: A TEMPORARY NUCLEAR POWER

1. Author's interview with Larry Napper, College Station, TX, 2012.

2. Author's interview with Napper.

3. Author's interview with William Courtney, Washington, DC, 2018.

4. Author's interview with Napper.

5. Author's interview with Napper.

6. Author's interview with Napper.

7. Letter from President Bush to President Nazarbayev, December 26, 1992, George H. W. Bush Presidential Library and Museum; Russian copy of the letter from President Bush to President Nazarbayev, December 26, 1992, f. 5H, o. 1, d. 1361, Archive of the President of the Republic of Kazakhstan.

8. Letter from President Bush to President Nazarbayev, December 26, 1991; Russian copy of the letter from President Bush to President Nazarbayev, December 26, 1992.

9. "Letters to Presidents Yeltsin, Kravchuk, Nazarbayev, and Shushkevich," memorandum for Brent Scowcroft from Rich Davis and Nicholas Burns, National Security Council, December 27, 1991, George H. W. Bush Presidential Library and Museum.

10. Statement of Secretary Brady on Membership of the New States of the Former Soviet Union in the IMF and the World Bank, January 3, 1992, George H. W. Bush Presidential Library and Museum.

11. Author's interview with Courtney.

12. Author's interview with Courtney.

13. Author's interview with Courtney.

14. Author's interview with Courtney.

15. Author's interview with Courtney.

16. Author's interview with Tulegen Zhukeev, Almaty, 2017.

17. "Defining American Interests in Kazakhstan," cable from the US embassy in Alma-Ata, written by William Courtney, February 1992, George H. W. Bush Presidential Library and Museum.

18. "Defining American Interests in Kazakhstan."

19. Moscow Ostankino TV, February 16, 1992; *Izvestiia*, February 25, 1992, reported by FBIS Trends, June 2, 1992, George H. W. Bush Presidential Library and Museum.

20. Letter from the Minister of Foreign Affairs of the Republic of Kazakhstan T. Suleimenov to President Nazarbayev, "K pozitscii Kazakhstana o prisoedinenii k DNIaO" [On Kazakhstan's position on NPT adherence], April 13, 1992, f. 5H, o. 1, d. 1303, Archive of the President of the Republic of Kazakhstan.

21. "Kazakh President Nazarbayev Comments on Nuclear Weapons Issues," cable from the US embassy in Alma-Ata, March 3, 1992, George H. W. Bush Presidential Library and Museum.

22. "Kazakh President Nazarbayev Comments on Nuclear Weapons Issues."

23. "Kazakh President Nazarbayev Comments on Nuclear Weapons Issues."

24. Agence France Presse reporting, March 20, 1992.

25. NPT defines nuclear-weapon states (NWS) as those that had manufactured and detonated a nuclear explosive device prior to January 1, 1967.

26. Author's interview with Zhukeev.

27. Included in "Kazakhstan as Nuclear State," memorandum from Susan Koch for John Gordon and Daniel Poneman, National Security Council, March 20, 1992, George H. W. Bush Presidential Library and Museum.

28. "Kazakhstan as Nuclear State."

29. "Nazarbayev Says Kazakhstan Has a Right to Be in the Nuclear Club," cable from the US embassy in Alma-Ata, written by William Courtney, April 23, 1992, George H. W. Bush Presidential Library and Museum; "Kazakhstan May Publicly Seek to Enter the NPT as a Nuclear Weapon State," cable from the US embassy in Almaty, written by William Courtney, April, 1992, George H. W. Bush Presidential Library and Museum.

30. "Kazakh President Nazarbayev on Nuclear Weapons: Comments to . . . in a Meeting Yesterday, . . . Who Debriefed Me," cable from the US embassy in Alma-Ata, written by William Courtney, April 23, 1992, George H. W. Bush Presidential Library and Museum.

31. "RLRFE Alma Ata Symposium on Kazakhstan," cable from the US embassy in Alma-Ata, written by William Courtney, April 29, 1992, George H. W. Bush Presidential Library and Museum.

32. Daniel Snyder, "Kazakhstan Seeks U.S. Pact for Further Nuclear Cuts," *Christian Science Monitor*, April 27, 1992.

33. Snyder, "Kazakhstan Seeks U.S. Pact for Further Nuclear Cuts."

34. Snyder, "Kazakhstan Seeks U.S. Pact for Further Nuclear Cuts."

35. "Interview N. Nazarbayeva amerikanskoi gazete" [N. Nazarbayev's Interview to an American Newspaper], TASS-KazTAG, *Kazakhstanskaia Pravda*, April 29, 1992.

36. "Kazakhstan and Nazarbayev Go Public on the Nuclear Issue," cable from the US embassy in Alma-Ata, written by William Courtney, April 29, 1992, Nunn-Lugar Collection, National Security Archive.

37. "Kazakhstan and Nazarbayev Go Public on the Nuclear Issue.".

38. "Kazakhstan and Nazarbayev Go Public on the Nuclear Issue."

39. "The Nuclear Issue and Kazakh President Nazarbayev's Visit to Washington," cable from the US embassy in Alma-Ata, written by William Courtney, April 29, 1992, Nunn-Lugar Collection, National Security Archive.

40. Author's interview with Zhukeev and Courtney.

41. Memorandum from Suleimenov to Nazarbayev, April 13, 1992, Archive of the President of the Republic of Kazakhstan.

42. Aleksandr Gagua, "Liubye pogranichnye pretenzii segodnia—eto neimenuemoe krovoprolitie: esli kto-to dumaet, shto Nazarbayev iz straha vedet sebia po-druzheski, on gluboko oshibaetsia" [Any border claims today are an unavoidable bloodshed: If anyone thinks that Nazarbayev acts friendly out of fear, they are deeply mistaken], in-

terview with the president of the Republic of Kazakhstan, *Nezavisimaia Gazeta*, May 6, 1992.

43. "Possible Legal Consequences for a START Agreement," memorandum written by Jo Hunerwadel for National Security Council, September 6, 1991, George H. W. Bush Presidential Library and Museum.

44. Letter from James Baker to Nazarbayev, March 1992, f. 5H, o. 1, d. 1303, Archive of the President of the Republic of Kazakhstan.

45. Draft letter from Nazarbayev to James Baker, f. 5H, o. 1, d. 1303, March 1992, Archive of the President of the Republic of Kazakhstan.

46. James A. Baker, *The Politics of Diplomacy: Revolution, War, and Peace, 1989–1992* (New York: G. P. Putnam's Sons, 1995), 660.

47. Baker, *Politics of Diplomacy*, 662.

48. Baker, *Politics of Diplomacy*, 662–64.

49. Simon Clark and Selina Williams, "Chevron-Led Consortium to Invest Up to $37 Billion in Kazakh Oil Field," *Wall Street Journal*, May 26, 2016.

50. "Trade and Investment Issues with the USSR," Robert A. Mosbacher, the Secretary of Commerce, memorandum for Brent Scowcroft, July 12, 1991, George H. W. Bush Presidential Library and Museum.

51. Steve Levine, *The Oil and the Glory: The Pursuit of Empire and Fortune on the Caspian Sea* (New York: Random House, 2007), 115.

52. Memorandum of conversation, "Luncheon with President Mikhail Gorbachev of the USSR," the White House, July 30, 1991, George H. W. Bush Presidential Library and Museum.

53. Memorandum of conversation, "Luncheon with President Mikhail Gorbachev of the USSR," the White House, July 30, 1991, George H. W. Bush Presidential Library and Museum.

54. Levine, *The Oil and the Glory*, 137.

55. "Defining American Interests in Kazakhstan."

56. Steven Greenhouse, "Chevron to Spend $10 Billion to Seek Oil in Kazakhstan," *New York Times*, May 19, 1992; Levine, *The Oil and the Glory*, 137.

57. "Initial Response to Message from President," cable from the US embassy in Alma-Ata, March 18, 1992, George H. W. Bush Presidential Library and Museum.

58. "U.S. Objectives of Nazarbayev Visit [sent for agency referral]," National Security Council, 1992, George H. W. Bush Presidential Library and Museum.

59. "The Nazarbayev Visit: Desired Outcomes," National Security Council, 1992, George H. W. Bush Presidential Library and Museum.

60. "Presidential Event—Nazarbayev," March 24, 1992, memorandum, National Security Council, George H. W. Bush Presidential Library and Museum.

61. "Kazakh President Nazarbayev's Visit to U.S.," cable from the US embassy in Alma-Ata, written by William Courtney, April 1992, Nunn-Lugar Collection, National Security Archive.

62. Cable from the State Department to the US embassy in Alma-Ata, March 24, 1992, George H. W. Bush Presidential Library and Museum.

63. "Kazakh President Nazarbayev's Visit to U.S."

64. "Kazakh President Nazarbayev's Visit to U.S.".

65. "U.S. Visit of Kazakh President Nazarbayev," memorandum, National Security Council, April 17, 1992, George H. W. Bush Presidential Library and Museum (from the US embassy in Alma-Ata).

66. Many years later, Giffen would be arrested in the United States, accused of bribing the Kazakh government to secure oil contracts for Western companies and of depositing money in Swiss banks for Kazakh officials. After years of investigation and a trial, Giffen walked away with no punishment or fine. Throughout the ordeal, he maintained that the US government was aware of and supportive of his efforts to help American companies and US foreign policy goals. "United States v. James H. Giffen," US Department of Justice, 2003, https://www.justice.gov/criminal-fraud/case/united-states-v-james-h-giffen-et-al; "James Giffen's Trial Ends: A Slap on the Wrist, and the Triumph of American Putinism," *Foreign Policy*, August 6, 2010, https://foreignpolicy.com/2010/08/06/james-giffens-trial-ends-a-slap-on-the-wrist-and-the-triumph-of-american-putinism/.

67. "Kazakh President Nazarbayev's Visit to U.S.".

68. "Kazakh Proposal for a Joint Statement in Washington during Nazarbayev Visit," cable from the US embassy in Alma-Ata, May 6, 1992, George H. W. Bush Presidential Library and Museum.

69. "Kazakhstan on the Eve of Nazarbayev's Visit to America," cable from the US embassy in Alma-Ata, May 1992, Nunn-Lugar Collection, National Security Archive.

70. "Kazakhstan on the Eve of Nazarbayev's Visit to America."

71. "Kazakhstan on the Eve of Nazarbayev's Visit to America."

72. Collective Security Treaty, May 15, 1992, http://www.odkb-csto.org/documents/detail.php?ELEMENT_ID=1897.

73. ITAR TASS, May 18, 1992.

74. I. A. Akhtamzian, "Iadernyi faktor v Tsentral'noi Azii" [Nuclear factor in Central Asia], in M. M. Narinskii and A. V. Mal'chin, eds., *Iuzhnyi Flang SNG. Tsentral'naia Aziya-Kaspii-Kavkaz: Vozmozhnosti i vyzovy dlia Rossii* [Southern Flank of the CIS: Central Asia-Caspian-Caucasus: Opportunities and Challenges for Russia], vol. 2 (Moscow: Navona, 2005), 203.

75. Author's interview with Zhukeev.

76. Vladimir Desiatov, "Tulegen Zhukeev: 'My ne sdelaem pervogo shaga k razrusheniiu, no gotovy ko vsemu'" [Tulegen Zhukeev: 'We will not take the first step toward destruction, but we are ready for anything'], *Nezavisimaia Gazeta*, June 24, 1992.

77. Baker, *Politics of Diplomacy*, 664.

78. Viacheslav Srybyh, "Flag Kazakhstana nad Amerikoi: vpechatleniia o nedavnei poezdke v SShA" [Kazakhstan's flag above America: Impressions about the recent trip to the USA], *Kazakhstanskaia Pravda*, May 30, 1992.

79. Speech by Espy P. Price, Vice President of Chevron Overseas Petroleum Inc, 1994.

80. Ostankino TV, May 24, 1992, from FBIS Trends, June 2, 1992, George H. W. Bush Presidential Library and Museum.

81. "Readout from the Official Working Visit of President Nazarbayev to Washington, May 18–20, 1992," Secretary of State James Baker, State Department, George H. W. Bush Presidential Library and Museum.

82. Video footage from the meeting. George H. W. Bush Presidential Library and Museum, https://www.youtube.com/watch?v=meIRYKmDHNo.

83. Memorandum of conversation, Meeting with President Nursultan Nazarbayev of Kazakhstan, May 19, 1992, the Oval Office, George H. W. Bush Presidential Library and Museum.

84. Memorandum of conversation, Meeting with President Nursultan Nazarbayev of Kazakhstan, May 19, 1992.

85. Memorandum of conversation, Meeting with President Nursultan Nazarbayev of Kazakhstan, May 19, 1992.

86. Memorandum of conversation, Meeting with President Nursultan Nazarbayev of Kazakhstan, May 19, 1992.

87. Srybyh, "Flag Kazakhstana nad Amerikoi."

88. "Bilateral Investment Treaty between the United States and the Republic of Kazakhstan," the White House, May 19, 1992, George H. W. Bush Presidential Library and Museum.

89. "U.S.-Kazakhstan OPIC Agreement," the White House, May 19, 1992, George H. W. Bush Presidential Library and Museum.

90. "Agreement on Trade Relations between the United States and Kazakhstan," the White House, May 19, 1992, George H. W. Bush Presidential Library and Museum.

91. "U.S. Humanitarian Assistance," the White House, May 19, 1992, George H. W. Bush Presidential Library and Museum.

92. "U.S. Humanitarian Assistance," the White House.

93. Nursultan Nazarbayev, statement at the National Press Club, Washington, DC, May 19, 1992.

94. "Nazarbayev Meets Baker, Discusses Adherence to Treaties," report by ITAR-TASS correspondents Pavel Vanichkin and Ivan Lebedev, FBIS, May 19, 1992.

95. "Pervye itogi obnadezhivaiut: vizit Prezidenta Kazakhstana v SShA" [First results provide hope: The visit of the president of Kazakhstan to the USA], *Kazakhstanskaia Pravda*, no date available.

96. "Readout from the Official Working Visit of President Nazarbayev."

97. Srybyh, "Flag Kazakhstana nad Amerikoi."

98. Srybyh, "Flag Kazakhstana nad Amerikoi."

99. "FAA Taped Message from Aeroflot a/c re: Farewell Statement by N. Nazarbayev President of Kazakhstan," May 23, 1992, Memorandum from Tony Baker, Senior Duty Officer, White House Situation Room for General Scowcroft and Admiral Howe, George H. W. Bush Presidential Library and Museum.

100. Protocol to the Agreement between the Union of Soviet Socialist Republics and

the United States of America on the Reduction and Limitation of Strategic Offensive Weapons, signed in Lisbon, Portugal, on May 23, 1992.

CHAPTER 8: THE FINAL PUSH

1. Author's interview with Tulegen Zhukeev, Almaty, 2018.

2. Author's interview with Zhukeev.

3. Lesya Gak, "Denuclearization and Ukraine: Lessons for the Future," *Nonproliferation Review* 11, no. 1 (2004): 106–35.

4. Author's interview with William Courtney, Washington, DC, 2019.

5. Author's interview with Zhukeev.

6. Agreement reached during the visit of General Burns, November 5, 1992.

7. USEC, "Megatons to Megawatts," http://www.usec.com/russian-contracts/megatons-megawatts.

8. "Megatons to Megawatts Program Concludes," December 11, 2013, https://www.world-nuclear-news.org/ENF-Megatons-to-Megawatts-program-concludes-1112134.html.

9. Letter from V. S. Shkolnik general director of Atomic Energy Commission to G. A. Abilsiitov, deputy prime minister, April 19, 1993, Archive of the President of the Republic of Kazakhstan.

10. Author's interview with Zhukeev.

11. Letter from the Minister of Foreign Affairs of the Republic of Kazakhstan T. Suleimenov to Nazarbayev, December 25, 1992, 5H-1-849, 79, Archive of the President of the Republic of Kazakhstan.

12. Sergei Ryzhakov, "Hvatit boiat'sia slova 'soiuz'" [Enough of fearing the word "union"], [unidentified newspaper], January 19, 1993.

13. "Prezident Kazakhstana vnov' prizyvaet k sozdaniiu effektivnoi kollektivnoi zashchity Sodruzhestva" [Kazakhstan's president again appeals to create the commonwealth's common defense], *Krasnaia Zvezda*, April 30, 1993.

14. "Interv'iu s Nazarbayevym" [Interview with Nazarbayev], *Krasnaia Zvezda*, May 15, 1993.

15. Transcript of the main contents of the conversation with the special coordinator for CIS and plenipotentiary ambassador Strobe Talbott, June 9, 1993, Almaty, Kazakhstan, Archive of the President of the Republic of Kazakhstan.

16. Transcript of the main contents of the conversation with the special coordinator for CIS and plenipotentiary ambassador Strobe Talbott, June 9, 1993.

17. Transcript of the main contents of the conversation with the special coordinator for CIS and plenipotentiary ambassador Strobe Talbott, June 9, 1993.

18. Transcript of the conversation between President Nazarbayev and US Ambassador William Courtney, Almaty, July 18, 1993, transcribed by Gizzatov, Archive of the President of the Republic of Kazakhstan.

19. Transcript of the conversation between President Nazarbayev and US Ambassador William Courtney, Almaty, July 18, 1993.

20. Letter from William Courtney to the Ministry of Foreign Affairs, Documents on preparation and results of the visit of the plenipotentiary ambassador and special

coordinator for CIS Strobe Talbott to Almaty, September 11–12, 1993, Department of Americas and Europe, Ministry of Foreign Affairs, 75-H-1, 441, Archive of the President of the Republic of Kazakhstan.

21. Documents on preparation and results of the visit of Strobe Talbott, the plenipotentiary ambassador and special coordinator for CIS, to Almaty, Archive of the President of the Republic of Kazakhstan.

22. Documents on preparation and results of the visit of Strobe Talbott, the plenipotentiary ambassador and special coordinator for CIS, to Almaty, September 11–12, 1993, Archive of the President of the Republic of Kazakhstan.

23. Transcript of the meeting between President of Kazakhstan N. Nazarbayev and the special coordinator for CIS and plenipotentiary ambassador Strobe Talbott, September 12, 1993, Archive of the President of the Republic of Kazakhstan.

24. Letter from the ministry of foreign affairs (Suleimenov) to Nazarbayev, October 1993, f. 5H, o. 1, d. 2192, 5–6, Archive of the President of the Republic of Kazakhstan.

25. Elaine Sciolino, "Kazakh Uses America to Enhance His Stature," *New York Times*, October 25, 1993.

26. Author's interview with Zhukeev.

27. Author's interview with Zhukeev.

28. Author's interview with Zhukeev.

29. Senators Sam Nunn and Richard Lugar conceived the Nunn-Lugar Cooperative Threat Reduction program to help former Soviet republics reduce nuclear risks; it included US payment for dismantling nuclear weapons infrastructure.

30. James E. Goodby, *At the Borderline of Armageddon: How American Presidents Managed the Atom Bomb* (New York: Rowman and Littlefield, 2006), 167.

31. Author's interview with Zhukeev.

32. Author's interview with Courtney.

33. Author's interview with Zhukeev.

34. Author's interview with Zhukeev.

35. Author's interview with Zhukeev.

36. Author's interview with Zhukeev.

37. Author's interview with Zhukeev.

38. Author's interview with Zhukeev.

39. Author's interview with Zhukeev.

40. William Safire, "Gore's Audible in Bishkek," *New York Times*, August 17, 2000.

41. Report of the America Desk of Kazakhstan's Ministry of Foreign Affairs on work completed in 1993, f. 75H, o. 1, d. 430, Archive of the President of the Republic of Kazakhstan; "Kazakhstan i SShA budut nadezhnymi partnerami" [Kazakhstan and the USA will be trusted partners], *Kazakhstanskaia Pravda*, December 15, 1993.

42. Nursultan Nazarbayev statement at the Supreme Soviet, December 13, 1993.

43. Nursultan Nazarbayev statement at the Supreme Soviet.

44. Nursultan Nazarbayev statement at the Supreme Soviet.

45. "On the Results of U.S. Vice President Al Gore's Visit to Kazakhstan," memoran-

dum from Gani Kassymov to Nazarbayev, f. 5H, o. 1, d. 3577, 3–8, Archive of the President of the Republic of Kazakhstan.

46. Nursultan Nazarbayev statement at the Supreme Soviet.

47. Report of the America Desk of Kazakhstan's MFA; "Kazakhstan i SShA budut nadezhnymi partnerami," *Kazakhstanskaia Pravda.*

48. Author's interview with Courtney.

CHAPTER 9: PROJECT SAPPHIRE AND THE NUNN-LUGAR COOPERATIVE THREAT REDUCTION PROGRAM

1. Vitalii Mette, footage from 1992, in "Operatsiia Sapfir" [Operation Sapphire], Khabar TV channel documentary, 2015, https://youtu.be/kjHIj9K-4jc.

2. "Operatsiia Sapfir." By 2020, the Ulba plant had regained its former prominence in the nuclear field, ranking as one of only three facilities worldwide that make beryllium products and one of the largest making tantalum (as well as the only one in the former Soviet Union).

3. Vladimir Bozhko in "Operatsiia Sapfir."

4. Tuleitai Suleimenov, "Operatsiia Sapfir."

5. Vitalii Mette's press conference, November 23, 1994, cited in William C. Potter, "The Changing Nuclear Threat: The 'Sapphire' File," *Transitions Online,* November 17, 1995.

6. David Hoffman, *Dead Hand: The Untold Story of the Cold War Arms Race and Its Dangerous Legacy* (New York: Anchor, 2010), 439; Gerald F. Seib, "Kazakhstan Is Best for Diplomats Who Find Paris a Bore," *Wall Street Journal,* April 17, 1992; author's interview with Andy Weber, by email, Washington, DC, 2020.

7. "Operatsiia Sapfir."

8. Author's interview with Weber.

9. Author's interview with Weber.

10. Author's interview with Weber.

11. Potter, "Changing Nuclear Threat."

12. "Operatsiia Sapfir."

13. R. Jeffrey Smith, "U.S. Takes Nuclear Fuel," *Washington Post,* November 23, 1994.

14. Author's interview with Weber.

15. Hoffman, *Dead Hand,* 445.

16. E. H. Gift, National Security Programs Office, Martin Marietta Energy Systems, Inc., Oak Ridge, Tennessee, "Analysis of HEU Samples from the Ulba Metallurgical Plant," revised by A. W. Reidy, initially issued in July 1994, US Department of Energy, https://www.osti.gov/biblio/192548-analysis-heu-samples-from-ulba-metallurgical-plant.

17. William C. Potter, "Project Sapphire: U.S.-Kazakhstani Cooperation for Non-Proliferation," in *Dismantling the Cold War: U.S. and NIS Perspectives on the Nunn-Lugar Cooperative Threat Reduction Program,* ed. John M. Shields and William C. Potter (Cambridge, MA: MIT Press, 1997), 345–62; Potter, "Changing Nuclear Threat."

18. "Operatsiia Sapfir."

19. "Operatsiia Sapfir."

20. Potter, "Changing Nuclear Threat."

21. Project Sapphire After-Action Report, Defense Threat Reduction Agency. The document made available by the National Security Archive, Washington, DC, https://nsarchive2.gwu.edu/NSAEBB/NSAEBB491/docs/01%20-%20After%20Action%20report%20DTRA.pdf.

22. Project Sapphire After-Action Report.

23. Igor Liutovskii and Dmitrii Mytar' in "Operatsiia Sapfir."

24. "U.S. Team Worked Secretly to Get Uranium to Safety," *New York Times*, October 8, 2005.

25. Project Sapphire After-Action Report.

26. Author's interview with Weber.

27. Elaine Sciolino, "Iran Says It Plans 10 Nuclear Plants But No Atom Arms," *New York Times*, May 14, 1995, A1.

28. Project Sapphire After-Action Report.

29. "U.S. Team Worked Secretly to Get Uranium to Safety."

30. Lidiia Vavilova in "Operatsiia Sapfir."

31. Project Sapphire After-Action Report.

32. Project Sapphire After-Action Report.

33. Project Sapphire After-Action Report; author's interview with Weber.

34. Bozhko in "Operatsiia Sapfir."

35. Andy Weber, "Project Sapphire 20 Years Later: Cooperative Threat Reduction and Lessons for the Future" event, Center for Strategic and International Studies (CSIS), November 17-18, 2014, https://www.csis.org/events/project-sapphire-20-years-later-cooperative-threat-reduction-and-lessons-future.

36. Andy Weber in "Operatsiia Sapfir."

37. Project Sapphire After-Action Report.

38. John R. Tirpak, "Project Sapphire," *Air Force* 78, no. 8 (August 1995), http://www.afa.org/magazine/aug1995/0895sapphire.asp.

39. Ashton B. Carter and William J. Perry, *Preventive Defense: A New Security Strategy for America* (Washington, DC: Brookings Institution Press, 1999), 66.

40. Author's interview with Susan Koch, Washington, DC, 2003.

41. Author's interview with Tulegen Zhukeev, Almaty, 2018.

42. DOD News Briefing: Secretary of Defense William J. Perry et al., November 23, 1994, Nunn-Lugar Collection, National Security Archive.

43. DOD News Briefing: Secretary of Defense William J. Perry et al., November 23, 1994.

44. "Russian Kommersant: 'U.S. Version of Uranium Deal With Almaty Questioned,'" FBIS translated text of Aleksandr Koretskiy, "More Uranium Has Been Bought Than Was Actually Available," November 25, 1994.

45. Cable from the Embassy of the Republic of Kazakhstan in Washington, DC to the Foreign Minister Tokayev, written by Bolat Nurgaliev, October 29, 1996, f. 75H, o. 1, d. 2624, Archive of the President of the Republic of Kazakhstan.

46. "Kazakhstan: 'Missing' HEU, October 26, 1996," PM Press Guidance, f. 75H, o. 1, d. 2624, Archive of the President of the Republic of Kazakhstan.

47. Author's interview with Kim Savit, by phone, 2020.

48. Vladimir Shkolnik in "Operatsiia Sapfir."

49. Author's interview with Laura Holgate, Washington, DC, 2020.

50. K. K. Tokayev and V. S. Shkolnik, eds., *CTR v Kazahstane* [CTR in Kazakhstan], 23.

51. Tokayev and Shkolnik, *CTR v Kazahstane*, 23.

52. "Proekt 'Sapfir': vzgliad iz Kazahstana" [Project Sapphire: A view from Kazakhstan], an excerpt from *CTR v Kazahstane, Chelovek. Energiia* [CTR in Kazakhstan, Human, Energy], ed. K. K. Tokayev and V. S. Shkolnik, *Atom* 1, no. 19 (2013): 41.

53. Joseph P. Harahan, *With Courage and Persistence: Eliminating and Securing Weapons of Mass Destruction with the Nunn-Lugar Cooperative Threat Reduction Programs* (Washington, DC: Defense Threat Reduction Agency, 2014), 192.

54. Carter and Perry, *Preventive Defense*, 7.

55. Memorandum from the Ministry of Foreign Affairs to President Nazarbayev, November 23, 1994, f. 5H, o. 1, d. 3806, Archive of the President of the Republic of Kazakhstan.

56. Senator Sam Nunn, "Foreword: Changing Threats in the Post-Cold War World" in Shields and Potter, *Dismantling the Cold War*, xvi.

57. John Felton, "The Nunn-Lugar Vision: 1992–2002," Washington, DC, Nuclear Threat Initiative, 2002, 5; Harahan, *With Courage and Persistence*, 17.

58. Author's interview with William Courtney, Washington, DC, 2019.

59. Text of the Soviet Nuclear Threat Reduction Act of 1991, available at the Federation of American Scientists' website, http://www.fas.org/nuke/control/ctr/docs/hr3807.html.

60. "Disarmament Visits to Alma Ata: Update," cable from the US embassy in Almaty, no date available, George H. W. Bush Presidential Library and Museum.

61. "Codel Nunn/Lugar Meeting with Kazakhstan President Nazarbayev, November 21, 1992," cable from the US embassy in Almaty, written by William Courtney, November 1992, George H. W. Bush Presidential Library and Museum.

62. "SSD: Alma Ata Bilateral Sessions," cable from the US embassy in Almaty, November 1992, George H. W. Bush Presidential Library and Museum.

63. Author's interview with James Goodby, Washington, DC, 2019.

64. Author's interview with Goodby.

65. Author's interview with Goodby.

66. Author's interview with Holgate.

67. Author's interview with Savit.

68. Laura Holgate, "Project Sapphire 20 Years Later: Cooperative Threat Reduction and Lessons for the Future."

69. Emily E. Daughtry, "Forging Partnerships, Preventing Proliferation: A Decade of Cooperative Threat Reduction in Central Asia," in Dan Burghart and Theresa Sabonis-Helf, eds., *In the Tracks of Tamerlane: Central Asia's Path to the 21st Century* (Washington: National Defense University, 2004), 327.

70. Anonymous former senior Kazakh official, 2015.

71. Laura Holgate, Second International Conference on the Nunn-Lugar Program, A Critical Oral History Project of the National Security Archive, Astana, June 2015.

72. Carter, Perry, *Preventive Defense*, 72–76.

73. Author's interview with Holgate.

74. Author's interview with Royal Gardner, by phone, 2019.

75. Author's interview with Holgate.

76. Author's interview with Gardner.

77. Author's interview with James Turner, Washington, DC, 2019.

78. Author's interview with Turner.

79. Weber, "Project Sapphire 20 Years Later."

CHAPTER 10: FAREWELL TO BOMBS

1. Letter from General-Lieutenant Yuri Konovalenko to the President of the Republic of Kazakhstan Nursultan Nazarbayev, December 28, 1992, f. 5H, o. 1, d. 2017, Archive of the President of the Republic of Kazakhstan.

2. Letter from Akezhan Kazhegeldin, 1993, f. 5H, o. 2, d. 351, Archive of the President of the Republic of Kazakhstan.

3. Letter from Akezhan Kazhegeldin.

4. "Spravka po ugolovnomu delu v otnoshenii komandira v/ch 52605 general-leitenanta Konovalenko Yu.V." [Memorandum on the criminal case against the commander of the 52605 military unit general-lieutenant Yu. V. Konovalenko], signed by A. F. Dudkin, deputy military prosecutor of the Republic of Kazakhstan and N. Tlemissov, chief of the defense section of the presidential administration and the council of ministers of the Republic of Kazakhstan, Archive of the President of the Republic of Kazakhstan.

5. "Spravka po ugolovnomu delu."

6. Author's interview with Thomas Simons, by phone, 2020.

7. "Meeting with Kazakhstan President Nursultan Nazarbayev," memorandum from Anthony Lake, National Security Council, February 12, 1994, William J. Clinton Presidential Library and Museum.

8. Background briefing by senior administration officials, the White House, February 1994, William J. Clinton Presidential Library and Museum.

9. The exact numbers vary between sources. In his remarks, President Clinton mentioned $311 million in economic assistance. Source: President Clinton and President Nazarbayev of Kazakhstan in Signing Ceremony and Press Availability, the White House, February 14, 1994, William J. Clinton Presidential Library and Museum. In a briefing for media, a senior official gave the following numbers for 1994: economic aid of $226 million, Nunn-Lugar—$170 million, total—$396 million. Source: Background briefing by a senior administration official, February 14, 1994, William J. Clinton Presidential Library and Museum.

10. Charter on Democratic Partnership between the United States of America and the Republic of Kazakhstan, Article 3.

11. Charter on Democratic Partnership, Article 5.

12. Charter on Democratic Partnership, Article 6.

13. Memorandum on Security Assurances in Connection with the Republic of Kazakhstan's Accession to the Treaty on the Non-Proliferation of Nuclear Weapons, December 5, 1994.

14. Memorandum from the Ministry of Foreign Affairs, November 23, 1994, f. 5H, o. 1, d. 3806, Archive of the President of the Republic of Kazakhstan.

15. Document from f. 5H, o. 1, d. 3376, Archive of the President of the Republic of Kazakhstan. Two other nuclear powers—China and France—also followed up with their own statements on security assurances to all three new states.

16. INMARSAT Technology Safeguards Agreement, Fact Sheet, White House Press Office, February 16, 1994, William J. Clinton Presidential Library and Museum; Agreement between the Government of the Republic of Kazakhstan and the Government of the Russian Federation and the Government of the United States of America on Technological Safeguards Associated with the Launch of the INMARSAT-3 Satellite, February 14, 1994, https://aerospace.org/sites/default/files/policy_archives/Tech%20Safeguards%20Agreement%20-%20Kazakhstan%20Feb94.pdf.

17. Background briefing by senior administration officials, the White House, February 1994, William J. Clinton Presidential Library and Museum.

18. Joseph P. Harahan, *With Courage and Persistence: Eliminating and Securing Weapons of Mass Destruction with the Nunn-Lugar Cooperative Threat Reduction Programs* (Washington, DC: Defense Threat Reduction Agency, 2014), 18.

19. Harahan, *With Courage and Persistence*, 186.

20. Soglashenie mezhdu Rossiiskoi Federatsiei i Respublikoi Kazakhstan o strategicheskih iadernyh silah, vremenno raspolozhennyh na territorii Respubliki Kazakhstan [Agreement between the Russian Federation and the Republic of Kazakhstan on strategic nuclear forces temporarily located on the territory of the Republic of Kazakhstan], March 28, 1994, http://base.spinform.ru/show_doc.fwx?rgn=8636.

21. The Kazakhstan-Russia agreement on cooperation and mutual [financial] settlements as part of the dismantlement of nuclear ammunition went into force in 1995, and the in 2017 Kazakhstan and Russia signed the protocol to the agreement.

22. "Military treaty with Russia ratified" [article by Sergey Kozlov, "Treaty for Military Cooperation with Russia Ratified. But Its Fate Remains in Question"] *Nezavisimaia Gazeta*, October 11, 1994, via FBIS.

23. "Possible Nuclear Weapon Emplaced at Semipalatinsk," cable from the US State Department to the US embassy in Alma-Ata, written by Lawrence Eagleburger, October 1992, George H. W. Bush Presidential Archives and Library.

24. "Possible Nuclear Weapon Emplaced at Semipalatinsk," cable from the US State Department to the US embassy in Alma-Ata.

25. Letter from S. Tereshchenko, Prime Minister of the Republic of Kazakhstan to S. Abdildin, Chair of the Supreme Soviet, November 30, 1992, f. 5H, o. 1, d. 1958, Archive of the President of the Republic of Kazakhstan.

26. Yuri Fomenko, "V toi gore zaryt ne klad—prosto iadernyi zariad" [Not a treasure but simply a nuclear device is buried in the mountain], *Kazakhstanskaia Pravda*, November 4, 1993.

27. Deputy Chair of the State Committee of the Russian Federation on Economic Cooperation with CIS (M. Khusnutdinov) to the Council of Ministers of the Republic of Kazakhstan, December 23, 1993. The Council of Ministers sent it to the Atomic Energy Agency (Vladimir Shkolnik), the Ministry of Defense (Sagadat Nurmagambetov) and the Ministry of Foreign Affairs (Tuleitai Suleimenov), f. 75H, o. 1, d. 602, Archive of the President of the Republic of Kazakhstan.

28. André Grabot, "Kazakhstan Officially Non-Nuclear But Legacy Remains," Agence France Presse, June 6, 1995.

29. N. A. Nazarbayev et al., *Provedenie kompleksa nauchno-tekhnicheskih i inzhenernyh rabot po privedeniiu byvshego Semipalatinskogo ispytatel'nogo poligona v bezopasnoe sostoianie* [Scientific-technical measures and engineering work to transform the former Semipalatinsk testing Polygon into a safe state] (Kurchatov: National Nuclear Center, 2016), 1:97.

30. John R. Matzko, "Inside a Soviet ICBM Silo Complex: The SS-18 Silo Dismantlement Program at Derzhavinsk," US Department of Interior, US Geological Survey National Center, prepared for the Defense Threat Reduction Agency, August 2000, https://apps.dtic.mil/dtic/tr/fulltext/u2/a388848.pdf.

31. Author's interview with a former manager of CTR projects in Kazakhstan, by phone, 2020.

32. Harahan, *With Courage and Persistence*, 200.

33. Background briefing by senior administration officials, the White House, February 1994, William J. Clinton Presidential Library and Museum.

34. Author's interview with Jim Reid, by phone, 2020.

35. Oumirserik T. Kasenov, Dastan Eleukenov, and Murat Laumulin, "Implementing the CTR Program in Kazakhstan," in John M. Shields and William C. Potter, eds., *Dismantling the Cold War: U.S. and NIS Perspectives on the Nunn-Lugar Cooperative Threat Reduction Program* (Cambridge, MA: MIT Press, 1997), 196.

36. Kasenov, Eleukenov, and Laumulin, "Implementing the CTR Program in Kazakhstan," 197.

37. Kasenov, Eleukenov, and Laumulin, "Implementing the CTR Program in Kazakhstan," 197.

38. Matzko, "Inside a Soviet ICBM Silo Complex," 15.

39. Matzko, "Inside a Soviet ICBM Silo Complex," 18.

40. Matzko, "Inside a Soviet ICBM Silo Complex," 17.

41. *Radiological Conditions at the Semipalatinsk Test Site, Kazakhstan: Preliminary Assessment and Recommendations for Further Study*, IAEA (Vienna, 1998), 1, 10.

42. Harahan, *With Courage and Persistence*, 195.

43. N. A. Nazarbayev et al., *Provedenie kompleksa nauchno-tekhnicheskih i inzhenernyh rabot*, 1:39, 70.

44. Harahan, *With Courage and Persistence*, 197.

45. N. A. Nazarbayev et al., *Provedenie kompleksa nauchno-tekhnicheskih i inzhen-ernyh rabot*, 1:87, 89.

46. Nicholas Priest and Robert Murley, "Radiological Conditions Prevailing at Technical Area 4A on the Semipalatinsk Nuclear Test Site: Hazards Presented by Radionuclide Deposits," December 2006, IAEA, 1998, https://www-pub.iaea.org/MTCD/Publications/PDF/Pub1063_web.pdf.

47. Eben Harrell and David Hoffman, *Plutonium Mountain: Inside the 17-Year Mission to Secure a Legacy of Soviet Nuclear Testing*, Managing the Atom Project (Cambridge, MA: Belfer Center, Harvard University, 2013), 14; Siegfried S. Hecker, "The Semipalatinsk Project: A Trilateral Cooperation to Secure Fissile Materials at the Former Soviet Semipalatinsk Nuclear Test Site," in *Doomed to Cooperate: How American and Russian Scientists Joined Forces to Avert Some of the Greatest Post–Cold War Nuclear Dangers*, ed. Siegfried S. Hecker (Los Alamos: Bathtub Row Press, 2016), 1:452.

48. Hecker, "Semipalatinsk Project," 1:452.

49. The formal name of the U.S.-Kazakhstan agreement: Joint Work on Eliminating the Nuclear Weapons Testing Infrastructure and Improving the Ecological Situation on the Territory of the Former Semipalatinsk Test Site.

50. Author's interview with Siegfried Hecker, by phone, 2020.

51. Kairat Kadyrzhanov, *V pamiati moei . . . rodnym, druz'iam, kollegam* [My memories . . . for loved ones, friends, and colleagues] (Astana: Master PO, 2015), 263.

52. Author's interview with Hecker.

53. Kadyrzhanov, *V pamiati moei . . . rodnym, druz'iam, kollegam*, 264–65.

54. Author's interview with Hecker.

55. Harrell and Hoffman, *Plutonium Mountain*, 14.

56. *Doomed to Cooperate*, ed. Hecker, 1:461–62.

57. Author's interview with Hecker.

58. Harrell and Hoffman, *Plutonium Mountain*, 17; Kairat K. Kadyrzhanov, "Kazakhstan Semipalatinsk Test Site: A Turning Point" in *Doomed to Cooperate*, ed. Hecker, 1:512.

59. Viktor S. Stepanyuk, "Liquidation of the Consequences of Nuclear Tests at the Semipalatinsk Test Site (STS) in Trilateral Collaboration (Russian Federation, Republic of Kazakhstan, United States)," in *Doomed to Cooperate*, ed. Hecker, 1:483–84.

60. Hecker, "Semipalatinsk Project," 1:466.

61. Harrell and Hoffman, *Plutonium Mountain*, 20–21; Philip H. Hemberger, "The Semipalatinsk Project: A Los Alamos Scientist's Perspective," in *Doomed to Cooperate*, ed. Hecker, 1:476.

62. Richard Stone, "Plutonium Fields Forever," *Science* 300 (2003): 1220–24.

63. N. A. Nazarbayev et al., *Provedenie kompleksa nauchno-tekhnicheskih i inzhen-ernyh rabot*, 1:207.

64. N. A. Nazarbayev et al., *Provedenie kompleksa nauchno-tekhnicheskih i inzhen-ernyh rabot*, 1:112–14, 117; Stepanyuk, "Liquidation of the Consequences of Nuclear Tests," 1:492.

65. Harrell and Hoffman, *Plutonium Mountain*, 25.

66. Stepanyuk, "Liquidation of the Consequences of Nuclear Tests," 1:495.

67. N. A. Nazarbayev et al., *Provedenie kompleksa nauchno-tekhnicheskih i inzhen-ernyh rabot*, 1:150; Stepanyuk, "Liquidation of the Consequences of Nuclear Tests," 1:493–94.

68. Author's interview with a US CTR project manager, by phone, 2020.

69. N. A. Nazarbayev et al., *Provedenie kompleksa nauchno-tekhnicheskih i inzhen-ernyh rabot*, 1:184, 170.

70. Hemberger, "The Semipalatinsk Project: A Los Alamos Scientist's Perspective," 1:479.

71. N. A. Nazarbayev et al., *Provedenie kompleksa nauchno-tekhnicheskih i inzhen-ernyh rabot*, 1:278–79, 282–83.

72. Joint Statement of the Presidents of Kazakhstan, the Russian Federation and the United States of America Regarding the Trilateral Cooperation at the Former Semipalatinsk Test Site, The White House, March 26, 2012, https://obamawhitehouse.archives.gov/the-press-office/2012/03/26/joint-statement-presidents-republic-kazakhstan-russian-federation-and-un.

73. Author's interview with Byron Ristvet, by phone, 2020.

74. *Nuclear Successor States of the Soviet Union: Status Report on Nuclear Weapons, Fissile Material, and Export Controls*, Monterey Institute of International Studies and the Carnegie Endowment for International Peace, no. 5 (March 1998): 38–42; I. A. Akhtamzian, "Iadernyi faktor v Tsentral'noi Azii" [Nuclear factor in Central Asia], in M. M. Narinskii and A. V. Mal'chin, eds., *Iuzhnyi flang SNG. Tsentral'naia Aziia-Kaspii-Kavkaz: vozmozhnosti i vyzovy dlia Rossii* [Southern Flank of the CIS: Central Asia-Capsian-Caucasus], vol. 2 (Moscow: Navona, 2005), 94–195.

75. Author's interview with Andy Weber, by email, Washington, DC, 2020.

76. Author's interview with John Ordway, by phone, 2019.

77. Author's interview with Eric Howden, by phone, 2020.

78. Author's interview with Howden.

79. Author's interview with Howden.

80. Author's interview with Howden.

81. R. Case et al., "Nuclear Material, Control, and Accounting Program at the Mangyshlak Atomic Energy Complex, Aktau, Republic of Kazakhstan."

82. Author's interview with Howden.

83. Case et al., "Nuclear Material, Control, and Accounting Program."

84. Author's interview with Joyce Connery, by phone, 2020.

85. Shaiakhmet Shiganakov, "BN-350 Reactor Spent Fuel Handling," presentation at the IAEA, April 26–28, 2006; Author's interview with Howden.

86. Author's interview with Howden.

87. Author's interview with Howden.

88. "Moving Kazakh Nuclear Cache a Massive Undertaking," *All Things Considered*, National Public Radio, November 17, 2010.

89. Author's interview with Howden.

90. "Kazakhstan Has Completed Disposal of Spent Nuclear Fuel," National Technical Information Service, Moscow, Russia, November 12, 2010.

91. "Soviet Nuclear Test Site Now a Model for Safeguards," *All Things Considered*, National Public Radio, November 19, 2010.

92. Bagila Bukharbayeva, "Joint Effort Taking Nuclear Materials out of Commission," October 9, 2005, https://www.seattletimes.com/nation-world/joint-effort-taking-nuclear-materials-out-of-commission/.

93. Author's interview with Laura Holgate, by phone, 2020.

94. BN-350 Decommissioning Plan for International Peer, K-513 ISTC Project, "Introduction."

95. D. Newton, J. Connery, and P. Wells, "U.S. Experience in the Decommissioning of the BN-350 Fast Breeder Reactor in Kazakhstan," Office of International Nuclear Safety and Cooperation, US Department of Energy, Nunn-Lugar Collection, National Security Archive.

96. Newton, Connery, and Wells, "U.S. Experience in the Decommissioning of the BN-350 Fast Breeder Reactor in Kazakhstan."

97. Harahan, *With Courage and Persistence*, 210.

98. Newton, Connery, and Wells, "U.S. Experience in the Decommissioning of the BN-350 Fast Breeder Reactor in Kazakhstan"; Joyce Connery, "Kazakhstan: Living with a Nuclear Legacy," September 27, 2001.

99. Author's interview with Connery.

100. *Nuclear Successor States of the Soviet Union*, 38–42; "Baykal-1 (Baikal) Research Reactor Complex," NTI, https://www.nti.org/learn/facilities/453/.

101. "Baykal-1 (Baikal) Research Reactor Complex."

102. "Baykal-1 (Baikal) Research Reactor Complex"; Second National Report of the Republic of Kazakhstan on Compliance with Obligations Subsequent upon the Convention on Nuclear Safety, Astana, 2016, https://www.iaea.org/sites/default/files/kazakhstan_nr-7th-rm.pdf.

103. "IGR Nuclear Research Reactor," NTI, https://www.nti.org/learn/facilities/455/.

104. "Kazakhstan and U.S. Cooperate to Eliminate Highly Enriched Uranium in Kazakhstan," September 22, 2020, National Nuclear Security Administration, https://www.energy.gov/nnsa/articles/kazakhstan-and-us-cooperate-eliminate-highly-enriched-uranium-kazakhstan.

105. Kadyrzhanov, *V pamiati moei . . . rodnym, druz'iam, kollegam*, 132.

106. "Institute of Nuclear Physics," NTI, https://www.nti.org/learn/facilities/738/.

107. Boris Kuznetsov, "Implementation of Material Control and Accounting at the Nuclear Facilities in Kazakhstan," *Partnership for Nuclear Security: United States/Former Soviet Union Program of Cooperation on Nuclear Material Protection, Control, and Accounting* (Washington, DC: Department of Energy, September 1998), 1–2.

108. "Kazakhstan Removes Research Reactor HEU," October 3, 2014, https://www.world-nuclear-news.org/RS-Kazakhstan-removes-research-reactor-HEU-03101401.html.

109. "Kazakhstan and U.S. Cooperate to Eliminate Highly Enriched Uranium in Kazakhstan."

110. "NNSA Partners with Kazakhstan Research Institute to Remove All of its Highly Enriched Uranium," National Nuclear Security Administration, September 19, 2017, https://www.energy.gov/nnsa/articles/nnsa-partners-kazakhstan-research-institute-remove-all-its-highly-enriched-uranium; "Russia Prepares to Accept Spent Fuel of Kazakhstan's VVR-K Reactor," International Panel on Fissile Materials, September 29, 2016, http://fissilematerials.org/blog/2016/09/russia_prepares_to_accept.html; "Kazakhstan and U.S. Cooperate to Eliminate Highly Enriched Uranium in Kazakhstan."

EPILOGUE: REIMAGINING THE ATOMIC STEPPE

Epigraph translated by Galina Kim.

1. Author's interviews with Dmitrii Vesselov, Semey, 2019–2020.

2. Treaty on the Prohibition of Nuclear Weapons, Office for Disarmament Affairs, United Nations, https://www.un.org/disarmament/wmd/nuclear/tpnw/.

3. "U.S. Urges Nations to Withdraw Support for U.N. Nuclear Weapons Ban Treaty," October 22, 2020, https://www.cbsnews.com/news/us-urges-nations-to-withdraw-support-for-un-nuclear-weapons-prohibition-treaty-ap/.

4. Eric Johnston, "U.N. Nuke Ban Treaty to Enter Effect Jan. 22, Heaping Pressure on Japan to Join," *Japan Times*, https://www.japantimes.co.jp/news/2020/10/25/national/un-nuclear-ban-treaty-japan/.

5. Marc Finaud, "Nuclear Testing: An Example to Follow," *Astana Times*, August 28, 2020, https://astanatimes.com/2020/08/nuclear-testing-an-example-to-follow/.

6. "Spanning 116 States, World's Five Nuclear Weapon Free Zones Must Use Political Capital to Advance Common Disarmament Goals, Speakers Tell First Committee," United Nations, October 17, 2018, https://www.un.org/press/en/2018/gadis3604.doc.htm.

7. Letter of Oumirserik Kasenov to Tulegen Zhukeev, "On Possibility of Creating an NWFZ in Central Asia," October 3, 1994, Archive of the President of the Republic of Kazakhstan.

8. For challenges facing the establishment of a Central Asian Nuclear-Weapon-Free Zone in the 1990s, see Oumirserik Kasenov, "On the Creation of a Nuclear-Weapon-Free Zone in Central Asia," *Nonproliferation Review* 6, no. 1 (1998): 144–147.

9. Togzhan Kassenova, "The Struggle for a Nuclear-Weapon-Free Zone in Central Asia," *Bulletin of Atomic Scientists*, December 22, 2008, https://thebulletin.org/2008/12/the-struggle-for-a-nuclear-weapon-free-zone-in-central-asia/.

10. Kassenova, "Struggle for a Nuclear-Weapon-Free Zone in Central Asia."

11. The treaties establishing other nuclear-weapon-free zones call upon their members to sign comprehensive safeguards agreements with the International Atomic Energy Agency (IAEA)—the required standard for all NPT non-nuclear-weapon states. Under these comprehensive safeguards agreements, the countries declare nuclear facilities and material to the IAEA, and the IAEA inspectors confirm that these *declared* facilities and material are not diverted to military use. But the Central Asian treaty ob-

ligates its members to sign the IAEA's Additional Protocol—a much more intrusive regime under which IAEA inspectors can check for *undeclared* activity and have access to more facilities.

12. "Status of Signature and Ratification," CTBTO, https://www.ctbto.org/the-treaty/status-of-signature-and-ratification/.

13. "Overview of the Verification Regime," CTBTO, https://www.ctbto.org/verification-regime/background/overview-of-the-verification-regime/.

14. N. A. Nazarbayev et al., *Provedenie kompleksa nauchno-tekhnicheskih i inzhenernyh rabot po privedeniiu byvshego Semipalatinskogo ispytatel'nogo poligona v bezopasnoe sostoianie* [Scientific-technical measures and engineering work to transform the former Semipalatinsk Polygon into a safe state] (Kurchatov: National Nuclear Center, 2016), 1:57.

15. "On-Site Inspection: Integrated Field Exercise 2008," CTBTO, https://www.ctbto.org/specials/integrated-field-exercise-2008/.

16. "IAEA Low Enriched Uranium Bank," IAEA, https://www.iaea.org/topics/iaea-low-enriched-uranium-bank.

17. David Dalton, "Kazakhstan Offers to Host International Fuel Bank," Nucnet, April 8, 2009, https://www.nucnet.org/news/kazakhstan-offers-to-host-international-fuel-bank.

18. Yerbolat Uatkhanov, "IAEA LEU Bank Completes Second Shipment of Low Enriched Uranium," *Astana Times*, December 12, 2019, https://www.iaea.org/newscenter/pressreleases/iaea-leu-bank-becomes-operational-with-delivery-of-low-enriched-uranium.

19. "Kazatomprom," https://www.kazatomprom.kz/en.

20. Author's interview with Gennadii Bartashevich, Chagan, 2020.

21. "Largest Military Aircraft by Weight, Operational Bomber," Guinness World Records, https://www.guinnessworldrecords.com/world-records/largest-military-aircraft-by-weight-operational-bomber.

22. Author's interview with Bartashevich.

23. Kazakhstan's former senior official, author's interview, Nur-Sultan, 2020.

24. Catherine Alexander, "A Chronotope of Expansion: Resisting Spatio-temporal Limits in a Kazakh Nuclear Town," *Ethnos: Journal of Anthropology* (2020): 8.

25. "Gorodok Kurchatov: Iz proshlogo—v budushchee", *Chelovek, Energiia, Atom* 2, no. 4 (2009): 48–53.

26. "O Natsional'nom iadernom tsentre i Agentstve to atomnoi energii Respubliki Kazakhstan" [On the National Nuclear Center and the Agency on Atomic Energy of the Republic of Kazakhstan], Presidential Decree No. 779, 1992; "O merah po obespecheniiu deiatel'nosti Natsional'nogo iadernogo tsentra Respubliki Kazakhstan," Regulation No. 55 adopted by the Council of Ministers of the Republic of Kazakhstan, January 21, 1993.

27. "Sergey Lukashenko: nerazrushaemoe—v liudiah," interview recorded by Evgenii Panov, *Chelovek, Energiia, Atom* 2, no. 4 (2009): 46–47.

28. "Uslugi i produktsiia" [Services and products], Park of Nuclear Technologies, http://pnt.kz/ru/services.html.

29. "V Kurchatove Park Iadernyh Tekhnologii ne smogli prodat' s chetvertoi

popytki," January 9, 2019, InformBuro, https://informburo.kz/novosti/v-kurchatove-park-yadernyh-tehnologiy-ne-smogli-prodat-s-chetvyortoy-popytki.html.

30. "Tokamak KTM," National Nuclear Center, https://ktm.nnc.kz.

31. "Baykal-1 (Baikal) Research Reactor Complex," Nuclear Threat Initiative, https://www.nti.org/learn/facilities/453/.

32. "IGR Reactor," National Nuclear Center, https://www.nnc.kz/en/facilities/igr. html; Kairat Kadyrzhanov, *V pamiati moei . . . rodnym, druz'iam, kollegam* [My memories . . . for loved ones, friends, and colleagues] (Astana: Master PO, 2015), 124.

33. The Institute of Radiation Safety and Ecology, part of the National Nuclear Center, carried out comprehensive studies of the Polygon. Author's interview with Sergey Lukashenko, by phone, 2020.

34. Kadyrzhanov, *V pamiati moei . . . rodnym, druz'iam, kollegam,* 276.

35. Kadyrzhanov, *V pamiati moei . . . rodnym, druz'iam, kollegam,* 205.

36. Kadyrzhanov, *V pamiati moei . . . rodnym, druz'iam, kollegam,* 198.

37. Draft Law of the Republic of Kazakhstan, On Semipalatinsk Nuclear Safety Zone, 2021, Adilet dabatase, https://adilet.zan.kz/rus/docs/P2100000185.

38. "Semipalatinskii ispytatel'nyi polygon: sovremennoe sostoianie" [Semipalatinsk testing Polygon: Current condition], ed. Sergey Lukashenko (Kurchatov : National Nuclear Center, 2011), 12.

39. Author's interview with Lukashenko.

40. Kadyrzhanov, *V pamiati moei . . . rodnym, druz'iam, kollegam,* 201, 204.

41. Letter from the General Director of the National Nuclear Center of the Republic of Kazakhstan G. A. Batyrbekov addressed to the Main Military-Medical Department of the Russian Federation, October 21, 1993, f. 5H, o. 1, d. 2017, Archive of the President of the Republic of Kazakhstan; Letter from the Chief of the Main Military-Medical Department of the Russian Federation General-Lieutenant I. Chizh addressed to the General Director of the National Nuclear Center of the Republic of Kazakhstan G. A. Batyrbekov, November 20, 1993, f. 5H, o. 1, d. 2017, Archive of the President of the Republic of Kazakhstan; Letter from the Acting General Director of the National Nuclear Center of the Republic of Kazakhstan Sh. T. Tukhvatullin addressed to the Chief of the Main Military-Medical Department of the Russian Federation General-Lieutenant I. Chizh, December 12, 1993; Letter from Kazakhstan's acting Health Minister E. K. Argymbaev addressed to Kazakhstan's Minister of Defense General S. N. Nurmagambetov and Kazakhstan's State Counselor K. Suleimenov, January 21, 1994, f. 5H, o. 1, d. 2017, Archive of the President of the Republic of Kazakhstan; Letter from the Deputy Minister of Foreign Affairs of the Republic of Kazakhstan K. Zhigalov addressed to the Cabinet of Ministers of the Republic of Kazakhstan, February 21, 1994, f. 5H, o. 1, d. 2017, Archive of the President of the Republic of Kazakhstan; Letter from the Prime Minister of the Republic of Kazakhstan S. Tereshchenko addressed to the Chairman of the Council of Ministers-Government of the Russian Federation V. S. Chernomyrdin, March 2, 1994, f. 5H, o. 1, d. 2017, Archive of the President of the Republic of Kazakhstan; Letter from the Deputy Chairman of the Government of the Russian Federation S. Shahrai addressed to the Prime Minister of the Republic of Kazakhstan S. Tereshchenko, April 29, 1994, f.

5H, o. 1, d. 2017, Archive of the President of the Republic of Kazakhstan; Letter from the Minister of Health of the Republic of Kazakhstan V. Deviatko addressed to the Cabinet of Ministers of the Republic of Kazakhstan, with a copy to the Agency on Atomic Energy of the Republic of Kazakhstan, July 5, 1994, f. 5H, o. 1, d. 2017, Archive of the President of the Republic of Kazakhstan; Letter from the Minister Ecology and Bioresources of the Republic of Kazakhstan S. A. Medvedev addressed to the Cabinet of Ministers of the Republic of Kazakhstan, July 13, 1994, f. 5H, o. 1, d. 2017, Archive of the President of the Republic of Kazakhstan.

42. "Istoriia radioekolochigeskih issledovanii, provodimyh NII RMiE v zone vliianiia SIIaP [History of radioecological studies conducted by the Institute of Radiation Medicine and Ecology in the area affected by the Semipalatinsk Nuclear Testing Polygon], Institute of Radiation Medicine and Ecology, http://rirme.kz/science/nauchnaya-deyatelnost.

43. This section is based on "Primenenie perechnia zabolevanii, imeiushchih sviaz' s oposredstvennym radiatsionnym vozdeistviem u lits, rozhdennyh ot obluchennyh roditelei v rezul'tate ispytanii iadernogo oruzhiia na Semipalatinskom iadernom poligone v rabote mezhvedomstvennyh ekspertnyh sovetov" [On the use of the list of diseases related to radiation exposure among the descendants of parents exposed to ionizing radiation as a result of nuclear weapons tests at the Semipalatinsk Nuclear Polygon in the work of interagency expert councils]," Institute of Radiation Medicine and Ecology, Astana, 2014, http://rirme.kz/assets/images/resources/11/metodicheskie-rekomendacii.pdf. For the institute's more detailed findings published in international scientific journals, see, e.g., Nadejda Y. Mudie et al., "Twinning in the Offspring of Parents with Chronic Radiation Exposure from Nuclear Testing in Kazakhstan," *Radiation Research Society* (2010): 829–36; L. M. Pivina et al., "Development of a Cause-of-Death Registry among the Population of Several Rayons in the East-Kazakhstan Oblast Exposed to Radiation Due to Nuclear Weapons Testing at the Semipalatinsk Test Site," final report of the Project "Health Effects of Nuclear Weapons Testing at Semipalatinsk Test Site, Kazakhstan, on the Population in Semipalatinsk Oblast (Semipalatinsk Follow-Up)," 2002; and K. N. Apsalikov et al., "Analiz i retrospektivnaia otsenka rezul'tatov tsitogeneticheskih obsledovanii naseleniia Kazakhstana, podvergavshegosia radiatsionnomu vozdeistviiu v rezul'tate ispytanii iadernogo oruzhiia na Semipalatinskom poligone, i ih potomkov" [The analysis and retrospective evaluation of the cytogenic studies of Kazakhstan's population exposed to radiation as a result of nuclear weapons testing at Semipalatinsk Polygon and of their descendants], *Mediko-biologicheskie problemy zhiznedeiatel'nosti* 1, no. 9 (2013): 42–48.

44. "Some Comparative Whole-Body Radiation Doses and Their Effects," World Nuclear Association, http://www.world-nuclear.org/uploadedFiles/org/WNA/Publications/Nuclear_Information/pocket_guide_radiation.pdf.

45. "Primenenie perechnia zabolevanii."

46. Author's interview with Talgat Muldagaliev, Semey, 2020.

47. The following section is based on author's interviews with Baian and Muratkali, Karaul, 2019–2020.

48. The following section is based on author's interviews with Bolatbek Baltabek, Sarzhal, 2019–2020.

49. The following section is based on author's interviews with Baltabek.

50. Milana Guzeeva, "Doza ostaetsia navsegda" [Dose stays forever], *Vremia*, August 14, 2019, https://time.kz/articles/risk/2019/08/14/doza-ostayotsya-navsegda.

51. Guzeeva, "Doza ostaetsia navsegda."

BIBLIOGRAPHY

ARCHIVAL SOURCES

Archive of the President of the Republic of Kazakhstan
(Almaty, Kazakhstan)

Cable from the Embassy of the Republic of Kazakhstan in Washington, DC, to the Foreign Minister Tokayev, written by Bolat Nurgaliev, October 29, 1996, f. 75H, o. 1, d. 2624, Archive of the President of the Republic of Kazakhstan.

Decree of the Council of Ministers of the USSR on speeding up economic and social development in Semipalatinsk Oblast; from the Council of Ministers of the Kazakh SSR to the President of the Kazakh SSR Nazarbayev N. A., signed by the chairman of the Council U. Karamanov, July 27, 1990, f. 7, o. 1, d. 88, Archive of the President of the Republic of Kazakhstan.

Deputy Chair of the State Committee of the Russian Federation on Economic Cooperation with CIS (M. Khusnutdinov) to the Council of Ministers of the Republic of Kazakhstan, revised draft of Russia-Kazakhstan agreement, December 23, 1993. The Council of Ministers sent it to the Atomic Energy Agency (Vladimir Shkolnik) and the Ministry of Defense (Sagadat Nurmagambetov) and the Ministry of Foreign Affairs (Tuleitai Suleimenov), f. 75H, o. 1, d. 602, Archive of the President of the Republic of Kazakhstan.

Document from f. 5H, o. 1, d. 3376, Archive of the President of the Republic of Kazakhstan.

Documents on preparation and results of the visit of Strobe Talbott, the plenipotentiary ambassador and special coordinator for CIS, to Almaty, September 11–12, 1993, Archive of the President of the Republic of Kazakhstan.

Draft letter from Nazarbayev to James Baker, March 1992, f. 5H, o. 1, d. 1303, Archive of the President of the Republic of Kazakhstan.

"Informatsciia nachal'nika UKGB pri Sovete Ministrov Kazakhskoi SSR po Semipalatinskoi obl. M. Dzhandil'dinova pervomu sekretariu Semipalatinskogo obkoma KP Kazakhstana M. P. Karpenko ob otritsatel'noi reaktsii naseleniia na atomnye ispytania" [Information from the chief of the department of KGB at the Council of Minister of

Kazakh SSR M. Dzhandil'dinov on the Semipalatinsk Oblast for the First Secretary of Semipalatinsk Oblast Executive Committee of Kazakhstan's Communist Party M. P. Karpenko on the population's negative reaction to nuclear tests], August 19, 1966, Semipalatinsk, secret, signed by Dzhandil'dinov, f. 708, o. 36/1, d. 4, 166–176, Archive of the President of the Republic of Kazakhstan.

"Informatsiia o press-konferentsii, sostoiavsheisia pered otkrytiem mezhdunarodnogo kongressa 'Izbirateli mira protiv iadernogo oruzhiia,' sozdannogo po initsiative antiiadernogo dvizheniia 'Nevada-Semipalatinsk' i mezhdunarodnoi organizatsii 'Vrachi mira za predotvrashchenie iadernoi voiny'" [Information on the press conference held on the eve of the International Congress of International Voters for the Prevention of Nuclear War Established on the Initiative of the Antinuclear Movement Nevada-Semipalatinsk and the International Organization of International Physicians for the Prevention of Nuclear War], May 24, 1990, f. 7, o. 1, d. 156, 24–25, Archive of the President of the Republic of Kazakhstan.

"Kazakhstan: 'Missing' HEU, October 26, 1996," PM Press Guidance, f. 75H, o. 1, d. 2624, Archive of the President of the Republic of Kazakhstan.

Kazakhstan's government commission, Akt Proverki materialov o kolichestve iadernyh vzryvov, provedennyh na Semipalatinskom iadernom poligone, c 1949 g. po 1989 g. [A record of inspection of materials on the quantity of nuclear explosions conducted at the Semipalatinsk Nuclear Polygon, 1949–1989], February 28, 1992, f. 5H, o. 1, d. 1020a, Archive of the President of the Republic of Kazakhstan.

Letter from the Acting General Director of the National Nuclear Center of the Republic of Kazakhstan Sh. T. Tukhvatullin addressed to the Chief of the Main Military-Medical Department of the Russian Federation General-Lieutenant I. Chizh, December 12, 1993, f. 5H, o. 1, d. 2017, Archive of the President of the Republic of Kazakhstan.

Letter from the Acting Minister of Health of the Republic of Kazakhstan E. K. Argymbaev addressed to the Minister of Defense of the Republic of Kazakhstan General S. N. Nurmagambetov and Kazakhstan's State Counselor K. Suleimenov, January 21, 1994, f. 5H, o. 1, d. 2017, Archive of the President of the Republic of Kazakhstan.

Letter from Akezhan Kazhegeldin, 1993, f. 5H, o. 2, d. 351, Archive of the President of the Republic of Kazakhstan.

Letter from the Chief of the Main Military-Medical Department of the Russian Federation General-Lieutenant I. Chizh addressed to the General Director of the National Nuclear Center of the Republic of Kazakhstan G. A. Batyrbekov, November 20, 1993, f. 5H, o. 1, d. 2017, Archive of the President of the Republic of Kazakhstan.

Letter from the Deputy Chairman of the Government of the Russian Federation S. Shahrai addressed to the Prime Minister of the Republic of Kazakhstan S. Tereshchenko, April 29, 1994, f. 5H, o. 1, d. 2017, Archive of the President of the Republic of Kazakhstan.

Letter from the Deputy Minister of Foreign Affairs of the Republic of Kazakhstan K. Zhigalov addressed to the Cabinet of Ministers of the Republic of Kazakhstan, February 21, 1994, f. 5H, o. 1, d. 2017, Archive of the President of the Republic of Kazakhstan.

Letter from the General Director of the National Nuclear Center of the Republic of Ka-zakhstan G. A. Batyrbekov addressed to the Main Military-Medical Department of the Russian Federation, October 21, 1993, f. 5H, o. 1, d. 2017, Archive of the President of the Republic of Kazakhstan.

Letter from General-Lieutenant Yuri Konovalenko to the President of the Republic of Kazakhstan Nursultan Nazarbayev, December 28, 1992, f. 5H, o. 1, d. 2017, Archive of the President of the Republic of Kazakhstan.

Letter from James Baker to Nazarbayev, f. 5H, o. 1, d. 1303, Archive of the President of the Republic of Kazakhstan.

Letter from the Minister of Ecology and Bioresources of the Republic of Kazakhstan S. A. Medvedev addressed to the Cabinet of Ministers of the Republic of Kazakh-stan, July 13, 1994, f. 5H, o. 1, d. 2017, Archive of the President of the Republic of Kazakhstan.

Letter from the Minister of Foreign Affairs of the Republic of Kazakhstan T. Suleimenov to President Nazarbayev, December 25, 1992, 5H-1-849, 79, Archive of the President of the Republic of Kazakhstan.

Letter from the Minister of Foreign Affairs of the Republic of Kazakhstan T. Suleimenov to President Nazarbayev, "K pozitscii Kazakhstana o prisoedinenii k DNIaO" [On Kazakhstan's position on NPT adherence], April 13, 1992, f. 5H, o. 1, d. 1303, Archive of the President of the Republic of Kazakhstan.

Letter from the Minister of Foreign Affairs of the Republic of Kazakhstan T. Suleimenov to President Nazarbayev, October 1993, f. 5H, o. 1, d. 2192, 5–6, Archive of the Presi-dent of the Republic of Kazakhstan.

Letter from the Minister of Health of the Republic of Kazakhstan V. Deviatko addressed to the Cabinet of Ministers of the Republic of Kazakhstan, with a copy to the Agency on Atomic Energy of the Republic of Kazakhstan, July 5, 1994, f. 5H, o. 1, d. 2017, Ar-chive of the President of the Republic of Kazakhstan.

Letter from Oumirserik Kasenov to Tulegen Zhukeev, "On Possibility of Creating an NWFZ in Central Asia," October 3, 1994, Archive of the President of the Republic of Kazakhstan.

Letter from President Bush to President Nazarbayev, December 26, 1991, f. 5H, o. 1, d. 1361, Archive of the President of the Republic of Kazakhstan.

Letter from the Prime Minister of the Republic of Kazakhstan S. Tereshchenko ad-dressed to the Chairman of the Council of Ministers of the Russian Federation V. S. Chernomyrdin, December 24, 1993, f. 5H, o. ½, d. 2818, Archive of the President of the Republic of Kazakhstan.

Letter from the Prime Minister of the Republic of Kazakhstan S. Tereshchenko ad-dressed to the Chairman of the Council of Ministers-Government of the Russian Federation V. S. Chernomyrdin, March 2, 1994, f. 5H, o. 1, d. 2017, Archive of the President of the Republic of Kazakhstan.

Letter from S. Tereshchenko, Prime Minister of the Republic of Kazakhstan, to S. Ab-dildin, Chair of the Supreme Soviet, November 30, 1992, f. 5H, o. 1, d. 1958, Archive of the President of the Republic of Kazakhstan.

Letter from V. Shkolnik, General Director of Atomic Energy Commission to G. A. Abil-siitov, Deputy Prime Minister, April 19, 1993, Archive of the President of the Republic of Kazakhstan.

Letter from William Courtney to the Ministry of Foreign Affairs of the Republic of Kazakh-stan, Documents on preparation and results of the visit of Strobe Talbott, the plenipo-tentiary ambassador and special coordinator for CIS, to Almaty, September 11–12, 1993, Department of Americas and Europe, Ministry of Foreign Affairs of the Republic of Kazakhstan, 75-H-1, 441, Archive of the President of the Republic of Kazakhstan.

Memorandum, Council of Ministers of the Kazakh SSR to the President of the Kazakh SSR Nazarbayev N. A., signed by the chairman of the Council U. Karamanov, July 27, 1990, f. 7, o. 1, d. 88, Archive of the President of the Republic of Kazakhstan.

Memorandum from Yu. Sheiko, deputy head of the socioeconomic section of the Cen-tral Committee of the Kazakhstan Communist Party, March 1, 1989, Archive of the President of the Republic Kazakhstan.

Memorandum from the Ministry of Foreign Affairs of the Republic of Kazakhstan to President Nazarbayev, November 23, 1994, f. 5H, o. 1, d. 3806, Archive of the Presi-dent of the Republic of Kazakhstan.

"On the Results of U.S. Vice President Al Gore's Visit to Kazakhstan," memorandum from Gani Kassymov to President Nazarbayev, f. 5H, o. 1, d. 3577, 3–8, Archive of the President of the Republic of Kazakhstan.

Open Statement to the USSR Supreme Soviet and Kazakhstan's Supreme Soviet, signed by O. Suleimenov, S. Muratbekov, D. Snegin, K. Myrzaliev, February 25, 1989, Ar-chive of the President of the Republic of Kazakhstan.

"Pis'mo pervogo sekretaria Semipalatinskogo obkoma KP Kazakhstana, narodnogo deputata SSSR K. B. Boztaeva Prezidentu Kazakhskoi SSR N. A. Nazarbayevu po vo-prosu Semipalatinskogo iadernogo poligona" [Letter from the First Secretary of the Semipalatinsk Oblast Committee of Kazakhstan's Communist Party, USSR People's Deputy K. B. Boztaev to the President of the Kazakh SSR N. A. Nazarbayev on the Semipalatinsk Nuclear Polygon], April 29, 1990, f. 708, o. 140, d. 78, 1–5, Archive of the President of the Republic of Kazakhstan.

"Pis'mo rukovoditelei soiuznykh ministerstv A. I. Burnaziana i E. P. Slavskogo pervomu sekretariu TsK KP Kazakhstana D. A. Kunaevu o bezopasnosti dlia naseleniia po-sledstvii provedeniia eksperimental'nyh vzryvov" [Letter from the Soviet ministers A. I. Burnazian and E. P. Slavskii to the First Secretary of the Central Committee of Kazakhstan's Communist Party D. A. Kunaev on the safety of experimental explo-sions for the population], February 8–9, 1965, f. 708, o. 36/1, d. 3, 113–14, Archive of the President of the Republic of Kazakhstan.

Report of the America Desk of Kazakhstan's MFA on work completed in 1993, 75-H-1, 430, Archive of the President of the Republic of Kazakhstan.

"Spravka po ugolovnomu delu v otnoshenii komandira v/ch 52605 general-leitenanta Konovalenko Yu. V." [Memorandum on the criminal case against the Commander of the military unit Yu. V. Konovalenko], signed by A. F. Dudkin, Deputy Military Prosecutor of the Republic of Kazakhstan and N. Tlemissov, Chief of the Defense

Section of the Presidential Administration and the Council of Ministers of the Republic of Kazakhstan, Archive of the President of the Republic of Kazakhstan.

Transcript of the conversation between President Nazarbayev and US Ambassador William Courtney, Almaty, July 18, 1993, transcribed by Gizzatov, Archive of the President of the Republic of Kazakhstan.

Transcript of the main contents of the conversation with Strobe Talbott, the special coordinator for CIS and plenipotentiary ambassador, June 9, 1993, Almaty, Kazakhstan, Archive of the President of the Republic of Kazakhstan.

Transcript of the meeting between President of Kazakhstan N. Nazarbayev and Strobe Talbott, the special coordinator for CIS and plenipotentiary ambassador, September 12, 1993, Archive of the President of the Republic of Kazakhstan.

Ustinov, A. "O mitinge obshchestvennosti g. Alma-Aty v konferents-zale Soiuza Pisatelei Kazakhstana 28 fevralia 1989 goda" [On the public rally in Alma-Ata in the conference hall of Kazakhstan's writers' union on February 28, 1989], internal memo, Central Committee of Kazakhstan's Communist Party, Archive of the President of the Republic of Kazakhstan.

"Vyvody mezhvedomstvennoi komissii, obrazovannoi Minzdravom SSSR v sootvetstvii s rasporiazheniem zamestitelia predsedatelia Soveta Ministrov SSSR" [Conclusions by the interagency commission created by the USSR Ministry of Health by the decree of the Deputy Chairman of the USSR Council of Ministers], signed by the correspondent member of the USSR Academy of Medical Scientists USSR Professor A. F. Tsyb, f. 708, o. 139, d. 1718, 41–44, Archive of the President of the Republic of Kazakhstan.

Center for Modern History Documentation of Eastern Kazakhstan (Semey, Kazakhstan)

"Informatsiia glavnogo vracha radiologicheskogo dispansera MZ SSSR, kandidata meditsinskih nauk B. I. Guseva o radiatsionno-gigienicheskoi obstanovke na territoriiah, prilegaiushchih k iadernomu poligonu, sostoianii zdorov'ia liudei, podvergavshihsia oblucheniiu ioniziruiushchih izluchenii v real'nyh usloviiah nazemnyh i vozdushnyh vzryvov (1949–1965 gg.)" [Information of the chief doctor of the USSR Ministry of Health's Radiological Clinic, candidate of medical sciences B. I. Gusev on the radiological-hygienic situations on the territories in the vicinity of the Nuclear Polygon, health of the residents exposed to ionizing radiation during ground and air explosions], September 6, 1990, Center for Modern History Documentation of Eastern Kazakhstan.

"Informatsiia pervogo sekretaria Semipalatinskogo obkoma partii, narodnogo deputata SSSR K. B. Boztaeva v Verhovnyi Sovet SSSR A. I. Luk'ianovu o destabilizatsii politicheskoi obstanovki v Semipalatinskoi oblasti" [Information of the First Secretary of the Semipalatinsk Oblast Committee of the Communist Party, USSR People's Deputy K. B. Boztaev for the USSR Supreme Soviet for the attention of A. I. Lukianov on the destabilization of political situation in Semipalatinsk Oblast], June

14, 1990, f. 103, o. 73, d. 21, 99–101, Center for Modern History Documentation of Eastern Kazakhstan.

"Informatsiia zaveduiushchei oblzdravotdelom Semipalatinskogo oblispolkoma F. Ab-dykhalykovoi sekretariu Semipalatinskogo obkoma KP Kazakhstana M. P. Karpenko ob obnaruzhenii povyshennogo gamma-fona i vypadeniia radioaktivnyh produktov vzryva" [Information from the head of the health unit of the Semipalatinsk Oblast Executive Committee of Kazakhstan's Communist Party F. Abdykhalykova to the Secretary of Semipalatinsk Oblast Committee of Kazakhstan's Communist Party M. P. Karpenko on the detection of elevated gamma- levels and post-explosion radioactive fallout], dated after January 21, 1965, f. 103, o. 73, d. 12, 44–45, Center for Modern History Documentation of Eastern Kazakhstan.

"Iz zaiavleniya zhitelia sela Karaul Abaiskogo raiona T. Sliambekova invalida Velikoi Otechestvennoi Voiny sekretariu Semipalatinskogo obkoma kompartii Kazakh-stana K. B. Boztaevu o provedenii iadernyh vzryvov na SIIaP" [From a letter of the resident of Karaul of Abaiskii raion T. Sliambekov—World War II veteran—to the Secretary of the Semipalatinsk Oblast Executive Committee of Kazakhstan's Com-munist Party Boztaev about the nuclear explosions at the Semipalatinsk Nuclear Testing Site], May 29, 1988, f. 103, o. 21, d. 73, 31–35, Center of Modern History Doc-umentation of Eastern Kazakhstan.

Letter from B. N. Ledenev (Ministry of Medium Machine-Making), I. N. Gureev (com-mander of the military division 52605), M. I. Voskoboinikov (12th Main Directorate of the Soviet Ministry of Defense), and Yu. P. Makshakov (3rd Main Directorate of the Soviet Ministry of Health) to the First Secretary of Semipalatinsk Oblast Com-mittee of Kazakhstan's Communist Party M. P. Karpenko, August 23, 1962, f. 103, o. 12, d. 73, 43, Center for Modern History Documentation of Eastern Kazakhstan.

Letter from M. Karpenko to First Secretary of the Central Committee of Kazakhstan's Communist Party D. A. Kunaev, August 25, 1962, f. 103, o. 12, d. 73, 40–41, Center for Modern History Documentation of Eastern Kazakhstan.

Letter from M. Karpenko to First Secretary of Kazakhstan's Communist Party D. A. Kunaev on supplying the population of Semipalatinsk with dwelling, August 18, 1962, f. 103, o. 12, d. 73, 45–47, Center for Modern History Documentation of Eastern Kazakhstan.

Memorandum written by Fomichev, head of the special unit of the KGB, August 23, 1962, f. 103, o. 12, d. 73, 42, Center for Modern History Documentation of Eastern Kazakhstan.

"Obrashchenie vrachei Semipalatinskoi oblasti k ministru zdravoohraneniia SSSR E. I. Chazovu o vliianii podzemnyh iadernyh ispytanii na zdorov'e liudei" [Appeal of doctors from the Semipalatinsk Oblast to the USSR Minister of Health E. I. Chazov on the impact of underground nuclear tests on population health], May 1989, f. 387, o. 7, d. 941, 36–37, Center for Modern History Documentation of Eastern Kazakhstan.

"Poiasnitel'naya zapiska zamestitelia predsedatelia ispolkoma Zhanasemeiskogo raion-nogo soveta narodnyh deputatov B. Golintseva v Semipalatinskii oblastnoi sovet

narodnyh deputatov ob ushcherbe, nanesennom hoziaistvam i naseleniiu Zhanasemeiskogo raiona v rezul'tate ispytanii na SIIaP" [Explanatory note of the deputy
chairman of the Executive Committee of Zhanasemei Raion Soviet of People's Deputies B. Golintsev to Semipalatinsk Oblast Soviet of People's Deputies on the damage
from nuclear tests inflicted on households and population], June 7, 1990, f. 771, o. 8,
d. 1075, 2–4, Center for Modern History Documentation of Eastern Kazakhstan.
"Rekomendatsii nauchno-prakticheskoi konferentsii 'Zdorov'ye naseleniia i ekologicheskaia obstanovka v g. Semipalatinske i Semipalatinskoi obl. Kazakhskoi SSR"
[Recommendations from the scientific-practical conference "Population Health and
Ecological Situation in Semipalatinsk and Semipalatinsk Oblast"], Semipalatinsk,
July 17–19, 1989, f. 409, o. 12, d. 1807, 1–10, Center for Modern History Documentation of Eastern Kazakhstan.
"Spravka kollektiva vrachei dispansera #4 sekretariu Semipalatinskogo obkoma KP Kazakhstana M. A. Suzhikovu o radiologicheskoi obstanovke oblasti i ee vliianiia na
liudei" [Memorandum of the staff doctors of the Dispensary #4 for the Secretary of
Semipalatinsk Oblast Committee of Kazakhstan's Communist Party M. A. Suzhikov
on the radiological situation in the Oblast and its impact on the population], top
secret, February 24, 1958, f. 103, o. 73, d. 12, 2–12, Center for Modern History Information of Eastern Kazakhstan.
"Spravka o rabote gruppy nauchnyh sotrudnikov Instituta Biofiziki Akademii meditsinskih nauk SSSR po obsledovaniiu naseleniia Semipalatinskoi obl." [Memorandum
on the work of the scientific staff of the Institute of Biophysics of the USSR Academy
of Health Science on the examination of the population in Semipalatinsk Oblast],
March 1, 1958, Semipalatinsk, top secret, f. 103, o. 73, d. 12, 13–17, Center for Modern
History Documentation of Eastern Kazakhstan.

Archive of the National Academy of Sciences
of the Republic of Kazakhstan

Aldanazarov, A. T., A. N. Butorina, and V. V. Varganov. "Kartina perifiricheskoi krovi u
sel'skohoziaistvennyh zhivotnyh (korov i ovets) v nekotoryh raionah tsentral'nogo
Kazakhstana (po dannym kompleksnoi ekspeditscii 1959 g.)" [An overview of periphery blood in livestock (cows and sheep) in some areas of central Kazakhstan
(data from the 1959 expedition)]. In *Radioaktivnost' vneshnei sredy i sostoianie
zdorov'ia naseleniia i selskohoziaistvennyh zhivotnyh v tsentral'nom Kazakhstane* [Ra-
dioactivity of environment and the health of population and livestock in central
Kazakhstan], ed. A. T. Aldanazarov and Kh. N. Kadybaeva, vol. 5. Almaty: Institute
of Regional Pathology, 1960.
Aldanazarov, A. T., Yu. I. Toropkina, and V. V. Varganov. "Sostoianie soprotivliaemosti kozhnyh kapiliarov u ovets v otdel'nyh hoziaistvah Severo-Vostochnoi zony
Kazakhstana" [Resistence of skin capillaries in sheep in some areas of northeast
Kazakhstan]. In *Radioaktivnost' vneshnei sredy i sostoianie zdorov'ia naseleniia i selskohoziaistvennyh zhivotnyh v tsentral'nom Kazakhstane* [Radioactivity of environment and the health of population and livestock in central Kazakhstan], ed. A. T.

Aldanazarov and Kh. N. Kadybaeva, vol. 5. Almaty: Institute of Regional Pathology, 1960.

Alekseev, E. N. "Beta-aktivnost' zhilyh pomeshchenii v poselkah Shchadrinsk, Tel'mana, Kainar i Abai" [Beta-activity of dwelling in the settlements of Shchadrinsk, Tel'mana, Kainar and Abai]. In *Radioaktivnost' vneshnei sredy sostoianie zdorov'ia naseleniia i selskohoziaistvennyh zhivotnyh v tsentral'nom Kazakhstane* [Radioactivity of environment and the health of population and livestock in central Kazakhstan], ed. E. N. Alekseev and S. A. Akkerman, vol. 1. Almaty: Institute of Regional Pathology, 1960.

Alekseev, E. N. "Radioaktivnoe zagriaznenie rastitel'nosti v obsledovannyh raionah" [Radioactive contamination of vegetation in examined areas]. In *Radioaktivnost' vneshnei sredy i sostoianie zdorov'ia naseleniia i selskohoziaistvennyh zhivotnyh v tsentral'nom Kazakhstane*, ed. E. N. Alekseev and S. A. Akkerman, vol. 1. Almaty: Institute of Regional Pathology, 1960.

Atchabarov, B. A., T. Kh. Aitbaev, Zh. A. Khairushev, and A. L. Pitiushin. "Opyt klinicheskogo izucheniia stareniia" [Experience in clinical study of aging]. In *Radioaktivnost' vneshnei sredy i sostoianie zdorov'ia naseleniia i selskohoziaistvennyh zhivotnyh v tsentral'nom Kazakhstane* [Radioactivity of environment and the health of population and livestock in central Kazakhstan], ed. A. S. Sokolova and V. S. Mashkevich, vol. 4. Almaty: Institute of Regional Pathology, 1960.

Atchabarov, B. A., and S. A. Peisakh. "Khronicheskaia nedostatochnost' golovnogo mozga" [Chronic brain deficiency]. In *Radioaktivnost' vneshnei sredy i sostoianie zdorov'ia naseleniia i selskohoziaistvennyh zhivotnyh v tsentral'nom Kazakhstane* [Radioactivity of environment and the health of population and livestock in central Kazakhstan], ed. E. A. Khairushev and S. A. Peisakh, vol. 3. Almaty: Institute of Regional Pathology, 1961.

Bul'vakhter, Ia. L., and A. A. Karpov. "Nekotorye dannye radiokhimicheskih issledovanii pochvy, rastenii i organov zhivotnyh" [Data on radiochemical studies of soil, vegetation, and animal organs]. In *Radioaktivnost' vneshnei sredy i sostoianie zdorov'ia naseleniia i selskohoziaistvennyh zhivotnyh v tsentral'nom Kazakhstane* [Radioactivity of environment and the health of population and livestock in central Kazakhstan], ed. E. N. Alekseev and S. A. Akkerman, vol. 1, Almaty: Institute of Regional Pathology, 1960.

Kadyrbaeva, Kh. M. "Gistologicheskie issledovaniia vnutrennih organov po materialu ekspeditsii 1959 g." [Histological study of internal organs based on the data from the 1959 expedition]. In *Radioaktivnost' vneshnei sredy i sostoianie zdorov'ia naseleniia i selskohoziaistvennyh zhivotnyh v tscentral'nom Kazakhstane* [Radioactivity of environment and the health of population and livestock in central Kazakhstan], ed. A. T. Aldanazarov and Kh. N. Kadybaeva, vol. 5. Almaty: Institute of Regional Pathology, 1960.

Khairushev, E. A. "Rezul'taty issledovaniia taktil'no-bolevoi chuvstvitel'nosti kozhnogo analizatora" [Research findings of tactile-pain sensitivity of skin analyzer]. In *Radioaktivnost' vneshnei sredy i sostoianie zdorov'ia naseleniia i selskohoziaistvennyh zhivotnyh v tsentral'nom Kazakhstane* [Radioactivity of environment and the health of population and livestock in central Kazakhstan], ed. E. A. Khairushev and S. A. Peisakh, vol. 3. Almaty: Institute of Regional Pathology, 1961.

Makarov, M. A., L. M. Kisseleva, T. N. Sailibaev, S. F. Kurashov, V. M. Makarov, T. V. Gerasenko, "Stressovoe vozdeistvie faktorov okruzhayushchei sredy na chastotu samoubiistv" [Stress impact of environmental factors on suicide frequency] in *Zdorov'ye liudei, prozhivaiushchih v raione prilegaiushchem k Semipalatinskomu poligonu* [Health of residents in the vicinity of Semipalatinsk Polygon], collection of articles, vol. 2, Semipalatinsk, 1994.

Makarov, M. A., T. N. Sailibaev, L. M. Kisseleva, S. F. Kurashov, T. V. Gerasenko, and V. M. Makarov. "Sravnitel'naia kharakteristika suicidov po raionam s preimushchestvennym prozhivaniem kazakhskogo naseleniia v Semipalatinskom regione" [Comparative characteristics of suicides in the areas in the Semipalatinsk region with a predominantly Kazakh population]. In *Zdorov'ye liudei, prozhivaiushchih v raione prilegaiushchem k Semipalatinskomu Poligonu* [Health of residents in the vicinity of Semipalatinsk Polygon], collection of articles, vol. 2, Semipalatinsk, 1994.

Makashev, K. K., and A. S. Sokolov. "Materialy radiologicheskogo obsledovaniia nekotoryh raionov Kazakhstana" [Data of the radiological examination in some areas of Kazakhstan]. In *Radioaktivnost' vneshnei sredy i sostoianie zdorov'ia naseleniia i selskohoziaistvennyh zhivotnyh v tsentral'nom Kazakhstane* [Radioactivity of environment and the health of population and livestock in central Kazakhstan], vol. 2. Almaty: Institute of Regional Pathology, 1958.

Moshkevich, V. S. "Kraevye osobennosti patologii v LOR organah u zhitelei tsentral'nogo Kazakhstana" [Regional pathologies of respiratory organs among residents of central Kazakhstan]. In *Radioaktivnost' vneshnei sredy i sostoianie zdorov'ia naseleniia i selskohoziaistvennyh zhivotnyh v tsentral'nom Kazakhstane* [Radioactivity of environment and the health of population and livestock in central Kazakhstan], ed. A. S. Sokolova and V. S. Mashkevich, vol. 4. Almaty: Institute of Regional Pathology, 1960.

Murzamadiev, A. "Issledovanie tsentral'noi nervnoi sistemy ovets i sobak (po materialam ekspeditsii za 1959 g.)" [Study of central nervous system in sheep and dogs (data from the 1959 expedition)]. In *Radioaktivnost' vneshnei sredy i sostoianie zdorov'ia naseleniia i selskohoziaistvennyh zhivotnyh v tsentral'nom Kazakhstane* [Radioactivity of environment and the health of population and livestock in central Kazakhstan], ed. A. T. Aldanazarov and Kh. N. Kadybaeva, vol. 5. Almaty: Institute of Regional Pathology, 1960.

Peisakh, S. A., and I. I. Velikanov. "Nevrologicheskie kharakteristiki obsledovannogo naseleniia nekotoryh raionov Semipalatinskoi i Pavlodarskoi oblastei" [Neurological characteristics of the studied populations in some areas of Semipalatinsk and Pavlodar Oblasts]. In *Radioaktivnost' vneshnei sredy i sostoianie zdorov'ia naseleniia i selskohoziaistvennyh zhivotnyh v tsentral'nom Kazakhstane* [Radioactivity of environment and the health of population and livestock in central Kazakhstan], ed. E. A. Khairushev and S. A. Peisakh, vol. 3. Almaty: Institute of Regional Pathology, 1961.

Sokolova, A. S., S. N. Nugmanov, and Kh. D. Abtieva. "Kharakteristika ginekologicheskih zabolevanii u obsledovannyh zhenshchin" [Characteristics of gynecological diseases among examined women]. In *Radioaktivnost' vneshnei sredy i sostoianie zdorov'ia naseleniia i selskohoziaistvennyh zhivotnyh v tsentral'nom Kazakhstane* [Radioactivity of environment and the health of population and livestock in central Kazakhstan], ed. A. S. Sokolova and V. S. Mashkevich, vol. 4. Almaty: Institute of Regional Pathology, 1960.

Sokolova, A. S., S. N. Nugmanov, and Kh. D. Abtieva. "Rezul'taty akushersko-geneticheskogo obsledovaniia nekotoryh raionov tsentral'nogo Kazakhstana" [Results of obstetric-genetic examinations in some areas of central Kazakhstan]. In *Radioaktivnost' vneshnei sredy i sostoianie zdorov'ia naseleniia i selskohoziaistvennyh zhivotnyh v tsentral'nom Kazakhstane* [Radioactivity of environment and the health of population and livestock in central Kazakhstan], ed. A. S. Sokolova and V. S. Mashkevich, vol. 4. Almaty: Institute of Regional Pathology, 1960.

George H. W. Bush Presidential Archives and Library (College Station, Texas)

"Agreement on Trade Relations between the United States and Kazakhstan," the White House, May 19, 1992, George H. W. Bush Presidential Library and Museum.

"America and the Collapse of the Soviet Empire: What Has to Be Done," address by Secretary of State James A. Baker III at Princeton University, December 12, 1991, George H. W. Bush Presidential Library and Museum.

"Baker-Yeltsin Meeting," memorandum from R. Nicholas Burns for Florence E. Gantt, Wilma G. Hall, and Kristen K. Cicio, December 16, 1991, National Security Council, George H. W. Bush Presidential Library and Museum.

"Bilateral Investment Treaty between the United States and the Republic of Kazakhstan," the White House, May 19, 1992, George H. W. Bush Presidential Library and Museum.

Cable from the State Department to the US embassy in Almaty, March 24, 1992, George H. W. Bush Presidential Library and Museum.

"Chronology of the President's Warning to President Gorbachev Concerning a Possible Coup Attempt," Nick Burns for General Scowcroft, National Security Council, November 13, 1991, including a memorandum of telephone conversation between President Bush and Mikhail Gorbachev, President of the Soviet Union, June 21, 1991, the Oval Office, George H. W. Bush Presidential Library and Museum.

"Codel Nunn/Lugar Meeting with Kazakhstan President Nazarbayev, November 21, 1992," cable from the US embassy in Almaty, written by William Courtney, November 1992, George H. W. Bush Presidential Library and Museum.

"The Coup Two Months Later," cable from the US embassy in Moscow, written by Ambassador Strauss, October 1991, George H. W. Bush Presidential Library and Museum.

"Defining American Interests in Kazakhstan," cable from the US embassy in Almaty, written by William Courtney, February 1992, George H. W. Bush Presidential Library and Museum.

"Disarmament Visits to Alma Ata: Update," cable from the US embassy in Almaty, no date available, George H. W. Bush Presidential Library and Museum.

"FAA Taped Message from Aeroflot a/c re: Farewell Statement by N. Nazarbayev President of Kazakhstan," May 23, 1992, memorandum from Tony Baker, Senior Duty Officer, White House Situation Room for General Scowcroft and Admiral Howe.

"Initial Response to Message from President," cable from the US embassy in Almaty, March 18, 1992, George H. W. Bush Presidential Library and Museum.

"Kazakh President Nazarbayev Comments on Nuclear Weapons Issues," cable from the US embassy in Almaty, March 3, 1992, George H. W. Bush Presidential Library and Museum.

"Kazakh President Nazarbayev on Nuclear Weapons: Comments to . . . in a Meeting Yesterday, . . . Who Debriefed Me," cable from the US embassy in Almaty, written by William Courtney, April 1992, George H. W. Bush Presidential Library and Museum.

"Kazakh Proposal for a Joint Statement in Washington during Nazarbayev Visit," cable from the US embassy in Almaty, May 6, 1992, George H. W. Bush Presidential Library and Museum.

"Kazakhstan as Nuclear State," memorandum from Susan Koch for John Gordon and Daniel Poneman, National Security Council, March 20, 1992, George H. W. Bush Presidential Library and Museum.

"Kazakhstan May Publicly Seek to Enter the NPT as a Nuclear Weapon State," cable from the US embassy in Almaty, written by William Courtney, April 1992, George H. W. Bush Presidential Library and Museum.

"Key Points in Secretary Baker's Meetings in the USSR and the Baltics: September 11–16, 1991," National Security Council, no date, George H. W. Bush Presidential Library and Museum.

"Letters to Presidents Yeltsin, Kravchuk, Nazarbayev, and Shushkevich," memorandum for Brent Scowcroft from Rich Davis and Nicholas Burns, National Security Council, December 27, 1991, George H. W. Bush Presidential Library and Museum.

Memorandum, National Security Council, June 21, 1991, George H. W. Bush Presidential Library and Museum.

Memorandum of conversation, "Luncheon with President Mikhail Gorbachev of the USSR," the White House, July 30, 1991, George H. W. Bush Presidential Library and Museum.

Memorandum of conversation, meeting with President Nursultan Nazarbayev of Kazakhstan, the Oval Office, May 19, 1992, George H. W. Bush Presidential Library and Museum.

Memorandum of telephone conversation between President Bush and President Yeltsin, the Oval Office, December 23, 1991, George H. W. Bush Presidential Library and Museum.

Memorandum of telephone conversation between President Gorbachev and President Bush, December 25, 1991, George H. W. Bush Presidential Library and Museum.

Memorandum of telephone conversation with Prime Minister Brian Mulroney of Canada, Kennebunkport, Maine, August 19, 1991, George H. W. Bush Presidential Library and Museum.

Memorandum of telephone conversation, Telcon with Leck Walesa, President of Poland, the White House, August 19, 1991, George H. W. Bush Presidential Library and Museum.

Memorandum of telephone conversation, Telcon with President Boris Yeltsin of the Republic of Russia, the Oval Office, August 20, 1991, George H. W. Bush Presidential Library and Museum.

Memorandum of telephone conversation, Telcon with President Boris Yeltsin of the Republic of Russia, the White House, December 8, 1991, George H. W. Bush Presidential Library and Museum.

Memorandum of telephone conversation, Telcon with President Mikhail Gorbachev of the USSR, August 21, 1991, Kennebunkport, Maine, George H. W. Bush Presidential Library and Museum.

Memorandum of telephone conversation, Telcon with Vaclav Havel, President of Czechoslovakia, the White House, August 19, 1991, George H. W. Bush Presidential Library and Museum.

Moscow Ostankino TV, February 16, 1992; *Izvestiia*, February 25, 1992 reported by FBIS Trends, June 2, 1992, George H. W. Bush Presidential Library and Museum.

Moscow Ostankino TV, May 24, 1992, from FBIS Trends, June 2, 1992, George H. W. Bush Presidential Library and Museum.

"Nazarbayev Resigns from the Politburo and the CPSU Central Committee, Accusing the Secretariat of Collaborating with the Leaders of the Putsch," Interfax News Agency, August 22, 1991, George H. W. Bush Presidential Library and Museum.

"Nazarbayev Says Kazakhstan Has a Right to Be in the Nuclear Club," cable from the US embassy in Almaty, written by William Courtney, April 23, 1992, George H. W. Bush Presidential Library and Museum.

"The Nazarbayev Visit: Desired Outcomes," National Security Council, 1992, George H. W. Bush Presidential Library and Museum.

"PNI: Nuclear Weapons, the Former Soviet Union, and Independent Republics," memorandum, National Security Council, December 6, 1991, George H. W. Bush Presidential Library and Museum.

"Possible Legal Consequences for a START Agreement," memorandum written by Jo Hunerwadel for the National Security Council, September 6, 1991, George H. W. Bush Presidential Library and Museum.

"Possible Nuclear Weapon Emplaced at Semipalatinsk," cable from the US State Department to the US embassy in Almaty, written by Lawrence Eagleburger, October 1992, George H. W. Bush Presidential Archives and Library.

"President Nazarbayev Interviewed," translation from Russian by FM FBIS, George H. W. Bush Presidential Library and Museum.

"Presidential Event—Nazarbayev," memorandum, March 24, 1992, National Security Council, George H. W. Bush Presidential Library and Museum.

"Readout from the Official Working Visit of President Nazarbayev to Washington, May 18–20, 1992," Secretary of State James Baker, State Department, George H. W. Bush Presidential Library and Museum.

"RLRFE Alma Ata Symposium on Kazakhstan," cable from the US embassy in Almaty, written by William Courtney, April 29, 1992, George H. W. Bush Presidential Library and Museum.

"SSD: Alma Ata Bilateral Sessions," cable from the US embassy in Almaty, November 1992, George H. W. Bush Presidential Library and Museum.

Statement of Secretary Brady on Membership of the New States of the Former Soviet Union in the IMF and the World Bank, January 3, 1992, George H. W. Bush Presidential Library and Museum.

"Trade and Investment Issues with the USSR," Robert A. Mosbacher, Secretary of Commerce, memorandum for Brent Scowcroft, July 12, 1991, George H. W. Bush Presidential Library and Museum.

"U.S. Humanitarian Assistance," the White House, May 19, 1992, George H. W. Bush Presidential Library and Museum.

"U.S.-Kazakhstan OPIC Agreement," the White House, May 19, 1992, George H. W. Bush Presidential Library and Museum.

"U.S. Objectives of Nazarbayev Visit [sent for agency referral]," National Security Council, 1992, George H. W. Bush Presidential Library and Museum.

"U.S. Visit of Kazakh President Nazarbayev," National Security Council memorandum, from the US embassy in Almaty, April 17, 1992, George H. W. Bush Presidential Library and Museum.

William J. Clinton Presidential Library and Museum (Little Rock, Arkansas)

Background briefing by senior administration officials, the White House, February 1994, William J. Clinton Presidential Library and Museum.

INMARSAT Technology Safeguards Agreement, Fact Sheet, White House Press Office, February 16, 1994, William J. Clinton Presidential Library and Museum.

"Meeting with Kazakhstan President Nursultan Nazarbayev," memorandum from Anthony Lake, National Security Council, February 12, 1994, William J. Clinton Presidential Library and Museum.

President Clinton and President Nazarbayev of Kazakhstan in Signing Ceremony and Press Availability, the White House, February 14, 1994, William J. Clinton Presidential Library and Museum.

National Security Archive (Washington, DC)

"Alleged Nuclear Weapons Tests near Semipalatinsk." Central Intelligence Agency, secret, excised copy of information report, April 1, 1957, National Security Archive.

Burr, William, and Hector L. Montford. "The Making of the Limited Test Ban Treaty, 1958–1963," National Security Archive.

Chernyaev, Anatoly Diary, 1991, translated by Anna Melyakov, edited by Svetlana Savranskaya, National Security Archive.

DOD News Briefing: Secretary of Defense William J. Perry et al., November 23, 1994, Nunn-Lugar Collection, National Security Archive.

"Kazakh President Nazarbayev's Visit to U.S.," cable from the US embassy in Almaty, written by William Courtney, April 1992, Nunn-Lugar Collection, National Security Archive.

"Kazakhstan and Nazarbayev Go Public on the Nuclear Issue," cable from the US embassy in Almaty, written by William Courtney, April 29, 1992, Nunn-Lugar Collection, National Security Archive.

"Kazakhstan on the Eve of Nazarbayev's Visit to America," cable from the US embassy in Almaty, May 1992, Nunn-Lugar Collection, National Security Archive.

Newton, D., J. Connery, and P. Wells. "U.S. Experience in the Decommissioning of the BN-350 Fast Breeder Reactor in Kazakhstan," Office of International Nuclear Safety and Cooperation, US Department of Energy, Nunn-Lugar Collection, National Security Archive.

"The Nuclear Issue and Kazakh President Nazarbayev's Visit to Washington," cable from the US embassy in Almaty, written by William Courtney, April 29, 1992, Nunn-Lugar Collection, National Security Archive.

Project Sapphire After-Action Report, Defense Threat Reduction Agency, National Security Archive.

Hoover Institution Library and Archives (Stanford, California)

Decree of the Central Committee of the Communist Party of the Soviet Union, "On the situation in Kazakh SSR in regards to underground nuclear tests at Semipalatinsk Polygon," Secretary of CCCPSU. Kataev collection, 2335, Hoover Institution Library and Archives, Stanford University.

Memorandum on the Soviet-American Negotiations on Limiting and Banning Nuclear Tests, Hoover Institution Library and Archives, Stanford University.

"Ob obstanovke v Kazakhskoi SSR v sviazi s podzemnymi iadernymi vzryvami na Semipalatinskon poligone" [On the situation in the Kazakh SSR in relation to underground nuclear explosions at the Semipalatinsk Polygon], signed by D. Yazov, O. Baklanov, I. Beloussov G. Kolbin, L. Ryabev, and N. Nazarbayev. Kataev collection, 2335, Hoover Institution Library and Archives, Stanford University.

"O voprosah v sviazi s vozobnovleniem Sovetskim Soiuzom iadernyh ispytanii i argumentatsii prichin etogo shaga" [On the issues related to the restart of nuclear testing by the Soviet Union and the argumentation in support of this development], Central Committee of the USSR Communist Party, signed by L. Zaikov, E. Shevardnadze, V. Chebrikov, A. Yakovlev, V. Kataev, box 8, folder 9; Postanovlenie TsK KPSS [Decree of the Central Committee of the Communist Party of the Soviet Union], V. Kataev, box 8, folder 9, Hoover Institution Library and Archives, Stanford University.

John F. Kennedy Presidential Library and Museum (Boston, Massachusetts)

"Commencement Address at American University, June 10, 1963," John F. Kennedy Presidential Library and Museum.

"Nuclear Test Ban Treaty," John F. Kennedy Presidential Library and Museum.

PERIODICALS

Astana Times
Christian Science Monitor
Ekspress-K
European
Guardian
Irtysh
Izbiratel'
Japan Times
Karavan
Kazakhstanskaia Pravda
Kommersant
Krasnaia Zvezda
Kyzylordinskie Vesti
Leninskaia Smena
Los Angeles Times
Megapolis
Medical Post
Moscow News
New York Times
Nezavisimaia Gazeta
Novaia Gazeta
Ogni Alatau
Philadelphia Inquirer
Rudnyi Altai
Sovetskaia Rossiia
Vechernii Almaty
Vremia
Wall Street Journal
Washington Post
Xinhua

PUBLISHED SOURCES

Abai. Public Foundation National Bureau of Translations in Partnership with Cambridge University Press, 2020.

Abishev, Maidan. "Dvizhenie Nevada-Semipalatinsk" [Nevada-Semipalatinsk movement]. *Prostor*, no date available.

Aitken, John. *Nazarbayev and the Making of Kazakhstan: From Communism to Capitalism*. London: Continuum, 2009.

Akchurin, I. A. *Semipalatinskii iadernyi poligon: Sozdanie, stanovlenie, deiatel'nost'* [Semipalatinsk Nuclear Polygon: Creation, development, activity]. Moscow: Ministry of Defense of the Russian Federation, 2007.

Akhtamzian, I. "Iadernyi faktor v Tsentral'noi Azii" [The nuclear factor in Central Asia]. In *Flang SNG. Tsentral'naia Aziia—Kaspii—Kavkaz: vozmozhnosti i vyzovy dlia Rossii* [CIS southern flank. Central Asia—Caspian—Caucasus: Opportunities and challenges for Russia], ed. M. Narinskii and A. Mal'gin. Moscow: Navona, 2005.

Alekseev, V. V. "Vo imia iadernogo shchita strany" [In the name of the country's nuclear shield]. In *Istoriia atomnogo proekta* [History of atomic project], ed. Sergei Davydov, issue 3, 57–75. Moscow: Kurchatovskii Institut, 1995.

Alexander, Catherine. "A Chronotope of Expansion: Resisting Spatio-temporal Limits in a Kazakh Nuclear Town." *Ethnos: Journal of Anthropology* (2020): 1–24.

Apsalikov, K. N., T. Zh. Muldagaliev, T. I. Belikhina, Z. A. Tanatova, and L. B. Kenzhina, "Analiz i retrospektivnaia otsenka rezul'tatov tsitogeneticheskih obsledovanii naseleniia Kazakhstana, podvergavshegosia radiatsionnomu vozdeistviiu v rezul'tate ispytanii iadernogo oruzhiia na Semipalatinskom poligone, i ih potomkov" [The analysis and retrospective evaluation of the cytogenic studies of Kazakhstan's population exposed to radiation as a result of nuclear weapons testing at Semipalatinsk Polygon and of their descendants]. *Mediko-biologicheskie problemy zhiznedeiatel'nosti* 1, no. 9 (2013): 42–48.

Aseev, I. D. "Iadernyi vzryv v mirnyh tsceliah" [Nuclear explosion for peaceful purposes]. In *Istoriia atomnogo proekta* [History of atomic project], ed. Sergei Davydov, issue 4, 193–201. Moscow: Kurchatovskii Institut, 1995.

Atchabarov, B. A. *Zabluzhdeniia, lozh' i istina po voprosu otsenki vliianiia na zdorov'ye liudei ispytaniia atomnogo oruzhiia na Semipalatinskom iadernom poligone* [Fallacies, lies, and truth in assessing impact of nuclear weapons testing at Semipalatinsk Nuclear Polygon on population's health]. Almaty: Karzhy-Karazhat, 2002.

Atomnyi proekt SSSR, vol. 2: *Atomnaia bomba, 1945–1954* [USSR atomic project: documents and materials, vol. 2: Atomic bomb, 1945–1954]. Sarov: RFNC and VNIIEF, 1999.

Ayazbekov, Anuar. "Kazakhstan's Decision-Making, 1991–92." *Nonproliferation Review* 21, no. 2 (2014): 149–68.

Baker, James A. *The Politics of Diplomacy: Revolution, War, and Peace, 1989–1992.* New York: G. P. Putnam's Sons, 1995.

Balmukhanov, Saim B. "The Semipalatinsk Nuclear Test Site—Through My Own Eyes." DTRA Technical Report (July 2014).

Blair, Bruce. *The Logic of Accidental Nuclear War.* Washington, DC: Brookings Institution Press, 2011.

BN-350 Decommissioning Plan for International Peer, K-513 ISTC Project. "Introduction."

Bonnel, Victoria E., Ann Cooper, and Gregory Freidin. *Russia at the Barricades: Eyewitness Accounts of the August 1991 Coup.* Abingdon-on-Thames: Routledge, 2015.

Boztaev, Keshrim. *29 avgusta* [August 29th]. Almaty: Atamura, 1998.

———. *Sindrom Kainara* [Kainar syndrome]. Almaty, 1994.

Brietich, Samantha. "The Crimea Model: Will Russia Annex the Northern Region of Kazakhstan?" *Modern Diplomacy*, October 16, 2014, https://moderndiplomacy.

eu/2014/10/16/the-crimea-model-will-russia-annex-the-northern-region-of-kazakhstan/.

Burkitbayev, Mukhambetkali, and Jukka Lehto, eds. *Environmental Radioactivity in Central Asia*. Almaty: Kazakh National University, 2012.

Cameron, Sarah. *The Hungry Steppe: Famine, Violence, and the Making of the Kazakh Steppe*. Ithaca, NY: Cornell University Press, 2018.

Carter, Ashton B., and William J. Perry. *Preventive Defense: A New Security Strategy for America*. Washington, DC: Brookings Institution, 2000.

Carter, Ashton, Kurt Campbell, Steven E. Miller, and Charles E. Zraket. *Soviet Nuclear Fission: Control of the Nuclear Arsenal in a Disintegrating Soviet Union*. Cambridge, MA: Belfer Center for Science and International Affairs, Harvard University, 1991.

Case, R., F. Crane, A. Atkins, J. Mason, D. Olsen, V. Bolgarin, V. Aniken, A. Bushmakin, N. Atsharbarov, G. Tittemore, J. K. Halbig, J. K. Sprinkle Jr., P. Staples, S. Buck, R. Parker, S. Klosterbuer, P. Reass, C. Horley, R. Brad Steele, W. Mitchell, and M. Barham. "Nuclear Material, Control, and Accounting Program at the Mangyshlak Atomic Energy Complex, Aktau, Republic of Kazakhstan." Albuquerque, NM: Sandia National Laboratories, 1998.

Chernyaev, Anatoly S. *My Six Years with Gorbachev*. University Park: Pennsylvania University Press, 2000.

Cochran, Thomas B., and Robert S. Norris. *Making the Russian Bomb: From Stalin to Yeltsin*. Boulder, CO: Westview Press, 1995.

Daughtry, Emily E. "Forging Partnerships, Preventing Proliferation: A Decade of Cooperative Threat Reduction in Central Asia." In *In the Tracks of Tamerlane: Central Asia's Path to the 21st Century*, ed. Dan Burghart and Theresa Sabonis-Helf, 321–39. Washington, DC: National Defense University, 2004.

Davydov, S. L. "Zadacha, stavshaia delom zhizni" [Task of a lifetime]. In *Istoriia atomnogo proekta* [History of atomic project], ed. Sergei Davydov, issue 2, 159–302. Moscow: Kurchatovskii Institut, 1995.

De Andreis, Marco, and Francesco Calogero. *The Soviet Nuclear Weapon Legacy*. SIPRI Research Report No. 10. Oxford: Oxford University Press, 1995.

Draft Law of the Republic of Kazakhstan, *On Semipalatinsk Nuclear Safety Zone*, 2021, in Russian, Adilet dabatase, https://adilet.zan.kz/rus/docs/P2100000185.

Elegant, Robert. "Fallout: In Kazakhstan, the Human Wreckage of Soviet Nuclear Tests." *National Review* 54, no. 16 (2002): 30–32.

"Estimation of the Baseline Number of Cancers among Marshallese and the Number of Cancers Attributable to Exposure to Fallout from Nuclear Weapons Testing Conducted in the Marshall Islands." Division of Cancer Epidemiology and Genetics, National Cancer Institute, National Institutes of Health, Department of Health and Human Services, 2004, http://marshall.csu.edu.au/Marshalls/html/Radiation/NCI-report.pdf.

Evangelista, Matthew. "The Paradox of State Strength: Transnational Relations, Domestic Structures, and Security Policy in Russia and the Soviet Union." *International Organization* 49, no. 1 (1995): 1–38.

Felton, John. "The Nunn-Lugar Vision: 1992–2002." Washington, DC: Nuclear Threat Initiative, 2002.

Gak, Lesya. "Denuclearization and Ukraine: Lessons for the Future." *Nonproliferation Review* 11, no. 1 (2004): 106–35.

Gift, E. H. National Security Programs Office, Martin Marietta Energy Systems, Inc., Oak Ridge, Tennessee, "Analysis of HEU Samples from the Ulba Metallurgical Plant," revised by A. W. Reidy. US Department of Energy; initially issued in July 1994.

Goodby, James E. *At the Borderline of Armageddon: How American Presidents Managed the Atom Bomb.* New York: Rowman and Littlefield, 2006.

Gorbachev, Mikhail. *The August Coup: The Truth and the Lessons.* New York: Harper Collins, 1991.

Gordeev, K., I. Vasilenko, A. Lebedev, André Bouville, Nickolas Luckyanov, Steven Simon, Y. Stepanov, S. Shinkarev, and Lynn Anspaugh. "Fallout from Nuclear Tests: Dosimetry in Kazakhstan." *Radiation and Environmental Biophysics* 41, no. 1 (March 2002): 61–67.

Gordin, Michael. *Red Cloud at Dawn.* New York: Farrar, Straus and Giroux, 2009.

"Gorodok Kurchatov: Iz proshlogo—v budushchee." *Chelovek, Energiia, Atom* 2, no. 4 (2009): 48–53. Kurchatov: National Nuclear Center.

Gusev, B. I. "Radiatsionno-giginiecheskaia kharakteristika raionov, prilegaiush-chih k Semipalatinskomu ispytatel'nomu Poligonu" [Radiation-hygienic char-acteristics of the districts adjacent to the Semipalatinsk Polygon]. In *Mediko-biologicheskie posledstviia iadernyh ispytanii na Semipalatinskom Poligone* [Medical-biological consequences of nuclear tests at the Semipalatinsk Poly-gon], collection of papers, vol. 5, Ministry of Health of the Republic of Kazakh-stan, Semipalatinsk, 1994.

Gusliarov, Evgenii. "Shto zhe eto bylo togda v poselke Karaul?" [What happened back then in Karaul village?] *Prostor*, no. 11 (1989): 130–31.

Harahan, Joseph P. *With Courage and Persistence: Eliminating and Securing Weapons of Mass Destruction with the Nunn-Lugar Cooperative Threat Reduction Programs.* Washington, DC: Defense Threat Reduction Agency, 2014.

Harrell, Eben, and David Hoffman. *Plutonium Mountain: Inside the 17-Year Mission to Secure a Legacy of Soviet Nuclear Testing.* Managing the Atom Project, Belfer Center. Cambridge, MA: Harvard University, 2013.

Hecker, Siegfried S. "The Semipalatinsk Project: A Trilateral Cooperation to Secure Fis-sile Materials at the Former Soviet Semipalatinsk Nuclear Test Site." In *Doomed to Cooperate: How American and Russian Scientists Joined Forces to Avert Some of the Greatest Post–Cold War Nuclear Dangers*, ed. Siegfried S. Hecker, 1:451–72. Los Ala-mos: Bathtub Row Press, 2016.

Hemberger, Philip H. "The Semipalatinsk Project: A Los Alamos Scientist's Perspective." In *Doomed to Cooperate: How American and Russian Scientists Joined Forces to Avert Some of the Greatest Post–Cold War Nuclear Dangers*, ed. Siegfried S. Hecker, 1:473–80. Los Alamos: Bathtub Row Press, 2016.

Hibbs, Mark. "'Vulnerable' Soviet Nuclear Experts Could Aid Clandestine Weapons Aims." *Nuclear Fuel* (October 28, 1991).

Hoffman, David. *Dead Hand: The Untold Story of the Cold War Arms Race and Its Dangerous Legacy.* New York: Anchor, 2010.

Holloway, David. *Stalin and the Bomb: The Soviet Union and Atomic Energy 1939–1956.* New Haven, CT: Yale University Press, 1994.

Iadernye ispytaniia SSSR: Semipalatinskii poligon [Nuclear tests in the USSR: Semipalatinsk Polygon]. Moscow: Midbioextrem, 1997.

Iakubovskaia, E. L., V. I., Nagibin, and V. P. Suslin. *Semipalatinskii iadernyi poligon: 50 let* [Semipalatinsk Nuclear Polygon: 50 years]. Novosibirsk: Sovetskaia Sibir', 1998.

Ipatkin, I. S. "Metodika KT" [CT methodology]. In *Istoriia atomnogo proekta* [History of atomic project], ed. Sergei Davydov, issue 11, 150–60. Moscow: Kurchatovskii Institut, 1997.

"Istoriia radioekolochigeskih isledovanii, provodimyh NII RMiE v zone vliianiia SIIaP" [History of radioecological studies conducted by the Institute of Radiation Medicine and Ecology in the area affected by the Semipalatinsk Nuclear Testing Polygon], Kurchatov: Institute of Radiation Medicine and Ecology, n.d.

Joint Statement of the Presidents of Kazakhstan, the Russian Federation and the United States of America Regarding the Trilateral Cooperation at the Former Semipalatinsk Test Site, The White House, March 26, 2012, https://obamawhitehouse.archives.gov/the-press-office/2012/03/26/joint-statement-presidents-republic-kazakhstan-russian-federation-and-un.

Kabdrakhmanov, Kairat. *470 bomb v serdtse Kazakhstana* [470 bombs in the heart of Kazakhstan]. Almaty, 1994.

Kadyrzhanov, Kairat. *V pamiati moei . . . rodnym, druz'iam, kollegam* [My memories . . . for loved ones, friends, and colleagues]. Astana: Master PO, 2015.

Kasenov, Oumirserik. *The Fragile Future of the NPT.* Unpublished paper, 1992, copy in author's possession.

———. "Iadernoe oruzhie i bezopasnost' Kazakhstana" [Nuclear weapons and Kazakhstan's security]. *Mysl'*, no. 6 (1992): 25–28.

———. "On the Creation of a Nuclear-Weapon-Free Zone in Central Asia." *Nonproliferation Review* 6, no. 1 (1998): 144–47.

Kasenov, Oumirserik T., Dastan Eleukenov, and Murat Laumulin. "Implementing the CTR Program in Kazakhstan." In *Dismantling the Cold War: U.S. and NIS Perspectives on the Nunn-Lugar Cooperative Threat Reduction Program*, ed. John M. Shields and William C. Potter, 193–207. Cambridge, MA: MIT Press, 1997.

Kashliak, V. N. *Semipalatinskie arabeski* [Semipalatinsk arabesques]. Semey, 2010.

"Kazakhstan Has Completed Disposal of Spent Nuclear Fuel." National Technical Information Service. Moscow, Russia, November 12, 2010.

Kedrov, K. P. "Sluchai ostroi luchevoi bolezni na Semipalatinskom poligone" [A case of acute radiation sickness at Semipalatinsk Polygon]. In *Istoriia atomnogo proekta* [History of atomic project], ed. Sergey Davydov, issue 5. Moscow: Kurchatovskii Institut, 1996.

Kennedy, Robert F. *Thirteen Days: A Memoir of the Cuban Missile Crisis*. New York: W. W. Norton, 1969.

Khariton, Yuli, Viktor Adamskii, and Yuri Smirnov. "The Way It Was." *Bulletin of the Atomic Scientists* 52, no. 6 (November/December 1996): 55.

Khariton, Yuli, and Yuri Smirnov. "The Khariton Version." *Bulletin of the Atomic Scientists* 49, no. 4 (1993): 20–31.

———. *Mify i real'nost' sovetskogo atomnogo proekta* [Myths and realities of the Soviet atom project]. Arzamas-16: VNIIEF, 1994.

Kholin, F. A. "Radost' truda i bol' veterana" [Joy of labor and veteran's pain]. In *Istoriia atomnogo proekta* [History of atomic project], ed. Sergei Davydov, issue 4, 49–72. Moscow: Kurchatovskii Institut, 1995.

Khovanovich, A. I. "RDS-1 i vsia zhizn'" [RDS-1 and the entire life]." In *Istoriia atomnogo proekta* [History of atomic project], ed. Sergei Davydov, issue 3, 103–42. Moscow: Kurchatovskii Institut, 1995.

Kindler, Robert. *Stalin's Nomads: Power and Famine in Kazakhstan*. Pittsburgh: University of Pittsburgh Press, 2018.

Kniazev, G. I. "13 Let na iadernom poligone" [13 years at the nuclear Polygon]. In *Istoriia atomnogo proekta* [History of atomic project], ed. Sergei Davydov, issue 2, 126–42. Moscow: Kurchatovskii Institut, 1995.

Kozlov, N. A. "Koe-shto o sebe i sluzhbe bezopasnosti" [A bit about myself and the safety service]. In *Istoriia atomnogo proekta* [History of atomic project], ed. Sergei Davydov, issue 5, 152–83. Moscow: Kurchatovskii Institut, 1995.

Kruglov, Arkadii. *The History of the Soviet Atomic Industry*. London: Taylor and Francis, 2002.

Kuznetsov, Boris. "Implementation of Material Control and Accounting at the Nuclear Facilities in Kazakhstan." Partnership for Nuclear Security: United States/Former Soviet Union Program of Cooperation on Nuclear Material Protection, Control, and Accounting. Washington, DC: Department of Energy, September 1998.

Levine, Steve. *The Oil and the Glory: The Pursuit of Empire and Fortune on the Caspian Sea*. New York: Random House, 2007.

Logachev, V. A., ed. *Iadernye ispytaniya SSSR: Sovremennoe radioekologicheskoe sostoianie Poligonov* [Nuclear tests of the USSR: Current radioecological state of Polygons]. Moscow: Izdat, 2002.

Lukashenko, Sergey. *Aktual'nye voprosy radioekologii Kazakhstana* [Topical issues of radioecology of Kazakhstan], vol. 1, issue 3. Kurchatov: Institute of Radiation Safety and Ecology, 2011.

Lukashenko, Sergey, ed. *Semipalatinskii ispytatel'nyi polygon: Sovremennoe sostoianie [Semipalatinsk testing Polygon: current condition]*. Kurchatov: National Nuclear Center, 2011.

Maliutov, V. M. "Tak my nachinali" [That is how we started]. In *Istoriia atomnogo proekta* [History of atomic project], ed. Sergei Davydov, issue 2, 99–115. Moscow: Kurchatovskii Institut, 1995.

Margulan A. Kh., K. A. Akishev, M. K. Kadyrbaev, and A. M. Orazbaev. *Drevniaia kul'tura Tscentral'nogo Kazakhstana* [Ancient culture of central Kazakhstan]. Alma-Ata: Nauka, 1966.

"Marshall Islands: Status of the Nuclear Claims Trust Fund," Government Accountability Office, 2002.

Martynenko, N., ed. *Alash Orda*. Alma-Ata: Aikap, 1992.

Massanov, N. E., Zh. B. Abylkhozhin, I. V. Erofeeva, A. N. Alekseenko, and G. S. Baratova. *Istoriia Kazakhstana: Narody i kul'tury* [History of Kazakhstan: People and culture]. Almaty: Dike Press, 2000.

Mather, Ian, and Paul Lowe. "Life and Death under a Cloud in Radiation City." *European* (June 1–3, 1990).

Mathers, Jennifer G. *The Russian Nuclear Shield from Stalin to Yeltsin*. London: Palgrave Macmillan, 2000.

Matlock, Jack. *Autopsy for an Empire: The American Ambassador's Account of the Collapse of the Soviet Union*. New York: Random House, 1995.

Matsuo, Masatsugu, Noriyuki Kawano, Kyoko Hirabayashi, Yasuyuki Tooka, Kazbek Apsalikov, and Masaharu Hoshi. "A Full-Text English Database of Testimonies of Those Exposed to Radiation Near the Semipalatinsk Nuclear Test Site, Kazakhstan." *Hiroshima Peace Science* 26 (2004): 75–99.

Matzko, John R. "Inside a Soviet ICBM Silo Complex: The SS-18 Silo Dismantlement Program at Derzhavinsk." US Department of Interior, US Geological Survey National Center, prepared for the Defense Threat Reduction Agency, August 2000.

Mikhailov, V. N., ed. *Iadernye ispytaniia SSSR* [Nuclear tests of the USSR]. Sarov: Russian Federal Nuclear Center, 1997.

"Moving Kazakh Nuclear Cache: A Massive Undertaking." *All Things Considered*, National Public Radio, November 17, 2010.

Mudie, Nadejda Y., Anthony J. Swerdlow, Boris I. Gusev, Minouk J. Schoemaker, Ludmila M. Pivina, Svetlana Chsherbakova, Almaqul Mansarina, Susanne Bauer, Yuri Jakovlev, and Kazbek N. Apsalikov. "Twinning in the Offspring of Parents with Chronic Radiation Exposure from Nuclear Testing in Kazakhstan." *Radiation Research Society* (2010): 829–36.

Nazarbayev, N. A., V. S. Shkolnik, E. G. Batyrbekov, S. A. Berezin, S. N. Lukashenko, and M. K. Skakov. *Provedenie kompleksa nauchno-tekhnicheskih i inzhenernyh rabot po privedeniiu byvshego Semipalatinskogo ispytatel'nogo poligona v bezopasnoe sostoianie* [Scientific-technical measures and engineering work to transform the former Semipalatinsk Polygon into a safe state], vol. 1. Kurchatov: National Nuclear Center, 2016.

Nazarbayev, Nursultan. Statement at the National Press Club, Washington, DC, May 19, 1992.

———. Statement at the Supreme Soviet of the Republic of Kazakhstan, December 13, 1993.

Nerushenko, V. M. "Esche odin porazhaiushchii faktor" [One more striking factor]. In *Istoriia atomnogo proekta* [History of atomic project], ed. Sergei Davydov, issue 4, 272–85. Moscow: Kurchatovskii Institut, 1995.

Nordyke, M. D. *The Soviet Program for Peaceful Uses of Nuclear Explosions*. Livermore, CA: Lawrence Livermore National Laboratory, 2000.

Norris, Robert, and William Arkin. "Soviet Nuclear Testing, August 29, 1949–October 24, 1990." *Bulletin of the Atomic Scientists* 54, no. 3 (May–June, 1998): 69–71.

Norris, Robert S., and Thomas B. Cochran. "Nuclear Weapons Tests and Peaceful Nuclear Explosions by the Soviet Union." Draft report, Natural Resource Defense Council, October 1996.

Norris, Robert, and Hans Kristensen. "Global Nuclear Stockpiles, 1945–2006." *Bulletin of the Atomic Scientists* 62, no. 4 (2006): 64–67.

Nuclear Successor States of the Soviet Union: Status Report on Nuclear Weapons, Fissile Material, and Export Controls. Monterey Institute of International Studies and the Carnegie Endowment for International Peace, no. 5, March 1998.

Nunn, Sam. "Foreword: Changing Threats in the Post–Cold War World." In *Dismantling the Cold War: U.S. and NIS Perspectives on the Nunn-Lugar Cooperative Threat Reduction Program*, ed. John M. Shields and William C. Potter, ix–xx. Cambridge, MA: MIT Press, 1997.

Olcott, Martha Brill. *The Kazakhs*. 2nd ed. Stanford, CA: Hoover Institution Press, 1995.

"O merah po obespecheniiu deiatel'nosti Natsional'nogo Iadernogo Tsentra Respubliki Kazakhstan" [On the measures to support functioning of the National Nuclear Center of the Republic of Kazakhstan], Regulation No. 55 adopted by the Council of Ministers of the Republic of Kazakhstan, January 21, 1993.

"O Natsional'nom Iadernom Tsentre i Agentstve to atomnoi energii Respubliki Kazakhstan" [On the National Nuclear Center and the Agency on Atomic Energy of the Republic of Kazakhstan], Presidential Decree No. 779, 1992.

Parish, Scott, and Tamara Robinson. "Efforts to Strengthen Export Controls and Combat Illicit Trafficking and Brain Drain." *Nonproliferation Review* 7, no. 1 (Spring 2000): 112–24.

Pearce, Fred. "Exposed: Soviet Cover-Up of Nuclear Fallout Worse Than Chernobyl." *New Scientist* 233 (2017): 16.

Peyrouse, Sebastien. "'The Imperial Minority': An Interpretative Framework of the Russians in Kazakhstan." *Nationalities Papers* 36, no. 1 (2008): 105–23.

Pivina, L. M., B. I. Gusev, S. Bauer, R. A. Winkelmann, and K. Apsalikov. "Development of a Cause-of-Death Registry among the Population of Several Raions in the East-Kazakhstan Oblast Exposed to Radiation Due to Nuclear Weapons Testing at the Semipalatinsk Test Site." Final report of the Project "Health Effects of Nuclear Weapons Testing at Semipalatinsk Test Site, Kazakhstan, on the Population in Semipalatinsk Oblast (Semipalatinsk Follow-Up)," 2002.

Polygon. Documentary film, in Russian, produced by Oraz Rymzhanov, codirected by Oraz Rymzhanov and Vladimir Rerikh, 1990.

Population Health in Regions Adjacent to the Semipalatinsk Nuclear Test Site. Institute of Biophysics, Physical Training Center, 1998.

Potter, William C. "The Changing Nuclear Threat: The 'Sapphire' File." *Transitions On-*

line (November 17, 1995), https://tol.org/client/article/1440-the-changing-nuclear-threat-the-sapphire-file.html.

——. "Nuclear Insecurity in the Post-Soviet States." Congressional testimony, *Nonproliferation Review* 1, no. 3 (Spring–Summer 1994): 61–65.

——. "The Politics of Renunciation: The Case of Belarus, Kazakhstan, and Ukraine." Henry L. Stimson Center, occasional paper no. 22, 1995.

——. "Project Sapphire: U.S.-Kazakhstani Cooperation for Non-Proliferation." In *Dismantling the Cold War: U.S. and NIS Perspectives on the Nunn-Lugar Cooperative Threat Reduction Program*, ed. John M. Shields and William C. Potter, 345–62. Cambridge, MA: MIT Press, 1997).

Potter, William C., and Elena Sokova. "Illicit Nuclear Trafficking in the NIS: What's New? What's True?" *Nonproliferation Review* 9, no. 2 (Summer 2002): 112–20.

Price, Espy P. Vice President of Chevron Overseas Petroleum Inc, speech, 1994.

Priest, Nicholas, and Robert Murley. "Radiological Conditions Prevailing at Technical Area 4A on the Semipalatinsk Nuclear Test Site: Hazards Presented by Radionuclide Deposits." IAEA, December 2006.

"Primenenie perechnia zabolevanii, imeiushchih sviaz' s oposredstvennym radiatsionnym vozdeistviem u lits, rozhdennyh ot obluchennyh roditelei v rezul'tate ispytanii iadernogo oruzhiia na Semipalatinskom iadernom poligone v rabote mezhvedomstvennyh ekspertnyh sovetov" [On the use of the list of diseases related to radiation exposure among the descendants of parents exposed to ionizing radiation as a result of nuclear weapons tests at the Semipalatinsk Nuclear Polygon in the work of interagency expert councils], Astana: Institute of Radiation Medicine and Ecology, 2014.

Protocol to the Agreement between the Union of Soviet Socialist Republics and the United States of America on the Reduction and Limitation of Strategic Offensive Weapons. Signed in Lisbon, Portugal, on May 23, 1992, https://2009-2017.state.gov/documents/organization/27389.pdf.

Radiological Conditions at the Semipalatinsk Test Site, Kazakhstan: Preliminary Assessment and Recommendations for Further Study. Vienna: IAEA, 1998.

Rappaport, Helen. *Joseph Stalin: A Biographical Companion.* Santa Barbara, CA: ABC-CLIO, 1999.

Reiss, Mitchel. *Bridled Ambition: Why Countries Constrain Their Nuclear Capabilities.* Washington, DC: Woodrow Wilson Press, 1995.

Robbins, Christopher. *Apples Are from Kazakhstan: The Land That Disappeared.* London: Atlas, 2008.

"Russian Kommersant: 'U.S. Version of Uranium Deal with Almaty Questioned,'" FBIS translated text of Aleksandr Koretskiy, "More Uranium Has Been Bought Than Was Actually Available," November 25, 1994.

Ryzhikov, I. A. "Na stroitel'stve poligona" [Building the Polygon]. In *Istoriia atomnogo proekta* [History of atomic project], ed. Sergei Davydov, issue 2, 72–98. Moscow: Kurchatovskii Institut, 1995.

Sadovskii, M. A. "Institut khimicheskoi fiziki" [Institute of Chemical Physics]. In *Istoriia atomnogo proekta* [History of atomic project], ed. Sergei Davydov, issue 11, 45–64. Moscow: Kurchatovskii Institut, 1997.

Sagadiev, K. A. "Akhmet Baitursynov i ekonomicheskie vzgliady liderov Alash Ordy" [Akhmet Baitursynov and Alash Orda leaders' views on economy]. *Otechestvennaia Istoriia (1998)*: 29–33. Almaty: Institute of History and Ethnology named after Chokan Valikhanov.

Sakharov, Andrei. *Memoirs*. New York: Knopf Doubleday, 1992.

Sakharov, V. N. "Nevidomoe porazhaiushchee izluchenie" [Invisible ionizing radiation]. In *Istoriia atomnogo proekta* [History of atomic project], ed. Sergei Davydov, issue 11. Moscow: Kurchatovskii Institut, 1997.

Saktaganova, Z., B. Omarova, K. Ilyassova, Z. Nurligenova, B. Abzhapparova, A. Zhalmurzina, and Zh. Mazhitova. "Alash Party: The Historiography of the Movement." *Space and Culture, India* 7, no. 4 (2020): 208–18.

Sarseke, Medeu. *Semipalatinskaia tragediia* [Semipalatinsk tragedy]. Astana: Foliant, 2016.

"Sergey Lukashenko: Nerazrushaemoe—v liudiah." Interview recorded by Evgenii Panov, *Chelovek, Energiia, Atom* 2, no. 4 (2009): 46–47. Kurchatov: National Nuclear Center.

Shakarimov, Zharkyn. *Amre v Parizhe* [Amre in Paris]. N.p.: Signet Press, 2016.

Shepel', V., ed., with A. E. Assanbaeva and E. M. Gribanova, contributors. *Kazakhstan za bez'iadernyi mir: Sbornik dokumentov i materialov* [Kazakhstan for a nuclear-free world: A compilation of documents and materials]. Almaty: Archive of the President of the Republic of Kazakhstan, 2011.

Sherwin, Martin. *Gambling with Armageddon: Nuclear Roulette from Hiroshima to the Cuban Missile Crisis*. New York: Knopf, 2020.

Shevchenko, A. D. "Vzryvaem zemnye zvezdy" [Exploding earth stars]. In *Istoriia atomnogo proekta* [History of atomic project], ed. Sergei Davydov, part 3, issue 4. Moscow: Kurchatovskii Institut, 1995.

Shields, John M., and William C. Potter. *Dismantling the Cold War: US and NIS Perspectives on the Nunn-Lugar Cooperative Threat Reduction Program*. Cambridge, MA: MIT Press, 1997.

Shiganakov, Shaiakhmet. "BN-350 Reactor Spent Fuel Handling." Presentation at the IAEA, April 26–28, 2006.

Shkolnik, Vladimir S., ed. *The Semipalatinsk Test Site: Creation, Operation, and Conversion*. Albuquerque: Sandia National Laboratories, 2002.

Skootsky, Mark D. "An Annotated Chronology of Post-Soviet Nuclear Disarmament 1991–1994." *Nonproliferation Review* (Spring–Summer, 1995).

Solzhenitsyn, Alexander. *Rebuilding Russia: Reflections and Tentative Proposals*. New York: Farrar, Straus and Giroux, 1991.

"Sounding an Alarm: Soviet Disunion and Threats to American National Security," letter written by Graham Allison to Brent Scowcroft, September 6, 1991, https://www2.jiia.or.jp/kokusaimondai_archive/2000/2006-09_007.pdf?noprint.

"Soviet Nuclear Test Site Now a Model for Safeguards." *All Things Considered*, National Public Radio, November 19, 2010.

"Soviet People Speak: Interviews and Letters to William Mandel." *Station Relay* 5, nos. 1–5 (1989–91).

"Soviet Union to Close Testing Site." *Arms Control Today* (April 1990): 31.

Stepankov, Valentin, and Evgenii Lisov. *Kremlyovskii zagovor* [Kremlin conspiracy]. Moscow: Ogonek, 1992.

Stepanyuk, Viktor S. "Liquidation of the Consequences of Nuclear Tests at the Semi-palatinsk Test Site (STS) in Trilateral Collaboration (Russian Federation, Republic of Kazakhstan, United States)." In *Doomed to Cooperate: How American and Russian Scientists Joined Forces to Avert Some of the Greatest Post–Cold War Nuclear Dangers*, ed. Siegfried S. Hecker, 1:481–506. Los Alamos: Bathtub Row Press, 2016.

Stern, Jessica Eve. "Cooperative Activities to Improve Fissile Material Production, Control, and Accounting." In *Dismantling the Cold War: U.S. and NIS Perspectives on the Nunn-Lugar Cooperative Threat Reduction Program*, ed. John M. Shields and William C. Potter. Cambridge, MA: MIT Press, 1997, 314.

Stone, Richard. "Plutonium Fields Forever." *Science* 300 (2003): 1220–24.

Sukhanov, Lev. *Kak Yeltsin stal prezidentom: Zapiski pervogo pomoshchnika* [How Yeltsin became a president: Notes of the chief assistant]. Moscow: Eksmo-Algoritm, 2011.

Tirpak, John A. "Project Sapphire." *Air Force* 78, no. 8 (August 1995).

Tokayev, K. K., and V. S. Shkolnik, eds. *CTR v Kazakhstane* [CTR in Kazakhstan], monograph.

Treaty on the Prohibition of Nuclear Weapons. Office for Disarmament Affairs, United Nations.

Tsukerman, Veniamin, and Zinaida Azarkh. *Arzamas-16: Soviet Scientists in the Nuclear Age: A Memoir*. Nottingham: Bramcote Press, 1999.

Vakulchuk, Roman, and Kristian Gjerde, with Tatiana Belikhina and Kazbek Apsalikov. *Semipalatinsk Nuclear Testing: The Humanitarian Consequences*. Norwegian Institute of International Affairs, NUPI Report, no. 1, 2014.

Van der Vink, Gregory E., and Christopher E. Paine. "The Politics of Verification: Limiting the Testing of Nuclear Weapons." *Science and Global Security* 3 (1993): 261–88.

Viukov, A. N. "Na grani osobogo riska" [On the brink of special risk]. In *Istoriia atomnogo proekta* [History of atomic project], ed. Sergei Davydov, issue 4, 73–130. Moscow: Kurchatovskii Institut, 1995.

Viukova, L. P. "Byt' vmeste liuboi tsenoi" [To be together at any price]. In *Istoriia atomnogo proekta* [History of atomic project], ed. Sergei Davydov, issue 4, 131–53. Moscow: Kurchatovskii Institut, 1995.

Wellerstein, Alex, and Edward Geist. "The Secret of the Soviet Hydrogen Bomb." *Physics Today* 4, no. 40 (April 2017): 40–47.

Werner, Cynthia, and Kathleen Purvis-Roberts. "Unravelling the Secrets of the Past: Contested Versions of Nuclear Testing in the Soviet Republic of Kazakhstan." National Council for Eurasian and East European Research, 2005.

Where the Wind Blew. Documentary film, directed by André Singer, 2017.

Yeltsin, Boris. *The Struggle for Russia*. New York: Crown, 1994.

Young, Daniel. "Thousands in Alma-Ata Demand Test Ban." Physicians for Social Responsibility, *PSR Reports* 10, no. 2 (Summer 1990).

Zdorov'ye liudei, prozhivaiushchih v raione prilegaiushchem k Semipalatinskomu poligonu [Health of residents in the vicinity of Semipalatinsk Polygon], collection of articles, vol. 2, Semipalatinsk, 1994.

Zhuchkov, V. P. "Na strazhe atomnoi" [On nuclear guard]. In *Istoriia atomnogo proekta* [History of atomic project], ed. Sergei Davydov, issue 2. Moscow: Kurchatovskii Institut, 1995.

Zorin, G. F. "I vse zhe . . . rabota i zhizn' byli interesnymi" [And still . . . work and life . . . were interesting]. In *Istoriia atomnogo proekta* [History of atomic project], ed. Sergei Davydov, issue 4. Moscow: Kurchatovskii Institut, 1995.

INDEX

Note: Page numbers in italics indicate illustrative material.

249; Cuban missile crisis, 45; establishment of post-Soviet embassies,
145–49; and HEU Deal, 174, 177, 252;
Joint Verification Experiment, 51–53;
mixed signals on Kazakhstan's nuclear
position, 151–56, 159; and MPC&A
program, 233, 234, 235, 236, 241–42;
Nazarbayev's visits to, 161–64, 165–71,
167, 190, 213–17, *215*; nuclear program,
21, 29, 32, 43, 44, 48, 54–55, 245; and
nuclear-weapon-free zones, 247–49;
and Nunn-Lugar CTR program, 179,
183, 185–86, 189, 199–205, 222, 225,
229–30, 309n29; oil industry involvement, 160 (*see also* Chevron); and
OSCE memorandum, 216–17; purchase
of LEU from Russia, 219; scenarios for
possible post-Soviet nuclear outcomes,
116–17; and Soviet coup attempt, 108,
109, 110; and START I, 156–59, 165, 166,
171, 172–73, 175–76, 221–22; test ban
treaties, 43–44, 45–46, 50–51, 53. *See
also* NPT; Project Sapphire
uranium: conversion to LEU, 174, 219, 233,
239–42, 252; dismantlement compensation, 174, 177, 183, 197–98, 219; and
HEU Deal, 174, 177, 252; in peaceful
nuclear programs, 254; production of,
126, 300n4; vulnerability of nuclear
material, 126–29. *See also* Project
Sapphire; plutonium
Ust-Kamenogorsk, 60, 126, 129, 192
Uzbekistan: and Central Asian Nuclear-
Weapon-Free Zone, 246–49; and
Tashkent Treaty, 164, 248

Vasilevskii, Marshal, 36
Velikhov, Evgenii, 7
verification methods, 44, 45, 46, 51–53,
192, 250
Voronov, Vitalii, 108
Vozrozhdenie Island, 130

Washington Times (newspaper), 196–97
Wayne, John, 55
weather monitoring, 25, 40, 57, 75
Weber, Andy, 188–90, 193, 194–95, 207, 234
workers' strikes, 87, 88
World War II, 21

Yanayev, Gennadii, 104–5, 106, 108
Yazov, Dmitrii, 110, 112
Yegai, Anatolii, 46–47
Yeltsin, Boris: and Alma-Ata Declaration,
120–21; and CIS, 117–18; on joint nuclear command with Kazakhstan, 143;
mentioned, 133; Nazarbayev compared
to, 214; and New Union Treaty, 102–3,
112; nuclear arsenal removal negotiations, 219; and Project Sapphire, 191;
and Soviet coup attempt, 104, 105–7,
109, 111
Young, Dan, 93

"Zaman-Ai" (hymn of Nevada-
Semipalatinsk movement), 78–79
Zaveniagin, Avraami, 55–56
Zhangiz Tobe, 218, 221, 222, 223
Zhirinovskii, Vladimir, 135
Zhovtis, Evgenii, 107
Zhukeev, Tulegen: background, 132; and
Christopher's visit to Kazakhstan,
178, 179; on Courtney, 149; on for-
eign relations ambitions, 163; HEU
compensation negotiations, 174, 183;
international reputation concerns, 125,
138; NPT negotiations, 165, 172, 179–81,
202; on nuclear position strategy, 152,
155, 165, 172; nuclear-weapon-free zone
negotiations, 247; and orphan nuclear
device in Polygon, 220; and START
I, 158, 171; on Ukraine, 173; visits to
Washington, 180–81, 214
Zhukov, Georgy, 32
Znamenka (Kokentau), 48

9 781503 632431